Missouri Genealogical Gleanings

1840 and Beyond
Volume 7

Sherida K. Eddlemon

HERITAGE BOOKS
2009

HERITAGE BOOKS
AN IMPRINT OF HERITAGE BOOKS, INC.

Books, CDs, and more—Worldwide

For our listing of thousands of titles see our website
at
www.HeritageBooks.com

Published 2009 by
HERITAGE BOOKS, INC.
Publishing Division
100 Railroad Ave. #104
Westminster, Maryland 21157

Copyright © 2001 Sherida K. Eddlemon

Index Copyright © 2001 Heritage Books, Inc.

All rights reserved. No part of this book may be reproduced or transmitted in any form or by any means, electronic or mechanical, including photocopying, recording or by any information storage and retrieval system without written permission from the author, except for the inclusion of brief quotations in a review.

International Standard Book Numbers
Paperbound: 978-0-7884-1391-9
Clothbound: 978-0-7884-8221-2

Dedication

To David Ray Helms who has brought new found serenity and happiness into my life. He is the son of Bailey Wesson Helms, Jr. and Barbara Jane Johnson, born December 3, 1958, Memphis, Shelby County, Tennessee.

TABLE OF CONTENTS

	Page

ADAIR COUNTY
(Founded 1841 from Macon County)

Marriage Records	152

BOONE COUNTY
(Founded 1820 from Howard County)

Draft, 1864	90

BUTLER COUNTY
(Founded 1849 from Wayne County)

Rural Directory of Taxpayers, 1923	26

CALDWELL COUNTY
(Founded 1836 from Ray County)

Delinquent Tax List, 1855	85

CARTER COUNTY
(Founded 1859 from Ripley and Shannon Counties)

Marriage book B, 1890-1898	115

CHRISTIAN COUNTY
(Founded 1859 from Greene, Taney and Webster Counties)

Prison Records, 1887 - 1889	76
Green Valley Cemetery	140

CLARK COUNTY
(Founded 1838 from Lewis County)

Tax Receipt for John Stull, 1901	109

CLINTON COUNTY
(Founded 1833 from Clay County)

1840 Census Index	140

FRANKLIN COUNTY
(Founded 1818 from St. Louis County)

Obituary of Norrell Tyler Triplett   90

GENTRY COUNTY
(Founded 1841 from Clinton County)

Automobile Registration for Claude L. David   85

HENRY COUNTY
(Founded 1834 from Lafayette County)

Hickory Grove Cemetery   190

JACKSON COUNTY
(Founded 1826 from Lafayette County)

Fishing License of Ruth M. Beshears   98

JASPER COUNTY
(Founded 1841 from Newton County)

Fishing License of E. L. Holden   98
1850 Census Index   101
Vehicle Registration Millard Bryan   190

LAFAYETTE COUNTY
(Founded 1820 from Cooper County)

Slave Bill, 1854   190
Vehicle Registration Ira Banks   190

LIVINGSTON COUNTY
(Founded 1837 from Carroll County)

Deceased World War I Veterans   95

MILLER COUNTY
(Founded 1837 from Cole County)

Enrolled Militia, 73rd Reg., Co. I   99

MISSISSIPPI COUNTY
(Founded 1845 from Scott County)

Obituary of Nellie Ann Barrett Brewer   89

SCOTT COUNTY
(Founded 1821 from New Madrid)

Fishing Licenses of Mathie D. Daniel   98

STE. GENEVIEVE COUNTY
(Founded 1812, Original District)

1890 Special Census   144

ST. LOUIS COUNTY
(Founded 1812, Original District)

Students of Ballwin School, 1895	95
Fishing License, Raymond C. Jennings	98
Deceased Veterans, Korean War	109
1928-1929 Roster, Mt. Moriah Temple	114
1913 Membership, Kirkwood Chapter Eastern Star	152
Attendees of Home Guard Dance, 1916	185

SCHUYLER COUNTY
(Founded 1845 from Adair County)

Queen City Telephone Directory   185

SHANNON COUNTY
(Founded 1841 from Ripley and Washington Counties)

Obituary of J. A. Tohline   198

VERNON COUNTY
(Founded 1851 from Bates County)

Postcard from W. T. Ballagh   85

WASHINGTON COUNTY
(Founded 1813 from Ste. Genevieve County)

Obituary of Hazel Harvey   94

D - Date	GR - Grantor
GE - Grantee	IN - Instrument
P - Page	I - Issue
R - Range	C - Court Cases
AP - Application	Dis - Dismissed
MOC - Missouri Connection	SUS - Suspended
TWP - Township	APP - Appraiser
A - Age	St - Martial Status
BP - Birth Place	RES - Residence
OC - Occupation	ADM/AD - Admission
MD - Marriage Date	MG - Minister
CMTS - Comments	SVC - Service
SVCCP - Service Branch	FAC - Faculty
YSUP - Years Superintendent	SUP - Superintendent
SEC - Secretary	Reg - Regiment
PO - Post Office	

Good luck in finding your ancestors within these pages.

PREFACE

Missouri was a gateway to the west. Both the Santa Fe Trail to the southwest and the Oregon Trail to the northwest began at Independence, Missouri. Settlers and new immigrants from Germany, Switzerland, Ireland, England, Poland, Bohemia and Italy flooded into Missouri when statehood was granted in 1821. Many of these new arrivals often did not list a destination on the ship passenger list. If a destination was indicated, it may mean that their were other relatives already there or that the family had already purchased property in advance.

Kansas was part of the Missouri Territory until 1821, but it was not until 1854 that the territory of Kansas was created luring new immigrants and settlers from Illinois, Ohio, Indiana and Missouri. So many Missourians relocated to Kansas that in 1855 Kansas was voted into the Union as a slave state.

Missouri was plagued with outlaws and raiders that had their beginnings even before the Civil War. The 1857 Dred Scott Decision helped to inflame the anti-slavery feelings in Missouri. During the Civil War, raiders and outlaws such as William Clarke Quantrill, Frank and Jesse James and the Cole Younger gangs terrorized Missouri. In the eyes of some these outlaws were heroes, but the law prevailed in the end.

Each new Gold Rush lured more people to Missouri on their way to make their fortune. There was a California Gold Rush in 1848; the Colorado Gold Rush in 1858 and the Klondike Gold Rush in the Yukon in 1896-1897. Many lost sons went to look for gold as well as whole families with only a child born in Missouri to show their passing through the state.

St. Joseph, Missouri was the starting point for the Pony Express. It promised delivery of the mail to Sacramento, California in eight to ten days. Although it was only in operation for eighteen months, these riders gained a glamorous spot in Missouri history.

Although there are extant census records for Missouri starting in 1830 many travelers and pioneering settlers were missed in the census years or only lived in the state between the census years. The purpose of this collection is to help the researcher pinpoint his ancestor between the census years.

All names appear as written on the records including the abbreviations of given names. The surnames appearing in the parentheses are included in the index. No attempt has been made to make corrections in spelling. Cemetery listings and mortality schedules include only persons born in 1840 or later.

In some instances it was necessary to use abbreviations. They are as follows:

m - Month
d - Day/Died
b - Born

y - Year
RD - Recorded Date
CLK - Clerk

MISCELLANEOUS RAILROAD MISSOURIANA

Railroad passes issued from the Missouri Pacific Railway, Terre Haute, Alton & St. Louis Railroad, North Missouri Railroad, St. Louis, Kansas City & Northern Railroad, Missouri River, St. Scott & Gulf Railroad, Missouri-Kansas & Texas Railway, St. Louis Coal Railway, Kansas-St. Joseph & Council Bluffs railroad, Chicago-Peoria & St. Louis Railway, St. Louis & San Francisco Railway, Minneapolis & St. Louis railroad, St. Louis Southwestern Railway, Missouri Oklahoma & Guld Railway, Kansas City-Clinton & Springfield Railroad, and others   83

MISCELLANEOUS MISSOURIANA

Notes on the Third Missouri Cavalry	85
Obituary of Job Standerfer	89
Correspondence of Gen. Thomas Jordan	94
Washita Cattle Company Bond	98
1851 Passport issued to Wade Woodson	98
Missouri Paymaster's General's Office payment to James Case	99
Military Service Voucher for Triphemiah Smith	108
Missourians in Grant Co., KS World War I Draft	143
Veterinary Department, 1915-1916	187
Civil War Letter of Henry Klice	197

Butler County, Missouri, Rural Directory of Taxpayers, 1923, Eddlemon Collection.

Name	Address
Kert Adkins	Qulin
J. W. Agee	Poplar Bluff
S.B. Agee	Poplar Bluff
G.W. Akers	Neelyville
H. E. Albert	Hendrickson
Wm. Albert	Poplar Bluff
A. M. Albright	Poplar Bluff
Ivan Aldridge	Rombauer
J. E. Aldrich	Hendrickson
Scott Alcorn	Ellsinore
J. F. Alexander	Broseley
L. Alexander	Neelyville
S. P. Alexander	Broseley
W.A. Alexander	Chaonia
Jas. Alford	Poplar Bluff
W.H. Alford	Poplar Bluff
F. Allen	Broseley
Elijah Allen	Poplar Bluff
John Allen	Poplar Bluff
G.W. Allen	Poplar Bluff
W.E. Allen	Poplar Bluff
M.M. Allen	Hendrickson
G. Allen	Harviell
C.P. Allensworth	Neelyville
C.P. Allensworth (sic)	Neelyville
O. Allensworth	Neelyville
C.W. Allison	Harviell
M.L. Allison	Harviell
J.L. Alread	Harviell
Henry Alread	Vastus
W.A. Alread	Neelyville
R.N. Alsup	Broseley
H.G. Alt	Fairdealing
Sam Alvey	Neelyville
Jerry Amo	Poplar Bluff
C.E. Anderson	Poplar Bluff
Frank Anderson	Poplar Bluff
Fred Anderson	Poplar Bluff
Henry Anderson	Poplar Bluff
J.A. Anderson	Vastus

J.M. Anderson	Qulin
John Anderson	Rombauer
Lee Anderson	Poplar Bluff
Lizzie Anderson	Broseley
Mrs. O.W. Anderson	Poplar Bluff
Will Anderson	Poplar Bluff
Hobart Andrews	Wappapello
George Andrews	Wappapello
H. Anmon	Poplar Bluff
Geo. Angdon	Qulin
Wade Anthony	Poplar Bluff
Henry Appleby	Poplar Bluff
Ray Apette	Qulin
G.A. Archer	Neelyville
J.R. Arga	Qulin
Harve Armour	Broseley
J.E. Armour	Fisk
B.F. Armstrong	Poplar Bluff
Mrs. M.E. Armstrong	Poplar Bluff
Curry Armstrong	Poplar Bluff
J.A. Armstrong	Fisk
Jas. Arnold	Qulin
J.W. Arterberry	Poplar Bluff
A.C. Ashby	Fisk
Wm. Ashby	Fisk
Bertha Ashcraft	Poplar Bluff
John Ashcroft	Qulin
Frank Asher	Poplar Bluff
T.E. Asher	Poplar Bluff
W.W. Asher	Neelyville
R.L. Ashworth	Qulin
Sam Atkins	Neelyville
R.E. Atkinson	Harviell
O.E. Aud	Poplar Bluff
C. Austill	Poplar Bluff
J.W. Autry	Poplar Bluff
Dennis Avant	Neelyville
E.W. Avant	Neelyville
John Ayers	Poplar Bluff
C. Baccus	Vastus
Ellen Baccus	Vastus
L. Baccus	Vastus
Jams Baccus	Vastus

C. W. Bachs	Poplar Bluff
Edward Bacon	Poplar Bluff
Jasper Bacon	Poplar Bluff
R.L. Badgett	Neelyville
Rufus Badgett	Rombauer
Frank Bagby	Poplar Bluff
Jas. Baggett	Fisk
Alex Bagwell	Fagus
W.A. Bailey	Fagus
C.C. Bain	Fagus
R.R. Bain	Broseley
Bert Baker	Qulin
Edwin Baker	Hendrickson
M.H. Baker	Poplar Bluff
Oscar Baker	Poplar Bluff
R.L. Baker	Rombauer
W.K. Baker	Poplar Bluff
Aden Baldridge	Fisk
H.M. Baldridge	Fisk
W.A. Baldridger	Fisk
H. C. Ball	Neelyville
John Ballard	Neelyville
Mrs. M. Ballheimer	Harviell
Jos. Ban	Poplar Bluff
Elizabeth Banks	Qulin
C.D. Barber	Poplar Bluff
John Barber	Poplar Bluff
Jeff Barcliff	Upalika
Hugh Barcliff	Upalika
Herman Barcliff	Upalika
Harry Bardsley	Neelyville
Mrs. A.L. Bardsley	Neelyville
A.S. Barger	Rombauer
F.S. Barger	Poplar Bluff
Mrs. Fannie Barger	Poplar Bluff
Mrs. J.A. Barks	Poplar Bluff
A.L. Barker	Harviell
Arvil Barker	Neelyville
F.S. Barker	Vastus
J.H. Barker	Poplar Bluff
J.S. Barker	Narviell
Phillip Barker	Neelyville
R.A. Barker	Poplar Bluff

Frank Barnes	Qulin
A. J. Barnes	Poplar Bluff
Lou Barnes	Poplar Bluff
C. Barnett	Broseley
J.W.P. Barnett	Poplar Bluff
Martha Barrett	Poplar Bluff
T.C. Barnett	Poplar Bluff
Henry Barns	Qulin
S.W. Barns	Qulin
Geo. Barrett	Harviell
Jas. Barriner	Poplar Bluff
N. F. Barriner	Poplar Bluff
E. J. Barrow	Poplar Bluff
Joe Barth	Fisk
Levi Barth	Poplar Bluff
Ben Barton	Poplar Bluff
J. W. Basinger	Fisk
F. M. Bass	Vastus
Claud Bates	Poplar Bluff
George W. Bates	Fisk
H. Bates	Fisk
W. A. Bates	Fisk
Perry Bates	Harviell
Albert Batson	Broseley
F. R. Batten	Broseley
W. B. Batten	Broseley
W. J. Batten	Broseley
T. B. Baugh	Poplar Bluff
Wm. H. Baugh	Poplar Bluff
H. C. Baumeister	Poplar Bluff
J. A. Baumgardner	Poplar Bluff
J. P. Baumgardner	Poplar Bluff
E. Baxter	Poplar Bluff
J. W. Baxter	Poplar Bluff
Tom Bayes	Broseley
Molly Bealer	Neelyville
W. E. Beacham	Neelyville
Luce Bedoll	Poplar Bluff
R. W. Bedoll	Poplar Bluff
H. W. Beecher	Harviell
Edgar Beers	Qulin
Sam Beenthall	Neelyville
Ed Beck	Rombauer

Guy D. Beck	Fisk
Jos. W. Beck	Rombauer
J. H. Belamy	Poplar Bluff
J. P. Belcher	Harviell
G. W. Belcher	Poplar Bluff
Claud Bell	Neelyville
George Bell	Neelyville
George Bell (sic)	Neelyville
Jasper Bellew	Hendrickson
Jas. Bellew	Chaonia
L. Bell	Fisk
Elmer Benner	Poplar Bluff
O. E. Bennet	Poplar Bluff
C. R. Bennet	Poplar Bluff
Grant Bennet	Poplar Bluff
John Bennett	Poplar Bluff
W. C. Bennett	Harviell
Mrs. B. E. Benthall	Neelyville
Mrs. M. E. Benthall	Neelyville
Robert Benton	Neelyville
Amel Berger	Qulin
Max Berger	Qulin
Otto Berger	Qulin
Ed Berient	Fagus
L. B. Berney	Harviell
H. Berringer	Rombauer
A. Berry	Neelyville
A. L. Berry	Poplar Bluff
J. W. Berry	Upalika
Oscar Berry	Poplar Bluff
R. T. Berry	Neelyville
T. C. Berry	Upalika
T. M. Berry	Upalika
W. D. Berry	Neelyville
Will Berry	Poplar Bluff
Will Berry (sic)	Poplar Bluff
I. W. Berryman	Rombauer
Sam Bertucci	Poplar Bluff
Leon Besand	Qulin
Chas. Bess	Poplar Bluff
John Best	Poplar Bluff
Wm. Best	Poplar Bluff
Frank Beumer	Poplar Bluff

L. Beumer	Poplar Bluff
C. A. Biggs	Neelyvlle
F. J. Biggs	Neelyville
J. A. Bissett	Neelyville
R. T. Biggs	Neelyville
W. L. Biggs	Neelyville
S. Billingsley	Harviell
W. H. Bilsky	Poplar Bluff
Wm. Bilsky	Poplar Bluff
Geo. Birdsong	Poplar Bluff
N. F. Bishop	Naylor
Rainey Bishop	Naylor
D. H. Black	Qulin
Elsworth Black	Qulin
Eugene Black	Qulin
L. A. Black	Poplar Bluff
W. R. L. Blackburn	Upalika
Martha Blackwell	Qulin
W. S. Blackwell	Poplar Bluff
Mrs. T. E. Bledsoe	Poplar Bluff
C. Blagg	Harviell
Doff Blagg	Harviell
L. Blagg	Harviell
C. W. Blanford	Fisk
J. A. Bland	Fisk
Sam Bland	Fisk
E. H. Blankenship	Poplar Bluff
Mrs. T. E. Bledsoe (sic)	Poplar Bluff
W. T. Bloodworth	Poplar Bluff
C. N. Board	Fisk
E. L. Board	Vastus
Het Board	Fisk
Paul Bocek	Poplar Bluff
Chas. Bodine	Neelyville
W. G. Boeving	Fagus
S. W. Boggs	Qulin
Robt. Boles	Neelyville
Albert Bolin	Harviell
R. A. Bolin	Qulin
Z. A. Bolin	Qulin
Mrs. C. Bollinger	Qulin
J. R. Boly	Harviell
Joseph Boly	Harviell

J. L. Book	Fisk
J. H. Boor	Neelyville
J. B. Booten	Vastus
J. E. Booten	Vastus
Frank Boozer	Poplar Bluff
G. W. Bond	Harviell
V. J. Borntrager	Poplar Bluff
Ben T. Borntrager	Poplar Bluff
H. R. Borntrager	Poplar Bluff
R. D. Borntrager	Poplar Bluff
Sam Borntrager	Poplar Bluff
Lee Bosek	Rombauer
S. C. Bounds	Ellsinore
A. G. Boyd	Harviell
E. Boyd	Harviell
Zelpha Boyd	Vastus
B. F. Boyer	Poplar Bluff
C. Boyer	Poplar Bluff
H. H. Boyer	Poplar Bluff
R. J. Boyer	Poplar Bluff
V. C. Boyer	Broseley
C. H. Boyet	Harviell
J. F. Box	Upalika
Luther Box	Ten Mile
W. H. Box	Upalika
J. Bozark	Harviell
A. L. Bracken	Qulin
J. C. Brackin	Qulin
Lizzie Bradford	Poplar Bluff
W. A. Bradford	Poplar Bluff
P. J. Brady	Poplar Bluff
J. W. Bragg	Qulin
Jas. Bragg	Fagus
M. C. Braidy	Poplar Bluff
Susan Brake	Harviell
Vernon Brake	Harviell
Bumic Branch	Fisk
Halley Branch	Fisk
Luther Branch	Fisk
W. D. Branch	Broseley
D. W. Brandon	Poplar Bluff
Albert Brandt	Broseley
Gus Brandt	Broseley

R. L. Brannon	Poplar Bluff
Arthur Brannum	Harviell
C. F. Brannum	Harviell
Jas. Brannum	Poplar Bluff
J. W. Brannum	Poplar Bluff
Oscar Brannum	Poplar Bluff
H. L. Bratcher	Poplar Bluff
Fred Braznik	Harviell
John Braznik	Harviell
Benny Brent	Broseley
Ed Brent	Broseley
James Brent	Broseley
Wm. Brent	Broseley
T. E. Brickell	Poplar Bluff
T. E. Brickle	Poplar Bluff
Dona Bridgman	Poplar Bluff
J. B. F. Briggs	Poplar Bluff
J. W. Brightwell	Poplar Bluff
F. W. Brink	Harviell
R. B. Britt, Jr.	Neelyville
R. B. Britt	Neelyville
E. L. Brickett	Harviell
Geo. Brogg	Qulin
Geo. Brokoetter	Poplar Bluff
G. W. Brooks	Poplar Bluff
J. M. Brooks	Poplar Bluff
J. M. Brooks (sic)	Poplar Bluff
A. F. Brothers	Fisk
J. R. Brothers	Fisk
A. G. Brown	Poplar Bluff
Bluford Brown	Poplar Bluff
C. A. Brown	Poplar Bluff
C. F. Brown	Broseley
C. S. Brown	Broseley
C. W. Brown	Harviell
Daisy Brown	Fagus
Dewey Brown	Rombauer
Ed Brown	Qulin
E. L. Brown	Rombauer
Eugene Brown	Poplar Bluff
Frank Brown	Rombauer
F. M. Brown	Qulin
Geo. H. Brown	Poplar Bluff

Gordon Brown	Fisk
G. F. Brown	Hendrickson
H. C. Brown	Neelyville
Jay Brown	Qulin
John D. Brown	Poplar Bluff
John Brown	Poplar Bluff
John Brown (sic)	Poplar Bluff
J. W. Brown	Poplar Bluff
J. Tom Brown	Rombauer
J. S. Brown	Fisk
J. I. Brown	Fisk
Junia Brown	Poplar Bluff
Lewis Brown	Hendrickson
Maggie Brown	Broseley
Malissa J. Brown	Qulin
Paul Brown	Qulin
Sarah Brown	Broseley
S. C. Brown	Poplar Bluff
Tom Brown	Poplar Bluff
Wm. M. Brown	Qulin
W. C. Brown	Hendrickson
W. H. H. Brown	Harviell
W. J. Brown	Fisk
W. S. Brown	Poplar Bluff
Katy Browning	Harviell
Earl Browning	Fisk
Jas. Broyles	Poplar Bluff
M. B. Bruce	Harviell
P. T. Bruce	Harviell
W. A. Brummitt	Fisk
N. E. Brunson	Neelyville
E. D. Bryan	Poplar Bluff
J. W. Bryan	Poplar Bluff
Forrest Bryant	Vastus
J. E. Bryant	Hendrickson
Theo. Bryant	Poplar Bluff
Henry Buchanan	Poplar Bluff
J. E. Buchanan	Poplar Bluff
John Bucher	Poplar Bluff
J. W. Bucu	Broseley
Claud Buffington	Harviell
Henry Buhler	Harviell
W. I. Bumpuss	Poplar Bluff

I. W. Burgman	Poplar Bluff
Mrs. D. L. Burke	Neelyville
C. M. Burkeen	Poplar Bluff
Jesse Burkett	Rombauer
Maudie Burkett	Rombauer
Wm. Burkett	Rombauer
W. R. Burkett	Hendrickson
J. R. Burnes	Rombauer
George Burnett	Neelyville
L. V. Burnett	Neelyville
Fred Burpo	Poplar Bluff
M. Burpo	Poplar Bluff
Ben Burris	Qulin
George E. Burris	Fisk
H. C. Burris	Fisk
M. W. Buriss	Fisk
N. B. Burriss	Qulin
T. M. Burris	Fisk
J. M. Bourroughs	Neelyville
Mrs. A. L. Burson	Neelyville
Dave Burson	Neelyville
Frank Burton	Poplar Bluff
George Burton	Broseley
G. H. Burton	Poplar Bluff
Jas. Burton	Poplar Bluff
J. B. Burton	Poplar Bluff
R. R. Burton	Neelyville
R. F. Busby	Poplar Bluff
Henry Buschman	Rombauer
W. R. Buster	Neelyville
C. D. Butler	Poplar Bluff
Wm. Butler	Bastus
Jennie Butts	Broseley
C. F. Byord (sic)	Broseley
Alva B. Byrd	Broseley
John Byrd	Vastus
J. H. Byrd	Vastus
M. D. Caldwell	Poplar Bluff
Mrs. M. E. Caldwell	Vastus
T. N. Caldwell	Poplar Bluff
T. T. Caldwell	Harviell
Thomas Calhoun	Neelyville
Will Call	Poplar Bluff

J. H. Caloway	Qulin
C. O. Calvin	Broseley
C. W. Calvin	Qulin
S. E. Calvin	Broseley
Eva Camden	Harviell
G. M. Camden	Harviell
A. J. Campbell	Harviell
B. Campbell	Neelyville
Lee Campbell	Poplar Bluff
L. Campbell	Rombauer
S. A. Campbell	Qulin
T. E. Campbell	Harviell
W. E. Campbell	Ten Mile
Wm. Campbell	Poplar Bluff
Wm. Campbell (sic)	Poplar Bluff
E. Cambron	Harviell
Tom Candler	Fisk
C. C. Canley	Neelyville
A. R. Cannell	Poplar Bluff
C. S. Cannell	Poplar Bluff
H. J. Cannell	Poplar Bluff
Chas. Cantrell	Chaonia
W. M. Cantrell	Naylor
C. Capper	Poplar Bluff
J. H. Capper	Poplar Bluff
M. S. Carder	Fisk
Abe Cardwell	Poplar Bluff
C. Cardwell	Poplar Bluff
Jas. Cardwell	Neelyville
J. A. Cardwell	Poplar Bluff
J. L. Cardwell	Poplar Bluff
A. Carmon	Poplar Bluff
H. M. Carpenter	Poplar Bluff
John R. Carpenter	Poplar Bluff
J. D. Carpenter	Poplar Bluff
J. W. Carpenter	Poplar Bluff
J. S. Carpenter	Neelyville
Sam Carpenter	Qulin
Wm. Carpenter	Fisk
Ed Carrico	Poplar Bluff
Ed Carrico (sic)	Qulin
J. N. Carroll	Poplar Bluff
Ray Carroll	Harviell

Roy Carroll	Poplar Bluff
Willis Carroll	Poplar Bluff
S. A. Carson	Poplar Bluff
B. T. Carter	Harviell
Chas. Carter	Vastus
Chas. R. Carter	Vastus
E. A. Carter	Rombauer
G. B. Carter	Poplar Bluff
H. E. Carter	Qulin
Jess Carter	Fagus
J. W. Caruthers	Ten Mile
G. S. Cary	Fisk
J. J. Cash	Poplar Bluff
Roy Cash	Poplar Bluff
David Casey	Poplar Bluff
Ed Casey	Poplar Bluff
E. R. Casey	Fisk
Henry Casey	Poplar Bluff
John Casey	Hendrickson
J. R. Casey	Chaonia
Tom Casey	Hendrickson
M. Casey	Poplar Bluff
W. A. Cason	Poplar Bluff
James Casper	Rombauer
C. T. Cassinger	Vastus
Jos. Cassinger	Vastus
Dan Castillo	Poplar Bluff
Toby Cato	Neelyville
W. A. Cato	Broseley
W. E. Cato	Fisk
W. Cato	Broseley
Earl Cave	Poplar Bluff
J. B. Chadwick	Qulin
J. B. Chadwick	Poplar Bluff
Tom Chafinn	Fisk
Ab Chaffman	Fisk
J. B. Chalk	Qulin
A. C. Chapman	Neelyville
H. L. Chapman	Qulin
J. E. Chapman	Neelyville
Cora Chaney	Qulin
R. E. Chard	Moark
J. M. Chatam	Poplar Bluff

Chas. Chatman	Harviell
Franklie Chatman	Poplar Bluff
Lude Chatman	Harviell
Wm. Chatman	Poplar Bluff
H. C. Chediester	Neelyville
George Cheeks	Poplar Bluff
C. S. Chenault	Poplar Bluff
Etta Chenault	Poplar Bluff
John Chenault	Poplar Bluff
Robt. Chenoweth	Fairdealing
J. U. Cherry	Fisk
Mary Chilcutt	Ellsinore
W. L. Chilcutt	Upalika
A. Childress	Poplar Bluff
Jas. Childress	Rombauer
Jno. Childress	Poplar Bluff
Sam Childress	Rombauer
W. A. Childress	Rombauer
George Chitler	Qulin
C. T. Choisser	Poplar Bluff
W. M. Christian	Harviell
T. Christopher	Poplar Bluff
J. W. Christy	Fagus
D. W. Chronister	Poplar Bluff
John D. Chronister	Hendrickson
S. A. Chronister	Hendrickson
N. S. Chupp	Poplar Bluff
C. M. Clark	Poplar Bluff
Ed Clark	Wappapello
Everett Clark	Broseley
J. A. Clark	Neelyville
J. H. Clark	Ellsinore
J. P. Clark	Poplar Bluff
J. W. Clark	Ten Mile
Miles Clark	Neelyville
Theo Clark	Rombauer
W. W. Clark	Broseley
G. N. Clawson	Poplar Bluff
H. D. Clawson	Poplar Bluff
George Cleaver	Qulin
A. L. Clemons	Harviell
C. W. Clements	Poplar Bluff
Harve Clemons	Harviell

Eva Clevlen	Rombauer
Dan Click	Poplar Bluff
John Clifton	Fagus
R. G. Cline	Neelyville
Lawrence Cloin	Poplar Bluff
J. H. Coble	Poplar Bluff
S. W. Coble	Poplar Bluff
J. Cochran	Harviell
R. E. Cochran	Harviell
Sarah R. Cochran	Poplar Bluff
Willis Colcher	Poplar Bluff
D. M. Cole	Moark
F. S. Cole	Hendrickson
J. R. Cole	Poplar Bluff
Louie Cole	Poplar Bluff
M. C. Coley	Poplar Bluff
S. W. Coleman	Ten Mile
W. S. Coleman	Chaonia
J. W. Collard	Poplar Bluff
L. E. Collier	Fisk
Geo. Collins	Poplar Bluff
George Collins (sic)	Hendrickson
H. A. Collins	Harviell
H. L. Collins	Poplar Bluff
Lee Collins	Poplar Bluff
W. A. Colter	Qulin
Louis Colwell	Harviell
Oscar Colwell	Harviell
W. T. Colwell	Naylor
Mrs. E. A. Combs	Harviell
J. E. Combs	Harviell
Milo Conger	Poplar Bluff
G. L. Connor	Neelyville
J. A. Connor	Neelyville
Matt Connor	Wappapello
Pearlie Conner (sic)	Rombauer
Roy Connor	Wappapello
Floyd Conover	Qulin
Mabel Conover	Poplar Bluff
Wm. Conover	Poplar Bluff
Ed Cook	Qulin
Fred Cook	Broseley
H. A. Cook	Neelyville

Newton Cook	Qulin
Scott Cook	Qulin
Geo. Cooley	Qulin
W. C. Coolidge	Upalika
Chas. Coonce	Poplar Bluff
D. W. Coonce	Broseley
Geo. Coonce	Broseley
Lee Coonce	Broseley
L. R. Coonce	Fisk
S. M. Coonce	Poplar Bluff
W. A. Coonce	Harviell
W. F. Coonce	Poplar Bluff
E. L. Cooper	Poplar Bluff
E. L. Coopers (sic)	Ten Mile
J. R. Cooper	Poplar Bluff
Nancy J. Cooper	Harviell
Rhea Cooper	Harviell
Rosa Cooper	Poplar Bluff
T. J. Cooper	Poplar Bluff
Ben Copeland	Poplar Bluff
Ben Copeland (sic)	Poplar Bluff
T. V. Copeland	Poplar Bluff
W. E. Copeland	Hendrickson
J. J. Corder	Fagus
Chas. Cordon	Naylor
W. R. Corey	Poplar Bluff
Amos Corfford	Poplar Bluff
Wm. Cornelius	Neelyville
J. E. Costin	Harviell
H. L. Couch	Poplar Bluff
E. F. Coward	Hendrickson
J. M. Cown	Poplar Bluff
Mrs. J. M. Cown	Poplar Bluff
R. Cowsert	Fisk
F. L. Cox	Poplar Bluff
F. L. Cox (sic)	Poplar Bluff
I. M. Cox	Harviell
Jos. Cox	Fagus
R. F. Cox	Poplar Bluff
W. D. Cox	Poplar Bluff
Harrison Cozort	Fisk
J. D. Cozort	Fisk
W. C. Cozort	Fisk

A. Crabtree	Neelyville
Mack Crabtree	Harviell
Curtis Crady	Fisk
Jas. Crafford	Fisk
Jas. Craford (sic)	Poplar Bluff
Elbert Craft	Qulin
George Craft	Hendrickson
H. C. Craft	Fagus
J. R. Craft	Qulin
Philip Craft	Poplar Bluff
T. J. Craft	Qulin
Will Craft	Qulin
Will Craft (sic)	Qulin
C. W. Cragle	Ten Mile
Chas. Craig	Fisk
Curtis Craig	Fagus
C. P. Craig	Fisk
L. Craig	Poplar Bluff
Robt. L. Craig	Poplar Bluff
Alva Crain	Rombauer
C. B. Crain	Rombauer
Noah Crain	Rombauer
L. L. Crain	Wappapello
Eli Cravens	Poplar Bluff
G. T. Cravens	Poplar Bluff
Wm. Cravens	Poplar Bluff
W. A. Cravens	Fisk
Jas. Creek	Poplar Bluff
Grant Crews	Rombauer
Harve Crews	Broseley
Allen Crips	Poplar Bluff
J. W. Crislip	Poplar Bluff
John Crivitz	Poplar Bluff
E. L. Crockett	Poplar Bluff
Amos Crofford	Poplar Bluff
Andy A. Crofford	Poplar Bluff
Chas. Cross	Poplar Bluff
Wm. Crossfield	Harviell
James Crossin	Neelyville
J. A. Crow	Neelyville
Jasper Crowder	Fagus
Dr. A. Crump	Broseley
Ab Crunk	Harviell

Albert Crunk	Poplar Bluff
Sam Crunk	Harviell
Thos. Crunk	Poplar Bluff
Tom Culbertson	Qulin
H. R. Culp	Poplar Bluff
B. Cunningham	Neelyville
Jale Cunningham	Qulin
W. J. Cunningham	Upalika
A. C. Curdt	Neelyville
A. Curdt	Neelyville
H. C. Curnel	Poplar Bluff
Addie Curry	Neelyville
L. C. Curtis	Qulin
Wm. Dabrico	Harviell
F. W. Dages	Poplar Bluff
E. A. Dalton	Poplar Bluff
Edgar Dalton	Fisk
Henry Datton (sic)	Qulin
L. F. Dalton	Poplar Bluff
G. Daniels	Vastus
T. F. Daniels	Poplar Bluff
E. V. English (Out of Order, sic)	Neelyville
W. D. Darby	Fisk
D. H. Dare	Hendrickson
S. N. Dare	Williamsville
Belle Darham	Poplar Bluff
Joel W. Daughette	Poplar Bluff
W. T. Daughette	Poplar Bluff
N. E. Davenport	Williamsville
A. L. Davidson	Poplar Bluff
Cora Davidson	Neelyville
E. M. Davidson	Hendrickson
F. G. W. Davidson	Fisk
I. L. Davidson	Hendrickson
Jas. Davidson	Poplar Bluff
S. Davidson	Hendrickson
T. F. Davidson	Harviell
Alfred Davis	Qulin
Andrew Davis	Qulin
Arthur Davis	Qulin
Bert Davis	Neelyville
George C. Davis	Poplar Bluff
Geo. N. Davis	Poplar Bluff

G. F. Davis	Chaonia
G. H. Davis	Qulin
Graddie Davis	Fagus
H. C. Davis	Fisk
John Davis	Qulin
J. H. Davis	Poplar Bluff
J. O. Davis	Neelyville
J. R. Davis	Neelyville
J. T. Davis	Neelyville
J. W. Davis	Qulin
Leonard Davis	Fisk
L. E. Davis	Neelyville
Merret Davis	Poplar Bluff
M. A. Davis	Poplar Bluff
Nye Davis	Poplar Bluff
Robt. Davis	Fisk
Rosa Davis	Fisk
Roy Davis	Poplar Bluff
R. C. Davis	Poplar Bluff
R. L. Davis	Fisk
Silas Davis	Poplar Bluff
Sirena Davis	Fagus
Stephen Davis	Neelyville
Tommy Davis	Neelyville
T. M. Davis	Fisk
Walter Davis	Chaonia
W. B. Davis	Neelyville
W. C. Davis	Fisk
W. D. Davis	Poplar Bluff
W. H. Davis	Fisk
W. H. Davis (sic)	Poplar Bluff
W. H. Davis, Jr.	Poplar Bluff
E. E. Deak	Poplar Bluff
George Deal	Poplar Bluff
G. W. Deal	Poplar Bluff
Henry Deal	Poplar Bluff
H. L. Deal	Poplar Bluff
Frances Deal	Poplar Bluff
J. L. Deaton	Poplar Bluff
M. L. Deal	Vastus
L. Deaton	Poplar Bluff
L. Deaton (sic)	Hendrickson
V. S. Deaton	Poplar Bluff

R. Deckard	Harviell
J. C. Decker	Poplar Bluff
Osa Decker	Broseley
Wm. DeGroot	Poplar Bluff
Susan E. Deitz	Qulin
H. Deitzer	Poplar Bluff
Chas. A. Deken	Glennonville
Chas. Deken (sic)	Glennonville
J. M. Deken	Glennonville
Chas. Delaney	Harviell
L. H. Delaney	Neelyville
M. Delaney	Neelyville
Ed Demaris	Poplar Bluff
J. F. Dement	Broseley
Wm. Denhardt	Poplar Bluff
Clark Denning	Poplar Bluff
John F. Denning	Poplar Bluff
G. P. Dennis	Poplar Bluff
G. P. Dennis (sic)	Henderickson
Wm. Denny	Poplar Bluff
J. J. Depoyster	Broseley
C. A. Depriest	Naylor
Ollie Derrington	Poplar Bluff
G. E. Devall	Poplar Bluff
W. A. Diamond	Qulin
W. A. Diamond	Broseley
F. R. Dickens	Neelyville
H. C. Dickens	Harviell
H. Dietzer	Poplar Bluff
J. H. Dickey	Qulin
A. W. Divinnie	Fisk
Wm. Dixon	Poplar Bluff
W. H. Dixon	Poplar Bluff
Fred Dobbs	Fisk
Hattie Dobbs	Qulin
Rena Dobbs	Fisk
Vernon Dobbs	Poplar Bluff
W. R. Dobbs	Fisk
M. A. Dockins	Broseley
J. W. Dodd	Harviell
F. A. Dodson	Brosley
F. A. Dodson (sic)	Fisk
J. A. Dodson	Poplar Bluff

J. A. Dodson (sic)	Fisk
John Doggett	Fisk
G. W. Dollins	Neelyville
John Dollins	Neelyville
Lee Dollins	Neelyville
Lizzie Dollins	Neelyville
Ross Dollins	Neelyville
Roy Dollins	Neelyville
John Dolz	Poplar Bluff
J. R. Donica	Fisk
D. O. Donovan	Poplar Bluff
Tell Doolin	Neelyville
Jas. Dorsett	Poplar Bluff
Walter Dotts	Neelyville
R. L. Doudy	Neelyville
S. M. Doudy	Neelyville
Mrs. R. A. Dougherty	Fisk
A. Douglas	Fisk
Wm. Douglass	Poplar Bluff
A. Douthett	Fisk
B. F. Douthett	Fisk
Delphia Douthitt	Fisk
Arthur Dover	Broseley
C. E. Dover	Poplar Bluff
George Dover	Poplar Bluff
Ed Dowd	Poplar Bluff
O. L. Dowd	Poplar Bluff
Amos Doyle	Fagus
A. Doyle	Fagus
P. R. Doyle	Qulin
Bennie Drake	Poplar Bluff
A. W. Drennon	Poplar Bluff
M. Dreuall	Rombauer
A. D. Drew	Qulin
Ed Drew	Qulin
Fred Drew	Rombauer
P. V. Drury	Poplar Bluff
A. C. Dry	Poplar Bluff
C. A. Dry	Poplar Bluff
L. A. Duckett	Poplar Bluff
Mrs. T. J. Duckett	Poplar Bluff
Allen Duckworth	Neelyville
Walter Duckworth	Neelyville

W. M. Duckworth	Neelyville
T. J. Dudley	Neelyville
C. D. Duffy	Broseley
Chas. Duke	Fisk
M. M. Duke	Fisk
N. W. Duke	Poplar Bluff
Ollie Duke	Poplar Bluff
T. E. Dull	Vastus
Mrs. J. L. Duly	Poplar Bluff
J. F. Duncan	Poplar Bluff
Jess Dunehoo	Broseley
Lon Durham	Qulin
C. C. Dunlap	Harviell
Levi Dunlap	Harviell
Mary E. Dunlap	Harviell
H. E. Dunlapp	Harviell
J. A. Dunlapp	Harviell
Lonnie Dunlapp	Harviell
T. W. Dunlap	Poplar Bluff
Grover Dunlay	Harviell
A. M Dunn	Poplar Bluff
John Dunn	Harviell
Ernest Dunning	Poplar Bluff
F. J. Dunning	Broseley
G. W. Dunning	Poplar Bluff
H. W. Dunning	Poplar Bluff
John F. Dunning	Poplar Bluff
J. W. Dunning	Poplar Bluff
Mrs. M. J. Dunning	Qulin
Marvin Eaker	Neelyville
Otto Earl	Broseley
E. W. Earleman	Vastus
W. Earp	Qulin
J. H. Eastin	Harviell
Owen F. Eastin	Harviell
Mrs. H. Easton	Poplar Bluff
Alex Eastwood	Neelyville
Claud Eastwood	Qulin
Claude Eastwood	Fisk
Ed Eastwood	Broseley
L. D. Eastwood	Poplar Bluff
L. G. Eaton	Fisk
R. Edington	Neelyville

Ermon Edwards	Poplar Bluff
Harve Edwards	Poplar Bluff
John E. Edwards	Poplar Bluff
Thos. Edelman	Poplar Bluff
N. J. Edmonston	Hendrickson
Virgil Edwards	Fisk
Walter Edwards	Fisk
W. J. Edwards	Poplar Bluff
E. Ehlers, Sr.	Poplar Bluff
E. Ehlers, Jr.	Poplar Bluff
Chas. Ehrsam	Neelyville
A. G. Elan	Poplar Bluff
R. B. Elan	Poplar Bluff
Jos Elfers	Fisk
Pos. (sic) Elfers	Fisk
L. D. Elder	Qulin
W. J. Ellerman	Poplar Bluff
Howard Elliott	Hendrickson
H. B. Elliott	Hendrickson
F. Elliott	Hendrickson
K. L. Ellis	Harviell
W. F. Ellis	Hendrickson
Alex Emerson	Poplar Bluff
Dennis Emerson	Poplar Bluff
Frank Emerson	Poplar Bluff
G. A. Emerson	Poplar Bluff
H. H. Emerson	Poplar Bluff
J. A. Emerson	Rombauer
Robt. Emerson	Poplar Bluff
R. E. Emerson	Rombauer
Nancy Emery	Neelyville
Wm. Engles	Fagus
E. English	Fisk
Jas. English	Poplar Bluff
J. D. Enlow	Poplar Bluff
Ben Ennis	Neelyville
Joe Ennis	Neelyville
C. D. Epps	Poplar Bluff
C. R. Epps	Poplar Bluff
C. V. Epps	Poplar Bluff
J. A. Epps	Poplar Bluff
Thomas D. Epps	Harviell
T. A. Epps	Poplar Bluff

H. Epply	Hendrickson
Harry Ervin	Neelyville
W. A. Ervin	Neelyville
M. Erznoknik	Poplar Bluff
J. D. Esmon	Poplar Bluff
J. B. Essman	Poplar Bluff
M. Etheridge	Poplar Bluff
Ray Etheridge	Poplar Bluff
J. E. Eudaley	Upalika
M. A. Eudaley	Upalika
Mrs. A. Evans	Poplar Bluff
L. E. Everett	Fisk
N. L. Everhart	Ten Mile
Emma J. Every	Fisk
S. F. Ewing	Poplar Bluff
Mary Eye	Poplar Bluff
C. G. Ezell	Poplar Bluff
F. C. Fairless	Poplar Bluff
Robt. Fairless	Poplar Bluff
W. C. Fairless	Poplar Bluff
T. P. Faith	Harviell
Chas. Fann	Poplar Bluff
O. D. Fann	Poplar Bluff
Edgar Farmer	Qulin
Jas. Farmer	Qulin
J. A. Farmer	Vastus
J. W. Faucett	Harviell
M. F. Fauklin	Qulin
C. J. Felkins	Poplar Bluff
Jennie Felts	Harviell
E. Ferguson	Neelyville
J. H. Ferguson	Ellsinore
L. M. Ferguson	Poplar Bluff
T. J. Ferguson	Fairdealing
W. K. Ferguson	Poplar Bluff
F. C. Ferrill	Broseley
W. C. Fesler	Neelyville
D. B. Fields	Neelyville
R. L. Fields	Neelyville
W. M. Fielder	Rombauer
B. P. Finney	Poplar Bluff
Harry Fisher	Henderickson
R. L. Fisher	Poplar Bluff

S. E. Fisher	Neelyville
Carmin Flanakin	Hendrickson
R. E. Flanakin	Hendrickson
E. W. Floyd	Neelyville
Lou Fondle	Qulin
Doyle Forrest	Broseley
J. A. Forrest	Broseley
A. B. Foster	Qulin
C. E. Foster	Fisk
C. W. Foster	Neelyville
G. T. Foster	Poplar Bluff
L. W. Foster	Fisk
M. A. Foster	Broseley
M. A. Foster (sic)	Fisk
Mrs. M. E. Foster	Broseley
Mrs. M. Foster	Rombauer
Roy Foster	Broseley
V. Foster	Fisk
B. Foust	Poplar Bluff
C. A. Foust	Poplar Bluff
C. E. Foust	Poplar Bluff
Roy Foust	Vastus
M. M. Fouts	Neelyville
T. J. Fouts	Neelyville
Al Fowler	Neelyville
F. F. Fowler	Fagus
J. L. Fowler	Harviell
L. S. Fowler	Fagus
Richard Fowler	Neelyville
Roy Fowler	Neelyville
T. W. Fowler	Fagus
W. B. Fowler	Neelyville
Mrs. Jessie Fowlks	Qulin
Alfred Francis	Fisk
H. C. Francis	Poplar Bluff
A. Francisco	Poplar Bluff
E. Francisco	Poplar Bluff
Stanton Franey	Neelyville
George Franklin	Qulin
J. W. Franklin	Poplar Bluff
Mrs. John Franko	Poplar Bluff
W. D. Frasher	Fisk
Albert Fray	Harviell

F. Frazier	Fisk
M. Frazier	Harviell
Raymond Frazier	Fisk
D. C. Frederick	Poplar Bluff
S. D. Freeman	Harviell
S. D. Freeman (sic)	Neelyville
N. Freeman	Harviell
C. H. Freer	Poplar Bluff
J. G. Freer	Poplar Bluff
J. J. Freer	Poplar Bluff
George French	Neelyville
W. R. Friday	Hendrickson
Chas. Friend	Qulin
Lee Frizzell	Poplar Bluff
W. M. Frost	Broseley
J. T. Fry	Qulin
A. D. Fuller	Fagus
Chester Fuller	Rombauer
Ezra Fuller	Qulin
E. Fuller	Poplar Bluff
Jas. H. Fuller	Rombauer
Sarah E. Fuller	Rombauer
S. F. Fulton	Neelyville
J. P. Funk	Broseley
E. H. Funke	Poplar Bluff
Henry Funke	Poplar Bluff
A. B. Fuson	Fisk
Lee Gaden	Neelyville
G. L. Gage	Neelyville
J. N. Gaines	Broseley
Delmar Galbraith	Naylor
H. A. Gallimore	Poplar Bluff
J. A. Gamble	Poplar Bluff
J. H. Gamble	Poplar Bluff
C. L. Gandy	Poplar Bluff
W. R. Gandy	Poplar Bluff
A. Gann	Broseley
Pink Gann	Broseley
J. A. Gardner	Harviell
Robt. Gardner	Poplar Bluff
Walter Gardner	Poplar Bluff
Ed Garrett	Fisk
Ed Garrett (sic)	Poplar Bluff

Geo. Garrett	Poplar Bluff
Jessie Garrett	Neelyville
John Garrett	Poplar Bluff
J. M. Garrett	Williamsville
M. Garrett	Neelyville
S. E. Garrett	Neelyville
S. J. Garrett	Poplar Bluff
Wm. Garret (sic)	Poplar Bluff
W. M. Garrett	Poplar Bluff
Geo. Garrison	Poplar Bluff
Geo. W. Garver	Broseley
J. V. Garver	Broseley
W. L. Garver	Broseley
C. F. Gatewood	Fisk
C. L. Gatlin	Neelyville
Jas. Gaultney	Rombauer
Claud Gayle	Neelyville
F. E. Gayle	Neelyville
J. H. Gean	Rombauer
M. Glensloser	Poplar Bluff
Hettie Gentzen	Qulin
Arthur Gerdis	Neelyville
Katie Gerdis	Neelyville
E. A. George	Broseley
Mrs. C. O. Gerhart	Poplar Bluff
Jesse Gerten	Qulin
E. L. Gibbs	Harviell
J. W. Gibbs	Poplar Bluff
A. H. Gibson	Harviell
C. E. Gibson	Broseley
C. L. Gibson	Poplar Bluff
D. P. Gibson	Neelyville
C. F. Gibson	Neelyville
E. Gifford	Neelyville
W. H. Gilbreath	Fisk
C. F. Gillespie	Poplar Bluff
Joshua Gillespie	Poplar Bluff
Geo. S. Gilliam	Poplar Bluff
M. E. Gilliam	Poplar Bluff
T. B. Gilliam	Poplar Bluff
E. C. Gillihan	Fisk
W. D. Gillin	Fagus
Tom Gillion	Neelyville

J. R. Gillis	Taft
J. J. Gilman	Poplar Bluff
N. L. Ginnis	Neelyville
D. M. Githens	Neelyville
J. A. Givens	Fisk
N. F. Gladden	Poplar Bluff
M. C. Glass	Broseley
Mary Glasebrook	Neelyville
W. L. Glasgow	Neelyville
Irvin Glass	Poplar Bluff
H. L. Glass	Poplar Bluff
Luke Glass	Neelyville
Wm. Glenn	Poplar Bluff
Wm. Glover	Neelyville
F. Goble	Fisk
John Goddard	Rombauer
J. A. Godwin	Poplar Bluff
R. Goff	Broseley
Isaac Goings	Poplar Bluff
J. B. Goings	Poplar Bluff
Wm. F. Goings	Poplar Bluff
S. Goins	Poplar Bluff
J. V. Golden	Broseley
J. H. Goldsmith	Neelyville
Ethan Gomer	Neelyville
J. H. Gonterman	Poplar Bluff
B. W. Goodman	Fagus
J. W. Goodman	Broseley
A. C. Goodrich	Harviell
Earl G. Gordinier	Neelyville
R. Gordon	Ten Mile
B. C. Goss	Neelyville
L. D. Gossett	Poplar Bluff
B. L. Gourley	Vastus
Claud Gourley	Taft
Ed Gourley	Harviell
Bert Gowen	Vastus
D. W. Gowen	Harviell
W. D. Gowen	Poplar Bluff
J. D. Gower	Poplar Bluff
J. L. Grable	Neelyville
Romine Grable	Naylor
W. H. Graham	Poplar Bluff

Ernest Gratz	Harviell
Enlas Gray	Fisk
Howard Gray	Rombauer
J. M. Gray	Fisk
Manvil (sic) Gray	Rombauer
Mary E. Gray	Harviell
R. W. Gray	Rombauer
Henry Gravis	Fisk
Bert L. Greason	Poplar Bluff
M. H. Greason	Poplar Bluff
Dr. V. L. Greathouse	Fisk
Daniel Gregory	Poplar Bluff
Geo. Gregory	Neelyville
C. R. Green	Rombauer
C. R. Green (sic)	Poplar Bluff
Joe Green	Fisk
L. Green	Neelyville
T. L. Green	Neelyville
H. Greentree	Poplar Bluff
J. A. Greenwood	Harviell
G. H. Greer	Poplar Bluff
John Greer	Fisk
Scott Greer	Fisk
H. A. Grider	Neelyville
J. C. Grider	Harviell
M. Gridley	Qulin
Mary Griffem (sic)	Poplar Bluff
E. Griffith	Poplar Bluff
N. L. Grimes	Neelyville
A. B. Grisham	Harviell
Geo. C. Grizzle	Neelyville
Mrs. M. A. Grizzle	Vastus
Carl Grobe	Poplar Bluff
Louis Grobe	Poplar Bluff
Sherman Groshart	Poplar Bluff
J. E. Grove	Neelyville
J. W. Grove	Neelyville
A. H. Guard	Poplar Bluff
L. Guess	Broseley
W. A. Guess	Broseley
Zelman Guess	Broseley
Will Guffy	Poplar Bluff
Clarence Gulledge	Broseley

D. B. Gulledge	Broseley
H. F. Gulledge	Broseley
J. D. Gulledge	Broseley
L. H. Gulledge	Broseley
Clyde Gully	Poplar Bluff
U. K. Gully	Poplar Bluff
L. W. Guthrie	Neelyville
M. Guthrie	Rombauer
Robt. Gutherie	Rombauer
Geo. Haag	Poplar Bluff
John Haag	Poplar Bluff
M. D. Haag	Poplar Bluff
P. G. Haag	Fisk
A. R. Hager	Harviell
Jettie Hager	Harviell
J. H. Hagaer	Poplar Bluff
Will Hager	Poplar Bluff
John Hahn	Broseley
E. H. Hairer	Poplar Bluff
J. W. Haislip	Fisk
Robb Haley	Qulin
W. E. Haley	Poplar Bluff
Van Halferty	Fisk
C. A. Hall	Fisk
Ed Hall	Poplar Bluff
Everett Hall	Fisk
F. M. Hall	Poplar Bluff
Herman Hall	Vastus
Riley Hall	Vastus
T. J. Hall	Harviell
T. D. Hall	Poplar Bluff
Henry Halrath	Wappapello
L. E. Halter	Vastus
Eddie Ham	Rombauer
G. E. Ham	Rombauer
Ira Ham	Rombauer
J. A. Ham	Rombauer
J. R. Ham	Rombauer
K. L. Ham	Poplar Bluff
Lige Ham	Rombauer
C. E. Hamilton	Poplar Bluff
E. T. Hammons	Qulin
L. V. Hammons	Neelyville

D. P. Hampton	Poplar Bluff
J. D. Hampton	Poplar Bluff
Robt. Hamilton	Fairdealing
B. F. Hancock	Poplar Bluff
Scott Hancock	Vastus
W. E. Hancock	Poplar Bluff
H. Hanley	Broseley
Roy Hanley	Broseley
F. L. Hannoh	Harviell
G. H. Hannan	Broseley
W. W. Hardesty	Harviell
L. Harducek	Poplar Bluff
Geo. B. Hardin	Poplar Bluff
C. O. Hardin	Poplar Bluff
J. H. Hardin	Poplar Bluff
C. H. Hargrove	Poplar Bluff
C. S. Hargrove	Poplar Bluff
D. W. Hargrove	Poplar Bluff
J. L. Harman	Ten Mile
C. F. Harmon	Poplar Bluff
F. L. Harmon	Harviell
E. H. Harned	Poplar Bluff
Fay Harned	Poplar Bluff
Thos. Harold	Poplar Bluff
G. W. Harper	Qulin
Mrs. M. F. Harper	Poplar Bluff
H. O. Harrawood	Poplar Bluff
J. F. Harrell	Poplar Bluff
J. W. Harrell	Poplar Bluff
J. H. Harrelson	Broseley
C. S. Harris	Vastus
J. N. Harris	Fisk
Luther Harris	Poplar Bluff
M. Harris	Neelyville
M. V. Harris	Broseley
W. H. Harris	Harviell
W. L. Harris	Harviell
A. Harshberger	Hendrickson
G. W. Harshberger	Hendrickson
A. C. Hart	Harviell
A. H. Hart	Poplar Bluff
W. J. Harrignton	Fisk
D. A. Hart	Harviell

J. A. Harvey	Poplar Bluff
Lawrence Harvey	Poplar Bluff
J. H. Harwell, Sr.	Hendrickson
J. H. Harwell	Poplar Bluff
S. G. Harwell	Hendrickson
W. M. Harwell	Hendrickson
Emery Haskins	Neelyville
A. Hast	Qulin
Mike Hast	Poplar Bluff
Wm. Hast	Qulin
F. E. Hastings	Rombauer
J. C. Hastings	Hendrickson
Mrs. R. Hastings	Rombauer
F. M. Hathaway	Poplar Bluff
G. L. Hawkins	Harviell
Mae Hawkins	Qulin
Robt. Hawthorn	Poplar Bluff
Ed Hay	Harviell
Mrs. Belle Hayes	Fisk
Chris Hayes	Fisk
C. C. Hayes	Broseley
C. H. Hayes	Fisk
C. R. Hayes	Fisk
Geo. C. Hayes	Fisk
Hiram Hayes	Fisk
Joseph Hayes	Harviell
Mrs. J. C. Hayes	Broseley
Mrs. J. C. Hayes (sic)	Qulin
J. M. Hayes	Broseley
Louis Hayes	Broseley
M. Haynes	Wappapello
Sanford Hayes	Fisk
G. C. Hayman	Neelyville
H. C. Hayman	Harviell
J. G. Hayman	Vastus
J. H. Hayman	Harviell
C. Haynes	Poplar Bluff
F. A. Haynes	Poplar Bluff
Ralph Haynes	Poplar Bluff
Sam Haynes	Neelyville
W. R. Haynes	Neelyville
Chester Hays	Broseley
C. H. Hays	Fisk

Dave Hays	Poplar Bluff
H. Hays	Harviell
J. J. Hays	Poplar Bluff
J. W. Hays	Moark
W. C. Hays	Qulin
Anna Heacox	Fisk
Elbert Heacox	Fisk
Ira Heacox	Fisk
Hayward Head	Poplar Bluff
John Head	Poplar Bluff
J. L. Head	Poplar Bluff
Sidney Head	Poplar Bluff
T. M. Head	Poplar Bluff
Will Head	Poplar Bluff
John Headrick	Hendrickson
J. A. Heady	Hendrickson
S. P. Heady	Hendrickson
V. A. Heartley	Poplar Bluff
???? Heartline	Rombauer
Mrs. E. J. Hease	Harviell
R. A. Heath	Broseley
C. Hedspeth	Williamsville
Ira Hedspeth	Williamsville
Alfred Hefner	Fagus
John F. Hefner	Qulin
J. A. Hefner	Qulin
H. L. Helleman	Harviell
J. U. Hellums	Poplar Bluff
T. D. Hellums	Poplar Bluff
Dennis Helm	Poplar Bluff
Ed Helm	Poplar Bluff
H. Helm	Poplar Bluff
M. W. Helm	Poplar Bluff
W. E. Helm	Neelyville
R. H. Helton	Rombauer
Mrs. L. Helvy	Poplar Bluff
Aubrey Hemby	Qulin
Henry Hembry	Fagus
Jesse Hemmick	Neelyville
Adam Hencil	Poplar Bluff
W.H. Henderson	Harviell
W.R. Henderson	Fisk
E.P. Hendrickson	Poplar Bluff

Jas. Hendrickson	Hendrickson
Joe Hendrickson	Poplar Bluff
N. W. Hendrickson	Hendrickson
Austin Hendrix	Harviell
Geo. Hendrix	Broseley
J. L. Hendrix	Poplar Bluff
L. S. Hendrix	Poplar Bluff
Fred Henry	Romabauer
Gus Henry	Romabauer
John Henry	Poplar Bluff
P. H. Henry	Romabauer
Earl Hensley	Harviell
Leonard Hensley	Harviell
W. S. Hensley	Harviell
Ed Henson	Poplar Bluff
G. A. Henson	Broseley
John Henson	Fisk
J. R. Henson	Harviell
Walter Henson	Broseley
W. T. Henson	Harviell
E. F. Herrignton	Poplar Bluff
Edgar Hert	Poplar Bluff
J. E. Hert	Poplar Bluff
John Hesselrode	Poplar Bluff
John Hesselrode (sic)	Poplar Bluff
J. S. Hesselrode	Fisk
Wm. Hesselrode	Fisk
A. T. Hester	Poplar Bluff
W. D. Hester	Rombauer
Elmer Hicks	Fisk
Elvis Hicks	Broseley
Geo. W. Hicks	Poplar Bluff
John Hicks	Qulin
J. H. Hicks	Broseley
Robt. Hicks	Poplar Bluff
T. E. Hicks	Naylor
T. L. Hicks	Rombauer
C. L. Hickson	Poplar bluff
R. R. Hickson	Poplar Bluff
Geo. Highland	Fisk
J. F. Higga	Harviell
J. W. Hightower	Broseley
Fred Hildrich	Broseley

Robert Hildrich	Fisk
Andrew Hill	Poplar Bluff
A. B. Hill	Fisk
A. T. Hill	Broseley
J. W. Hill	Poplar Bluff
Riley Hill	Poplar Bluff
R. B. Hill	Fisk
S. L. Hill	Broseley
W. C. Hill	Broseley
W. S. Hill	Fisk
C. F. Hillis	Poplar Bluff
G. P. Hillis	Poplar Bluff
Henry Hillis	Poplar Bluff
Luther Hillis	Poplar Bluff
Sam Hillis	Fagus
E. J. Hines	Neelyville
S. Hines	Harviell
J. D. Hinkle	Moark
Elmer Hirby	Fagus
L. C. Hitchcock	Qulin
C. L. Hixon	Poplar Bluff
John Hodapp	Poplar Bluff
S. Hodapp	Poplar Bluff
H. F. Hodge	Hendrickson
J. M. Hodge	Poplar Bluff
R. H. Hodges	Poplar Bluff
Tom Hodge	Fisk
W. H. Hodge	Poplar Bluff
Fred Hodler	Neelyville
J. H. Hodler	Neelyville
Will Hodson	Poplar Bluff
F. W. Hoelscher	Poplar Bluff
Adam Hoerr	Neelyville
T. J. Hoff	Harviell
John Hoffman	Wappapello
J. A. Hoffman	Chaonia
J. L. Hoffman	Poplar Bluff
Sidney Hoffman	Chaonia
Carrie Hogan	Poplar Bluff
John Hogan	Vastus
L. Hogan	Harviell
J. H. Hoguse	Harviell
W. E. Hohn	Neelyville

H. H. Holford	Poplar Bluff
J. A. Holland	Poplar Bluff
J. W. Holland	Poplar Bluff
M. J. Holliday	Chaonia
Alice Hollis	Neelyville
A. D. Hollman	Broseley
E. O. Holloway	Poplar Bluff
Chester Holloway	Poplar bluff
J. T. Holman	Poplar Bluff
J. T. Holmes	Poplar Bluff
John Holsapple	Poplar Bluff
Chas. Hooberry	Broseley
E. I. Hood	Poplar Bluff
E. M. Hood	Rombauer
Jas. Hoops	Wappapello
H. A. Hoover	Poplar Bluff
T. E. Hopkins	Fisk
H. A. Hoppe	Poplar Bluff
S. A. Hoppe	Poplar Bluff
C. F. Horn	Harviell
O. Horton	Poplar Bluff
Chas. Hosfelt	Wappapello
Earl Hosfelt	Wappapello
L. M. Hough	Broseley
R. L. Houks	Poplar Bluff
H. House	Fagus
Bert Housman	Fisk
J. E. Houts	Poplar Bluff
Paul C. Houts	Poplar Bluff
C. A. Hover	Hilliard
C. F. Howard	Poplar Bluff
D. F. Howard	Poplar Bluff
J. J. Hower	Harviell
P. C. Howell	Poplar Bluff
Chas. Hoyle	Qulin
Jas. Hoyle	Qulin
John Hribshek	Harviell
Elmer Hubbs	Harviell
John Hubeck	Rombauer
Mace Huddleston	Neelyville
D. Hudgins	Poplar Bluff
J. S. Hudgins	Poplar Bluff
F. N. Hudson	Poplar Bluff

G. A. Hudson	Neelyville
J. W. Hudson	Neelyville
O. R. Hudson	Harviell
R. C. Hudson	Poplar Bluff
J. H. Hughy	Qulin
E. V. Huff	Poplar Bluff
S. W. Huff	Qulin
T. H. Huff	Fagus
Ben Humphrey	Poplar Bluf
Isaac Humphrey	Poplar Bluff
O. M. Humphrey	Fagus
Guy Hunley	Harviell
Mrs. C. A. Hunnicutt	Fisk
Alf Hunt	Poplar Bluff
Ben Hunt	Fisk
Chester Hunt	Neelyville
C. H. Hunter	Neelyville
Mary Hunter	Neelyville
A. J. Huskey	Poplar Bluff
B. Huson	Poplar Bluff
S. W. Huson	Poplar Bluff
J. S. Hutchison	Fairdealing
V. S. Hutchison	Fairdealing
M. B. Hutson	Poplar Bluff
E. O. Hyde	Neelyville
H. Inman	Poplar Bluff
H. Inman (sic)	Poplar Bluff
Hoy Inman	Chaonia
J. A. Inman	Elsinore
J. A. Inman (sic)	Poplar Bluff
Chas. Irny	Williamsville
D. B. Irby	Poplar Bluff
W. H. Irby	Poplar Bluff
N. M. Ivy	Harviell
B. Jackson	Neelyville
Curnel Jackson	Neelyville
H. A. Jackson	Harviell
J. Jackson	Neelyville
Marian Jackson	Fisk
Martha Jackson	Neelyville
M. M. Jackson	Poplar Bluff
W. D. Jackson	Broseley
Ambers James	Broseley

G. B. James	Broseley
H. N. James	Broseley
T. J. James	Harviell
Joe Jaminik	Poplar Bluff
John Jansen	Poplar Bluff
J. H. Jeffords	Harviell
Roy Jeffords	Harviell
Geo. Jenkins	Harviell
Homer Jenkins	Fisk
M. C. Jenkins	Harviell
R. Jenkins	Harviell
S. T. Jennings	Neelyville
H. L. Jett	Poplar Bluff
E. C. Jewel	Ten Mile
Basil Jiles	Qulin
Ruby Jiles	Qulin
T.M. Johns	Qulin
Archie Johnson	Neelyville
Arthur Johnson	Fisk
C. Johnson	Poplar Bluff
C. T. Johnson	Poplar Bluff
Frank Johnson	Poplar Bluff
G. B. Johnson	Poplar Bluff
G. H. Johnson	Neelyville
G. H. Johnson (sic)	Wappapello
G. J. Johnson	Wappapello
G. W. Johnson	Fisk
Isaac Johnson	Neelyville
Isaac Johnson (sic)	Poplar Bluff
L. H. Johnson	Neelyville
Jas. Johnson	Poplar Bluff
Joseph Johnson	Poplar Bluff
J. H. Johnson	Neelyville
J. H. Johnson (sic)	Fagus
J. P. Johnson	Qulin
J. T. Johnson	Poplar Bluff
J. W. Johnson	Fisk
K. H. Johnson	Harviell
L. B. johnson	Poplar Bluff
Mat Johnson	Broseley
M. E. Johnson	Harviell
Odie Johnson	Poplar Bluff
O. D. Johnson	Poplar Bluff

Sam Johnson	Neelyville
Silas Johnson	Poplar Bluff
W. M. Johnson	Ten Mile
J. T. Johnston	Fisk
John Joiner	Fisk
H. S. Joines	Qulin
Sam Joiner	Rombauer
Chas. Joines	Naylor
Chas. Joins (sic)	Naylor
Frank J. Jolly	Fisk
John F. Jolly	Fisk
John S. Jolly	Fisk
Ben Jonas	Poplar Bluff
E. C. Jonas	Poplar Bluff
W. B. Jonas	Harviell
W. J. Jonas	Harviell
Arthur Jones	Qulin
Chas. H. Jones	Fisk
C. T. Jones	Poplar Bluff
E. Jones	Fisk
E. B. Jones	Neelyville
E. I. Jones	Neelyville
E. S. Jones	Fagus
Helen Jones	Poplar Bluff
H. H. Jones	Fisk
H. H. Jones (sic)	Neelyville
Joe H. Jones	Fisk
J. C. Jones	Fisk
J. T. Jones	Poplar Bluff
Marion Jones	Qulin
Perry Jones	Poplar Bluff
S. J. Jones	Vastus
T. B. Jones	Harviell
Will Jones	Qulin
W. H. Jones	Fisk
W. M. Jones	Poplar Bluff
Hubert Jordan	Broseley
John F. Jordan	Fisk
M. W. Jordan	Neelyville
O. M. Jordan	Fisk
Wm. Jordan	Elsinore
Will Jordan	Broseley
O. Jordan	Fisk

Abby Joseph	Fisk
Ed Judy	Neelyville
George Julian	Upalika
W. C. Justice	Fisk
Albert Kaich	Qulin
B. F. Karsner	Poplar Bluff
Obe Kassinger	Poplar Bluff
Albert Kearbey	Ten Mile
B. C. Kearbey	Poplar Bluff
Carl Kearbey	Williamsville
Ellen E. Kearbey	Ten Mile
E. H. Kearbey	Ten Mile
F. L. Kearbey	Ten Mile
John Kearbey	Poplar Bluff
J. A. Kearbey	Poplar Bluff
J. E. Kearbey	Poplar Bluff
I. M. Kearbey	Poplar Bluff
W. H. Kearbey	Poplar Bluff
J. W. Keck	Ten Mile
A. L. Keel	Hendrickson
Ben Keel	Hendrickson
George Keel	Hendrickson
H. B. Keel	Hendrickson
John Keener	Poplar Bluff
R. T. Keener	Poplar Bluff
B. Keibardm (sic)	Taft
J. C. Keith	Fisk
George Kellogg	Poplar Bluff
Wm. Kellums	Poplar Bluff
W. F. Kelly	Fisk
W. K. Kelsaw	Broseley
Amos Kemp	Elsinore
E. M. Kennedy	Fisk
E. Kennedy	Broseley
Chas. Kenner	Poplar Bluff
E. H. C. Kenner	Poplar Bluff
J. R. Kent	Vastus
C. W. Kerr	Fisk
M. C. Kersting	Poplar Bluff
John Kerzek	Harviell
Chas. Ketchum	Poplar Bluff
Cora Ketchum	Poplar Bluff
W. P. Kilgore	Poplar Bluff

W. H. Killian	Poplar Bluff
E. H. Kinder	Chaonia
I. C. Kindrick	Upalika
Jas. Kinder	Chaonia
Jas. Kinder (sic)	Poplar Bluff
Arch King	Rombauer
A. J. King	Fagus
E. D. King	Williamsville
Frank King	Fagus
G. R. King	Qulin
J. D. King	Upalika
Manville King	Rombauer
Q. R. King	Qulin
William King	Fisk
W. R. King	Williamsville
Otis Kingery	Harvey
H. W. Kingree	Harvey
L. Kingree	Harvey
A. B. Kingsley	Poplar Bluff
John Kinkead	Poplar Bluff
C. J. Kinsey	Harviell
T. E. Kinsey	Harviell
H. M. Kipper	Broseley
A. Kirkley	Harviell
H. F. Kirkley	Harviell
Isaac Kirkley	Neelyville
J. H. Kirkley	Neelyville
A. D. Kirkman	Poplar Bluff
D. A. Kirkman	Poplar Bluff
E. V. Kirkman	Poplar Bluff
R. Kirkpatrick	Neelyville
Albert Kiser	Poplar Bluff
Geo. Kiser	Poplar Bluff
Jack Kiser	Poplar Bluff
L. J. Kiseer	Poplar Bluff
Max Kiser	Poplar Bluff
Roy Kiser	Poplar Bluff
R. L. Kiser	Poplar Bluff
D. C. Kittredge	Harviell
Lydia Knapp	Wappapello
S. M. Knier	Poplar Bluff
J. H. Knight (sic)	Fisk
J. H. Knight	Broseley

Selmon Knight	Vastus
J. L. Knowles	Fisk
August Koehler	Naylor
W. C. Koehler	Naylor
Frank Kovach	Harviell
Henry Kramer	Poplar Bluff
John Krevits	Poplar Bluff
W. S. Kriegbaum	Poplar Bluff
Geo. Kulkbrenner	Poplar Bluff
W. A. Kurz	Poplar Bluff
Fred Labrier	Poplar Bluff
N. Labrier	Poplar Bluff
Chas. Lacewell	Fisk
Perry Lacewell	Wappapello
Victor Lade	Poplar Bluff
T. J. Ladd	Poplar Bluff
Wm. Lafferty	Neelyville
Chas. Lambert	Qulin
C. M. Lampkin	Poplar Bluff
Carl Lampkin	Poplar Bluff
James Lampkin	Poplar Bluff
Frank Lancaster	Qulin
Plumer Lancaseter	Broseley
Henry Land	Upalika
John Land	Fisk
Riley Landreth	Fisk
Will Landreth	Poplar Bluff
D. G. Landrum	Poplar Bluff
J. M. Landrum	Taft
R. Landrum	Fisk
R. E. Landrum	Fisk
Sam Landrum	Fisk
Alex Lane	Poplar Bluff
Elmer Lane	Vastus
E. Lane	Poplar Bluff
F. E. :Lane	Poplar Bluff
F. E. Lane (sic)	Poplar Bluff
Joe Lane	Poplar Bluff
L. W. Lane	Poplar Bluff
M. M. Lane	Harviell
W. B. Lane	Poplar Bluff
Chas. Langley	Neelyville
E. S. Langley	Harviell

Geo. Langley	Neelyville
Jesse L. Langdon	Hendrickson
Jeff Langley	Neelyville
Rebecca Langley	Harviell
R. W. Langley	Neelyville
T. M. Langley	Harviell
David Lankford	Fisk
Tim Lantfort	Fisk
F. E. Latham	Poplar Bluff
J. G. Laughlin	Poplar Bluff
J. R. Laughlin	Poplar Bluff
Hulda Lawrence	Vastus
Lee E. Lawrence	Poplar Bluff
W. N. Lawrence	Harviell
Ed Lawson	Neelyville
J. A. Lawson	Neelyville
A. W. Lazalier	Neelyville
Ed Lazalier	Neelyville
C. C. Leach	Poplar Bluff
C. W. Leach	Williamsville
G. H. Leach	Poplar Bluff
J. A. Leach	Poplar Bluff
E. B. Leader	Poplar Bluff
Mrs. M. E. Leader	Harviell
H. W. Leatherman	Poplar Bluff
R. L. Ledbetter	Qulin
R. L. Ledbetter (sic)	Broseley
H. A. Lee	Poplar Bluff
J. W. Lee	Poplar Bluff
J. W. Lee (sic)	Rombauer
Robert Lee	Neelyville
Will Lee	Neelyville
M. Leer	Neelyville
Fred Legrand	Williamsville
Reuben Legrand	Upalika
Wm. Legrand	Ellsinore
E. H. Lemberg	Poplar Bluff
J. E. Leming	Harviell
C. S. Lemmons	Poplar Bluff
C. B. Leonard	Poplar Bluff
Fred Leonard	Fagus
Ralph Leonard	Fagus
I. E. Leonard	Poplar Bluff

Robt. Leonard	Fagus
F. M. Leslie	Williamsville
S. D. Leslie	Harviell
Alfred Leutert	Qulin
Frank Leutert	Qulin
Herman Leutert	Qulin
John Levick	Poplar Bluff
Evelyn Lewis	Neelyville
J. H. Lewis	Poplar Bluff
R. E. Lewis	Neelyville
Susie Lewis	Neelyville
Thad Lewis	Neelyvillw
Thomas Lewis	Neelyville
Wm. J. Lewis	Poplar Bluff
John Liddle	Fagus
C. R. Lilly	Naylor
W. B. Lilly	Poplar Bluff
H. J. Limbaugh	Poplar Bluff
S. J. Linder	Poplar Bluff
C. T. Lindsay	Broseley
L. C. Lindsay	Poplar Bluff
R. P. Lindsay	Broseley
Fritz Linger	Neelyville
R. L. Lingo	Poplar Bluff
Moses Linville	Wappapello
Jacob Liposek	Neelyville
A. R. Lipscomb	Qulin
Fred Lisky	Qulin
Dick Little	Qulin
Joe Little	Fisk
Mrs. Louisa F. Little	Fisk
M. T. Little	Harviell
Mrs. L. E. Livingston	Poplar Bluff
O. D. Livingston	Poplar Bluff
Paul Lockwood	Harviell
L. E. Loflin	Neelyville
Frank Loge	Poplar Bluff
Otto Lohmeier	Poplar Bluff
E. T. Long	Neelyville
J. D. Long	Ellsinore
J. R. :Long	Ellsinore
W. H. Long	Poplar Bluff
W. P. Long	Neelyville

J. A. Longer	Fisk
Jesse Looney	Qulin
G. E. Lorton	Wappapello
W. R. Love	Poplar Bluff
J. C. Lovelace	Poplar Bluff
W. A. Lowery	Poplar Bluff
B. D. Lucas	Broseley
T. B. Lucas	Qulin
Frank Lumpkin	Neelyville
John Lumpkins	Neelyville
Luther Lumpkins	Moark
Sam Lumpkins	Neelyville
G. W. Lusk	Neelyville
Mat. Lusk	Neelyville
R. L. Luster	Neelyville
D. O. Lutes	Neelyville
M. Luttrell	Neelyville
G. C. Lynch	Poplar Bluff
Nobie Lynn	Poplar Bluff
William Lynn	Fagus
C. H. Lyons	Fisk
Sim (sic) Mabin	Poplar Bluff
W. G. Mackley	Neelyville
W. T. Mackley	Neelyville
Abner Macom	Poplar Bluff
Clarence Macom	Poplar Bluff
Edward Maddux	Qulin
E. P. Maddux	Qulin
Jas. Maddux	Poplar Bluff
J. H. Maddux	Hendrickson
F. E. Magill	Hendrickson
George Magill	Hendickson
Henry Magill	Hendrickson
W. H. Magill	Hendrickson
W. Magill	Hendrickson
L. Maines	Poplar Bluff
C. C. Maize	Poplar Bluff
L. C. Maize	Poplar Bluff
F. T. Malady	Poplar Buff
Henry Malady	Poplar Bluff
Frank J. Mangold	Harviell
Mrs. S. E. Mangold	Harviell
Wm. Mangram	Poplar Bluff

J. W. Manion	Fisk
William Manley	Fisk
C. E. Mann	Qulin
J. R. Mann	Poplar Bluff
J. G. Mann	Poplar Bluff
W. H. Mann	Fisk
W. M. Mann	Qulin
W. O. Manns (sic)	Poplar Bluff
Fred Mansbridge	Fisk
J. C. Mansfield	Harviell
J. Maple	Fisk
W. A. Markel	Neelyville
W. A. Markel (sic)	Neelyville
A. Marler	Broseley
Frank Marler	Broseley
J. L. Marler	Broseley
Sarah J. Marler	Fisk
Thomas Marler	Fisk
B. Marley	Poplar Bluff
H. E. Marris	Neelyville
C. W. Marshall	Broseley
H. N. Marshall	Wappapello
J. A. Marshall	Poplar Bluff
R. T. Marshall	Poplar Bluff
R. T. Marshall	Vastus
S. L. Marshall	Poplar Bluff
A. Marschand	Neelyville
Eli Martin	Broseley
H. E. Martin	Fairdealing
J. C. Martin	Fairdealing
J. L. Martin	Poplar Bluff
M. V. Martin	Poplar Bluff
Roy Martin	Fairdealing
R. T. Martin	Poplar Bluff
Wm. Martin	Poplar Bluff
Henry Martins (sic)	Poplar Bluff
Mary E. Mary (sic)	Harviell
A. L. Mason	Poplar Bluff
T. G. Masley	Hendrickson
E. B. Masters	Fisk
John Mathis	Rombauer
J. E. Mathis	Neelyville
L. L. Mathis	Broseley

Ned Mathis	Neelyville
W. R. Mathis	Poplar Bluff
M. Mattick	Harviell
J. M. Mattingly	Fisk
T. F. Mattingly	Fisk
Albert Mayberry	Fagus
D. Mayberry	Naylor
D. W. Mayberry	Qulin
F. M. Mayberry	Broseley
J. H. Mayberry	Broseley
J. M. Mayberry	Fisk
L. T. Mayberry	Fisk
S. H. Mayberry	Fisk
W. C. Mayberry	Broseley
L. Mayes	Moark
T. L. Mayes	Poplar Bluff
G. E. Mayhugh	Poplar Bluff
William Mayo	Poplar Bluff
Ode McAllister	Neelyville
W. N. McArthur	Poplar Bluff
G. S. McBroom	Vastus
S. C. McBroom	Vastus
J. P. McCabe	Poplar Bluff
W. H. McCain	Fisk
C. E. McCauley	Harviell
J. R. McCauley	Harviell
J. W. McCauley	Harviell
M. McCauley	Harviell
Chas. McCarter	Hendrickson
C. W. McCave	Neelyville
Ed McChristian	Broseley
C. McClanahan	Poplar Bluff
Hattie McClanahan	Poplar Bluff
Walter J. McCollum	Neelyville
W. J. McCollum	Neelyville
Wm. McConkey	Wappapello
John McCormack	Neelyville
J. A. McCormack	Neelyville
D. M. McDaniel	Poplar Bluff
Wm. McDaniel	Vastus
D. L. McDaniels	Qulin
D. M. McDaniels	Poplar Bluff
Earl McDaniels	Qulin

S. J. McDaniels	Broseley
D. C. McElhannon	Fagus
E. S. McElroy	Ellsinore
Bertha McGee	Poplar Bluff
A. E. McGowen	Poplar Bluff
F. M. McGowen	Poplar Bluff
H. A. McGowen	Poplar Bluff
J. P. Robert McGowen	Poplar Bluff
W. J. McGowen	Poplar Bluff
D. G. McIntyre	Neelyville
James McIver	Qulin
T. J. McIver	Poplar Bluff
Willis McIver	Qulin
Wm. McIver	Qulin
P. M. McKay	Qulin
J. F. McKee	Qulin
C. C. McKim	Harviell
F. T. McKinkey	Poplar Bluff
A. L. McKinney	Poplar Bluff
J. L. McKinney	Poplar Bluff
J. L. McKinzie	Fisk
Leslie McKinzie	Fisk
L. C. McKinzie	Fisk
J. H. McLaughlin	Glennonville
Wm. McLean	Neelyville
I. N. McManus	Harviell
S. A. McManus	Harviell
H. W. McMullen	Neelyville
John McNece	Qulin
C. F. McNeece (sic)	Broseley
C. F. McNice	Qulin
J. C. McReynolds	Fisk
Vera McReynolds	Fisk
C. P. McRill	Poplar Bluff
W. F. McVey	Neelyville
Ethel McWilliams	Fisk
L. McWilliams	Broseley
J. S. Medcalf	Poplar Bluff
C. W. Meddeck	Qulin
A. E. Medlin	Broseley
Elmer Medlock	Qulin
Bell Melton	Broseley
I. L. Melton	Fagus

W. S. Melton	Poplar Bluff
J. D. Mercer	Fisk
T. W. Mercer	Fisk
A. L. Merrell	Qulin
J. T. Merrett	Harviell
Lucy Merriman	Poplar Bluff
J. H. Merritt	Poplar Bluff
Oscar Merritt	Poplar Bluff
Pearl Merritt	Poplar Bluff
W. T. Morrow	Harviell
L. A. Metz	Vastus
W. E. Meyers	Fisk
Louis Middleton	Poplar Bluff
M. Middleton	Poplar Bluff
J. H. Miflin	Poplar Bluff
C. O. Miles	Poplar Bluff
Oscar Miles	Poplar Bluff
A. N. Miller	Fisk
Chas. F. Miller	Naylor
C. F. Miller	Neelyville
David Miller	Fisk
D. M. Miller	Fisk
D. W. Miller	Fagus
E. L. Miller	Fagus
Fred E. Miller	Poplar Bluff
G. M. Milner (sic)	Broseley
G. W. Miller	Vastus
Henry Miller	Neelyville
Harry Miller	Neelyville
H. F. Miller	Fagus
Jane Miller	Fisk
John J. Miller	Neelyville
J. D. Miller	Neelyville
J. E. Miller	Neelyville
J. M. Miller	Rombauer
J. P. Miller	Poplar Bluff
J. R. Miller	Poplar Bluff
K. G. Miller	Poplar Bluff
Luther Miller	Fisk
Mike Miller	Rombauer
Mina A. Miller	Fagus
O. J. Miller	Vastus
Robt. Miller	Poplar Bluff

R. G. Miller	Poplar Bluff
S. P. Miller	Naylor
J. E. Milster	Fagus
G. F. Minks	Qulin
N. G. Minten	Poplar Bluff
S. W. Minten	Poplar Bluff
C. E. Mitchell	Poplar Bluff
Elza Mitchell	Poplar Bluff
Frank Mitchelle	Poplar Bluff
Raymond Mitchell	Poplar Bluff
T. B. Mitchell	Polar Bluff
Walter Mitchell	Vastus
Geo. W. Mitchner	Poplar Bluff
Mrs. P. H. Mitchelle	Poplar Bluff
H. W. Mittelhauser	Neelyville
Ed Mobley	Broseley
D. A. Mobley	Broseley
J. P. Mobley	Broseley
Curtis Monday	Fisk
M. M. Monday	Fisk
Roy Monday	Fisk
Wm. Monica	Fisk
A. L. Montague	Poplar Bluff
B. F. Montgomery	Poplar Bluff
H. O. Montgomery	Polar Bluff
Ira Montgomery	Poplar Bluff
James Montgomery	Poplar Bluff
J. F. Montgomery	Fisk
S. P. Montgomery	Qulin
Wm. Montgomery	Poplar Bluff
W. P. Montgomery	Poplar Bluff
Leonard Moomaw	Neelyville
Alice Moore	Harviell
Arthur Moore	Neelyville
A. W. Moore	Neelyville
Chas. Moore	Hendrickson
Claud Moore	Poplar Bluff
Clifford Moore	Neelyville
E. R. Moore	Vastus
E. R. Moore (sic)	Neelyville
Gertrude Moore	Neelyville
Harry Moore	Neelyville
H. V. Moore	Fisk

John Moore	Ellsinore
J. F. Moore	Fisk
J. H. Moore	Poplar Bluff
J. H. Moore (sic)	Ellsinore
J. H. Moore (sic)	Hendrickson
Mary Moore	Ellsinore
Sandford Moore	Hendrickson
Seba Moore	Neelyville
S. L. Moore (sic)	Vastus
S. L. Moore (sic)	Ellsinore
William Moore (sic)	Hendrickson
William Moore (sic)	Wappapello
Will Moore	Poplar Bluff
V. R. Moore	Fisk
Arno Moran	Fisk
Guy Morey	Harviell
George Morgan	Wappapello
Harry Morgan	Fisk
James Morgan (sic)	Harviell
James Morgan (sic)	Fisk
John Morgan	Fisk
J. W. Morley	Harviell
A. F. Morrison	Hendrickson
E. A. Morris (sic)	Fisk
E. A. Morris (sic)	Neelyville
George C. Morris	Harviell
Harry Morris	Broseley
Hugh Morris	Fisk
Mrs. James Morris	Broseley
John E. Morris	Poplar Bluff
John H. Morris	Poplar Bluff
J. L. Morris	Poplar Bluff
Mary E. Morrison	Poplar Bluff
M. Morris	Naylor
Naud Morris (sic)	Poplar Bluff
T. M. Morris	Broseley
W. L. Morris	Fisk
M. D. Morrison	Henderickson
C. V. Morrow	Poplar Bluff
G. W. Morrow	Harviell
R. F. Morrow	Harviell
J. H. Mosby	Fisk
Will Mosley	Poplar Bluff

G. W. Moss	Neelyville
Ira Moss	Neelyville
Roy Moss	Neelyville
S. L. Moss	Hendrickson
Alex Moton	Neelyville
L. A. Mott	Neelyville
Harry Mowery	Poplar Bluff
C. A. Murphy	Harviell
Joe Murphy	Poplar Bluff
Chas. Murray	Harviell
Emma Murray	Harviell
H. F. Murray	Neelyville
Ivan A. Murray	Poplar Bluff
James Murray	Neelyville
J. P. Murray	Neelyville
Logan Murray	Neelyville
Ross Murray	Harviell
Mrs. Sarah Murray	Harviell
Freddie Myers	Qulin
F. Myers	Fisk
F. S. Myers	Naylor
Henry Myers	Qulin
Hildegarde Myers	Fagus
B. F. Myrant (sic)	Neelyville
B. F. Myrant (sic)	Harviell
G. W. Myrant	Fagus
Jennie Myrant	Broseley
Doby Nash	Neelyville
Tom Nash	Neelyville
B. F. Nations	Broseley
Earl Nations	Broseley
Wade Nations	Broseley
Willie Nations	Broseley
B. F. Neel	Fisk
F. R. Neel	Vastus
L. C. Neal	Harviell
N. C. Neal	Poplar Bluff
W. A. Neal	Poplar Bluff
Howard Neely	Poplar Bluff
F. S. Neilson	Fisk
G. C. Nelson	Qulin
J. A. Nelson	Poplar Bluff
George Nentrup	Qulin

J. R. Nentrup	Qulin
Hannah Nesby	Neelyville
W. P. Nevill	Poplar Bluff
Fred Newingham	Poplar Bluff
A. Nichols	Poplar Bluff
C. P. Nichols	Poplar Bluff
N. N. Nichols	Poplar Bluff
W. F. Nichols	Williamsville
H. D. Niederstradt	Harviell
W. H. Niswanger	Poplar Bluff
M. P. Nixon	Harviell
R. L. Nixon	Poplar Bluff
T. F. Nixon	Poplar Bluff
W. D. Nixon	Harviell
J. F. Noah	Harviell
Mary E. Noah	Harviell
J. T. Noble	Qulin
M. F. Noble	Qulin
Robert Noble	Harviell
Chas. Nollman	Harviell
W. F. Nollman	Harviell
Chas. Nolty	Neelyville
M. H. Nolte	Poplar Bluff
Earnest Noon	Poplar Bluff
Thomas Noon	Poplar Bluff
George Norden	Fisk
E. Norden	Broseley
Fred W. Norden	Broseley
Jas. H. Norman	Qulin
John Norman	Qulin
L. Norman	Fagus
W. W. Norton	Qulin
Louis Nosse	Poplar Bluff
John Nunley	Poplar Bluff
P. E. Oakley	Poplar Bluff
E. Obemeier	Vastus
C. F. O'Connor	Poplar Bluff
E. O'daniel	Poplar Bluff
H. E. Odom	Harviell
H. W. Odom	Harviell
Tom Odom	Fisk
Wm. Odom	Fisk
L. V. O'Farrell	Poplar Bluff

A. L. Ogle	Qulin
Geo. O'Kane	Harviell
E. S. Old	Poplar Bluff
E. S. Old (sic)	Poplar Bluff
E. D. Oliver	Neelyville
L. J. Oliver	Neelyville
J. M. Oller	Qulin
P. J. Ookes (sic)	Neelyville
Frank O'Nal	Neelyville
Myrtle Ordway	Poplar Bluff
H. W. Osborne	Neelyville
J. F. Osborne	Neelyville
Mary E. Osborne	Hendrickson
O. O. Osborn	Harviell
R. G. Osborne	Hendrickson
S. N. Osborne	Hendrickson
V. osbirne	Fagus
Irvan (sic) Osbourne	Qulin
Isaac Osburner	Qulin
I. A. Osburne	Qulin
W. Osburne	Qulin
John Oster	Harviell
Louis Oster	Harviell
A. S. Overfield	Broseley
Matilda Overton	Rombauer
Will Overton	Rombauer
Luther Owen (sic)	Williamsville
A. R. Owens	Neelyville
C. C. Owens	Fisk
James Owens	Neelyville
Luther Owens (sic)	Williamsville
Louis Owens	Rombauer
M. W. Owens	Neelyville
Mrs. S. E. Owens	Neelyville
T. E. Owens	Poplar Bluff
L. E. Pace	Ellsinore
Wm. Page	Poplar Bluff
J. C. Page	Poplar Bluff
Angeline Palmer	Poplar Bluff
Colby Palmer	Qulin
George Palmer	Broseley
Henry Palmer	Broseley
J. C. Palmer	Broseley

J. E. Palmer	Broseley
Rosa Palmer	Hendrickson
Clel Pargin (sic)	Harviell
J. Pargin	Harviell
J. F. Parker	Broseley
L. Parker	Fisk
T. E. Parker	Poplar Bluff
Wallace Parkins	Poplar Bluff
E. B. Parks	Fagus
Harry Parks	Harviell
John Parks	Fagus
J. H. Parks	Fisk
C. M. Parrish	Neelyville
W. S. Parrish	Neelyville
G. P. Parsley	Poplar Bluff
Walter Parsley	Naylor
Ben Partenberry	Broseley
M. Partenberry	Broseley
V. Partridge	Poplar Bluff
Alice V. Patterson	Poplar Bluff
E. B. Patterson	Fagus
H. A. Patteson	Fagus
J. E. Patterson	Fagus
J. L. Patterson	Poplar Bluff
J. C. Patty	Poplar Bluff
Ira Payne	Neelyville
D. Payton	Vastus
Ed Pearce	Poplar Bluff
W. C. Pearson	Poplar Bluff
D. Pease	Neelyville
H. D. Pease	Harviell
Geo. W. Pedigo	Broseley
J. D. Penne;;	Hendrickson
Byrd Pennington	Harviell
Everett Pennington	Poplar Bluff
George Pennington	Fisk
Loy (sic) Pennington	Harviell
P. B. Pennington	Poplar Bluff
T. J. Pennington	Harviell
Wm. Pennington	Poplar Bluff
Mrs. W. J. Pennington	Harviell
W. L. Pennington	Poplar Bluff
A. C. Penrod	Fisk

F. E. Penrod	Fisk
Harry Penrod	Neelyville
Thomas Penrose	Moark
Anton Perc	Neelyville
Joe Perdosia	Poplar Bluff
Chas. Perdue	Poplar Bluff
Roy Perkins	Poplar Bluff
Chas. Pervis	Broseley
D. L. Peters	Neelyville
Louella Peters	Poplar Bluff
M. A. Peters	Neelyville
Wm. Peters	Neelyville
H. W. Peterson	Poplar Bluff
P. J. Peterson	Poplar Bluff
Chas. Petty	Qulin
Ed Petty	Qulin
Frank Petty	Broseley
M. J. Petty	Neelyville
W. H. Petty	Fisk
Amanda Pettypool	Fisk
Elbert Pettypool	Fisk
W. W. Pfrimmer	Poplar Bluff
R. D. Phelps	Poplar Bluff
William Phelps	Poplar Bluff
Bud Phillips	Hendrickson
F. M. Phillips	Broseley
Ira Phillips	Hendrickson
J. A. Phillips	Fisk
W. L. Phillips	Broseley
J. A. Piett	Poplar Bluff
Cora Pierce	Broseley
G. M. Pierce	Harviell
Ira Pierce	Broseley
James Pierce	Harviell
J. E. Pierce	Harviell
J. W. Pierce	Fisk
J. F. Piett	Qulin
G. L. Pigg	Harviell
G. W. Pigg	Hendrickson
H. W. Pigg	Harviell
John Pigg	Hendrickson
J. S. Pilkinton	Poplar Bluff
John Pinkston	Poplar Bluff

Roy Pipkin	Fagus
Sarah Pipkin	Fisk
Sid Pipkin	Fisk
Will Pipkin	Fisk
Roy Pitman	Qulin
A. Plunk	Poplar Bluff
Joe Pogjahin	Harviell
Jane Poke	Poplar Bluff
C. L. Pollard	Moark
G. T. Ponder	Harviell
J. A. Ponder	Poplar Bluff
I. N. Pool	Poplar Bluff
James K. Pool	Fisk
A. C. Poore	Harviell
Isom Pope	Fisk
Elmer Porch	Poplar Bluff
Chas. Port	Harviell
Dalton Porter	Poplar Bluff
Dennis Porter	Poplar Bluff
D. W. Porter	Poplar Bluff
Jas. Porter	Poppar Bluff
Jacob Potillo	Poplar Bluff
W. M. Potillo	Poplar Bluff
A. A. Potter	Poplar Bluff
Sam Potter	Fagus
A. E. Powell	Poplar Bluff
G. S. Powers	Poplar Bluff
G. W. Poers	Poplar Bluff
Mrs. Mary Pratt	Harviell
John Prenzel	Poplar Bkuff
A. L. Presson	Fisk
C. O. Presson	Broseley
Will Presson	Fisk
J. W. Prickard	Hendrickson
Joe Prickett	Poplar Bluff
G. W. Priest	Neelyville
G. P. Proctor	Harviell
E. Propse	Harviell
C. N. Pruett	Harviell
E. Pruett	Harviell
H. C. Pyles	Poplar Bluff
J. W. Pyles	Poplar Bluff
H. P. Qualls	Ellsinore

Chas. Queen	Rombauer
Julius Quiffinne	Poplar Bluff
L. B. Quigley	Poplar Bluff
O. Quigley	Fairdealing
Will Quigley	Poplar Bluff
W. J. Quigley	Fairdealing
J. F. Radcliff	Poplar Bluff
J. H. Radcliff	Poplar Bluff
T. D. Ragsdale	Neelyvillle
Fred Raines	Upalika
J. W. Raines	Ten Mile
Wesley Raines	Upalika
Walter Rainey	Neelyville
Earl Randalls	Poplar Bluff
Janie Randalls	Poplar Bluff
A. L. Raulston	Poplar Bluff
Chas. Raulston	Poplar Bluff
Hubert Raulston	Poplar Bluff
Alex Ravelette	Broseley
A. Rawlwy	Fisk
G. W. Ray	Broseley
James Ray	Poplar Bluff
J. G. Ray	Hendrickson
Ira Ryamer	Poplar Bluff
T. L. Read	Poplar Bluff
Jay Reading	Poplar Bluff
Joe Reading	Poplar Bluff
Tom Reason	Rombauer
T. A. Reciter	Fisk
A. B. Reddins	Broseley
J. A. Redford	Poplar Bluff
Otis Redford	Polar Bluff
Harry Reed	Harviell
H. E. Reed	Hendrickson
H. E. Reed (sic)	Poplar Bluff
Rosa Reed	Broseley
W. C. Reed	Fisk
W. E. Reed	Fisk
William Reed	Qulin
E. M. Reeder	Broseley
G. I. Reeder	Broseley
Ralls Reeder	Broseley
John Reese	Fisk

A. Reeves	Fisk
Jack Reeves	Fisk
S. B. Reeves	Qulin
T. A. Renfro	Poplar Bluff
Freank Repotee	Fairdealing
John Resnik	Poplar Bluff
A. Restle	Neelyville
C. R. Revelle	Ten Mile
Ollie Reynolds	Qulin
Jas. Rhodes	Poplar Bluff
William Rhodes	Poplar Bluff
Mrs. M. R. Risinger	Fisk
Ralph Risinger	Rombauer
George Risley	Poplar Bluff
C. H. Roach	Harviell
J. B. Roach	Poplar Bluff
B. D. Roark	Poplar Bluff
J. E. Roark	Ellsinore
W. B. Roark	Poplar Bluff
W. T. Roark	Ellsinore
Richards (sic) Rpbbins	Poplar Bluff
R. H. Robbs	Neelyville
John Roberts	Fisk
J. W. Roberts	Fisk
W. D. Roberts	Neelyville
Jack Roberson	Poplar Bluff
C. E. Robertson	Poplar Bluff
F. L. Robertson	Poplar Bluff
H. Robertson	Poplar Bluff
T. R. Robertson	Broseley
A. C. Robinson	Poplar Bluff
Frank Robinson	Poplar Bluff
H. G. Robinson	Poplar Bluff
Jess Robinaon	Harviell
Mary F. Robinson	Chaonia
Walter Robinson	Harviell
Wm. Robinson	Qulin
Albert Rodawald	Qulin
E. W. Robison	Poplar Bluff
V. C. Roden	Neelyville
John Roe	Broseley
C. R. Rogers	Fisk
C. F. Rogers	Poplar Bluff

M. Rogers	Harviell
W. D. Rogers	Poplar Bluff
H. F. Rohlfing	Naylor
H. L. Rohlfing	Naylor
Rempt. (sic) Rohlfs	Harviell
A. R. Roland	Qulin
W. A. Roland	Poplar Bluff
C. V. Rommell	Poplar Bluff
J. R. Rone	Poplar Bluff
E. Z. Rouse	Neelyville
J. C. Roper	Hendrickson
F. M. Rose	Poplar Bluff
Howard Rose	Hendrickson
James Rose	Neelyville
H. F. Roseman	Poplar Bluff
A. C. Rose	Qulin
Carroll Ross	Vastus
J. P. Rowark	Broseley
Clarence Ross	Broseley
B. S. Royal	Neelyville
B. B. Bowden	Fisk
Martin Bribar	Fairdealing
E. Z. Rubottom	Williamsville
W. L. Rubottom	Upalika
W. D. Rudisil	Poplar Bluff
C. K. Rudolph	Poplar Bluff
J. D. Ruser	Poplar Bluff
D. A. Rush	Qulin
Fred Rush	Qulin
Alice Rushin	Harviell
Mary Rushin	Harviell
Robert Rushin	Harviell
J. W. Rushing (sic)	Neelyville
Frank Russell	Poplar Bluff
Geo. Russell	Poplar Bluff
W. S. Russell	Poplar Bluff
Will Rust	Poplar Bluff
F. X. Ryan	Poplar Bluff
S. E. Ryan	Poplar Bluff
J. W. Saddler	Broseley
P. Saltzman	Fisk
Clarence Sanders	Poplar Bluff
D. W. Sanders	Poplar Bluff

J. R. Sanders	Vastus
Ollie Sanders	Poplar Bluff
G. P. Sanderson	Fisk
Carl Sappington	Harviell
H. S. Sappington	Harviell
John G. Sappington	Harviell
Rhode Sarver	Chaonia
Henry Sasse	Ten Mile
I. M. Sauer	Ten Mile
James Savage	Neelyville
Hugh Saylors	Poplar Bluff
T. W. Scates	Ellsinore
Fred Schach	Harviell
O. J. Schalk	Poplar Bluff
A. Schenewerk	Poplar Bluff
C. A. Schenewerk	Poplar Bluff
P. C. Schenewerk	Poplar Bluff
Christ Schisler	Poplar Bluff
F. L. Schisler	Poplar Bluff
Henry Schisler	Poplar Bluff
H. J. Schisler	Poplar Bluff
W. A. Schloterback	Poplar Bluff
H. J. Schmerbauch	Poplar Bluff
J. H. Schmidt	Poplar Bluff
P. C. Schrader	Fisk
Will C. Schroeder	Harviell
Harry Schuber	Poplar Bluff
T. J. Schumaker	Poplar Bluff
Ed Schumer	Qulin
John Schumer	Qulin
H. M. Schull	Poplar Bluff
Arthur Scofield	Wappapello
John Scofield	Wappapello
J. A. Scofield	Wappapello
Chester Scoggins	Poplar Bluff
H. A. Scoggins	Poplar Bluff
J. Q. Scoggins	Poplar Bluff
Andrew Scott	Poplar Bluff
A. O. Scott	Harviell
Bert Scott	Neelyville
Chas. Scott	Poplar Bluff
Clint Scott	Neelyvillle
E. O. Scott	Poplar Bluff

F. A. Scott	Neelyville
Grant Scott	Neelyville
J. H. Scott	Poplar Bluff
J. M. Scott	Neelyville
Will Scott	Neelyville
W. E. Scott	Neelyville
W. H. Scott	Fisk
W. J. Scott (sic)	Fisk
W. J. Scott	Broseley
J. H. Secrets (sic)	Wappapello
J. H. Secrets	Rombauer
Alice E. Seger	Moark
Ed Seger	Moark
S. K. Seger	Neelyville
H. E. Seeley	Williamsville
Wm. Seiberts	Qulin
Mary Sert	Fisk
A. G. Seypohltowsky (sic)	Poplar Bluff
Ed Shackleford	Harviell
Fred Shaffer	Poplar Bluff
Geo. Shaffley	Neelyville
O. U. Shain	Fisk
Verlin Shain	Fisk
C. A. Shamblin	Hendrickson
Odie Shanks	Rombauer
W. O. Sharp	Poplar Bluff
C. L. Shaw	Poplar Bluff
L. M. Shaw	Poplar Bluff
Martin Sheckler	Ten Mile
Jesse Sheehy	Poplar Bluff
W. H. Sheehy	Poplar Bluff
J. E. Sheely	Hendrickson
J. T. Sheffield	Fisk
C. C. Shehane	Upalika
B. F. Shelton	Poplar Bluff
W. O. Shelton	Poplar Bluff
E. S. Sheppard	Poplar Bluff
L. Sheppard	Neelyville
John Sheridan	Ten Mile
Luther Sheridan	Ten Mile
W. O. Sheridan	Ten Mile
W. H. Sherman	Poplar Bluff
W. S. Sherry	Poplar Bluff

R. M. Shiffley	Fagus
J. E. Shipp	Poplar Bluff
J. J. Shively	Neelyville
J. J. Shoat	Hendrickson
R. A. Shoat	Williamsville
R. L. Short	Harviell
W. J. Short	Fagus
James Shoup	Poplar Bluff
Adam Shrout	Harviell
Frank Shrum	Harviell
J. T. Shrum	Harviell
E. S. Shull	Qulin
J. Shull	Qulin
Noah Shurell	Chaonia
John H. Sickles	Fisk
W. A. Silkwood	Vastus
F. H. Simmering	Hendrickson
Frank Simmons	Poplar Bluff
H. E. Simmons	Poplar Bluff
Jas. Simmons	Harviell
M. D. Simmons	Poplar Bluff
J. H. Simms	Harviell
J. W. Simms	Harviell
Lee Simms	Harviell
C. B. Simpson	Naylor
E. B. Simpson	Haylor
Sam Sinks	Poplar Bluff
Sidney Sinks	Poplar Bluff
Earl Sisco	Fisk
Thomas Sisco	Broseley
Frank Sisney	Poplar Bluff
John Sisney	Poplar Bluff
J. B. Sizemore	Poplar Bluff
J. B. Sizemore	Poplar Bluff
J. H. Summers	Poplar Bluff
D. M. Skelton	Neelyville
Fannie Skaggs	Neelyville
M. L. Skaggs	Poplar Bluff
Ed Slabaugh	Broseley
John Slabaugh	Hendrickson
J. L. Slabaugh	Poplar Bluff
L. F. Slabaugh	Broseley
L. M. Slabaugh	Hendrickson

S. S. Slade	Poplar Bluff
Anton Slance	Neelyville
P. W. Slayton	Fairdealing
C. B. Sliger	Poplar Bluff
J. M. Sliger	Poplar Bluff
S. M. Sliger	Hendrickson
Z. B. Sliger	Poplar Bluff
Chas. Sloan	Poplar Bluff
M. F. Sloan	Neelyville
W, M. Sloan	Neelyville
John Slovinsky	Poplar Bluff
John Smart	Neelyville
A. B. Smith	Qulin
Ben Smith	Neelyville
B. B. Smith	Poplar Bluff
Chas. Smith (sic)	Vastus
Chas. Smith	Hendrickson
Clarence Smith	Vastus
C. E. Smith	Poplar Bluff
C. F. Smith	Harviell
C. L. Smith	Neelyville
C. L. Smith (sic)	Hendrickson
E. A. Smith	Ellsinore
Fred Smith	Harviell
George Smith	Poplar Bluff
George W. Smith	Qulin
Geo. Smith	Hendrickson
Herman Smith	Harviell
Harry Smith	Neelyville
Henry Smith	Neelyville
H. L. Smith	Neelyville
H. V. Smith	Neelyville
I. C. Smith	Poplar Bluff
Joe Smith	Neelyville
Joseph Smith	Fisk
J. R. Smith	Harviell
J. W. Smith	Fisk
Lon Smith	Qulin
Martha J. Smith	Poplar Bluff
M. R. Smith	Poplar Bluff
Mary J. Smith	Fisk
Nannie F. Smith	Hendrickson
Mrs. Nora Smith	Broseley

Odie Smith	Poplar Bluff
O. L. Smith	Poplar Bluff
P. G. Smith	Poplar Bluff
Mrs. Rena Smithers	Fairdealing
Rosco Smith	Fisk
Ruth Smith	Poplar Bluff
T. H. Smith	Fisk
Willie Smith	Neelyville
Wm. Smith	Fisk
W. M. Smith	Fagus
W. T. Smith	Neelyville
W. V. Smith	Poplar Bluff
C. A. Smock	Neelyville
Frank Smoody	Harviell
Cyrena Smother	Naylor
Robt. Sneathern	Poplar Bluff
W. H. Sneed	Fisk
A. W. Snider	Broseley
John W. Snider	Ten Mile
L. M. Snider	Fisk
M. Snider	Fisk
W. H. Snyder	Poplar Bluff
Frank Soli	Neelyville
A. Somerlott	Fisk
J. S. Somerlott	Fisk
Chas. Sommers	Poplar Bluff
C. L. Sommers	Harviell
J. L. Sommers	Fagus
Mrs. George P. Spangler	Rombauer
C. N. Sparkman	Poplar Bluff
J. E. Sparkman, Sr.	Poplar Bluff
J. E. Sparkman, Jr.	Poplar Bluff
Leslie Sparkman	Poplar Bluff
Mrs. Leslie Sparkman	Hendrickson
Nannie Sparkman	Poplar Bluff
T. H. Sparkman	Hendrickson
William Sparkman	Poplar Bluff
Ed Spell	Fairdealing
Ernest Spell	Fairdealing
Lena Spelts	Poplar Bluff
Rena Spelts	Poplar Bluff
Harold Spencer	Neelyville
J. D. Spencer	Poplar Bluff

J. H. Spencer	Poplar Bluff
J. J. Spencer	Poplar Bluff
J. P. Spencer	Poplar Bluff
J. J. Spitzig	Neelyville
Ben Spradling	Poplar Bluff
E. S. Spradling	Poplar Bluff
James Spradling	Poplar Bluff
Joe Spradling	Poplar Bluff
John Spradling	Poplar Bluff
H. S. Spradling	Poplar Bluff
M. S. Spradling	Poplar Bluff
M. T. Spradling	Poplar Bluff
Robert Spradling	Poplar Bluff
Guy Springer	Neelyville
D. L. Spurlock	Poplar Bluff
Alonzo Stage	Poplar Bluff
John Stage	Poplar Bluff
Lucinda Stage	Poplar Bluff
Samuel Stage	Poplar Bluff
Clint Stallings	Fagus
J. T. Stamp	Fisk
A. A. Stanley	Poplar Bluff
Harve Stanley	Poplar Bluff
Jack Stanley	Poplar Bluff
R. L. Steed	Poplar Bluff
Mack Steed	Poplar Bluff
John Steele	Poplar Bluff
J. G. Steele	Poplar Bluff
John Steenks	Fairdealing
Walter Steinberg	Fagus
Joe Stepp	Poplar Bluff
A. B. Stevens	Poplar Bluff
E. R. Stevens	Poplar Bluff
Frances Stevens	Poplar Bluff
J. O. Stevens	Fisk
D. F. Stevenson	Hendrickson
Ed Steward	Poplar Bluff
Alfred Stewart	Hendrickson
T. E. Stewart	Hendrickson
Will Stewart	Hendrickson
R. A. Stilley	Poplar Bluff
Wm. Stinger	Harviell
C. C. Stinson	Poplar Bluff

T. M. Stitt	Neelyville
B. A. Stoker	Neelyville
James Stoker	Fisk
Henry Stone	Poplar Bluff
Mrs. M. E. Stone	Poplar Bluff
R. H. Stoner	Fisk
G. E. Stout	Harviell
H. G. Stout	Harviell
J. D. Stout	Taft
J. L. Stout	Harviell
W. A. Stout	Harviell
J. L. Strayhorn	Neelyville
Henry Street	Neelyville
Wm. Street	Hendrickson
John Stringfel	Poplar Bluff
V. Stringfel	Poplar Bluff
B. W. Stroud	Broseley
Noah Stroud	Moark
Rey (sic) Stroud	Broseley
D. A. Stucker	Poplar Bluff
Elmer Stucker	Poplar Bluff
George Stucker	Poplar Bluff
Geo. Stucker (sic)	Poplar Bluff
J. G. Stucker	Poplar Bluff
J. B. Stull	Vastus
C. H. Stults	Vastus
E. L. Stults	Vastus
Chas. St. Cin	Neelyville
David St. Cin	Neelyville
J. H. St. Clair	Fairdealing
Tom St. Clair	Poplar Bluff
Anton Suder	Neelyville
W. H. Sutherland	Poplar Bluff
J. S. Sutt	Fisk
W. H. Sutt	Fisk
M. A. Sutton	Williamsville
J. N. Swan	Broseley
J. W. Swan	Poplar Bluff
Lawrence Swan	Neelyville
Tom Swafford	Broseley
L. S. Swan	Neelyville
W. J. Swan	Broseley
James Swank	Harviell

J. D. Swanson	Poplar Bluff
Frank Talley	Broseley
J. L. Talley	Broseley
R. J. Talley	Broseley
Tom Talley	Broseley
James Talton	Rombauer
Lee Tarpley	Poplar Bluff
Nathan Tarpley	Rombauer
William Tarpley	Rombauer
J. L. Tate (sic)	Fisk
J. L. Tate	Neelyville
J. W. Tate	Fisk
J. Tatman	Neelyville
J. W. Tatman	Neelyville
D. W. Taylor	Poplar Bluff
F. B. Taylor	Poplar Bluff
J. B. Taylor	Poplar Bluff
J. H. Taylor	Fisk
J. T. Taylor	Harviell
L. Taylor	Ellsinore
Lawrence Taylor	Upalika
O. D. Taylor	Poplar Bluff
S. C. Taylor	Poplar Bluff
Mrs. S. J. Taylor	Poplar Bluff
Wesley Teel	Fisk
John Templemere	Poplar Bluff
James Terry	Neelyville
J. N. Terry	Rombauer
John Tesowick	Neelyville
Eva Thedford	Poplar Bluff
A. J. Thies	Poplar Bluff
William H. Thies	Poplar Bluff
A. J. Thomas	Hendrickson
Chas. Thomas	Broseley
C. C. Thomas	Fisk
George Thomas	Fisk
James Thomas	Fagus
L. B. Thomas	Neelyville
J. H. Thomas	Poplar Bluff
J. L. Thomas	Poplar Bluff
Nancy Thomas	Fisk
W. R. Thomas	Poplar Bluff
John W. Thomason	Fagus

C. T. Thomeure	Harviell
Andy Thompson	Poplar Bluff
A. J. Thompson	Harviell
J. F. Thompson	Fisk
J. M. Thompson	Fisk
Lon G. Thompson	Poplar Bluff
Lon Thompson	Poplar Bluff
L. R. Thompson	Broseley
M. C. Thompson	Fisk
P. W. Thompson	Fisk
Sam Thompson	Poplar Bluff
Toney Thompson	Fisk
W. M. Thompson	Fisk
David Thorn	Poplar Bluff
A. A. Thurman	Poplar Bluff
E. E. Thurman	Poplar Bluff
M. Thurman	Poplar Bluff
Frank Tibbs	Poplar Bluff
J. H. Tibbs	Poplar Bluff
Perry Tidwell	Harviell
Lee Tilly	Poplar Bluff
S. T. Tilly	Chaonia
A. W. Timmerman	Qulin
Joe Timmons	Poplar Bluff
M. W. Timmons	Poplar Bluff
Sanford Timmons	Vastus
H. Tinker	Hendrickson
L. C. Tinker	Hendrickson
William Tinker	Williamsville
W. C. Tinker	Williamsville
Earl Tinsley	Harviell
F. M. Tisdial	Neelyville
F. M. Tisdial	Naylor
Monroe Tittle	Qulin
D. F. Todd	Neelyville
Ed Todd	Poplar Bluff
E. L. Todd	Poplar Bluff
Jesse F. Todd	Vastus
E. L. Toliver	Neelyville
J. W. Tollum	Ten Mile
S. B. Toliver	Neelyville
D. M. Tomerlin	Fisk
Jas. Tomerlin	Poplar Bluff

R. C. Tomes	Broseley
G. E. Tomlin	Poplar Bluff
P. E. Tomlin	Hendrickson
Wm. Tommerlin	Qulin
J. W. Tomurlin	Poplar Bluff
Dow Tompkins	Qulin
Mrs. M. E. Toutant	Hendrickson
L. L. Towns	Neelyville
R. B. Towns	Neelyville
Bert Townsend	Neelyville
Dan Townsend	Fisk
Louis Townsend	Neelyville
N. E. Townsend	Neelyville
M. A. Track	Moark
D. A. Trebble	Taft
N. T. Tremble	Ten Mile
George Trent	Poplar Bluff
Harry Trent	Poplar Bluff
J. W. Trent	Poplar Bluff
Harry Trentleman	Neelyville
Martin O. Tripp	Fisk
A. O. Trostle	Poplar Bluff
W. A. Trostle	Poplar Bluff
Mary Trusty	Poplar Bluff
W. G. Trousdale	Poplar Bluff
George F. Tubb	Poplar Bluff
George M. Tubb	Poplar Bluff
Leona Tubb	Poplar Bluff
L. A. E. Tubb	Poplar Bluff
William Tucker	Vastus
T. A. Tune	Chaonia
C. B. Turley	Poplar Bluff
George Turner	Neelyville
G. W. Turner, Sr.	Poplar Bluff
Henry Turner	Neelyville
Jack Turner	Neelyville
James Turner	Neelyville
J. C. Turner	Neelyville
Mrs. L. F. Turner	Fisk
Mary Turner	Neelyville
Nola Turner	Harviell
R. L. Turner	Neelyville
L. W. Twaddle	Broseley

John Uebelein	Poplar Bluff
Leo Uhl	Poplar Bluff
Tony Ule	Poplar Bluff
Evert Upton	Poplar Bluff
Will Urich	Poplar Bluff
W. Vance	Poplar Bluff
C. H. Vandover	Fairdealing
R. Vandover	Fairdealing
M. M. Vankirk	Rombauer
E. W. Vansel	Qulin
Floyd Vansel	Qulin
Chas. D. Vaughn	Fisk
Sam Vaughn	Hendrickson
Guy Van Vulkenburg	Vastus
Mary A. Verble	Fisk
Allie Vinson	Chaonia
Claud Vinson	Fagus
Jas. Vinson	Fagus
J. W. Vinson	Poplar Bluff
S. D. Vinson	Poplar Bluff
Will Vinson	Poplar Bluff
F. E. Vroman	Poplar Bluff
J. R. Wade	Fisk
W. C. Wade	Fisk
J. W. Wadlington	Neelyville
Mrs. J. A. Waggoner	Vastus
R. M. Waggoner	Neelyville
J. M. Waggoner	Fisk
Mrs. J. P. Waggoner	Poplar Bluff
J. L. Wagster	Qulin
J. W. Walker	Fisk
S. W. Walker	Neelyville
T. J. Walker	Harviell
Wylie Walker	Poplar Bluff
W. B. Walker	Wappapello
W. H. Walker	Qulin
Isaac Waller	Poplar Bluff
Pearl Waller	Qulin
L. E. Walls	Neelyville
Sylvester Walls	Poplar Bluff
Ammon Walter	Qulin
Elmer Walter	Neelyville
George Walters	Neelyville

Chas. Walton	Qulin
Chester Walton	Ellsinore
D. R. Walton	Ellsinore
T. H. Walton	Qulin
W. L. Walton	Ellsinore
A. W. Warbington	Rombauer
Bell Warbington	Poplar Bluff
E. T. Warbington	Harviell
T. J. Warbington	Harviell
Z. T. Warbington	Harviell
Arthur Ward	Ten Mile
Chas. Ward	Poplar Bluff
D. A. Ward	Poplar Bluff
G. W. Ward	Poplar Bluff
John Ward	Ten Mile
J. A. Ward	Qulin
J. H. Ward	Harviell
J. V. Ward	Fisk
Robt. Ward	Poplar Bluff
S. A. Ward (sic)	Fairdealing
S. A. Ward	Harviell
Thomas Ward	Harviell
Will Ward	Neelyville
William Ward	Poplar Bluff
J. C. Warmack	Poplar Bluff
Louis Warmack	Poplar Bluff
Bert Warren	Neelyville
D. S. Warren	Broseley
Elva Warren	Poplar Bluff
Fred L. Warren	Poplar Bluff
Herbert Warren	Poplar Bluff
J. W. Warren	Fisk
R. W. Warren	Poplar Bluff
George Washington	Neelyville
G. W. Waterall	Poplar Bluff
A. W. Waters	Qulin
B. F. Waters	Fisk
J. W. Waters	Broseley
C. H. Watkins	Harviell
J. O. Watkins	Poplar Bluff
V. H. Watkins	Poplar Bluff
D. Watson	Poplar Bluff
D. Watson (sic)	Poplar Bluff

G. W. Watson	Rombauer
W. A. Watson	Poplar Bluff
W. C. Watson	Poplar Bluff
Thos. Watts	Fisk
J. L. Weaver	Poplar Bluff
J. W. Weaver	Neelyville
Ernest Webb	Neelyville
E. F. Webb	Harviell
H. H. Webb	Poplar Bluff
I. N. Webb	Harviell
J. G. Webb	Poplar Bluff
J. G. Webbn(sic)	Qulin
L. W. Webb	Poplar Bluff
William Webb	Qulin
T. E. Webber	Neelyville
A. J. Weishrod	Poplar Bluff
F. X. Weishrod	Poplar Bluff
C. L. Wellemeyer	Neelyville
J. L. Weller	Poplar Bluff
George Wells	Broseley
James Wells	Poplar Bluff
Jasper Wells	Fisk
L. A. West	Neelyville
McCoy Wells	Rombauer
Mrs. N. E. Wells	Harviell
Richard Wells	Fisk
W. J. West	Poplar Bluff
J. E. Weston	Poplar Bluff
George A. Whalen	Poplar Bluff
James Whalen	Ten Mile
N. W. Whalen	Ten Mile
J. C. Wheatley	Moark
S. A. Whetley	Moark
bert Wheeling	Hendrickson
M. Wheelis	Poplar Bluff
R. E. Whiffen	Poplar Bluff
U. R. Whiffen	Poplar Bluff
W. S. Whiffen	Poplar Bluff
Joseph Whistler	Qulin
C. C. White	Poplar Bluff
Ed White	Fisk
Grant White	Fisk
E. E. White	Poplar Bluff

H. L. White	Fisk
James White	Hendrickson
John White	Poplar Bluff
J. L. White	Neelyville
Leb White	Poplar Bluff
R. M. White	Poplar Bluff
Walter White	Poplar Bluff
Walter W. White	Rombauer
W. A. White	Poplar Bluff
W. F. White	Fisk
A. E. Whiteside	Ellsinore
Ed Whitehead	Neelyville
J. E. Whitley	Poplar Bluff
W. W. Whitlow	Qulin
Andy Whitmer	Poplar Bluff
Wm. Whitmer	Poplar Bluff
J. H. Whitsed	Poplar Bluff
Frank Whittington	Broseley
Frank Whittington (sic)	Neelyville
James Whittington	Broseley
T. F. Whitworth	Poplar Bluff
G. H. Wicks	Fisk
George Widmer	Neelyville
T. A. Wilcutt	Poplar Bluff
T. S. Wilcutt	Poplar Bluff
Frank Wilkerson	Fisk
Frank Wilkerson (sic)	Rombauer
George T. Wilkerson	Fagus
Lawrence Wilkerson	Fisk
W. A. Wilkerson	Fisk
Sam Wilkins	Broseley
C. R. Wilks	Qulin
J. A. Wilks	Qulin
C. W. Williams	Poplar Bluff
Etta Williams	Neelyville
H. Williams	Broseley
James Williams	Poplar Bluff
Jas. Williams	Hendrickson
John Williams	Fisk
J. H. Williams	Qulin
J. H. Williams (sic)	Fisk
W. M. Williams	Broseley
B. F. Williamson	Fisk

Geo. Williamson	Fisk
James Williamson	Fisk
John Williamson	Fisk
Mary P. Williamson	Fisk
R. C. Williford	Fisk
Charles Willis	Fisk
Mat Willoughby	Poplar Bluff
Anderson Wilson	Poplar Bluff
Brown Wilson	Poplar Bluff
C. M. Wilson	Poplar Bluff
Dovie Wilson	Williamsville
E. B. Wilson	Poplar Bluff
John Wilson	Poplar Bluff
J. D. Wilson	Qulin
J. J. Wilson	Poplar Bluff
Milam Wilson	Poplar Bluff
N. E. Wilson	Harviell
William Wilson	Broseley
William Wilson (sic)	Poplar Bluff
William R. Wilson	Poplar Bluff
W. A. Wilson	Poplar Bluff
W. F. Wilson	Naylor
W. H. Wilson	Broseley
Earl C. Winder	Fisk
Jack Windel	Rombauer
J. C. Winder	Fisk
Lizzie Winder	Poplar Bluff
Chas. Windle	Harviell
George Wisdon	Harviell
H. A. Wisdom	Harviell
H. O. Wisdom	Harviell
Fred Wisecarver	Upalika
G. N. Wisecarver	Upalika
Henry Wisecarver	Upalika
J. R. Wisecarver	Upalika
Steven Wisecarver	Williamsville
W. W. Wiseman	Harviell
Clyde Withrow	Poplar Bluff
Jess Withrow	Poplar Bluff
Chas. W. Witte	Poplar Bluff
O. W. Witte	Poplar Bluff
Irvin Wood	Upalika
J. T. Wood	Vastus

J. W. Wood	Upalika
Robt. Wood	Poplar Bluff
J. E. Woodall	Qulin
A. L. Woodruff	Poplar Bluff
W. H. Woodruff	Poplar Bluff
Ben Woods	Neelyville
Henry Woods	Hendrickson
Hugh Woods	Hendrickson
J. C. Woods	Poplar Bluff
J. R. Woods	Qulin
W. A. Woolsey	Neelyville
J. F Wooly	Harviell
George Wooten	Poplar Bluff
Clyde Worley	Naylor
C. E. Worley	Naylor
James Wormack	Poplar Bluff
William Wormack	Poplar Bluff
Clarence Wright	Poplar Bluff
Curnel Wright	Poplar Bluff
Jerry Wright	Fick
J. C. Wright	Neelyville
Marion Wright	Wappapello
Mary Wright	Rombauer
Nathan Wright	Poplar Bluff
Robert Wright	Poplar Bluff
Samuel Wright	Poplar Bluff
C. W. Wyley	Neelyville
C. W. Yates	Qulin
M. York	Poplar Bluff
S. R. York	Poplar Bluff
Henry Young	Poplar Bluff
James Young	Poplar Bluff
W. D. Young	Fisk
Frank Zadniz	Neelyville
William Zeigler	Williamsville
William Zimmerman	Neelyville
A. W. Zoll	Rombauer
J. H. Zuck	Poplar Bluff
Samuel Zumalt	Ellsinore

<u>Additional Names Section</u>

Julia Allen	Fisk
Geo. Bailey	Chaonia
Edwin Baker	Williamsville

John Batton	Naylor
Lee Batton	Naylor
J. W. Beck	Wappapello
J. M. Bennett	Wappapello
L. W. Bennett	Wappapello
T. A. Black	Hendrickson
P. J. Bounds	Wappapello
C. L. Boyer	Wappapello
Emma Bullis	Naylor
E. B. Bullis	Naylor
W. T. Caldwell	Harviell
W. D. Carter	Fisk
J. E. Chapman	Harviell
H. E. Cook	Harviell
H. J. Corner	Broseley
G. W. Cross	Broseley
Flint Curd	Broseley
Fred davis	Ellsinore
Oscar Denman	Wappapello
C. M. Dunhapp	Fairdealing
A. R. Earls	Broseley
J. W. Edwards	Broseley
J. C. Garrett	Hendrickson
Jas. Gean	Hendrickson
John Gilbert	Williamsville
J. C. Gilbert	Williamsville
L. R. Green	Naylor
Ed Groves	Williamsville
James Groves	Williamsville
R. E. Gulledge	Fisk

Christian County, Missouri, Prison Records, 1887 - 1889

Prisoner's Name	Age	Arrested	Charge
Wm. Roberts, Jr.	38	Mar. 13, 1887	Murder
Sam Preston	54	Mar. 13, 1887	Murder
Sam Preston, Jr.	23	Mar. 13, 1887	Murder
James Preson	24	Mar. 14, 1887	Murder
Bud Ray	30	Mar. 13, 1887	Murder
Jessie Robertson	21	Mar. 16, 1887	Murder
William Abbott	43	Mar. 15, 1887	Murder
J.R. McGuire	24	Mar. 17, 1887	Murder
Jack Hiles	24	Mar. 15, 1887	Murder
John Hiles	29	Mar, 15, 1887	Murder

Name	Age	Date	Crime
J.M. Nash	27	Mar. 18, 1887	Murder
G. Applegate	27	Mar. 17, 1887	Murder
J.S. Nash	19	Mar. 18, 1887	Murder
W.J. Johns	29	Mar. 18, 1887	Murder
John Mathews	39	Mar. 15, 1887	Murder
Wiley Mathews	23	Mar. 15, 1887	Murder
Jim Mathews	18	Mar. 15, 1887	Murder
Chas. Graves	37	Mar. 15, 1887	Murder
William Newton	25	Sep. 2, 1887	Murder
Amos Jones	20	Mar. 15, 1887	Murder
C. O. Simmons	30	Mar. 15, 1887	Murder
Wm. Stanley	38	Mar. 15, 1887	Murder
Andy Adams	27	Mar. 17, 1887	Murder
Lewis Davis	32	Mar. 17, 1887	Murder
Peter Davis	23	Mar. 17, 1887	Murder
*Wm. Walker	18	Mar. 29, 1887	Murder

*Executed May 29, 1889

Name	Age	Date	Crime
Joseph Hyde	26	Mar. 15, 1887	Murder
William Mapes	21	Apr. 29, 1887	Perjury
John Mapes	24	Apr. 29, 1887	Perjury
James King	??	Apr. 29, 1887	????
Harve Wheeler	??	Oct. 6, 1887	Concealed Weapon
Geo. Houston	??	Nov. 14, 1887	Arson
J.H. Riddle	??	Nov. 25, 1887	Petty Larceny
A.G. Riddle	??	Nov. 25, 1887	Petty Larceny
William Meadows	??	Dec. 14, 1887	Displaying a Firearm
Thomas Garrison	??	Dec. 23, 1887	Petty Larceny
Frank Kessinger	??	Dec. 30, 1887	Concealed Weapon
Lee Butler	??	Jan. 5, 1888	Arson
D.W. Rains	??	Jan. 7, 188	Selling liquor without a license
D.J. Gallagher		Feb. 1, 1888	Unlawful Conveyance
John Murphy	??	Feb. 11, 1888	Concealed Weapon
Wm. Prichard	??	Feb. 15, 1888	Concealed Weapon
Henry Trott	??	Feb. 27, 1888	Gambling
Guss Cloud	??	Feb. 27, 1888	Gambling
S.B. Caskey	??	Mar. 1, 1888	Concealed Weapon
Landon Whitlock	??	Mar. 2, 1888	Concealed Weapon
Frank Kessinger	??	Mar. 3, 1888	Concealed Weapon
Mat Nash	??	Mar. 3, 1888	Assault & Battery
Samuel Coin	??	Mar. 5, 1888	Concealed Weapon
Frank Williams	??	Mar. 11, 1888	False Pretense
John Nash	??	Mar. 12, 1888	Assault & Battery

Name	Age	Date	Offense
Andy Adams	??	Feb. 25, 1888	????
William Stillings	??	Mar. 14, 1888	Concealed Weapon
Joe M'Clughen	??	Mar. 14, 1888	Felonious Assault
Monroe Stillings	??	Mar. 15, 1888	????
Wm. Prichard	??	Mar. 11, 1888	Concealed Weapon
Henry Baimer	??	Mar. 16, 1888	Disturbing the Peace
Samuel Bolin	??	Mar. 23, 1888	Disturbing Religious Worship
J.M. Nash	??	Mar. 22, 1888	????
Jas. Kinney	??	Apr. 31, 1888	Battery & Larceny
M. Bright	??	May 3, 1888	Explosive Discharge of a Weapon
William Lee	??	May 3, 1888	Assault & Battery
Isaac Meadley	??	May 10, 1888	Petty Larceny
Wm. Bailey	??	May 10, 1888	Petty Larceny
G.W. Bailey	??	May 10, 1888	????
Edna Johnson	??	May 18, 1888	Larceny
John Smith	28	Jul. 2, 1888	Grand Larceny
Joseph Grayham	22	Jul. 2, 1888	Grand Larceny
Wm. Walton	??	Jul. 5, 1888	Disturbing Religious Worship
M. M. Inmon	??	Jul. 14, 1888	Disturbing the Peace
Willian Marley	??	Aug. 6, 1888	Assault & Battery
Albert Highly	??	Aug. 7, 1888	Explosive Discharge of a weapon
Andre Baily	??	Aug. 9, 1888	Battery & Larceny
James Carr	??	Aug. 25, 1888	Concealed Weapon
William Hemphill	??	Aug. 25, 1888	Larceny
Thomas Baily	??	Aug.28, 1888	Disturbing the Peace
Fletcher Guinn	??	Aug. 29, 1888	Concealed Weapon
Andy Bright	??	Sep. 3, 1888	????
Walter Todd	??	Sep. 3,1888	Assault & Battery
WilliamRoberts	??	Sep. 5, 1888	Assault & Battery
Colres Galloway	??	Sep. 10,1888	Exibiting a Dangerous Weapon
Wm. McCauly	??	Sep. 10, 1888	Distrubing Religious Worship
G.M. Rice	??	Sep. 25, 1888	Concealed Weapon
Sherman Walker	??	Sep. 25, 1888	Concealed Weapon
Emla Erb	??	Oct. 3, 1888	Petty Larceny
J.C. Rucker	??	Oct. 8, 1888	False Pretence
Jim Barry	??	Oct. 11, 1888	1st Degree Murder

Name	Age	Date	Charge
Wm. Miles	??	Oct. 11, 1888	1st Degree Murder
R. D. Johnson	??	Nov. 12, 1888	Disturbing the Peace
W. P. Halberslebew	21	Nov. 30, 1888	Grand Larceny
Frank Johnson	20	Nov. 30, 1888	Grand Larceny
Wm. Bedford	18	Nov.30, 1888	Grand Larceny
Thos. Rooney	??	Dec. 4, 1888	Grand Larceny
William Lawson	??	Dec. 4, 1888	Grand Larceny
Wm. Walton	??	Feb. 2, 1889	Distrubing the Peace
Frank B. Ambrose	??	Feb. 22, 1889	1st Degree Murder
William M. Ambrose	??	Feb. 22, 1889	1st Degree Murder
Joe Stephens	??	Feb. 22, 1889	Assault and Battery
Wm. Shelton	??	Feb. 25, 1889	Assault and Battery
John Wetherman	??	Feb. 26, 1889	Disturbing Religious Worship
Daniel Redmond	??	Feb. 26, 1889	Disturbing Religious Worship
Thomas Sims	??	Feb. 26, 1889	Assault and Battery
William Sweringin	??	Feb. 27, 1889	Assault and Battery
John Hancock	??	Feb. 28, 1889	Assault and Battery
Frank Gideon	??	Feb. 28, 1889	Concealed Weapon
R.H.H. McCanley	??	Feb. 28, 1889	Selling Liquor without a License
Newton Hayes	??	Feb. 28, 1889	Disturbing Religious Worship
Wm. Tennis	??	Mar. 1, 1889	Concealed Weapon
John Mapes	??	Mar. 2, 1889	Assault and Battery
Joe Inman	??	Mar. 4, 1889	Riot
J.R. White	??	Apr. 1, 1889	Disurbing Religious Worship
Elijah White	??	Apr. 1, 1889	Disturbing Religious Worship
James Miles	??	Apr. 7, 1889	Murder Accesseror
Mike Gray	??	Apr. 13, 1889	Insane
William Prichard	??	Apr. 15, 1889	Concealed Weapon
N. B. Terry	??	Apr. 29, 1889	Concealed Weapon
W. Gibson	??	May 8, 1889	Notorious Lewdness
T. V. Gibson	??	May 8, 1889	Notorious Lewdness
Sarah Guinn	??	May 11, 1889	Assault and Battery
Martha Guinn	??	May 11, 1889	Assault and Battery
James Purssley (sic)	??	May 13, 1889	Disturbing Religious Worship
Davis Elis Dudley	??	May 25, 1889	False Pretense

Name		Date	Offense
Geo. Bright	??	Jun. 22, 1889	Concealed Weapon
Josh Vaughn	??	Jun. 22, 1889	Disturbing the Peace
N. B. Terry	??	Jun. 27, 1899	Breaking in the Post Office
Albert Combs	??	Aug. 7, 1889	Murder 1st Degree
James Miles	??	Aug. 7, 1889	Murder 1st Degree
Wm. Bohannan	??	Aug. 10, 1889	Concealed Weapon
Thos. Harp	??	Aug. 10, 1889	Concealed Weapon
James Pursley	??	Aug. 20, 1889	Concealed Weapon
Thos. Sims	??	Aug. 23, 1889	Assault and Battery
John Rains	??	Aug. 26, 1889	Disturbing the Peace
John Wigley	??	Aug. 27, 1889	Playing cards on Sunday
James Guinn	??	Aug, 27, 1889	Gambling
Al Guinn	??	Aug. 27, 1889	Gambling
Dan Redmond	??	Aug. 27, 1889	Disturbing Religious Worship
Ellis Scott	??	Sep. 5, 1889	Concealed Weapon
Frank Bleadsoe	??	Sep. 6, 1889	Sodomy
A. J. Carson	??	Sep. 5, 1889	Battery and Larceny
W. L. Maxwell	??	Sep. 5, 1889	Gambling
Wm. Harris	??	Sep. 5, 1889	Battery and Larceny
Thos. Davis	??	Aug. 27, 1889	Shooting on s public road
Catherine Hale	??	Sep. 10, 1889	Concealing Birth
W. W. Mathews	??	Sep. 15, 1889	Slander
James Pursley	??	Sep. 23, 1889	Breaking custody
W. G. Dewitt	??	Sep. 30, 1889	Grand Larceny
S. B. Nix	??	Oct. 17, 1889	Disturbing the Family Peace
James Miles	??	Aug. 7, 1889	Murder of C.E. Branson
Luther Carter	??	Nov. 12, 1889	Playing cards on Sunday
Newton Hayes	??	Dec. 2, 1889	????
W. J. Pierce	??	Dec. 22, 1889	Assault and Battery

<u>Railroad Passes and some other Railroad miscellaneous information.</u>
  1859 The Terre Haute, Alton, & St. Louis Railroad Co., St. Louis, Missouri, $5, No 240, Registered by A. Ware, Signed C. Murdock, treas.; James A. Raynn, vice-pres..

December 31, 1865 North Missouri Railroad issued to D. W. Kilbourne, Vice President, Des Monies Rail Road, No.342, signed Isaac H. Sturgeon.

1869 Raritan and Delaware Bay Rail Road issued to J. S. Wandell.

1870 Galveston, Houston & Henderson Rail Road issued to A.Y. Beach

Nov. 19, 1872 St. Louis, Kansas City & Northern Railroad receipt for certificate of preferred stock to John Jackson

1873 St. Louis, Alton & Terre Haute Rail Road Co., No.94, issued to W.W. Walker, Chief Engineer B.C. & M, Signed Jno. W. Parker

Misssouri River, Ft. Scott & Gulf Railroad Pass, No.309, issued to R. P. Dow.

March 7, 1879, Missouri, Kansas and Texas Railway Stock Certificate, 100 shares, No.B3235, issued to Price & Whitney, Chas. Cochran, attorney, Canceled date October 7, 1879.

June 1, 1880 Missouri, Kansas and Texas Extension Railroad Company Stock Certificate, No. 982, Issued to John Sevier

Apr. 20, 1881 St. Louis, Alton & Terre Haute Railroad Co. Dividend Bond Scrip issued to Edmond Sweet.

1885 St. Louis Coal Railroad, No.892, issued to L. A. Bowen.

1886 Missouri Pacific Railroad, No.3095 issued to Mr. E. Clark, Jt., General Freight Agent, N.Y.C. & H.R. Railroad.

1886 Missouri, Kansas Texas Stock Certificate, signed by George Gould, son of RR stock manipulator Jay Gould.

1887 Missouri, Kansas and Texas Railway Co., Stock Certificate No. A41597, 10 Shares, Issued to Adolph Boissevain, Canceled Dec. 2, 1887, Purchased Nov. 1, 1887.

September 22, 1887, Missouri, Kansas and Texas Railway Company, Stock Certificate 10 Shares, issued to Wertheim & Gompertz, No.A40859, assigned to Frederick P. Olcutt, Chariman, George W. Bastedo, attorney, Cancelled date May 26, 1890.

1889 Kansas, St. Joseph & Council Bluffs Railroad Pass No.2296, issued to F. M. Iron

1892 Indiana, Illinois and Iowa Railroad, No. 781, issued to S. B. Giddings. (See 1895 listing)

1895 Chicago, Peoria & St. Louis Railway, No.1267, S. B. Giddings, Signed E. H. Bosworth

1895 Elgin, Joliet and Eastern Railway, No.1126, issued to S. B. Giddings

1896 Burlington & Missouri River Railroad, No.E2490, issued to J. B. Fowler, Missouri Pacific

1899 Mississippi River and Bonne Terre Railway, No.1449, issued to Mr. R. E. Eaverson

1900 Wabash Railroad, No.B150, issued to S. B. Giddings. (See year 1895 listings)

1903 Missouri, Kansas and Texas Railway System, No.A1535 issued to Mr. W. G. Knittle, T.P.A. of C.C.C. & St.L Ry.

July 7, 1904 Missouri, Kansas & Texas Railway Co. of Texas, Office of Consulting Engineer, S. B. Fisher, from St. Louis, Mo

1905 Missouri Pacific Railway Co., No. 9544, Issued to Geo. D. Bennet.

December 17, 1905, Missouri Kansas and Texas Railway, Stock Certificate No. A091895, 10 Shares, R. Raphael & Sons, transferred William E Lauer, Transfer date July 6, 1909, John E. Corby, attorney.

1906 Missouri Kansas and Texas Railway System, No.A3992, issued to G. A. Gamble, Agent, Lehigh Valley Co.

1907 St.Louis & San Francisco Rail Road, Annual pass No.E1640, issued to CA Hunter, GA.

1908 Missouri, Kansas & Texas Railway, No.5540, issued to Mr. J. J. Livingston, Traveling Agt. C. & N. W. Railway

August 3, 1909, Missouri, Kansas and Texas Railway Co. 30 Share Stock Certificate, No.801832, issued to B. L. Forsyth

1910 Missouri, Kansas & Texas Railway, No.A2943, issued to Mr. J. J. Livingston, Traveling Agt., C & N. W.

1910 Toledo, St.Louis, and Western RR "Clover Leaf Route", Annual pass No.A3518, Issued to T. J Anderson, Wife, GPA.

1911 Missouri, Kansas & Texas Railway, No.B1044, issued to Mr. J. J. Livingston, Traveling Agt., C. & N. W. Railway.

1911, September, 1st Mortgage, 5% bond issued by Kansas City, Clay County and St. Joseph Railway Co., No.47, signed by H. F. Mays

1911 New York, Chicago,& St. Louis Raiload, No.B3698, issued to S. B. Giddings

1911 Missouri Pacific Railway, No. B2901 issused to Mr. T. C. Peck, Gen. Pass. Agent S.P.L. A. & S. L. R.R.

1911 Missouri, Texas and Kansas Railway Company, No.B3436, issued to Mr. A. H. Griswold, A. G. F. A. Vandalia Railroad.

1912 Wabash Railroad, No.A2476, issued to Mr F. C. Anderson, Missouri, Kansas & Texas Rail Road

1913 Missouri Pacific Railway Company, No.A2860, issued to Mr. M. A. Box, General Road Master, K.C. S. Railroad

1914 Minneapolis, St. Paul & Sault Ste. Marie Railway, No.B3431, issued to L. C. Rains, Grain and Flour Agent, Minneapolis & St. Louis Rail Road.

1914 Minneapolis & St. Louis Railroad Co., No.1296, issued to Mr. J. W. Skinner, Engr. M & St. L Rail Road and wife Mrs. J. W. Skinner, Signed S. Johnson and W. G. Bird

1915 Kansas City, Clinton, and Springfield Rail Road, Annual pass, No. G, Issued to Dr. Carl Doolin, Local Surgeon.

1915 Missouri, Oklahoma and Guld Railway Co., No.B291, issued to Mrs. E. E. McLellan.

1916 Missouri Pacific Railway and the St. Louis, Iron Mountain and Southern Railway, No. B11025, Issued to Mrs. L. A. David, Mabel David, Keith David, Lewis David, wife, daughter and sons of trainmaster.

1917 Pittsburgh, Cincinnati, Chicago, & St. Louis Railroad Scrip. Certificate is for $50, No. 115, issued for Elizabeth King,

1916 St. Louis Southwestern Railway, No.A1079, issued to Mr. C. D. Bowman, Depot ticket Agent

1918 Nashville, Chattanooga and St. Louis Railway Pass issued to Miss Margaret Kinningham, daughter of I. J. Kinningham.

1918 St. Louis Southwestern Railway Lines annual pass, No.A3396, issued to Mr. C. D. Bowman.

1921 Missouri Pacific Railroad, Annual Pass, No.A4987, Issued to Mr. S. C. Bushnell, Traf. Rep. DL & L RR.

1922 Kansas City, Mexico, & Orient RR, Annual pass No.A3834, issued to F. W. Trent

1923 Missouri Pacific Railroad $1000 Gold Bond, issued Josiah M. Vale.

1927 Atchison, Topeka & Santa Fe Railway Pass issued to L. A. Down.

1928, (A) 28Y Missouri Kansas & Texas Lines, No.7159 issued to Mr. H. P. Greenough, Supertindent CRI & RY.

1928, (A) 28Y Mt. Tamalpais & Muir Wood Railway, No.141r, Mrs. E. R. Anthony and daughter, Helen.

1929 Missouri Pacific Railway Co. Pass, No.A7389, issued to C. V. Jones, traveling Mechanical Inspector, IL Central System

1929 Missouri and North Arkansas Railway Pass, No.B2662, issed toMr. S. E. Gilderman, Ft. Smith & Western Kentucky

1930 Nashville, Chattanooga & St. Louis Railway Pass, No.4984 issued to Ralph Balisdell, Gen. Auditor

1930 The Pullman Co., No.E886 issued to J. L Howard, Trav. pass.
agent Mo Pac RR

1931 Missouri Pacific Railroad Company, No. B23671. Issued to Mr. R.B. Webb, Asst.B&B Foreman, Bet.Stas.on Arkanas, Memphis and Little Rock Division

1931 Missouri Pacific Railroad Company, No.B23681, Issued toMrs. R.B. Webb,wife of Asst.B&B Foreman, Bet.Stas.on Arkanas, Memphis and Little Rock Division

1931 St. Louis Southwestern Railway Company of Texas, No.A113, issued to Charles E. Denney, Jr., son of C. E. Denney, president of the Erie Railroad.

1931 Missouri Pacific Railroad Pass No. 10345 issued to V. J. Tannlund, Traffic Agent, Chicago Great Western Rail Road

1931 The Pullman Co., No. B5820, issued to A.C .Jackson Asst.L & I commr Missouri Pacific Railroad

1932 Kansas City, Clay County & St. Joseph Railway Co., No.B193, Mr. G. H. Hamilton, Asst. Frgt., Traffic Manager, Missouri Pacific, Signed by Robert P. Woods.

November 1, 1933 Pennsylvania Railroad, Roll of Honor certificate awarded to Harvey P. Hopkins, telegraph operator, St. Louis Division, after 47 11/12 years of service. Signed by PRR President, W.W. Atterbury.

1933-34 Missouri Pacific Lines, No. xJA35729 issued to W. L. Evans

1934 Missouri Texas Kansas Lines, No.X8070, issued to Mr. W. A. Pyle, Commercial Agent, Atlanta, Birmingham & Coast Railrodad.

1935 Chicago & Eastern Illinois Railway Co., No. C4323, A. C, Jackson, Asst. gen. passgr. agent, Mo Pac RR.

1935 Missouri-Kansas-Texas Lines, No.x9631, issued to Neil Norsworthy

1937 Missouri-Kansas-Texas Lines, X12040, issued to Mrs. S. E. Golderman, wife Asst. General Frt. Agent Ft. Smith & Western Kentucky

1937-38 Texas Mexican Railway, No.X575, issued to Mrs. A. C. Jackson and son, A. C. Jr., wife of A. C., Missouri Pacific Lines

1937 The Pullman Co., No.B8511, A. C Jackson, asst. general passenger agent, Mo Pacfic Rail Road.

1937 St. Louis, Southwestern Railway Lines, No.15394, issued to M. O. Truitt, claim agent.

1938 The Pullman Co., No.B886, issued to A. C. Jackson, asst .gen. pass.agent, Mo Pacific Rail RoAD

1938-1939 Missouri Pacific Lines Pass No.15268 Issued to Geo. B. Merrill, Asst. Freight Traffic Manager, New York, Chicago & St. Louis Railroad

1938-39 Northwestern Pacific Rail Road issued to Mr. E. R. Anthony and daughter, Helen, S.P. Retired

1938-1939 Missouri Pacific Lines annual pass, No.JA26662 issued to Mr. T.L Davism telegrapher, 27 years serviceSan Marcos, TX

1939 Carthage Central Railroad, No.857, issued to C. D. Bowman, General Passenger Agent, St. Louis Southwestern Railway Co.

1939 Missouri Kansas Texas Lines, No.7908, issued to Mr. D. W. Morris, Div. Passager Agent Mo. Pac.

1944 Missouri Texas Kansas Lines, No.30558, Issued Nov. 18, 1944 to Mrs. J. M. Hendrix travelling from New Franklin, MO to Kansas City, MO.

Postcards
    Printed for W. T. Ballagh of Nevada, MO, printed in 1910ca. in Germany showing a view of Cherry St., Nevada, MO.

Gentry County, Missouri, Automobile Registration, 1942.
    Claude L. David: (RES) Albany, (CAR) 1929 Chevelete, (LISC) 1234127, (REG No.) 273618, (DATE) Jan. 27, 1942.

Caldwell County, Missouri, Delinquent Tax List, 1855, "*Caldwell Banner of Liberty, Kingston,*" August 20, 1864
    M. Comstock, John S. Havter, A.D. McCoskie, D. McDowell, Robert Petre, G. Williams

Comments on the Third Missouri Cavalry
Col. John M. Glover: (CMTS) Called to service Aug. 5, 1861, (RES) Knox County, MO. Resigned Mar. 13, 1864.
Lt. Col. Walter C. Gannt: (CMTS) Joined the Regiment on Sep. 1, 1861. Discharged by order of the War Department on Sep. 4, 1862.
Maj. Robert Carick: (CMTS) Assigned to duty Aug. 15, 1861.
Chaplain Lester Janes: (CMTS) Appointed Sep. 12, 1861.
Adjutant William W. Grainger: (CMTS) Appointed Sep. 22, 1861.
John J. Allen: (CMTS) Appointed Quartermaster Sep. 22, 1861.
James T. Howland: (CMTS) Elected Captain of Co. A Sep. 20, 1861. Promoted to Major Feb. 2, 1863
Benjamin J. Triplett: (CMTS) Elected 1st Lt. of Co. A on Sep. 20, 1861.
George W. Moulder: (CMTS) Elected 2nd Lt. of Co. A on Sep. 20, 1861.
Albert D. Glover: (CMTS) Elected Captain of Co. B on Sep. 21, 1861. Promoted to Major Feb. 2, 1863. Maj. A. D. Glover resigned Mar. 13, 1864.
John W. Yates: (CMTS) Elected 1st Lt. of Co. B on Sep. 21, 1861
John Q. Agnew: (CMTS) Elected 2nd Lt. of Co. B on Sep. 21, 1861. 1st Lt. John Q. Agnew of Co. B promoted to Capt. of Co. D on Jul. 1, 1864.
Thomas G. Black: (CMTS) Elected Captain of Co. C on Oct. 22, 1861.
James Kirkpatrick: (CMTS) Elected 1st Lt. of Co. C on Oct. 22, 1861. Resigned Aug. 12, 1864.
Wm. Glover: (CMTS) Elected 2nd Lt. of Co. C on Oct. 22, 1861, Resigned in 1862..
John H. Reed: (CMTS) Elected Captain of Co.D on Sep. 26, 1861. Miss-

ing in action Apr. 26, 1864 at Mark's Mill, Ark. Promoted to Lt. Col. On Sep. 21, 1864,

Isaac C. Jewel: (CMTS) Elected 1st Lt. of Co. D on Sep. 26, 1861.

Jacob Snyder: (CMTS) Elected 2nd Lt. of Co. D on Sep. 26, 1861.

George D. Bradway: (CMTS) Elected Captain of Co. E on Oct. 29, 1861. Killed in action on Feb. 2, 1863.

Joseph F. Biggerstaff: (CMTS) Elected 1st Lt. of Co. E on Oct. 29, 1861.

Nelson Young: (CMTS) Elected 2nd Lt. of E on Oct. 29, 1861.

James Call: (CMTS) Transferred from 3rd Iowa Cavalry and took command as Captain of Co. F on Dec. 1, 1861 Resigned on Jun. 26, 1863.

F. M. Wilcox: (CMTS) Elected 1st Lt. Co. F on Nov. 30, 1861.

Surgeon John L. Taylor: (CMTS) Appointed Sep. 12, 1861.

Asst. Surgeon George Jones: (CMTS) Appointed Sep. 12, 1861. Resigned Sep. 30, 1862.

Battalion Adjutant James White: (CMTS) Appointed Oct. 12, 1861. Mustered out of service on Sep. 15, 1862.

Quatermaster Samuel T. Bronson: (CMTS) Appointed Oct. 12, 1861.

Richard Gentry: (CMTS) Appointed Sergeant-Major Nov. 10, 1861

William L. Johnson: (CMYS) Appointed. Regt. C. S. Sergeant on Nov. 25, 1861. Appinted to 1st Lt. on Sep. 22, 1862.

William McAfee: (CMTS) Appointed Regimental Quartermaster on Nov. 25, 1861.

Alonzo Jones: (CMTS) Appointed Hospital Steward on Sep. 12, 1861.

John A. Lennon: (CMTS) Elected 1st Lt. of Co. K on Jan. 6, 1862. Promoted to Captain of Co. I on Feb. 27, 1862. Promoted to Major of Co. I on Aug. 11, 1863. Resigned Aug. 3, 1864.

H. A. Gallup: (CMTS) Appointed Major on Sep. 4, 1861. Transferred with Battalion from Fremont Rangers to the 3rd MO on Dec. 3, 1861. Mar. H. A. Gallup was dismissed from service Jul. 31, 1863.

James Moffat: (CMTS) Elected 1st Lt. of Co. H on Dec. 1, 1861. Resigned Jun. 30, 1862.

Alex. H. Lacy: (CMTS) Promoted to 2nd Lt. of Co. I on Feb. 27, 1862. Promoted to 1st Lt Co. I Aug. 2, 1862.

Thomas J. Mitchel: (CMTS) Promoted to Captain of Co. K on Mar. 4, 1862. Promoted to Maj. on Sep. 19, 1864.

I. S. Crowel: (CMTS) Promoted to 1st lt. of Co. K on Mar. 6, 1862

Benjamin I. Clupp: (CMTS) Promoted to 2nd Lt. of Co. K on Mar. 6, 1862. Resigned Jan. 4, 1863

Simeon L. Graham: (CMTS) Promoted to 2nd Lt. of Co. H on Feb. 20, 1862.

George S. Avery: (CMTS) Promoted 1st Lt. of Co. I on Feb. 20, 1862, Promoted to Captain to Co. H on Jul. 15, 1862. Promoted to Maj. on Sep. 21, 1864.

Capt. Willard Wright: (CMTS) Resigned Jul. 20, 1862.
1st Lt. John S. Crowel: (CMTS) Resigned Jul. 20, 1862.
1st Lt. Timothy Willcox: (CMTS) Detached as provst marshal of Rolla, MO on Jul. 20, 1862, Promoted to Captain of Co. G on Aug. 2, 1862. Taken in action on Apr. 24, 1864 at Mark's Mill, Ark.
Orderly Sergeant James C. Miller: (CMTS) Appointed 2nd Lt. Co. C effective Aug. 2, 1862 replacing Vice Lt. Glover.
Capt. Willard Wright: (CMTS) 1862 resigned as Captain of Co. G.
Sergeant George W. Felt: (CMTS) Appointed 1st Lt. of Co. G.
William C. T. Davidson: (CMTS) Appointed from non-commissioned staff to 1st Lt. of Co. G. Vice Lt. Moffitt resigned.
Sergeant Louis Gaffeney: (CMTS) Co. F promoted to 1st Lt. of Co. K.
H. Reed: (CMTS) Sergeant of Co. D promoted to 2nd Lt. of Co. E on Sep. 12, 1862.
Battalion Adjt. Charlton H. Howe: (CMTS) Mustered out of service on Sep. 15, 1862.
Leander C. Gifford: (CMTS) Private on Co. D promoted to Captain of 36th Reg. MO Vol. on Dec. 11, 1862.
John S. Glover: (CMTS) Promoted to 1st Lt. Sep. 22, 1862.
W. W. Granger: (CMTS) Appointed Asst. Surgeon on Sep. 17, 1862. Resigned Mar. 13, 1864.
2nd Lt. George W. Moldin: (CMTS) Resigned Oct. 7, 1862.
Capt. John Ing: (CMTS) Commanding Co. L was transferred with company from the 9th MO Cavalry on Dec. 18, 1862.
1st Lt. Phillip Florick: (CMTS) Transferred with Capt. John Ing.
2nd Lt. Charles I. Hartman: (CMTS) Transferred with Capt. John Ing.
David R. Hindman: (CMTS) Appointed 2nd Lt. Dec. 16, 1862. 1st Lt. D. R. Hindman resigned Jul. 2, 1863 at Pilot Knob
William P. Hanes: (CMTS) Appointed from non-commissioned staff to 2nd Lt. Co. H. Vice Lt. Gray now resigned, effective Aug. 2, 1862.
William H. Bywater: (CMTS) Appointed 2nd Lt. Dec. 16, 1862.
Captain John D. Crabtree: (CMTS) Transferred with is company M from the 9th MO Cavalry. Attached to the 3rd MO on Dec. 18, 1862. Resigned from Co. M on Aug. 16, 1864.
William H. Harding: (CMTS) Appointed 2nd Lt. of Co. E on Feb. 5, 1863.
1st Lt. Francis Hyatt: (CMTS) Transferred with Capt. John D. Crabtree
Sergeant Henry Hickman: (CMTS) Appointed 2nd Lt. of Co. B on Feb. 2, 1862.
Sergeant N. N. Hill: (CMTS) Promoted to 2nd Lt. of Co. F on Apr. 8, 1863. Lt. Hill resigned on Feb. 6, 1864 at Little Rock.

2nd Lt. David H. Hindman: (CMTS) Promoted to 1st Lt. on Apr. 6, 1863.
Sergeant Watson Roberts: (CMTS) Appointed 2nd Lt. of Co. A on
    Feb. 2, 1863.
R. M. Griggs: (CMTS) Appointed 2nd Lt. Co. F on Feb, 5m 1863.
James C. White: (CMTS) Promoted to 2ns Lt. of Co. K on Feb. 5, 1863.
    1st Lt. James C, White resigned Mar. 13, 1864.
A. J. Prickett: (CMTS) 2nd Lt. of Co. F resigned on Feb. 1, 1863.
1st Lt. Nelson Young: (CMTS) Promoted to Capt. of Co. E replacing
    Capt. Bradway. Resigned Feb. 6, 1864 at Little Rock.
2nd Lt. H. Reed: (CMTS) Promoted to 1st Lt. Feb. 2, 1863.
1st Sgt. Charles W. Wolfe: (CMTS) Promoted to 2nd Lt. Co. I on
    Apr. 8, 1863.
1st Lt. Isaac C. Jewel: (CMTS) Resigned on Mar. 27, 1863 from Co. D
1st Sgt. G. E. Bailey: (CMTS) Appointed 2nd Lt. Mar. 11, 1863.
1st Lt. Alex. H. Lacy: (CMTS) Resigned Mar. 27,1863.
1st Lt. W. E. Davidson: (CMTS) 1863 Appointed to the General Command
    Staff.
Capt. Thomas I. Mitchel: (CMTS) Caputured by the enemy at Chalk Bluff
    on May 1, 1863.
Lt. Col. Robert Carrick: (CMTS) Resigned Jun. 26, 1863.
Capt. Thomas G. Black: (CMTS) Promoted to Lt. Col. On Jul. 2, 1863
Sgt. Charles H. Frost: (CMTS) Promotd to 2nd Lt. of Co. C on
    Jul. 2, 1863.
Lt. Wm. H. Harding: (CMTS) Of Co. F resigned on Jul. 8, 1863 at Pilot
    Knob.
Charles W. Coan: (CMTS) Promoted from Sgt. Maj. To 2nd Lt. of Co. E
    on Jul. 22, 1863 at Pilot Knob. Resigned Apr. 19, 1864 at Camden,
    Ark.
Maj. James T Howland: (CMTS) Resigned Jul. 21, 1863 at Pilot Knob.
Chaplain Reuben McCoy: (CMTS) Resigned Oct. 1, 1863 at Little Rock.
Regt. Q. M. James P. Agnew: (CMTS) Resigned Feb. 27, 1864.
B. J. Hodge: (CMTS) Sgt. Of Co. D promoted to Chaplain on
    Mar. 16, 1864.
Capt. C. V. Jacobs: (CMTS) Missing in action on Apr. 24, 1864 at Mark's
    Mill, Ark. Of Co. I resigned on Aug. 8, 1864.
Pvt. Samuel L. McAfee: (CMTS) Appointed regimental quartermaster on
    Apr. 18, 1864.
Asst. Surgeon Lafayette Avery: (CMTS) Appointed from civl life on
    Apr. 21, 1864
Sgt. Wm. H. Clyma: (CMTS) Promted to 2nd Lt. from Co. I on
    Jan. 20, 1864.
Sgt. Edward Glavin: (CMTS) Promoted to 1st Lt. of Co. E on
    Mar. 9, 1864.

Sgt. Francis Magher: (CMTS) Promoted to 2nd Lt. of Co. K on Jun. 13, 1864.
Sgt. James J. Hiles: (CMTS) Promoted to 2nd Lt. of Co. C on Jun. 13, 1864
Lt. Co. Thomas G. Black: (CMTS) Resigned Aug. 11, 1864 at Little Rock.
Sgt. Maj. Thomas Ortin: (CMTS) Promoted to 1st Lt. and regimental adjutant Sep. 21, 1864.
1st Sgt. James B. Yancy: (CMTS) Of Co. B promoted to 1st Lt. on Sep. 21, 1864.

Mississippi County, Charleston, Missouri Connection, *"Batesville Daily Guard,"*Batesville, Ark, Dec. 29, 1997..

Nellie Ann Barrett Brewer, 96, died Sunday, Dec.28, 1997 in Sikeston, Mo. She was born in Batesville on Oct. 5, 1901, daughter of Preston and Julia Mariah Cornish Barrett. Before moving to Missouri in 1989, she had lived in Batesville, AR and was a member of the West Baptist Church and the LLL Sunday School Class. She married Nelson Brewer in Batesville on Feb. 2, 1919. She lives behind a son and daughter-in-law, Leon and Mikki Brewer of Lake Charles, LA.; a daughter and son-in-law, Nelsene and Ray Hillhouse of Charleston, MO.; 10 grandchildren; 19 great-grandchildren; a great-great-granddaughter; and two stepgrandsons. Her parents; her husband; a daughter, Christene Brewer; and two grandsons, William Leon Brewer, and Benny Hillhouse.

The funeral is Thursday in Crouch Funeral Home of Batesville chapel with the Rev. Bob Dailey officiating. Burial will be in Mount Zion Cemetery.

Pallbearers are grandsons, John Hillhouse, David Brewer, James Brewer, Steven Brewer, great-grandsons, Mark Hurley and Mike Hurley.

Dahlgren Echo, IL September 9, 1920

Job Standerfer was born December 15, 1851 and died September 4, 1920. He was the son of John B. and Elizabeth Standerfer. He married Rebecca Trotter, September 7, 1869 in Hamilton County, Illinois. They had seven children, four dead. He leaves his wife, Rebecca, and three children: Laura Bolerjack, Morehouse, Missouri; Kelly Standerfer, Dexter, Missouri; Clarence Standerfer, at home; one sister, Mrs. Amanda Maulding, Belle City; One brother, Hugh Standerfer, Fairfield; one half-sister: Betty Dale, Centrailia; six half brothers: Robert, Delafield; Marshall, Dahlgren; Trap, Dahlgren; Charley, Chicago; Eb, Florida; and Ed, up north; one full brother is dead: Eld. Wilburn Standerfer, d. near Ewing. He is interred at Blooming Grove Cemetery in Hamilton County, Illinois.

Franklin County, Missouri, *"Centerville Journal,"* Centerville, IA, 10 Apr 1889, Obituary of Norrell Tyler Triplett.

Norrell Tyler Triplett was born in Montgomery County, IN, August 30, 1835, and died in Centerville, March 31st, 1889 at age 53 years and 7 months. He moved to Franklin county, Mo., in 1883, later to Putnam county in 1885, and then to Centerville last November. . He married Mary Jane Bear on June 1st, 1858. They had nine children. He was a member of the Disciples of Christ for several years.. He leaves six children, with other relatives and friends.. The funeral took place at his the residence on Monday afternoon. Service were conducted by Elder Lucas, assisted by Rev. Cole.

Boone County, Missouri, 1864 Citizens Drafted

Name	Comments
John Adair	supplied substitute for one year
Robert Henry	exempted from draft
James Pigg	did not report, bushwacker
Peter Palmer	did not report
Benjamin Mead, Jr.	did not report
Morgan Reams	exempted from draft
Robert R. McBain	supplied substitute for one year
John W. Asbury	did not report
Henry N. Esse	tutor in the State University, supplied substitute for one year
Henry Robinett	did not report
John R. Boulton	supplied substitute for one year
Daniel Phillips	did not report
Pollard W. Graves	supplied substitute for three years
John M. Samuel	supplied substitute for three years
Alfred Stephens	did not report
Andrew J. Bryson	did not report
Azariah Martin	did not support
George H. Akeman	supplied substitute for one year
Elias Elliott	did not report
William Barnes	did not report
Wm. Albright	did not report
Lewis M. Switzler	assistant editor of the Stateman, supplied substitute for one year
William H. Barnett	did not report
John F. Evans	supplied substitute for one year
Nathaniel Harris	did not report
David Vivion	supplied substitute for three years
W.A. Darnally	did not report

Elijah G. Taylor	did not report
Clay Ballew	did not report
Jacob Strawn	supplied substitute for three years
Riley Christian	did not report
Samuel M. Jones	tutor in the State University, exempted from draft
Milton A. Wiggington	did not report
James M. Smith	did not report
Asa C. Nichols	supplied substitute for three years
Eli Lanham	Confederate army
H.W. Richardson	did not report
Eward Mansfield	did not report
Samuel S. Hagan	did not report
Alfred E. Grubbs	Confederate army
Morrison Powell	did not report
Isaac Lamme	did not report
R.C. Dyson	exempted from draft
John M. Brown	supplied substitute for one year
Hiram Cowden	did not report
John E. Blakemore	did not report
William D. Oliver	held to personal service
James Petty	did not report
Peter Lyons	did not report
Thomas Gibson	did not report
William A. Harris	supplied substitute for three years
Robert T. Sapp	supplied substitute for three years
Joseph E. Proctor	supplied substitute for three years
Thomas L. Burdett	did not report
David Mead	Confederate army
Ashby Crump	supplied substitute for one year
Henry L. Cook	did not report
Horace W. Gold	did not report
Pleasant R. Nicholson	did not report
John E. Woolfolk	supplied substitute for one year
William J. Simms	did not report
Harry C. Summers	did not report
James E. Tucker	supplied substitute for one year
Wm. T. Shock	supplied substitute for one year
Thomas Milhollin	did not report in Gratiot Prison
Thomas Dunbar	did not report
James R. Hagan	did not report
Robert Melloway	did not report
Robert B. Coleman	Confederate army

John D. Patton	did not report
James A. McQuitty	did not report
Robert P. Waters	supplied substitute for three years
John Rogers	did not report
Lawson G. Drury	supplied substitute for one year
Augustus Levi	did not report
Jesse Claypole	did not report
James Harris	Confederate army
Wm. Bestwick	did not report
Nathan Roberts	did not report
Frank Thomas	held to personal service
Solomon Grindstaff	held to personal service
Wm. F. Hall	exempted from draft
Carter Chandler	supplied substitute for one year
James S. Yeager	did not report
John N. Ward	did not report
Michael Speilman	supplied substitute for one year
James J. Winscott	did not report
James J. Arnott	held to personal service
Wm. Allen, Sr.	did not report, reported by letter; very sick at home
Samuel Street	did not report
Benjamin Jenkins	did not report
Sydney Hume	supplied substitute for one year
Abraham Ewing	did not report
John R. Garth	supplied substitute for three years
L.W. Hendrix	held to personal service
Robert Gordon	did not report
Joseph Hall	did not report
Wm. Hunter	exempted from draft
James W. Singleton	did not report
James Slate	exempted from draft, later in U.S. Army
Andrew Peyton	did not report
Henry Grindstaff	exempted from draft
Samuel Simms	held to personal service
Robert H. Woolfolk	supplied substitute for three years
Wm. H. Crane	exempted from draft
Ambrose W. Hulen	did not report
Enoch C. Dooley	supplied substitute for three years
James Davis	did not report
Henry Colvin	did not report
Amos Bartley	did not report
Benjamin F. Davis	did not report

John L. Hines	did not report
Thomas Spillman	exempted from draft
Robert E. Smith	exempted from draft
Henry F. Williams	supplied substitute for one year
Liright Vandiver	supplied substitute for three years
James M. Dinwiddie	supplied substitute for three years
Ben. F. Williamson	did not report
Stephen W. Pigg	supplied substitute for one year
James M. Strode	supplied substitute for three years
Thomas H. Keene	supplied substitute for one year
James H. Turner	supplied substitute for one year
Samuel Clinton	held to personal service
Matthew Evans	exempted from draft
Simeon Christian	supplied substitute for one year
Alonzo Wright	supplied substitute for one year
Silas Senior	held to personal service
Joseph Sappington	did not report
Jacob Palm	exempted from draft
John M. Shock	supplied substitute for three years
Columbus Hunter	held to personal service
James R. Selby	supplied substitute for one year
John H. Seymour	did not report
Wm. Fagg	held to personal service
Samuel Boyd	did not report
Daniel Robinett	held to personal service
James B. Stansbury	did not report
Sylvester Dines	did not report
John F. Cato	in California
Jesse G. Long	did not report
Wm. Irvin	near Quincy, IL
Jeff. B. Ridgway	deceased

Colored

Lewis Vanhorn	colored held to personal service
Wallace Williams	colored, did not report, in U.S. Army
Lewis Ashbury	colored, did not report
William Beazley	colored, exempted from draft
Anthony Clarkson	colored, exempted from draft
Charles Todd	colored, held to personal service
John Conway	colored held to personal service
Lewis McAfee	colored, held to personal service
Harvey Parker	colored, held to personal service
Thomas Ballew	colored, exempted from draft
Silas Hudson	colored, exempted from draft

Isaac Henry	colored, held to personal service
Squire Searcy	colored, did not report
Joseph Roberts	colored, did not report
Edward Bass	colored, exempted from draft
Joel Kirtley	colored; held to personal service
Creed Conley	colored did not report in U.S. army
Jacob Smith	colored did not report
Frank Sappington	colored, held to personal service
Stephen Todd	colored, did not report
Levi Hickam	colored, held to personal service
Frederick Wilcox	colored did not report

Washington County, Missouri, *"The Detroit News,"* Tuesday, July 21, 1998, Obituary of Hazel L. Harvey

"Services for Hazel L. Harvey, who rode a horse to her first job as a school teacher in a one-room school house in Palmer, Mo., will be held at 2 p.m. Saturday in the Gum and Son Funeral Home in Potosi, Mo. Mrs. Harvey died of heart failure Tuesday, July 14, 1998, at Woodward Hills Nursing Home in Bloomfield Hills. She was 98.

"She was one of those people who loved to cook and entertain," said her daughter, Wilma Dellinger. Mrs. Harvey, a 1917 graduate of the Missouri State Teacher's College, was also a charter member of the Northbrook Presbyterian Church of Beverly Hills, and a Life Member of Loyalty Southfield Ionic 427 of the Order of the Eastern Star for 57 years.

After marrying her husband, the late Willis P. Harvey, she moved to Detroit in 1919 she lived in the city 55 years before moving with her husband back to Potosi, Mo. She returned to Detroit four years ago to be near her children. She is survived by her daughters, Wilma G. Dellinger and Betty Mood; sons, W. Paul and Dr. J. Edgar; a sister; four brothers; seven grandchildren; and 11 great grandchildren. Burial will be in The New Masonic Cemetery in Potosi, Mo."

Headquarters, Tallahassee, November 6, 1862, Correspondence toBrig. Gen. Thomas Jordan, Chief of Staff and Assistant Adjutant-General.

I have the honor to report the recapture of three abolitionist prisoners who made their escape from Macon, Ga. They were apprehended by our pickets on the Apalachicola River on their way to the gunboats of the enemy. Names, J. W. Woolley, Company B, Sixteenth Regiment Illinois Volunteers; James Baldwin, Twenty-third Missouri Volunteers, captured at Shiloh; Charles Hood, sailor, captured on the Aucilla River, Fla. In addition to the above I have a Spaniard who was wounded at Crystal River, where our men killed the captain and two of the crew of the blockading vessel and captured at the same time the balance of the boat's crew that landed. This man was shot through the body; he is now well enough to be exchanged; his name is Frank Russell. I respectfully ask instructions where I shall send these men.

I have the honor to be, your obedient servant, Joseph Finnegan.

St. Louis County, Missouri, Students of Ballwin School, 1895.

Lizzie Koehneman, Meta Woerther, Clara Eickerman, Louis Wussow, Sally Lash, Louise Zeiser, Tillie Strothkamp, Bill Zeiser, Dan Woerther, Bernice Zuppann, Fred Erke, Julia Koehneman, Walter Busch, Tille Krueger, Bill Hain, Sophie Oberback, Milton Bopp, Julie Busch, Eddie Fischbeck, Carrie Busch, ???? Banta, ???? Dahike, ???? Trapp

Livingston County, Missouri, " *Chillicothe Constitution-Tribune Centennial Edition,"* Chillicothe, MO," September 13, 1937 "Livingston County Boys Gave Their Lives in War " Many Lie in France After Trip to Europe During World Conflict Thirty-One of County's Best Died

Miles Abbott: Buried in Edgewood Cemetery, died August 30,1917.

Frank H. Bassett, Jr.: The son of Frank H. and Alice S. Bassett who enlisted in the Navy, died following an operation October 11, 1918. He became ill of bronchial pneumonia at the Great Lakes Naval Training Station, Chicago. He is buried in the South Wheeling Cemetery.

Jerry Broaddus: Son of the late Joseph Broaddus and Mrs. Jessie Broaddus of this city, died of bronchial pneumonia October 15 1918, at Camp Dodge Base Hospital. His grave is in Edgewood Cemetery.

Lester C. Burgard: Avalon, son of Samuel H. and Charity E. Burgard, was killed in action in the battle of Argonne Forest September 26, 1918. He is buried in France.

Roy Burkett: Chillicothe, son of Albert L. and Maggie Burkett, is buried in France. Killed in action near Charpentry, France, September 23, 1918.

Charles Burton: son of Mr. and Mrs. Emmett Burton, both deceased, died September 30, 1918. He is buried in Alphadelphia Cemetery south of Avalon.

Everett Bryan: Utica, son of William Columbus and Scottie Bell Bryan, died of bronchial pneumonia on his way to Europe on Sept. 25, 1918. He is interred in Bethel Church Cemetery near Ludlow.

John Francis Cleveland: Bedford, son of Alexander and Minnie Bell Cleveland, served with Company L, 159th Infantry, Coast Guard duty, when he contracted measles resulting in pneumonia, which caused his death. He is buried in South Wheeling Cemetery.

Archie J. Cox: son of Joseph B. and Lee A. Cox, Chillicothe, developed bronchial pneumonia at the Great Lakes Naval Training Station, Chicago, and died September 21, 1918. His body was returned for burial.

Vincent Eades: Son of J. E. and Tempa Eades, contracted pneumonia on his way to France in October, 1918. He was removed from shipboard at Brest and taken to the Base Hospital where he died on October 15, He is buried in France.

A. Morris Ellett: Chillicothe, son of W, H, and Grace Ellet, was buried with military honors at Linthal Cemetery, a French Military Cemetery after his death by accidental explosion of a hand grenade on August 8, 1918, in France. Ellett was captain of Company I when the boys were stationed on the Mexican border.

Edward G. Gladieux: Chillicothe, son of Joseph and Josephine Gladieux, died in an Officers' Training School in Florida, October 29, 1918, of bronchial pneumonia. He is buried in the Catholic cemetery.

Vernon R. Glick:, Son of Mrs. Isabelle Glick, was struck by enemy shrapnel joined Company I against the enemy in the Meuse-Argonne, October, 1918. A member of Company I, he was honored by the local American Legion post when his name was chosen as the name of this post. He is buried in Argonne Cemetery in France and his mother visited his grave there a few years ago.

Eugene V. Debbs Goldsworthy: Son of A. L. and Sarah Goldsworthy, died at Aricourt, France, October 29, 1918, He is buried in Edgewood cemetery. Young Goldsworthy trained at Camp Dodge, Ia.

Walter J. Gould: Son of James and Mary Jane Gould, Wheeling, is buried in
the U, S. Naval Cemetery, Brest, France. His death was caused by pneumonia.

Hobart Gray: Son of Mrs. J. W. Harper, Bridge Street, died September 25, 1918. He is buried in Edgewood Cemetery.

William Franklin Herring: Son of N. J. and Sarah Herring of Hickory, entered service here, later to be sent to France where he was killed in action October 21, 1918. He is buried on the field of battle.

Charles M. Hoge: buried at Edgewood, died of bronchial pneumonia, October 26, 1918 at the Great Lakes Naval Training Station, Chicago. He enlisted in the Navy. Hoge was the son of Israel and Ellen Hoge.

Glenn Humphreys: Of Sturges was killed in the battle of the Meuse-Argonne, November 10, 1918 near Pouilly, France. He was the son of S. J, and Mollie Humphreys of Sturges.

Everett William Mann: The son of Mr. and Mrs. William Mann,
died at the French-American Military Hospital at Hericourt, France of bronchial pneumonia, October 16, 1918.

Reuben Claude McKiddy: Died in Camp Doniphan, Okla., December 31, 1917. He was the son of W. F. and Alice B. McKiddy of Wheeling. His body was brought hack to his home for burial.

Henry Louis Miller: son of Mrs. Lena Gallagher, was killed in the battle of Belleau Wood between July 18 and 24, 1918. He is buried on a French battlefield. Miller enlisted from Genoa, Montana.

George Ostrander: was the first Livingston County boy to fall during the World War. He was at the front preparing a machine when an enemy plane dropped a bomb wounding him, March 22, 1918 resulting in his death two days later. He is buried at Rosier, France. Ostrander, son of G. A. and Elizabeth Ostrander, entered service in aviation. He is buried in Edgewood.

Walter S. Sherman: Son of Mr. and Mrs. William Sherman of Utica enlisted in the Navy. He was serving aboard the U. S. S. Black Arrow when he died accidently at Brooklyn, New York, March 13, 1919, He is buried at Utica.

William J. Singleton: Son of J. J, Singleton, Bedford, was killed in action in the Meuse-Argonne drive in September, 1918.

Earl Smith: Son of D. F. and Anna Smith, Chillicothe, entered service at Scolby, Montana.. He was wounded in the battle of the Argonne Forest, September 20,1918 . He died at the American Central Hospital at Florides Meuse, France Oct. 8, 1918. He is buried in American Military Cemetery located at Florides Meuse, France.

James H. Sparks: Killed in action in the battle of the Argonne Forest, September 26, 1918 and is buried there on that battlefield. He was the son of Mr. and Mrs. J. E. Sparks of Avalon and entered service in Chillicothe.

Delford E. Stephens: From Bedford. Entered the service in Chillicothe, is buried in the South Wheeling cemetery. He died in a hospital at Fort Riley, October 14, 1918. His death resulted in pneumonia, developing from influenza.

Harold Hoyle Sutherland: Enlisted in aviation in 1917 when he was a Junior at the University of Illinois. He was commissioned lieutenant in 1918 and at the time of his death he had been an instructor in the aviation school at Tours, France. He was killed in a plane accident at Tours, December 13, 1918. He is buried in Edgewood cemetery.

Archie R. Taylor: From Utica, son of R. W. and Nana L. Taylor. Enlisted with the marines in 1917. After the Armistice was signed he was sent to Coblenz, Germany with the Army of Occupation where he died May 13, 1919.

George K. Thompson: Son of Elliott W. and Alice J. Thompson, died of acute poisoning while in training at Fort Riley, February-24, l918. He is buried in Edgewood cemetery.

Missouri Fishing Permits

Mathie D. Daniel: (RES) Benton, (A) 42Y, (DES) Brown Hair, Blue Eyes, Height 5 ft, 11 in., (NO.) 304270, (YR) 1969, (CO) Scott.

Mathie Daniel: (RES) 2612 Compton St., St. Louis, MO, (A) 38Y, (DES) Brown Hair, Blue Eyes, Height 6 ft, Weight 165lb., (ISSUED) August 18, 1859, (NO.) 404045, (CO) St. Louis

Mathie D. Daniel: (RES) Benton, (A) 44Y, (DES) Brown Hair, Blue Eyes, Height 5 ft, 11 in, Weight 160lb., (ISSUED) May 30, 1965, (NO.) 898048, (CO) Scott.

Ruth M. Beshears: (RES) 122 N. Askew, Kansas City, MO, (ISSUED) July 4, 1953, (NO) M81672, (DES) 40Y, Brown Hair, Blue Eyes, Height 5 ft., 5 in., Weight 130lb, (CO) Jackson.

E. L. Holden: (RES) Joplin, (CO) Jasper, (DES) 36Y, Brown hair, Brown Eyes, 170 lbs., (ISSUED) Oct. 31, 1942, (NO) 298301

Raymond C. Jennings: (RES) St. Louis, (CMTS) Street Address not listed, (ISSUED) May 8, 1936, (NO) 218345, (DES) Blue Eyes, Black Hair, (A) 21 or 31Y?

1883 Washita Cattle Company Bond

1883 Washita Cattle Company Bond issued in Missouri. Signed by D.T. Parker and Erastus Wells.

Missouri Passport

Issued in 1851 by the Mayor of Vercruz to Wade Woodson. He was sailing around South America traveling from Missouri to California.

Missouri, Paymaster General's Office

Head Quarters, State of Missouri, Paymaster General's Office, dated Jan 7 1867?, a statement of a $57.60 payment to James Case to be sent by Negro Express. Signed by Gen. W. J. Nexsen.

Miller County, Missouri, Enrolled Missouri Militia, 73rd Reg., Co. L

Asalom McKinney: (RK) Capt., (A) 28Y
John W. Boyd: (RK)1st Lt., (A) 41Y
John B Yates: (RK) 2nd Lt., (A) 24Y
William Baskett: (RK) 1st Sgt., (A) 44Y

John L Lynch: (RK) 2nd Sgt., (A) 22Y
McCrager Keith: (RK) Comm. Sgt., (A) 43Y
Jacob Williams: (RK) Sgt., (A) 23Y
Samuel Thorn : (RK) Sgt, (A) 24Y
Joseph Allen : (RK) Sgt, (A) 37Y
William F. Cavness: (RK) Sgt, (A) 32Y
William Farley: (RK) Sgt, (A) 22Y
William B. Hill: (RK) Corp, (A) 37Y
Martin Gouge: (RK) Corp, (A) 33Y
Daniel L Williams: (RK) Corp, (A) 23Y
William M. Young: (RK) Corp, (A) 44Y
William J Briggs: (RK) Corp, (A) 26Y
Riley W. Adey: (RK) Corp, (A) 35Y
Isaac Moore: (RK) Corp, (A) 36Y
Robert W Worthington: (RK) Corp, (A) 34Y
Robert B. Reeves: (RK) Blacksmith, (A) 44Y
Francis L. Johnson: (RK) Blacksmith, (A) 47Y
William Austill: (RK) Pvt., (A) 35Y
Thomas Barnum: (RK) Pvt., (A) 41Y
William J. Brown: (RK) Pvt., (A) 20Y
Lawson Butcher: (RK) Pvt., (A) 33Y
George T. Briggs: (RK) Pvt., (A) 16Y
James R. Blankenship: (RK) Pvt., (A) 26Y
James Brown: (RK) Pvt., (A) 38Y
Charles M. Baskett: (RK) Pvt., (A) 18Y
David J. Chambers: (RK) Pvt., (A) 21Y
Henry Chambers: (RK) Pvt., (A) 23Y
John H. Coats: (RK) Pvt., (A) 34Y
Jackson Cobble: (RK) Pvt., (A) 23Y
Harvey Carlisle: (RK) Pvt., (A) 23Y
Benjamin Carter: (RK) Pvt., (A) 25Y
Wilson Coats: (RK) Pvt., (A) 21Y
Josephus Cavness: (RK) Pvt., (A) 20Y
William P. Dunlap: (RK) Pvt., (A) ., (A) 24Y
John T. Davis: (RK) Pvt., (A) 39Y
Milton B. Davis: (RK) Pvt., 28Y
William Flowers: (RK) Pvt., (A) 29Y
Jonathan F. Fry: (RK) Pvt., (A) 44Y
Jonathan F. Fry: (RK) Pvt., (A) 18Y
James Flowers: (RK) Pvt., (A) 26Y
David Frederick: (RK) Pvt., (A) 18Y
John C. Ford: (RK) Pvt., (A)31Y
Martines Gravens: (RK) Pvt., (A), (A) 28Y

William Jones: (RK) Pvt., (A) 19
John Kinser: (RK) Pvt., (A) 20Y
Alfred Kimrey: (RK) Pvt., (A) 31
William Lay: (RK) Pvt., (A), (A) 24Y
Thomas Lay: (RK) Pvt., (A) 32
Thomas Lemmons: (RK) Pvt., (A) 44Y
Monroe McKinney: (RK) Pvt., (A) 21Y
James A McElroy: (RK) Pvt., (A) 20Y
Henry Mayberry: (RK) Pvt., (A) 35Y
Charles Moreland: (RK) Pvt., (A) 26Y
George W. Moody: (RK) Pvt., (A), (A) 41Y
Morgan S. McGowen: (RK) Pvt., (A) 36Y
John D. McCain: (RK) Pvt., (A) 35Y
James A. Norman: (RK) Pvt., (A) 23Y
William D. Owens: (RK) Pvt., (A) 18Y
William Powell: (RK) Pvt., (A) 36Y
Isaac Purcell: (RK) Pvt., (A) 25Y
Robert Reeves: (RK) Pvt., (A) 47Y
Gabriel M. Pike: (RK) Pvt., (A), (A) 41Y
Napolean Stauislauce: (RK) Pvt., (A) 40Y
William Simmons: (RK) Pvt., (A) 34
Carrol Simmons: (RK) Pvt., (A) 34
Jacob Sanders: (RK) Pvt., (A) 24Y
Joel Smith: (RK) Pvt., (A) 38Y
William J. Smith: (RK) Pvt., (A) 35Y
Tillman Smith: (RK) Pvt., (A) 21Y
Bennett Smith: (RK) Pvt., (A) 31
George W. Taylor: (RK) Pvt., (A), (A) 28Y
Adlar A. Tweedy: (RK) Pvt., (A) ., (A) 28Y
Isaac Turner: (RK) Pvt., (A) 18Y
William Ward: (RK) Pvt., (A) 25Y
David H. White: (RK) Pvt., (A) 29Y
Moses Wilhite: (RK) Pvt., (A) 22Y
William H White: (RK) Pvt., (A)18Y
Thomas Young: (RK) Pvt., (A) 38Y

Jasper County, Missouri, 1850 Census Index.
Harrison Adkins (P) 375; Henry Adkins (P) 375; Thomas Akers (P) 363; Archibald N. Alexander (P) 406; William D. Alexander (P) 395; Robert E. Allison (P) 365; James L. Anderson (P) 371; Ann Archer (P) 383; Drusilla Archer (P) 383; Ferdinand S. Archer (P) 379; Jeremiah P. Archer (P) 398; Michael Archer (P) 368; Moses Archer (P) 383; William Archer (P) 383; George T. Arthur (P) 389; Thomas Arthur (P) 405;

Moses J. Baker (P) 381; Edward Barnes (P) 386; Ann Barnett (P) 390; Joseph Barnett (P) 361; Jane Barrick (P) 403; Nancy Barrick (P) 402; Reuben D. Basket (P) 362; David Baysinger (P) 360; James W. Beasley (P) 359; Rebecca Beasley (P) 359; Henry B. Belville (P) 405; Nancy Benham (P) 378; Noah Bennett (P) 401; George Bethel (P) 396; Lewis Bible (P) 377; John Bird (P) 38; John S. Bird (P) 366; John Bishop (P) 392; Edward W. Black (P) 394; Edgeman Blake (P) 360; John F. Blommenkemper (P) 404; Margaret Board (P) 390; John Bollen (P) 389; Margaret Bollen (P) 389; Nancy Bollen (P) 389; Gideon Bolling (P) 397; Daniel R. Boothby (P) 387; Mary Bourdeneau (P) 382; Rebecca Bowles (P) 394; Rhoda Bowlin (P) 377; Lundsford Boxley (P) 391; Thomas F. Boxley (P) 373; John W. Boyd (P) 368; Joseph Boyd (P) 405; Josiah Boyd (P) 359; Louisa A. Boyd (P) 369; Mary J. Boyd (P) 405; Milton M. Boyd (P) 370; Robert H. Boyd (P) 359; John Bozworth (P) 389; James M. Braly (P) 369; Thomas A. Braly (P) 361; George Brewer (P) 391; Elijah Bright (P) 379; Henderson Bright (P) 379; Abraham Bringolf (P) 365; John Britton (P) 369; Eliza Broam (P) 404; Samuel W. Broam (P) 403; Dicy A. Brock (P) 375; James Brock (P) 375; Alexander M. Brown (P) 370; Ben. Brown (P) 401; Elizabeth Brown (P) 401; Ivan Brown (P) 401; Josephus Brown (P) 366; Thomas Brown (P) 385; Thomas M. Brown (P) 366; William Brown (P) 401; Ira D. Broyles (P) 398; Mary Broyles (P) 398; Wiley D. Brown (P) 405; Daniel Bryant (P) 372; David Bryant (P) 361; Martha Bryanum (P) 384; John Buck (P) 367; Mary Buck (P) 367; Thomas Buck (P) 363; William Burden (P) 392; John Burnett (P) 406; Elida Burns (P) 364; Richard W. Burriss (P) 369; Josiah Buzby (P) 361; John Cabaness (P) 394; Edwin Cagel (P) 359; Elizabeth Cagle (P) 390; Lindsey Cagle (P) 390; Margaret Cagle (P) 364; Matthew J. Cagle (P) 364; Emma Caltrin (P) 379; William Capehart (P) 400; Meredith Carlisle (P) 395; William Carlisle (P) 396; Andrew Carmack (P) 371; William Carroll (P) 382; Isabella Carter (P) 361; James G. Carter (P) 387; Lindsey D. Carter (P) 376; Polly Carter (P) 369; Salathiel Carter (P) 387; Washington Carter (P) 387; Sarah Carton (P) 387; Selina Cash (P) 404; Henry Cather (P) 405; Sarah Cather (P) 405; William Cather (P) 405; Rice Challes (P) 382; Reuben Chapman (P) 390; Reuben Chapman (P) 393; James Chenault (P) 396; John R. Chenault (P) 390; Sarah Ellen Chenault (P) 391; Benjamin Chester (P) 395; Elihu Childers (P) 402; Joel E. Crenshaw (P) 384; John H. Crenshaw (P) 384; Nicholas Crenshaw (P) 384; Alonzo Clanton (P) 395; Elizabeth Clark (P) 373; O. R. Clark (P) 361; William Clark (P) 401; Joseph Clibourn (P) 368; James Clow (P) 366; James H. Clow (P) 371; Sarah Clow (P) 367; William Clow (P) 371; Hannah Clubb (P) 389; Jeremiah M. Clubb (P) 388; Peter W. Clubb (P) 367; Clement Coats (P) 360; David Cobbs (P) 391; William Cobbs (P) 390; Andrew J. Cockran (P) 401; Emely Coffelt (P) 406; Pleasant Coffelt (P) 406; T. W. Coffelt (P) 403; Nancy Colderon (P)

376; David Cole (P) 379; Elizabeth Combs (P) 396; Mahlon Combs (P) 396; Abijah Comer (P) 365; Joseph M. Conefax (P) 397; Henry Conklin (P) 403; John Connor (P) 397; Woolsey Conrad (P) 394; James H. Cook (P) 388; John W. Cooley (P) 387; Paradine A. Cooley (P) 387; Sarah Cooley (P) 374; Thomas J. Cooley (P) 374; William Cooley (P) 382; Adam M. Coonrod (P) 386; Robert P. Cooper (P) 369; Samuel Corby (P) 380; Isaiah Corwine (P) 381; Benjamin Cotton (P) 398; Jonathan Cotton (P) 397; Mary Cotton (P) 397; John Cox (P) 366; John C. Cox (P) 378; John H. Cox (P) 366; William W. Cox (P) 378; Lydia Crabtree (P) 375; Mason Crabtree (P) 399; Jesse P. Craigo (P) 364; Frederick Crambow (P) 405; James Cravens (P) 359; Retiarah Cravens (P) 359; Elizabeth Crawford (P) 365; Bernett J. Cristman (P) 372; Pleasant M. Crouch (P) 406; Anna Crow (P) 398; Levi Crow (P) 405; Moses Crow (P) 405; Henry H. Crowell (P) 380; Daniel H. Crumm (P) 389; Jacob Crumm (P) 388; Jesse Crumm (P) 373; Stephen Crumm (P) 388; James Culton (P) 403; John Culton (P) 403; Joseph Culton (P) 403; Sarah Culton (P) 403; James Cunningham (P) 393; Jacob Daisey (P) 406; Elijah P. Dale (P) 379; Elizabeth J. Dale (P) 371; John B. Dale (P) 371; Robert J. Dale (P) 378; Thomas A. Dale (P) 371; Charles Dameron (P) 363; Wesley Dameron (P) 361; Delilah Damerson (P) 363; Wesley Damerson (P) 363; John H. Darden (P) 363; Thomas Darr (P) 381; Thomas Darr (P) 400; Elizabeth Darrow (P) 364; Jesse Darrow (P) 364; J. Anderson Davis (P) 372; Alexander M. Dawson (P) 369; Thomas W. Dawson (P) 392; Barnabas D. Debolt (P) 380; Margaret Debolt (P) 383; John Degraffenreid (P) 381; Martha Degraffenried (P) 405; Martha G. Degraffenreid (P) 359; Robert Degraffenreid (P) 383; Stephen Degraffenreid (P) 405; John W. Delaney (P) 375; Jeremiah Deold (P) 377; Asbury Derham (P) 365; Louisa Derham (P) 366; Stephen F. Dewsenbury (P) 360; William G. Dewsenbury (P) 360; George Dickenson (P) 386; Levi Dickenson (P) 387; Levi Dickerson (P) 404; Isaac M. Dickey (P) 404; Vincent Digraffenreid (P) 405; Rebecca Dillender (P) 377; Edward S. Dillon (P) 359; Mary J. Dillon (P) 359; Ann Dollison (P) 384; James Dollison (P) 384; Cordelia A. Donnegan (P) 370; M. Donnegan (P) 370; John Dougherty (P) 402; Edward V. Downey (P) 384; George Downey (P) 374; Joseph Dowty (P) 402; Allen Driver (P) 363; George Duff (P) 369; Jenira Duke (P) 392; Mary Duke (P) 386; David Duncan (P) 394; John Duncan (P) 399; Joshua L. Duncan (P) 361; Melcena Duncan (P) 402; William Duncan (P) 361; Moses Duncan (P) 362; William Dunn (P) 372; Cornelius W. Dunnivan (P) 361; John Dunnivan (P) 361; John East (P) 397; Virginia A. Edmonds (P) 378; Margaret Edwards (P) 391; Samuel Elliott (P) 373; Cynthia A. Endicott (P) 378; Daniel Endicott (P) 387; Gabriel J. Endicott (P) 377; Samuel Endicott (P) 387; James Englehart (P) 385; Nancy J. Englehart (P) 385; Samuel Englehart (P) 384; Anderson Ennis (P) 382; Jacob Ennis (P) 382; James G. Ennis (P) 386; John Ennis

(P) 405; Margaret Ennis (P) 387; Celia Epperson (P) 397; Jonathan Eppright (P) 405; Napoleon Eppright (P) 405; Enoch Estep (P) 40; Enoch L. Estep (P) 401; Perma Evanse (P) 406; Hepsey Evans (P) 390; John Evanse (P) 381; Lewis Evert (P) 40; Thomas J. Ferguson (P) 386; Washington Ferguson (P) 395; Slawson Fetney (P) 365; John Fishburn (P) 363; Abraham Fisher (P) 359; Edward Fisher (P) 391; Henry Fisher (P) 363; Jesse Fisher (P) 365; John J. Fisher (P) 360; Richard Fisher (P) 367; Thomas Fisher (P) 360; William Fisher (P) 365; John Fitzgerald (P) 390; Sam Fitzpatrick (P) 400; Elijah Flanery (P) 375; Mary Ford (P) 398; James Forgy (P) 383; Dorcas Foster (P) 377; Jarrett Foster (P) 376; John Foster (P) 395; Abram P. Frasier (P) 369; Henry French (P) 397; John Fukgisson (P) 386; Adam Fulk (P) 405; Elizabeth Fulk (P) 39; John Fuller (P) 388; Samuel Fuller (P) 388; Jesse H. Fullerton (P) 366; John M. Fullerton (P) 387; John P. Fullerton (P) 388; Laban T. Fullerton (P) 370; James Fullington (P) 362; Sarh A. Fullington (P) 362; Frederick Garver (P) 399; Henry Garver (P) 400; Julia Ann Gebhart (P) 400; George Gersham (P) 404; John Gersham (P) 404; Isaac Gevear (P) 403; Isham Giboney (P) 391; Elizabeth J. Gibson (P) 376; John W. Gibson (P) 377; William Gibson (P) 375; Joseph C. Gilliland (P) 381; Jeremiah Gillstrap (P) 371; A. Ann Gilmore (P) 398; John T. Gilmore (P) 398; Robert Gilmore (P) 398; Peter Gilstrap (P) 370; John Girard (P) 363; Hiram Gist (P) 386; Andrew J. Glasscock (P) 375; Elijah Gordon (P) 384; Elijah Grace (P) 372; James M. Grace (P) 372; Livingston L. Graham (P) 381; Rebecca Graham (P) 381; Andrew J. Grant (P) 399; Edward Gray (P) 372; Edwin R. Griffith (P) 364; Joel Grubb (P) 372; David Guthrie (P) 378; John M. Haden (P) 395; Rebecca Hafer (P) 381; Rebecca Hafer (P) 400; Sarah Ann Hager (P) 359; William H. Hager (P) 360; Joseph Hall (P) 372; Joseph Hall (P) 376; Martin Hall (P) 376; Winston Hall (P) 374; William B. Hamilton (P) 365; Harrison Hammer (P) 370; Jaocb Hammer (P) 376; William Hammer (P) 376; William Hannum (P) 40; Grandville Hansford (P) 373; Hiram Hansford (P) 376; Nancy Hansford (P) 371; Samuel Hanson (P) 369; John Happy (P) 380; Stephen Hare (P) 394; Stephen Harper (P) 388; John Harris (P) 361; Jonathan Harris (P) 398; Elizabeth Harvey (P) 367; John Harvey (P) 360; Joseph E. Harvey (P) 360; Louisa Harvey (P) 363; Parthena Harvey (P) 365; Phoebe Harvey (P) 373; Rachel Harvey (P) 363; George W. Hawkins (P) 363; Susan Hawkins (P) 390; Thomas H. Hawkins (P) 376; Thomas Hays (P) 396; Minerva E. Hazelwood (P) 373; Thomas R. Hazelwood (P) 373; Sarah Hefton (P) 397; William Hefton (P) 397; Richard Henderson (P) 389; Madison Hendrick (P) 402; John Henry (P) 365; Paul Henson (P) 403; Emberson Herald (P) 393; Andrew Herley (P) 395; Joseph Herndon (P) 385; Mary H. Herndon (P) 385; Francis M. Hewett (P) 392; Joshua Hickey (P) 374; Middleton Hickey (P) 374; Lewis Hinds (P) 385; Lucretia A. Holcomb (P) 373; Martha Holcomb (P) 373;

Jerman D. Holloway (P) 368; Joel Hood (P) 366; John Hood (P) 366; Jesse B. Hopkins (P) 361; Thomas Hopkins (P) 380; James Hornbeck (P) 377; John Hornbeck (P) 393; Josephus Hornsinger (P) 366; Lewis Houghland (P) 390; Benedictor Howard (P) 382; Elvira Howard (P) 375; Jasper Howard (P) 383; George Hawk (P) 382; Edward H. Hubbard (P) 390; Jacob Huff (P) 379; Elisha M. Hurt (P) 359; Amelia J. Hushaw (P) 361; Adison Irvin (P) 385; William P. Irwin (P) 391; Jacob Iseley (P) 379; James Jackett (P) 399; Ellenor Jackson (P) 382; Isaac Jackson (P) 385; Joel P. Jackson (P) 385; Rachel Jackson (P) 396; William Jackson (P) 380; William Jackson (P) 391; Cynthain Jamerson (P) 390; Elwood B. James (P) 391; Hanibal James (P) 392; Eliza R. Jason (P) 375; Esther Jason (P) 375; Thomas W. Jameson (P) 374; Alexander Johnson (P) 367; Angelina Johnson (P) 374; Daniel Johnson (P) 372; Daniel Johnson (P) 374; Eli Johnson (P) 378; Gabriel Johnson (P) 391; Hubbard Johnson (P) 371; John Johnson (P) 375; Owen Johnson (P) 384; Peter R. Johnson (P) 381; William P. Johnson (P) 369; Bedford B. Jones (P) 381; Daniel J. Jones (P) 373; James G. Jones (P) 371; John D. Jones (P) 372; Jonah Jones (P) 401; Jonas M. Jones (P) 370; Nancy Jones (P) 378; Phoebe Jones (P) 365; Vincent Jones (P) 369; William Jones (P) 384; Alfred Jordan (P) 363; Gustavus Jordan (P) 362; Sarah Keith (P) 376; Charles Kelly (P) 392; Jesse Kelly (P) 401; Margaret Kelly (P) 401; Philip Kelly (P) 396; Sarah Kelly (P) 397; Sarah Kelly (P) 362; Lattimer Kendall (P) 365; Robert Kern (P) 386; Elizabeth Kerr (P) 367; Isaac Kerr (P) 389; John B. Kerr (P) 393; John J. Kerr (P) 361; Wesley Key (P) 372; Sam Killpatrick (P) 379; Sarah Killpatrick (P) 379; Aquilla King (P) 361; James T. King (P) 383; John King (P) 362; Joseph H. King (P) 383; William R. King (P) 36; Nelson Knight (P) 389; James L. Laforce (P) 390; Samuel B. Laforce (P) 390; Alexander Lamar (P) 404; Archibald Lambert (P) 397; Robert Lancaster (P) 382; James K. Langley (P) 394; Mary A. Langley (P) 394; Margaret Larson (P) 385; James S. Laughlin (P) 397; Joseph L. Laughlin (P) 397; Elizabeth Laxson (P) 377; Robert R. Laxton (P) 386; Lewis Ledbetter (P) 406; Mary E. Ledford (P) 375; Rhoda Lee (P) 372; Lucretia Lemaster (P) 377; John Lemons (P) 406; Mary Lemons (P) 403; Clark P. Levally (P) 368; David R. Lewis (P) 363; Elizabeth Lewis (P) 362; Iddings Lewis (P) 388; Moses Lewis (P) 362; Reuben Lewis (P) 362; Caroline J. Lofton (P) 384; James Lofton (P) 383; James B. Lofton (P) 403; Philip B. Logon (P) 380; Spotswood Longan (P) 383; Aaron Loving (P) 406; Thomas Lowry (P) 401; Robert Lowther (P) 382; Milton B. Lugg (P) 364; Alfred Lundsford (P) 364; George Lundsford (P) 368; David Lundy (P) 382; Robert Luwellen (P) 374; Mary Mabes (P) 393; Thomas Malone (P) 393; Peter Mann (P) 363; Josephus Manner (P) 384; Thomas Mansfield (P) 384; Thomas W. Margrave (P) 403; William Margrave (P) 396; Pamela Markham (P) 361; Holmes Marrison (P) 385; David Martin (P) 395;

George Martin (P) 376; Hartwell Martin (P) 362; Henry J. Martin (P) 397; James Martin (P) 384; Joseph Martin (P) 398; Joshua Martin (P) 381; Lewis G. Martin (P) 362; Louisa M. Martin (P) 383; Tillman W. Martin (P) 397; William Martin (P) 376; Ben F. Masie (P) 370; William Mason (P) 384; Rachel Mathews (P) 370; Elizabeth Matlock (P) 384; Henry Matthews (P) 402; Philip Matthews (P) 402; Mary Maupin (P) 392; Wilkerson Maupin (P) 392; James G. Maxey (P) 381; James W. Maxey (P) 378; John P. Maxey (P) 378; Vincent Maxey (P) 381; William Maxey (P) 381; William G. Maxey (P) 381; William H. Maxey (P) 378; John G. McCabe (P) 385; Mary E. McCabe (P) 387; Cornelia McClain (P) 404; Susannah McClay (P) 395; James McCollum (P) 385; Martin McCollum (P) 385; Samuel McConnell (P) 39; William McCrea (P) 376; John McCuen (P) 406; Elijah McDaniel (P) 405; Hiram McDaniel (P) 405; James McDaniel (P) 386; John McDaniel (P) 406; John McDaniels (P) 391; Elizabeth McDonald (P) 399; Joshua McDonald (P) 399; William McDonald (P) 401; John McDowell (P) 386; Caroline McFaa (P) 403; Harriett McFarland (P) 364; Robert McFarland (P) 390; Robert McFarland (P) 391; John G. McGinnes (P) 387; Harriet McGinnis (P) 388; John McGuire (P) 404; Nehemiah McGuire (P) 405; Lemuel McIntire (P) 367; Andrew M. McKee (P) 380; John R. McKinney (P) 397; James C. McLaughlin (P) 394; Joseph McLaughlin (P) 404; Susannah McLaughlin (P) 395; Moses McMannis (P) 399; James H. McPhatridge (P) 361; Austin Meador (P) 368; Moses G. Meador (P) 368; Timothy Meador (P) 363; Archibald Meadows (P) 404; Thomas J. Means (P) 371; Joseph W. Meligian (P) 365; Joseph A. Melugian (P) 364; Samuel Melugian (P) 363; Thomas Melugian (P) 363; Jacob Michael (P) 395; Micajah Michael (P) 395; James Miles (P) 400; Charles Miller (P) 390; Jacob Miller (P) 365; Virginia Mills (P) 359; Henry Mills (P) 378; Thomas Mills (P) 386; William Mills (P) 386; Willis Mills (P) 378; Hannah Miner (P) 398; John Miner (P) 397; Carville Mitchell (P) 394; Alexander Morehead (P) 396; Samuel Moreton (P) 374; Nancy J. Morgan (P) 362; Rudda Morgan (P) 389; George Morris (P) 402; William Morris (P) 402; John L. Morse (P) 371; David Martin (P) 381; David Moss (P) 373; Henry Moss (P) 392; Lucinda Moss (P) 368; Edwin C. Motley (P) 390; John S. Motley (P) 393; Sarah Motley (P) 365; William Mounts (P) 367; David Murphy (P) 379; Thomas Musser (P) 379; Robert D. Neale (P) 359; William Neale (P) 377; Elijah Nelson (P) 402; William Nelson (P) 402; Green Nicholas (P) 379; Frederick B. Nichols (P) 360; Jaocb Nickolson (P) 394; Elizabeth Noakes (P) 387; William A. Noakes (P) 387; Daniel Noland (P) 393; Thomas Norris (P) 369; Abraham Onstoll (P) 376; John Onstoll (P) 376; Alexander Orchard (P) 374; Claybourn Osborn (P) 405; William W. Osborn (P) 404; Miles Overton (P) 368; Richard Ozmant (P) 368; Augustus Page (P) 382; John Parcel (P) 394; William Henry Parrott (P) 369; Francis A. Patrick (P)

371; Wallace J. Patrick (P) 371; Thomas Paul (P) 364; Matthew Payne (P) 373; Fletcher Pearce (P) 396; Jackson B. Pearce (P) 396; John Pearce (P) 396; F. W. Pennington (P) 391; Jesse Perdue (P) 363; Virgil Perkinzer (P) 373; Sarah C. Perrington (P) 385; Alexander Perry (P) 372; Elisha Peters (P) 400; Luton Peters (P) 401; Allen Petty (P) 401; Nancy Petty (P) 397; Barbara Phoebus (P) 393; John Phoebus (P) 367; Sarah L. Pierce (P) 370; Josiah F. Pinson (P) 383; Andrew J. Pipkin (P) 363; Elijah Pool (P) 397; William A. Pool (P) 397; John Potts (P) 377; Louisa Potts (P) 403; John Powers (P) 369; Fields Prewett (P) 362; Daniel Prigmore (P) 366; Daniel Prigmore, Jr. (P) 370; James R. Prigmore (P) 370; John Prigmore (P) 366; Thomas Prigmore (P) 370; John Prior (P) 399; John F. Prior (P) 398; Martha Prior (P) 399; Stephen Prior (P) 398; John Pritchett (P) 402; Jacob Rader (P) 393; John Ragan (P) 373; Ellin Rains (P) 359; Margaret Rains (P) 359; Nathan D. Ralston (P) 373; Wesley Raney (P) 368; Jacob Rankin (P) 392; John Rankin (P) 382; Linnet Rankin (P) 392; Francis Reands (P) 382; James Releford (P) 397; Levi Reynolds (P) 374; James Rice (P) 362; B. W. Richardson (P) 360; E. H. Richardson (P) 391; Mark Richardson (P) 386; Moses Richardson (P) 376; Susannah Richardson (P) 391; Edward Rickets (P) 399; Jaocb Rickner (P) 388; Samuel Rickner (P) 388; Jamima Roaden (P) 364; Elizabeth Roberts (P) 406; Arthur Robertson (P) 362; Augustus Robertson (P) 374; Clisby Robertson (P) 374; John H. Robertson (P) 374; Martha Robertson (P) 375; Matthew L. Robertson (P) 383; Peter Robertson (P) 374; Samuel Robertson (P) 398; Samuel B. Robertson (P) 367; Washington Robertson (P) 374; William L. Robertson (P) 387; John Robinson (P) 366; John H. Robinson (P) 364; Mary A. Robinson (P) 364; Adaline Rogers (P) 396; Joseph Rogers (P) 395; Israel Rose (P) 401; Samuel Rose (P) 403; John E. Roson (P) 367; James H. Ross (P) 386; Margaret Ross (P) 386; Arthur P. Rosson (P) 367; William D. Rosson (P) 368; Isaac Roy (P) 383; Reuben Ruck (P) 382; Elliott Rucker (P) 375; James Rucker (P) 375; Margaret Rucker (P) 375; William Rucker (P) 382; David Rush (P) 396; Solomon Rushenborger (P) 383; Jonathan Rusk (P) 382; John Samples (P) 364; Mavor Sanders (P) 391; Sam D. Sanders (P) 369; Thomas Sanders (P) 388; William Scantling (P) 403; John J. Scott (P) 390; Nancy Scott (P) 361; William Scott (P) 387; William Scott (P) 40; William M. Scott (P) 387; William R. Scott (P) 369; Lewis H. Scruggs (P) 391; James Secrest (P) 404; John Secrest (P) 404; Joseph Secrest (P) 395; Thomas Secrest (P) 395; Isaac Sela (P) 388; H. W. Shanks (P) 389; William Shannon (P) 369; James A. Shaw (P) 361; Samuel Shaw (P) 371; Willis Shaw (P) 368; James Shelton (P) 394; John P. Shelton (P) 374; John Shirley (P) 396; Preston Shirley (P) 392; Edwin Shoemaker (P) 402; James Shoemaker (P) 400; Seth Shoemaker (P) 402; Wilson Shoemaker (P) 402; William A. Shroyer (P) 380; Albert Slater (P) 404; Joseph Slawson (P) 365; James A. Slinker (P) 368; Joel Slinker (P)

361; Merryman Slinker (P) 362; George Sly (P) 367; Thompson Smallwood (P) 379; Andrew Smith (P) 400; Calvin Smith (P) 400; Daniel Smith (P) 386; Edward Smith (P) 386; Eli Smith (P) 400; Elizabeth Smith (P) 380; F. P. Smith (P) 370; James Smith (P) 386; James Smith (P) 387; James Smith (P) 400; James B. Smith (P) 384; James W. Smith (P) 400; Joseph Smith (P) 399; Joseph M. Smith (P) 389; Lydia Smith (P) 386; Marcus Smith (P) 379; Moses Smith (P) 379; Samuel J. Smith (P) 372; Sarah Smith (P) 399; William Smith (P) 400; William Smith (P) 372; William Smith (P) 370; William B. Smith (P) 393; William Levi Smith (P) 360; William Snodgrass (P) 39; James Scott (P) 365; Ben H. South (P) 363; Richard South (P) 406; William B. Southard (P) 391; Adda Spears (P) 387; Lorenzo J. Speigle (P) 377; Priscilla Speigle (P) 377; Daniel Spence (P) 370; Lazarus Spence (P) 372; Samuel Spence (P) 373; Fleming Spencer (P) 382; Grenville Spencer (P) 382; Minerva J. Spencer (P) 373; Peleg Spencer (P) 36; William Spencer (P) 372; Noah Stanly (P) 401; Robert Stanly (P) 402; John Stanton (P) 361; Hector Steale (P) 377; Abraham Stephenson (P) 401; Milton Stephenson (P) 366; Terribae Sterrett (P) 368; Joel C. Stiels (P) 398; John Stiers (P) 385; David Stiles (P) 398; Ferman Stiles (P) 398; Edwin Stith (P) 394; Lucy Stith (P) 394; William F. Stith (P) 39; Sarah Stockton (P) 378; Preston Storms (P) 395; Ephraim Stout (P) 387; Francis Stribling (P) 359; John Struble (P) 385; Milton B. Sugg (P) 364; James Sullenger (P) 379; John Sullenger (P) 380; Thomas Sullenger (P) 380; Thomas Sullenger, Jr. (P) 380; James Summers (P) 392; John Summers (P) 392; Nancy Summers (P) 391; Jesse Summers (P) 376; Michael Sword (P) 380; John Tackett (P) 399; John K. Tapscott (P) 391; James Tate (P) 370; George W. Taylor (P) 401; Martha Teal (P) 402; John Terrell (P) 368; Lucinda Tharp (P) 392; William O. Tharp (P) 392; Daniel H. Thomas (P) 371; Thomas S. Thompson (P) 392; David Thompson (P) 396; Hiram Thompson (P) 378; Isaac M. Thompson (P) 404; James Thompson (P) 390; John Thompson (P) 384; John D. Thompson (P) 380; Joseph Thompson (P) 384; Joseph Thurman (P) 360; Ebenezer Torrence (P) 404; Eliza Torrence (P) 404; Jr. John Townsend (P) 378; John Townsend, Sr. (P) 384; John Triplett (P) 371; Sarah E. Triplett (P) 367; Allen L. Trotter (P) 406; James Trout (P) 391; Charles Tucker (P) 405; Harriett Tucker (P) 402; Harman Tuin (P) 359; David Tunnel (P) 385; James Tunnel (P) 406; Martha Tunnel (P) 406; Nicholas Tunnel (P) 386; Pamela Tunnel (P) 386; Solomon Turnipseed (P) 392; Perry M. Twitty (P) 381; William Twitty (P) 381; Cary E. Vance (P) 387; Joseph Vance (P) 404; Malissa Vernon (P) 401; Samuel J. Vestal (P) 367; Solomon Vester (P) 388; Stephen T. Videtoe (P) 365; Charles Vivion (P) 383; John M. Vivion (P) 385; Alanson D. Wade (P) 395; James Waldon (P) 372; Harrison Walker (P) 374; Jacob B. Walker (P) 374; James Walker (P) 39; James F. Walker (P) 400; John W. Walker (P) 400; John W. Walker (P)

373; Martha Ann Walker (P) 360; Rufus R. Walker (P) 360; Samuel Walker (P) 375; Samuel Walker (P) 360; John C. Walton (P) 370; John Q. Walton (P) 393; Thomas G. Walton (P) 390; William H. Walton (P) 390; Robert M. Ward (P) 394; Wilhelmina Ward (P) 394; Caroline Ware (P) 397; William N. Warren (P) 371; John D. Waters (P) 395; William R. Watson (P) 373; Elizabeth Wear (P) 397; Wesley Webb (P) 384; Daniel Wethers (P) 364; James Wethers (P) 379; John Wethers (P) 378; William Wethers (P) 368; Joel Whaley (P) 38; David A. Wheeler (P) 380; James R. Wheeler (P) 380; Mary White (P) 397; Oliver T. White (P) 396; Thomas White (P) 397; William White (P) 368; Francis Whitehead (P) 388; Elizabeth Whitlock (P) 394; Willburn Whitlock (P) 393; William Whitten (P) 377; John M. Wilkenson (P) 382; Morgan Wilkenson (P) 382; Elizabeth Williams (P) 398; John Williams (P) 375; Russell Williamson (P) 393; James Willis (P) 399; Andrew Wilson (P) 399; Daniel Wilson (P) 395; James M. Wilson (P) 369; Javin Wilson (P) 395; Sarah E. Wilson (P) 360; William Wilson (P) 395; William C. Wilson (P) 359; William C. Winters (P) 369; John H. Withers (P) 365; Rachel Wolf (P) 401; Eli W. Wolfe (P) 369; Hannah Wolfe (P) 398; Paris Woodcock (P) 363; Elijah Woodram (P) 389; Washington Woodram (P) 389; William Woodram (P) 373; John W. Woods (P) 369; James Woolson (P) 366; John Worley (P) 39; Eli Worthington (P) 400; Josiah Worthington (P) 400; Lewis M. Worthington (P) 370; Nancy Worthington (P) 400; William Worthington (P) 400; James Wright (P) 370; Josiah Wright (P) 380; Powell O. Wright (P) 380; William T. Wright (P) 360; Barbara Young (P) 390; Henry H. Young (P) 391; Susan Young (P) 389; Henry H. Zachary (P) 375; Henry Zellers (P) 367; John Zellers (P) 367; Mary Zellers (P) 367; Alexander Zevally (P) 399; John Zevelly (P) 399; Levi Zillers (P) 389.

Missouri, State Military Service Voucher, (Note: This item was at an auction. I lost the bid, but the buyer allowed me to copy the information.)
Triphemiah Smith, Co. F, 6threg., E.M.M. (Enrolled Missouri Militia), August 18, 1874, Cert. No. 2935, Amt. $520. Civil War Veteran Service Voucher

Clark County, Missouri, 1911 Property Receipt
1901 Property Tax receipt to John Stull of Jefferson Township in Clark Co., Missouri signed G.L. Roland, Collector for Clark County and F.M. Thompson, deputy collector. The property is 120 acres in three sections of Jefferson Township. The property tax total was $11.65. Dated Nov. 18, 1901.

Missouri Military Payment Certificate, 1874

State of Missouri Military Payment Certificate dated December 7, 1874, issued to B. B. Beck for $366.45 Certificate by The R. P. Studley Co., St. Louis. Sigened Silus Woodson, Governor.

St. Louis County, Missouri, Veterans Killed in Military Service in the Korean War.
Augustus A. Abbey: (Rank) Cpl., (Svc) Army
Augustus A. Abbey: (Rank) Cpl., (Svc) Army
Bill J. Acinelli: (Rank) Pvt., (Svc) Army
Raymond J. Adams: (Rank) Sfc., (Svc) Army
Barry E. Albright: (Rank) Maj., (Svc) Army
Glenn M. Anderson: (Rank) Pvt., (Svc) Army
Bob L. Arley: (Rank) Pvt., (Svc) Marines
John E. Ashby: (Rank) Cpl., (Svc) Army
Theron Clark Askew: (Rank) Pfc., (Svc) Marines
Joseph P. Avery: (Rank) Sgt., (Svc) Army
Walter J. Ball: (Rank) Pvt., (Svc) Army
Joseph L. Barnett: (Rank) Pvt., (Svc) Army
Jerry Barry: (Rank) 2ndLt., (Svc) Army
Dale L. Beishir: (Rank) Pfc., (Svc) Army
Robert E. Bell: (Rank) Cpl., (Svc) Army
Wardell A. Bell: (Rank) Pvt., (Svc) Army
Leon John Bernal: (Rank) Capt., (Svc) Marines
Henry J. Betz: (Rank) Pvt., (Svc) Army
Robert Joseph Betz: (Rank) Pfc., (Svc) Marines
Fred George Bevfoden: (Rank) Pfc., (Svc) Marines
Jerry Douglas Bingaman: (Rank) 1stLt., (Svc) Air Force
Junior Black: (Rank) Pvt., (Svc) Army
Zack A. Bone: (Rank) Pvt., (Svc) Army
Clarence Bonner: (Rank) Sgt., (Svc) Army
Joe J. Bookout: (Rank) Sfc., (Svc) Army
Charles Borum: (Rank) Pfc., (Svc) Marines
Norman L. Bounds: (Rank) Cpl., (Svc) Army
James A. Boyce: (Rank) Pvt., (Svc) Army
Victor Braud: (Rank) Pfc., (Svc) Army
Ernest J. Brendel: (Rank) Cpl., (Svc) Army
Dillman Lawrence Brendle: (Rank) SSgt., (Svc) Air Force
Walter B. Brown: (Rank) Pvt., (Svc) Army
Harold B. Brown: (Rank) Pfc., (Svc) Army
Lawrence Brunnert: (Rank) Capt., (Svc) Army
Edward J. Bruno: (Rank) Pfc., (Svc) Army
Ira Emmett Burnett: (Rank) Pfc., (Svc) Marines
Ralph W Burns: (Rank) Cpl., (Svc) Army

Sammie D. Calhoun: (Rank) Pvt., (Svc) Army
James F. Campbell: (Rank) Pfc., (Svc) Army
Gregory O. Canan: (Rank) Cpl., (Svc) Army
Joe L. Cardwell: (Rank) Pfc., (Svc) Army
Billie Carl Carothers: (Rank) Pfc., (Svc) Marines
Frederick Carrino: (Rank) Pfc., (Svc) Army
Taylor K. Castlen: (Rank) 1stLt., (Svc) Army
Alfredo G. Chavei: (Rank) Pfc., (Svc) Marines
Charles E. Clemons: (Rank) Sgt., (Svc) Army
Hubert F. Cochran: (Rank) Pfc., (Svc) Army
John E. Collins: (Rank) Pfc., (Svc) Army
John M. Collins: (Rank) Sfc., (Svc) Army
Robert Thomas Connell: (Rank) Cpl., (Svc) Marines
Robert K. Conner: (Rank) Pfc., (Svc) Army
Lamonte B. Cook: (Rank) Pfc., (Svc) Army
Charles W Costello: (Rank) Cpl., (Svc) Army
William E. Craig: (Rank) Pfc., (Svc) Army
Elmer E. Crawford: (Rank) Pfc., (Svc) Army
James F. Dairda: (Rank) Pvt., (Svc) Army
Curtis L. Daniels: (Rank) Pvt., (Svc) Army
Ralph H. Davioter: (Rank) Pvt., (Svc) Army
Joseph W Deller: (Rank) Pfc., (Svc) Army
Frank V. Doerr: (Rank) Pfc., (Svc) Army
Norrie C. Doolittle: (Rank) Sgt., (Svc) Army
Thomas E. Dowling: (Rank) Capt., (Svc) Army
Rutherford Early: (Rank) Pfc., (Svc) Army
Glennon W Eaton: (Rank) Pfc., (Svc) Army
Edgar A. Ehrlich: (Rank) 1stLt., (Svc) Air Force
Donald Earl Eichschlag: (Rank) Pfc., (Svc) Marines
William L. Farabee: (Rank) Pvt., (Svc) Army
Charles L. Farris: (Rank) Cpl., (Svc) Army
Chester A. Fields: (Rank) Cpl., (Svc) Army
Wilbert S Ford: (Rank) Cpl., (Svc) Army
Sherman E. Fowler: (Rank) Pvt., (Svc) Marines
Charlie Frazier: (Rank) Pfc., (Svc) Army
William Don Fugit: (Rank) Pfc., (Svc) Marines
Anthony Gary: (Rank) 1stLt., (Svc) Air Force
James E. Gebhart: (Rank) Cpl., (Svc) Army
Raymond Glass: (Rank) Pfc., (Svc) Army
Billy J. Graham: (Rank) Pvt., (Svc) Army
Richard A. Grundman: (Rank) Sgt., (Svc) Army
Charles H. Hagemier: (Rank) Pfc., (Svc) Army
Joseph F. Hagerty: (Rank) Sfc., (Svc) Army

Freddie L. Hamilton: (Rank) Pfc., (Svc) Army
Ronald W Hamilton: (Rank) Cpl., (Svc) Army
Alonzo R. Hammock: (Rank) 1stLt., (Svc) Army
Richard J. Handing: (Rank) Sgt., (Svc) Marines
Danny J. Handley: (Rank) Pvt., (Svc) Army
Edward E. Harber: (Rank) Pfc., (Svc) Army
Edward Calhoun Hardcastle: (Rank) Pfc., (Svc) Marines
Clode Marvin Harold: (Rank) Cpl., (Svc) Marines
Herbert Henderson: (Rank) Cpl., (Svc) Army
Elton Thomas Henry: (Rank) Sgt., (Svc) Marines
Walter L. Hentz: (Rank) Pvt., (Svc) Army
John F. Herdlick: (Rank) 1stLt., (Svc) Army
Alfred H. Herman: (Rank) 1stLt., (Svc) Army
Thomas Robert Higgins: (Rank) Pfc., (Svc) Marines
John F. Higgs: (Rank) SSgt., (Svc) Marines
Carter Hilgard: (Rank) Capt., (Svc) Army
Raymond Frederick Hill: (Rank) Cpl., (Svc) Marines
Eugene Tayor Hite: (Rank) SSgt., (Svc) Marines
Virgil L. Hodge: (Rank) Pfc., (Svc) Army
George M. Hoefeler: (Rank) Sgt., (Svc) Army
Billy E. Holdman: (Rank) Cpl., (Svc) Army
Jack Horn: (Rank) Pfc., (Svc) Marines
Jerome V. Hummel: (Rank) Pfc., (Svc) Army
Donald J. Hutton: (Rank) Cpl., (Svc) Army
Alan R. Jastram: (Rank) Sgt., (Svc) Army
Vernon D. Jenkins: (Rank) Sgt., (Svc) Army
Elijah L. Jennings: (Rank) Pvt., (Svc) Army
Elvis J. Jimes: (Rank) Pvt., (Svc) Army
Richard E. Johnston: (Rank) Pfc., (Svc) Army
William F. Kahrhoff: (Rank) Pfc., (Svc) Army
Anth Kapfensteiner: (Rank) Pvt., (Svc) Army
Harold L. Kay: (Rank) Pfc., (Svc) Army
Charles W Kellison: (Rank) Sgt., (Svc) Army
Roy L. Kirkpatrick: (Rank) Pvt., (Svc) Army
Leslie F. Klees: (Rank) Cpl., (Svc) Army
Louis J. Klein: (Rank) Cpl., (Svc) Army
Joseph Jude Knox: (Rank) Pfc., (Svc) Marines
Roy Eugene Koenig: (Rank) Pfc., (Svc) Marines
Richard A. Kolar: (Rank) Pvt., (Svc) Army
Charles Kolody: (Rank) Pvt., (Svc) Army
Don G. Krause: (Rank) Pvt., (Svc) Army
Graham H. Kreunen: (Rank) Cpl., (Svc) Army
Oliver B. Kupferle: (Rank) Pfc., (Svc) Army

Mastus Robert La: (Rank) Pfc., (Svc) Army
Leonard E. Lahm: (Rank) Pfc., (Svc) Army
Johnny D. Lange: (Rank) Pfc., (Svc) Army
James N. Larkin: (Rank) Pfc., (Svc) Army
George E. Laurence: (Rank) Pfc., (Svc) Army
Edwin J. Leary: (Rank) Pvt., (Svc) Army
Ernest A. Lee: (Rank) Pvt., (Svc) Army
Arthur E. Lewis: (Rank) Sfc., (Svc) Army
Herman O. Lewis: (Rank) Pfc., (Svc) Army
Loran K. Libbert: (Rank) Pfc., (Svc) Army
Leslie Donald Little: (Rank) Pfc., (Svc) Marines
Charles E. Logan: (Rank) Pfc., (Svc) Army
Thomas A. Lombardo: (Rank) 1stlt., (Svc) Army
Tommie L. Long: (Rank) MSgt., (Svc) Army
Charles M. Long: (Rank) Cpl., (Svc) Army
William P. Luyendyk: (Rank) Pfc., (Svc) Army
William E. Maddox: (Rank) Pfc., (Svc) Army
Harold R. Mann: (Rank) Pvt., (Svc) Army
Roberts Roy Mc: (Rank) Sfc., (Svc) Army
William C. Mead: (Rank) Pfc., (Svc) Army
Paul G. Mentzos: (Rank) Sgt., (Svc) Army
Jake Raymond Meyer: (Rank) Pfc., (Svc) Marines
Raymond J. Meyer: (Rank) Pvt., (Svc) Army
Alexander Midgett: (Rank) Pvt., (Svc) Army
Frederick H. Mihaupt: (Rank) 1stLt., (Svc) Air Force
Harold J. Miller: (Rank) Pfc., (Svc) Army
Robert Mitchell: (Rank) Pfc., (Svc) Army
Hercules Moore: (Rank) Pfc., (Svc) Army
Henry M. Moore: (Rank) 1stLt., (Svc) Army
James L. Moore: (Rank) Pfc., (Svc) Army
Lenzey Moore: (Rank) Pfc., (Svc) Army
Kenneth D. Murphy: (Rank) Sgt., (Svc) Army
Thomas Ellis Myers: (Rank) Maj., (Svc) Air Force
Edward J. Nagel: (Rank) Cpl., (Svc) Army
Mike E. Neisz: (Rank) Pfc., (Svc) Army
James L. Noe: (Rank) Pfc., (Svc) Army
Mike R. Novak: (Rank) Pfc., (Svc) Army
William H. Owens: (Rank) Cpl., (Svc) Army
Harry R. Painter: (Rank) 1stLt., (Svc) Air Force
David D. Parke: (Rank) Cpl., (Svc) Army
Harry F. Parsons: (Rank) Pfc., (Svc) Army
Lawrence A. Pauly: (Rank) Cpl., (Svc) Army
Dalko D. Pavletich: (Rank) Pfc., (Svc) Army

Arthur J. Perez: (Rank) Pfc., (Svc) Army
Clyde A. Perry: (Rank) Pvt., (Svc) Army
Armand A. Petersen: (Rank) Pvt., (Svc) Army
James Edmund Phillips: (Rank) Pfc., (Svc) Marines
Jackie L. Phillips: (Rank) Pvt., (Svc) Army
Marcel C. Poelker: (Rank) Sgt., (Svc) Army
Bill J. Porter: (Rank) Pfc., (Svc) Army
William R. Potter: (Rank) Pfc., (Svc) Marines
John E. Pree: (Rank) Pvt., (Svc) Army
Alfred A. Pucci: (Rank) Pvt., (Svc) Army
Sam Ramsey: (Rank) Sgt., (Svc) Army
John J. Rascher: (Rank) MSgt., (Svc) Army
Harold Reid: (Rank) Pfc., (Svc) Army
George Joseph Reitmeyer: (Rank) Pfc., (Svc) Marines
James A. Richardson: (Rank) Cpl., (Svc) Marines
Herman W Roesch: (Rank) Capt., (Svc) Army
Vincent Frank Rogers: (Rank) Pfc., (Svc) Marines
Tenney K. Ross: (Rank) 1stLt., (Svc) Army
Walter A. Ross: (Rank) Sgt., (Svc) Army
Joseph R. Roussin: (Rank) Pvt., (Svc) Army
Leo P. Russavage: (Rank) MSgt., (Svc) Army
John H. Russell: (Rank) Pfc., (Svc) Army
Rudy J. Santacruz: (Rank) Pfc., (Svc) Army
Henry C. Scharlott: (Rank) Pvt., (Svc) Army
Felix Scott: (Rank) Pvt., (Svc) Army
Leonard Scott: (Rank) Pfc., (Svc) Army
John Elsworth Semar: (Rank) Cpl., (Svc) Marines
Martin F. Seymour: (Rank) Pvt., (Svc) Army
Jim Shelton: (Rank) Pfc., (Svc) Army
Thurman Milton Shults: (Rank) Fn, (Svc) Navy
Richard Henry Sieckmann: (Rank) Cpl., (Svc) Marines
Roy Simmons: (Rank) Cpl., (Svc) Army
Frank P. Simon: (Rank) Cpl., (Svc) Army
Donald G. Smith: (Rank) Pfc., (Svc) Army
J D. Smith: (Rank) Pfc., (Svc) Army
Charles D. Smith: (Rank) Pvt., (Svc) Army
John E. Smith: (Rank) Pvt., (Svc) Army
Hugh N. Sommer: (Rank) Pvt., (Svc) Army
Edwin W Szwabo: (Rank) Cpl., (Svc) Army
Harvey Tarkow: (Rank) Cpl., (Svc) Army
Earl W Taylor: (Rank) Pvt., (Svc) Army
James Thomas: (Rank) Pvt., (Svc) Army
Theodore Thornton: (Rank) Cpl., (Svc) Army

Edward J. Thraum: (Rank) Pfc., (Svc) Army
Eugene F. Tross: (Rank) Pvt., (Svc) Army
Fredrick W Vach: (Rank) Cpl., (Svc) Army
William E. Vincent: (Rank) Pfc., (Svc) Army
Haar James Vonder: (Rank) Cpl., (Svc) Army
Tim E. Wade: (Rank) Sgt., (Svc) Army
Louie D. Walker: (Rank) Pvt., (Svc) Marines
James I. Walker: (Rank) Pvt., (Svc) Army
Charles Washington: (Rank) Pfc., (Svc) Army
Willie Wells: (Rank) Pvt., (Svc) Army
Waddell White: (Rank) Pvt., (Svc) Army
Roy N. Whited: (Rank) Sgt., (Svc) Army
Paul J. Wichman: (Rank) Pfc., (Svc) Army
James H. William: (Rank) Cpl., (Svc) Army
Clarence Williams: (Rank) Pfc., (Svc) Marines
Richard Charles Willmann: (Rank) Cpl., (Svc) Marines
Joseph D. Wills: (Rank) Pvt., (Svc) Army
Roy Cornelius Wilson: (Rank) Cpl., (Svc) Marines
James Wilson: (Rank) Cpl., (Svc) Army
Clifford J. Windom: (Rank) Pfc., (Svc) Army
Don Wolfe: (Rank) Cpl., (Svc) Army
Paul Henry Wulf: (Rank) Pfc., (Svc) Marines
John Paul Yellen: (Rank) Pfc., (Svc) Marines
Alphonse Zampier: (Rank) Pvt., (Svc) Army

St. Louis County, Missouri, 1928-1929, Roster Mt. Moriah Temple Chapter No. 6, Order of the Eastern Star.

Mrs. Ruanna Abbott, Harry A. Adam, Mrs. Helen A. Adam, Miss Anna Ahring, Mrs. Frances Ahring, Mrs. Orlean Alford (Chicago, IL), Mrs. Frances Allan, Mrs. Abbie Alsdorf, Miss Ethel Alsdorf, William Alsdorf, Mrs. Anna Anderson, Miss Bernice Anderson, Mrs. Lottie Andreas, Mrs. Carrie Aufderheide, Mrs. Mayme Axline, Mrs. Minnie Baegerman, Harvey M. Bajer, Mrs.Matilda Bajer, Mrs. Edna Baird, Mrs. Louise Baird, Mrs. Mabel baker, Mrs. Edna Balthasar, Mrs. Irene Bamford, Frank Banks, Mrs. Katherine Banks, Miss Kittie Barkley, Mrs. Bertha Barks, Mrs. Olga barnard, August Barthels, Mrs. Clara Barthels, August Bumgartner, Chas. Bumgartner, Mrs. Emma Baumgartner, Mrs. Olive Baugmgartner, Mrs. Rena Bealke, Mrs. Katherine Beaury, Mrs. Anna Beave, Chas. A. Beck, Mrs. Louise Beck, Miss Esther Becker, Mrs. Kather Becker, Miss Lucille Becker, Mrs. Viola becker, Mrs. Captola Bedsworth, Mrs. Frances Beenck, Chas. H. Begemann, Mrs. Frieda Begemann, Mrs. Margaret Begemann, Miss Mabel Behrend, Mrs. Frieda Beilsten (Los Angeles, CA), Miss Elizabeth Beltz, Mrs. Lettie Beltz, Miss

Sophia Benner, Mrs. Mae Bennett, Owen T. Bennett, Mrs. Florence Bensing, Fred Bensing, Mrs. Lulu Benson, Mrs. Elizabeth Berding, Mrs. Louise Berg,

Carter County Missouri Marriage Records, Book B, 1890-1898
Page 1
Amos Ball and Ann Short, (MD) May 11, 1890
John Carnahan and Loe E. Cutlerboth, Mill Springs, Wayne Co., MO, (MD) May 11, 1890
Jesse A. Skiep and Clairsiy Eggers, (MD) May 20, 1890,(CMTS) Johnathan Eggers, guardian.
Page 2
John H. Crouch and Mrs. Nancy E. Tucker; (RD) May 31, 1890
Henry Goings and Annie Agnes Miller, (MD) Jul. 22, 1890, (CMTS) Bride's Father, J. A. Miller
Page 3
T. J. Vance and Jennie Onman, (MD) Jun. 23, 1890
Page 4
William H. Farmer, Butler Co. MO and Rannie D. Fast, (MD) Jun. 22, 1890
Charles C. Linsenmeyer and Girtrude Austin, (MD) Jun. 11, 1890
Page 5
Martin Stogdell and Malisa Allen, both from, Reynolds Co. MO, (MD) Jul. 8, 1890
Thomas McPhee and Lou Pierce, Reynolds Co. MO, (MD) Jul. 6, 1890
Page 6
George F. Weldon and Mrs. Josephene McSpaden, (MD) Jul. 9, 1890
D.A. Burgin and Sarah Hedrick, (MD) Jul. 21, 1890
Page 7
James P. Farris and Florance Hampton, (MD) Jul. 24, 1890, (CMTS) Bride's father, S. P. Hampton
Joseph Barney and Geneva Dunn, (MD) Jul. 24, 1890
Page 8
John Goss and Mary L. Ridenhour, (MD) Jul. 24, 1890
L.C. Casey and Mrs. Jennette Foster, (MD) Jul. 28, 1890
Page 9
Frank Cleveland and Ida F. Shreve, (MD) Aug. 2, 1890
John A. Alward and Mary Hart, (MD) Aug. 2, 1890
Page 10
Peter A. Hanger and Rebecca Ann Moses, Both from Reynolds Co., MO, (MD) Aug. 17, 1890, (CMTS) Bride's father Frank Moses
Thornton H. Lacey and Arazela Gates, (MD) Aug. 17, 1890
Page 11

William A. Ballard and Alsay E. Moss, (MD) Aug. 17, 1890
J.A. Rongey and Malinda Vincent, (MD) Aug. 20, 1890
Page 12
Reson B. Brown and Annie Vermillion, (MD) Aug. 28, 1890
William A. Jarrett and Cordelia Boyer, (MD) Aug. 30, 1890
Page 13
William A. Partney and Viola J. Chilton, (MD) Sep. 10, 1890
John B. Vermillion and Mary F. Massie, (MD) Sep. 14, 1890
Page 14
Rev. Canterbery and Amanda Link, (MD) Sep. 14, 1890
L.T. Womack and Julia Moris, (MD) Sep. 11, 1890
Page 15
Elton Rodgers and Blanch V. Collins,(MD) Oct. 4, 1890, (CMTS) Consent of F.M. Rodgers and Joseph Collins, fathers
Frank Langley and Nellie Rush; (FD) Sep. 27, 1890
Page 16
Joseph L. Carter and Orena Walker, (MD) Oct. 12, 1890, (CMTS) Consent
    Jesse Robertson, stepfather of groom and Belle Walker mother of bride
Anthony Kirkland and Minnie Odell, (MD) Oct. 19, 1890
Page 17
Fred Siechmeyer and Patsey Stephens, (MD) Oct. 15, 1890
John Hill and Elizabeth J. Roper, (MD) Nov. 2, 1890
Page 18
George L. Nanna and Mary L. Webb,(CMTS) Consent of Eli Webb, father, (MD) Nov. 16, 1890
John M. Brawley and Jennette Leslie, (MD) Nov. 9, 1890, (CMTS) Consent of S.A.G. Brawley, father
Page 19
John R. Ging and Elizabeth Jane Greenwald, (MD) Nov. 17, 1890
Andrew Norris and Mary Pogue, (MD) Nov. 1, 1890
Page 20
Albert Ward and Lcuy Chapin, (CMTS) Both from Shannon Co. MO, (MD) Dec. 6, 1890
Elijah M. Smith and Lulu McPhee, (MD) Dec. 11, 1890
Page 21
William Ross and Clara Bell Ross, (MD) Dec. 18, 1890
Jesse R. Pratt and Ruminda J. Dickson, (MD) Dec. 25, 1890, (CMTS) Both
    from Reynolds Co. MO, Consent, William D. Dickson, guardian
Page 22
William C. Hicks and Fannie Brown, (MD) Dec. 18, 1890

J. P. Terry and Margaret A. Hampton, (CMTS) Consent of G. W.
    Hampton, father, (MD) Dec. 25, 1890

Page 23
J. Henry Darr and Victory Howard, (CMTS) both from, Reynolds Co.,
    MO, (MD) Dec. 25, 1890
Orrin L. Munger and Minnie Marvin Lee, Wayne Co. MO, (MD)
    Dec. 23, 1890

Page 24
Pleasant A. Gibbs and Sarah E. Brooks, (MD) Dec. 23, 1890
Anderson Woodward and Annie E. McFaddin(CMTS) Both from, Wayne
    Co. MO, Consent of Martha Woodward, mother (MD)
    Dec. 25, 1890

Page 25
Charles Gosnell and Dora V. Wilson, (MD) Jan. 4, 1891, (CMTS)
    Consent of Walter Gosnell and James K. Wilson
Cisero Wallin and Fannie Russell, Reynolds Co., MO, (MD) Dec. 31,
1890

Page 26
William Brakefield and Lidie Jane Harder, (MD) Jan. 4, 1891
David H. Allison and Mattie Franklin, (MD) Jan. 4, 1891

Page 27
F.A. Franklin and Mary Arnold, (MD) Jan, 3, 1891
John Smith and Mary A. Hanger, (MD) Jan. 6, 1891, (CMTS) Consent of
    M. J. Hanger, mother

Page 28
S.H. Hefraan and Sarah J. McGonnigal, (MD) Jan. 8, 1891
    (CMTS) Consent of Mr. E. McGonnigal,
Morgan Magness and Docia Gossett, (MD) Jan. 10, 1891, (CMTS)
Consent
    of B. Z. Gossett, father.

Page 29
William Short and Belle Lawthers, (CMTS) Consent of Mr. R.P. Lawthers,
    father, (MD) Jan. 11, 1891
R.T. Hutcherson and Mary Boyer, (MD) Jan. 11, 1891

Page 30
Levi Maberry and Manda Russell, (MD) Jan. 25, 1891
Jackson Smith and Vuenavista Sartin (CMTS) Consent of S. Sartin, father,
    (MD) Jan. 25, 1891

Page 31
Joel Freeman, Oregon Co., and Mary E. Entenman, (MD) Jan. 21, 1891
A.F. Shoulders and Virginia E. Klenn, (CMTS) Consent of bride's father,
    (MD) Feb. 4, 1891

Page 32

R.B. Canada and Braska N. Pruett, (MD) Feb. 1, 1891
H.B. Rightnowar and Luellen Hanners, (MD) Feb. 1, 1891
Page 33
Joseph B. Hampton and Belle Turnbow, (MD) Feb. 3, 1891
William Leadbetter and M.E. Hunt, (CMTS) Consent of bride's father, (MD) Feb. 15, 1891
Page 34
Lawson Hughs and Lusteller Coleman, (MD) Feb. 24, 1891
John Sharp and Mary M. Smith, (MD) Mar. 1, 1891
Page 35
Berry Yates and Mahalie J. Maberry, (CMTS) Consent of groom's mother, (MD) Mar. 5, 1891
John D. Stewart and Mrs. A.N. Kent, (MD) Mar. 19, 1891
Page 36
Ed Lewis, Shannon Co and Ida Cowen, (MD) Mar. 12, 1891
A. Mann and Jane W. Cotton, (CMTS) Both from Reynolds Co., (MD) Apr. 1, 1891
Page 37
P.N. Buchanan and Josie Sheets, (MD) Feb. 6, 1891
Willie A. McEntire and Ella Raymer consent, groom's father, (MD) Apr. 26, 1891
Page 38
A. Mann and Jane W. Cotton, both from Reynolds Co., (MD) Apr. 1, 1891
Anderson Chilton and Laura Smith, Reynolds Co., (MD) 26 Apr 1891
Page 39
Lloid Wright and Ollie Mitchell, both from Shannon Co., (MD) May 8, 1891
A.C. Arisman and Fannie Lore, (MD) May 13, 1891
Page 40
A.B. Collins and Ida M. Platt, (MD) May 14, 1891
Frank Shreeves and Mary Goolsley, (MD) May 17, 1891
Page 41
J. McCoy and Mary Everett, (MD) May 24, 1891
Francis H. Beamon and Albina Gunter, (MD) Jun 6, 1891
Page 42
J.D. Cole and Malissa Walker, (MD) May 28, 1891
F.M. Smith and M.A. Fowler, (MD) Jun. 4, 1891
Page 43
James Steel and Elizabeth Walker, (CMTS) Bride's Father, George Walker,
    father, (MD) Jun. 19, 1891
Albert Hunter, Texas Co. and Missouri Skyles, (MD) Jun. 14, 1891
Page 44

:John F. McCabe and Jennie Bowman, (MD) Jun. 22, 1891
Henry Whitaker and Mrs. Sarah A. Tucker, (MD) ?
Page 45
Nathan R. Tinsley and Cordie Hensen, (MD) Jul. 7, 1891
Eli Smith and Matilda Green, Texas Co., MO, (MD) Jul. 2, 1891
Page 46
J.G. Hall and Josie Smith, (MD) Jul. 7, 1891
Wash Decker and Susie Jane Huett, both from Reynolds Co., MO, (MD) Jul. 9, 1891
Page 47
J.D. Buchanan and Mrs. Tennessee Jackson, Reynolds Co., MO, (MD) Jul. 14, 1891
J.O. Kenworthy and Mary E. Smallwood, (MD) Jul. 29, 1891
Page 48
Joseph S. Gresham and GeorgeAnn Wallis, (MD) Jul. 31, 1891
M. E. Christian and Martha Morris, (MD) Aug. 6, 1891
Page 49
Barry I. James and Hattie Wallis both from, Wayne Co, (MD) Aug. 20, 1891
John P. Huett and Mary H. Christian, both from, Reynolds Co., (MD) Aug. 27, 1891, (CMTS) Consent of William Christian, father.
Page 50, (MD)
William Allison and Mrs. Mary Willis both from Shannon Co., (MD) ?
John Geisler andMiss Callie Pane, (MD) Aug. 30, 1891
Page 51
Oliver Segastian and Martha J. Smith, (CMTS) Consent of Martha Segastian, mother, (MD) Aug. 30, 1891
H. A. Sweeney and Lily Robertson (MD) Sep. 14, 1891
Page 52
George W. Brame and Minnie T. Webb, Reynolds Co, (MD) Sep. 20, 1891, (CMTS) consent, groom's father
Thomas G. Clay and Mattie Huett, (MD) Sep. 24, 1891
Page 53
Samuel Hanger and Louisa D'Spain, (MD) Aug. 15, 1891
Joseph H. Diamond and Alice Boyer, (MD) Oct. 18, 1891
Page 54
Samuel Huett and Ida Nunley, (MD) Oct. 18, 1891
William Farmer and Matilda D. Boyer, (MD) Oct. 25, 1891
Page 55
Fred P. Greene and Clara L. Clay, (MD) Oct. 31, 1891
P.B. Freeman, Greene Co and Maud L. Temple, Reynolds Co., (MD) Nov. 2, 1891
Page 56

Daniel Davis and Lorena Richardson, (MD) Nov. 10, 1891
W.P. Cotes and Oepha Harney, (MD) Nov. 15, 1891
Page 57
Edward A. Benning and Cornelia Laftey, (MD) Nov. 22, 1891
Charles Buchanan and Nora Rodgers, (MD) Nov. 29, 1891
Page 58
Thomas Cotes and Flora Conoway, (MD) Dec. 4, 1891
Howard Davis and Ellen Groves, (MD) Nov. 28, 1891
Page 59
James T. Widggers and Mary Lane, (MD) Nov. 6, 1891
Willie Chilton and Jennie Crandell, (MD) Dec. 13, 1891
Page 60
J.M. Eddington and Emma Wolfe, (MD) Dec. 17, 1891
James Arisman and Cora Lore, (MD) Dec. 24, 1891
Page 61
James T. Vandyke and Sarah J. Foster, (MD) Dec. 30, 1891
David E. Rutledge and Clara McPhee, (MD) Jan. 3, 1892
Page 62
S.H. Burnham, Reynolds Co., and Ellen Williams, Shannon Co., (MD) Jan. 3, 1892
J.W. Kunce and Agnes Jarrett, (MD) Jan. 19, 1892
Page 63
Frank Bristol and Jane Pulliam, (MD) Jan. 28, 1892
Charles Coleman and Mollie Coleman, (MD) Jan. 29, 1892
Page 64
Robert Maberry and Lydia Massie, (MD) Feb. 14, 1892
Mack Odom and Mary Stringer, (MD) Jan. 18, 1892
Page 65
Andrew McGhee, Wayne Co., and Anna E. Clayburn; (MD) Feb. 17, 1892
Sandford Stapp and Jennie Sutton, (MD) Mar. 6, 1892
Page 66
John T. Sartin and Mary E. Tinker, (MD) Mar. 13, 1892
Jacob Buckles and Ada Sutton, (MD) Mar. 3, 1892
Page 67
William Schrader and Belle Jackson, (MD) Mar. 16, 1892
John Brooks and Clara Hooper, (MD) Mar. 16, 1892
Page 68
William Pogue and Annie I. Fort, Reynolds Co.., (MD) Mar. 20, 1892
John Riley and Sarah Terry, (MD) Mar. 27, 1892
Page 69
John H Roy and Tennie F. Sheets; (MD) Mar. 27, 1892, (CMTS) Henderson

Roy and John Sheets, fathers
Henry Griffin and Ella Weldon; (MD) Mar. 31, 1892

Page 70
W.W. Martin, Shannon Co., and Elzadia Gibbs, (MD) Apr. 13, 1892
J.Y. Stephens and Annie Hill, (MD) Apr. 18, 1892

Page 71
J.H. Gassaway and Media Matkin, Reynolds Co., (MD) Apr. 16, 1892
C.E. Cambell, Shannon Co., and S.C. Julian, (MD) Apr. 19, 1892

Page 72
George C. Clyburn and Missouri Johnston, Reynolds Co., (MD) Apr. 24, 1892
John B., Gossett and Susie Elliott, (MD) May 1, 1892

Page 73
John Coleman and Tennie Smith, Reynolds Co., (MD) May 8, 1892
William E. Brinkley and Matilda Turnbough, (MD) May 15, 1892

Page 74
George E. Grafus and Amanda White, (MD) May 22, 1892
James H. Ethel and Ida M. White, (MD) May 22, 1892

Page 75
Lane Secrease and Jossie Hardin, (MD) May 20, 1892
Al Waits and Flora Hanks, (MD) Jun. 5, 1892

Page 76
Jno. M. Cook, Howell Co., and Mrs. Ellen Marshall, (MD) Jun. 29, 1892
J.H.Tibbs and Janie Schmick, (MD) Jul. 4, 1892

Page 77
J.W. Crallay and Lulu Hopkins, (MD) Jul. 12, 1892
James Cummins and Mary Cox, (MD) Jul. 17, 1892

Page 78
S.M. Casey and Annie Rodgers, (CMTS) Consent of Dora Green, bride's aunt, (MD) Jul. 26, 1892
Morgan Potter and Mary Gossett, both from Reynolds Co., (MD) Jun. 19, 1892

Page 79
W.S. Hutchings and Lizzie Fort, both from Reynolds Co., (MD) Aug. 3, 1892
J.S. Honea and Rachel Gentry, (MD) Aug. 14, 1892

Page 80
A.D. Rose and Nancy A. Keathley, Reynolds Co., (MD) Aug. 26, 1892
William Burns and Mrs. Lizzie Smart, (MD) Sep. 1, 1892

Page 81
Walter Massie and Telsie W. Cotton, Reynolds Co., (MD) Sep. 4, 1892
Thomas F. Street, Reynolds Co., and Annie Kindle, (MD) Sep. 11 1892

William Burns and Mrs. Lizzie Smart, (MD) Sep. 1, 1892

Page 81
Walter Massie and Telsie W. Cotton, Reynolds Co., (MD) Sep. 4, 1892
Thomas F. Street, Reynolds Co., and Annie Kindle, (MD) Sep. 11 1892
Page 82
John Marrs, Ripley Co., and Tracey E. Maine, (MD) Sep. 11, 1892, (CMTS) William R. Maine, father
William Blockley and Martha Cotes, (MD) Sep. 8, 1892
Page 83
Elmer C. Drake and Willie Sweazea, (MD) Sep. 11, 1892
William A. Hardy and Elizabeth Brown, (MD) Sep. 9, 1892
Page 84
James McClary and Mrs. Martha Turley, (MD) Sep. 15, 1892
C.M. Brown and Della Parker, Shannon Co., (MD) Sep. 18, 1892
Page 85
L.C. Taber and Bertha M. Pinyerd, both from Texas Co., (MD) Sep. 22, 1892
Dan Emins and Nellie Davis, (CMTS) Consent of groom's stepfather, (MD) Jun. 12, 1892

Page 86
James Norries and Alice Clark, Reynolds Co., (MD) Sep. 29, 1892
Harvey Huett and Mrs. Kisse Mossengill, both from Reynolds Co., (MD) Oct. 8, 1892
Page 87
Jno. R. Creasy and Hattie Parker, Shannon Co., (MD) Oct. 9, 1892
Henry Ball and Martha Graham, (MD) Oct. 11, 1892
Page 88
Lewis Carpenter and Ida Mulligan, (MD) Oct. 16, 1892
Thomas Hannars and Jane McGuire, (MD) Oct. 15, 1892
Page 89
James F. Green and Marietta Bucy, (CMTS) Consent of James Bucy, father,(MD) Oct. 27, 1892
W.W. Wrye and Sarah J. Harris, (MD) Oct. 2, 1892

Page 90
T. R. Tinsley and Jannie Barree, (MD) Oct. 23, 1892
Lewis Rutledge and Rosa Lennix, (MD) Nov. 13, 1892
Page 91
William Parsons and Sarah E. Edington, (MD) Nov. 6, 1892
John W. Dawson and Hariet E. Norman, (MD) Nov. 6, 1892

William Sanders and Sarah Johnston, (MD) Dec. 3, 1892, (CMTS) James Sanders, father
W.F. Thomas and Rachel McNeeley, (MD) Dec. 21, 1892

Page 94
Alvy Frazier and Jane Maberry, (MD) Dec. 22, 1892
Loy Fisher and Sarah R. Boyer, (MD) Dec. 11, 1892, (CMTS) Consent of D.M. Smith bride's brother-in-law.

Page 95
J.Q. Bowden, Douglas Co. and Mary Sherell, (MD) Jan. 3, 1893
D. J. Griffin, Shannon Co. and Janie Fowler, (MD) Jan. 3, 1893

Page 96
William G. Lashley and Sarah I. Hinkle, Howell Co., (MD) Jan. 7, 1893
William L. Morlan and Minnie Condray, (MD) Jan 1893

Page 97
William Orrick and Belle Lee, (MD) Jan. 1, 1893
J.A. Dulaney and Margaret Howell. (MD) Jan. 29, 1893

Page 98
Thomas Jones and Lulu Link, (MD) Jan. 22, 1893
S.M. Ray, Howell Co and Margaret House, (MD) Jan. 30, 1893

Page 99
J.N. Bennett and Delia Banister, (MD) Feb. 12, 1893
Paul Conoway and Ellen Dole, (MD) Feb. 19, 1893

Page 100
John D. Sanders, Jr., Reynolds Co. and Ida May Harvey, (MD) Feb. 19, 1893
Lee Pinwell and Sarah Maine, (MD) Mar. 11, 1893

Page 101
Thomas W. Cole and Mrs. Elizabeth Joplin, (MD) Mar. 30, 1893
Silas L. Pace and Hannah Baker, (MD) Apr. 3, 1893

Page 102
John Delcour and Maggie Clayton, (MD) Apr. 11, 1893
T.J. Bowers and Janie Gentry, (MD) Apr. 15, 1893

Page 103
William Mitchell and Mary E. Snider, (MD) Apr. 22, 1893
W.P. Brinkley and Julia A. Langley, Wayne Co., (MD) Apr. 11, 1893

Page 104
W.L.. Taylor and M.A. McBride, (MD) Apr. 30, 1893
J.W. Brooks and V.N. Jordan, both from Wayne Co., (MD) May 7, 1893

Page 105
Thomas C. Davis and Dicie A. Sanders, both from Reynolds Co., (MD) Apr. 9, 1893

B.P. Carther and Ernie Frazier, (MD) May 13, 1893
Page 106
J.F. Emmons and Maggie Nanna, (MD) May 2, 1893
William Davis and Samantha E. Long, (MD) May 21, 1893
Page 107
John Robertson and Rosa Marshbanks, (MD) Jun. 6, 1893
J.F. Collins and Sadie Morris, (MD) Jun. 12, 1893
Page 108
H.A. Banister and Sallie Lathim, (MD) Jun. 10, 1893
Golden Inman and Janey Sells, (MD) Jun. 21, 1893
Page 109
Jerry M. Christian and Rosie Allison, both from Reynolds Co., (MD) Jul. 2, 1893
Columbus Honea and Lucey Crownover, (MD) Jul. 7, 1893
Page 110
R. S. Ramba, Butler Co. and Maggie J. Long, (MD) Jul. 4, 1893
George Fowler and Mary J. Eddington, (MD) Jul. 15, 1893
Page 111
Henry Hall and Rosetta Bane, both from Reynolds Co., (MD) May 20, 1893
William Brooks and Mary J. Jordan, both from, Reynolds Co, (MD) May 21, 1893
Page 112
William R. Sullivan and Mary E. Robertson, (MD) Jul. 16, 1893
W.J. Bowen and Sarah L. Wallace, both from Shannon Co., (MD) Jul. 16, 1893
Page 113
Thomas W. Smith and Tennie Coleman, (MD) Jul. 25, 1893
F.M. Eaton and A.A. Corey, (MD) Jul. 27, 1893
Page 114
Elias Green and Ida Adams, (MD) Aug. 2, 1893
H.W. Wolfe and Sopha E. Smelser, (MD) Aug. 12, 1893
Page 115
John McCall and Minnie Stone, (MD) Aug. 13, 1893, (CMTS) Bride under age, parents dead; no legal guardian
Thomas M. Butler, Jr. and Nancy Proffit, (MD) Aug. 16, 1893
Page 116
C.W. Gunn, Wayne Co., and Carrie Wallace, (MD) Aug. 20, 1893
Daniel E. Mummert and Ida Delaney, (MD) Oct. 26, 1893, (CMTS) Consent
    John D. Mummert, father.
Page 117
Henry Luckenotte and Bertha Nitz, (MD) Aug. 30, 1893

John Baker and Cora Smith, both from Reynolds Co., (MD) Jul. 30, 1893

Page 118
Elmer Green and Alice Turley, (MD) Aug. 13, 1893
James M. Keevil and Margaret Carmichael, (MD) Sep. 13, 1893

Page 119
John Lamasther and Manda Tanners, (CMTS) Consent of Johnson Tanners,
    father, (MD) Sep. 19, 1893
James Wilder and Laura Powers, (MD) Sep. 16, 1893

Page 120
George W. Kinnard and Frances Mabeary, (MD) Oct. 1, 1893
Emery Taylor and Mariah Patterson, (MD) Oct. 4, 1893

Page 121
John F. Berry and Jessie Kindricks, (MD) Oct. 22, 1893
John L. Hill and Mary Gross, (MD) Oct. 14, 1893

Page 122
James Saunders and Mary Boyer, (CMTS) Groom underage but parents dead,
    (MD) Oct. 8, 1893
A.S. Boyd and Mollie Hassell, (MD) Oct. 16, 1893

Page 123
Joseph R. Meyers and Emmer Burnley, (MD) Nov. 12, 1893, (CMTS)
    Consent of Henry Burnley, father
M.T. Ryan and Rosa B. McDonald, (MD) Oct. 29, 1893

Page 124
A.D. Nickless and Elizabeth S. Clyburn, (MD) Nov. 5, 1893

Page 125
George Hoskins and Hannah Saunders, (MD) Nov. 14, 1893
James M. Taylor and Ettie Williams, (MD) Nov. 27, 1893

Page 126
W.T. Windle and Caroline Hugan, (MD) Dec. 10, 1893
J.C. Grist and Ollie Casteel, (MD) Dec. 13, 1893

Page 127
M. Harris and Luritia O'Dell, both from Reynolds Co., (MD) Oct. 10, 1893
N. Frank Nunnally and Emma Myrick, (MD) Dec. 17, 1893

Page 128
S. Morris, Ripley Co. and Mary Kunce 23 Dec 1893
Jonathan Smith, Laclede Co. and Mary Snider 31 Dec 1893

Page 129
M.B. Waller and Edie Bates, (MD) Jan. 1, 1894
Robert A. Williams, Ripley Co., and S.P. Richmond, (MD) Jan. 12, 1894

Page 130

R.L. Coleman and M.H. Rose, (MD) Jan. 7, 1894
William DeHaven and Julia Cole, (MD) Jan. 11, 1894
Page 131
R.H. Mason and Adie Dinning, (MD) Jan. 25, 1894
Amel Bugist and Mary Penson, (MD) Feb. 11, 1894
Page 132
J.T. McSpadden and Alice Lowther, (MD) Feb. 11, 1894
Tim Carney and Petresa R.L. Estept, (MD) Feb. 19, 1894
Page 133
James Bowen and Mary Moore, both from Shannon Co., (MD) Feb. 18, 1894.
D.C. Baker and Emma F. Rumberg, both from Reynolds Co., (MD) Feb. 19, 1894
Page 134
Raney Julian and Mary Link, (MD) Feb. 25, 1894
William Loyd and Hattie Piles, both from Reynolds Co., (MD) Feb. 18, 1894
Page 135
J.M. Bradshaw and Jennie Johnson, both from Wayne Co., (MD) Mar. 26, 1894
George M. Shreeves and Mollie Browning, (MD) Mar. 22, 1894
Page 136
George E. Campbell and Martha A. Gunn, (MD) Apr. 11, 1894
M. Chitwood and Sarah Shaw, both from Reynolds Co., (MD) Feb. 25, 1894
Page 137
Chris Fowler and Mollie Sharp, (MD) Apr. 15, 1894
James E. Casteel and Mrs. Amanda Groom, Jefferson Co., (MD) Apr. 24, 1894
Page 138
Charles W. Entenman and Julia F. Leslie, (MD) Apr. 15, 1894
E.L. Maberry and Jennie Laxton, (MD) Apr. 8, 1894
Page 139
J.W. Rodgers and Kansas A. Stephens, May 6, 1894
J.R. Gambill, Ripley Co., and Debby Main, (MD) May 13, 1894
Page 140
E.M. Baker and Lizzie Bryan, (MD) May 29, 1894
Chas A. Stokely and Katie Willett, Reynolds Co., (MD) May 23, 1894
Page 141
W.H. Rives and Lou Monroe, (CMTS) Bride under age. Parents dead, (MD) Jun. 14, 1894
John Smith and Rosa Parsons, consent, groom's father 17 Jun 1894
Page 142

Henry A. Crowley and Sarah Sherrer, consent for both parties. 17 Jun 1894

L.J. DePriest and Emma DePriest, both from, Oregon Co. 26 Jun 1894

Page 143

James M. Boyer and Ida Doyle, consnet, bride's father 08 Jul 1894

James M. Williams and Margaret Doyle 08 Jul 1894

Page 144

John W. Stratton and Sarah J. Richardson, (MD) Jun. 10, 1894

William Boyer and Ettie Gosnell, (MD) Aug. 19, 1894

Page 145

William Hughes and Cassie A. Lightfoot, Butler Co., (MD) Nov. 11, 1894

Jeff Leonard and Mary Alice Boyer, (MD) Aug. 26, 1894

Page 146

A. Clemmons and Lizzie Price, (MD) Aug. 19, 1894

John Moser and Martha J. Cowen, (CMTS) Consent of George W. Cowen, father, (MD) Sep. 1, 1894

Page 147

T.E. England and Ellen Blalock, both from Shannon Co., (MD) Sep. 9, 1894

Peter Tinker and Rachel R. Moore, both from Shannon Co., (MD) Aug. 11, 1894, (CMTS) Married at the home of Mark Moore. Parents deceased.

Page 148

Samuel Galbraith and Mrs. Oda Sheets, (MD) Sep. 2, 1894

Wesley C. Horton and Eliza E. Stapp, (MD) Oct. 14, 1894

Page 149

James M. Boyer and Amanda Condray, Wayne Co. (MD) Sep. 15,1894, (CMTS) Consent of bride's guardian, C. G. Gunn

Charles Spencer and Osia Cockrom , (MD) Sep. 13, 1894

Page 150

Richard Wolsey and S.M. Jones, (MD) Sep. 18, 1894

J. W. Eaton and Sophronia Boyer, (MD) Sep. 30, 1894

Page 151

Robert Jones and Emeline Vermillion, (MD) Sep. 11, 1894

H.Y. Tucker and Ellen Morelan, (MD) Oct. 7, 1894

Walter Wood and Laura Wagner, (MD) Oct. 27, 1894

Page 153

J.M. Harmon and Mrs. Lottie Stevenson, (MD) Oct. 30, 1894

John C. Pepmiller and Ida Clarlotta Johnson, (MD) Nov. 20, 1894

Page 154

Joseph E. Fleming and Mary L. Stephens, (MD) Nov. 4, 1894, (CMTS) Consent of Rufus Stephens, father.

Eli Boyer and Fannie Leach, (MD) Oct. 28, 1894

Page 155
J.W. Sams and Charity Lofty, (MD) Nov. 19, 1894
Thomas Shaw and Debby Chitwood, both from Reynolds Co., (MD) Nov. 25, 1894

Page 156
Andrew Woodard and Rosa B. Walker, (MD) Nov. 26, 1894
F.L. Akridge and M.E. Walker, both from Reynolds Co., (MD) Nov. 29, 1894

Page 157
John Ludlum and Mary Finney, (MD) Dec. 1, 1894
Lewis Bales and Florence Rector, (MD) Dec. 2, 1894

Page 158
S.R. Rector and Pearl McKinney, both from Shannon Co., (MD) Dec. 8, 1894
S. Windes and Alice Snider, (MD) Dec. 12, 1894

Page 159
Timon L. O'Dell and Charity Gowen, both from Reynolds Co., (MD) Dec. 16, 1894
George E. Howard and Emma Hackworth, both from Reynolds Co., (MD) Dec. 20, 1894

Page 160
James Lambert and Josie Yates, (MD) Jan. 2, 1895
Frank Harley and E. Jinkins, (MD) Jan. 14, 1895

Page 161
James A. Johnston, Butler Co., MO and Florence M. Barclay, (MD) Jan. 15, 1895
D.F. Allison and Effie Hake, both from Reynolds Co., MO, (MD) Jan. 24, 1895

Page 162
John Brown and Nancy Cates, (MD) Jan. 6, 1895
William Willhite and Laura E. Stineman, (MD) Jan. 23, 1895

Page 163
Charles P. Woolf and Docia Turley, (MD) Jan. 30, 1895
James M. Vermillion and Malinda J. Hollis, (MD) Feb. 5, 1895

Page 164
M.L. Sanders and Maggie Sweazea both from Reynolds Co., MO, (MD) Feb. 10, 1895
R. L. Rongey and Ida M. Parkhill, (MD) Feb. 10, 1895

Page 165
William Whitsell and Lilly May Duke, (MD) Feb. 17, 1895
Lee Horn and Mollie Pace, (MD) Feb. 17, 1895

Page 166
William A. Watson and Mary Hall, both from Reynolds Co., (MD)

Feb. 2, 1895
G.P. Kindrick and Arminty Masters, (MD) Feb. 17, 1895
Page 167
Robert Hampton and Jesse Nichols 22 Feb 1895
John W. Clark and Edith House consent bride's father Mar. 6, 1895
Page 168
Robert Hampton and Jesse Nichols, (MD) Feb. 22, 1895
John W. Clark and Edith House, (MD) Mar. 6, 1895
Page 169
Wiley Leach and Roda Lenard, (MD) Mar. 17, 1895
Thomas A. Wilson, Wayne Co., and Nancy C. Stephens, (MD) Mar. 17, 1895
Page 170
George Munger and Lotta Campbell, (MD) Mar. 20, 1895
Charles Phelps and Teritha E. Helvey, both from Reynolds Co, (MD) Mar. 24, 1895
Page 171
William Bowman and Margaret Jackson, (MD) Mar. 26, 1895
William Hughes and Cassie A. Lightfoot, (MD) Apr. 2, 1895
Page 172
Elmer E. Wheeler and Louisa Mitchell 13 Apr 1895
Mark Phelps and Cora B. Webb, both from Reynolds Co., (MD) Mar. 13, 1895
Page 173
Albert Bays and Maggie Joplin, (MD) May 16, 1895
Goerge F. Youngblood and Drusilda Baker, (MD) Jun. 16, 1895
Page 174
B.F. Goodson and Mary G. Youngblood, (MD) Jun. 16, 1895
Andrew Olson and Mrs. Sarah Cargel, (MD) Jun. 13, 1895
Page 175
James N. Thomas and Alice Allen, (MD) Jun. 14, 1895
B. F. Chilton, Wayne Co., MO and Dora Bales, (MD) Jun. 26, 1895
Page 176
Frank Wood, Butler Co., MO and Ada Henson, (MD) Jul. 3, 1895
Daniel Lewis, Iron Co., MO and N. Smith, Reynolds Co., (MD) Jul. 26, 1895
Page 177
Buck Smith, Reynolds Co., MO and Alice Clayton, (MD) Jun. 16, 1895
Ervin Mitchell and Laura Weldon, (MD) Jul. 18, 1895
Page 178
Henry Adier and Bettie A. Hedrick, both from Shannon Co., (MD) Jul. 9, 1895
John E. Raymer and Minnie A. Dunnegan, (MD) Jul. 14, 1895

Page 179
Henry Baldridge, Howell Co. and Lillie M. Jones, (MD) Sep. 4, 1894
A.H. Graves and Ida Zook, (MD) Sep. 4, 1895

Page 180
Robert Kendall and Janie Delcore, (MD) Sep. 15, 1895
Burris Wallice and Mary J. Chilton, (MD) Sep. 18, 1895

Page 181
J.M. Bruce and Belle Jones, (MD) Sep. 29, 1895
W.E. Condray and L.J. Stratton, (MD) Sep. 22, 1895

Page 182
John M. Leach, Wayne Co. and Margaret Boyer, (MD) Sep. 29, 1895
George Justice and Dora Hill, (MD) Oct. 6, 1895

Page 183
Jesse Thomas and Cora Adams, (MD) Oct. 6, 1895
William A. Moss and Sarah A. Box, (MD) Oct. 21, 1895

Page 184
John O. Sanner and Ava R. Grummett, (MD) Oct. 22, 1895
A.G. Shaw and Cordelia Chilton, both from Reynolds Co.; (MB) Sep. 8, 1895

Page 185
William S. Stephens and Minnie E. Hull, (MD) Oct. 20, 1895
Gordon A. Waldo and Blanche Greene, (MD) Oct. 26, 1895

Page 186
Jesse Gunn and Jennie Jorden, (MD) Oct. 27, 1895
George W. Million and Mariann Tucker, (MD) Oct. 27, 1895

Page 187
James A. Stratton and Nancy A. Hogg, (MD) Nov. 10, 1895
Enoch Turley and Katie Bales, (MD) Nov. 17, 1895

Page 188
Harry M. Green and Katie Lassen, Ripley Co., (MD) Nov. 25, 1895
James Morris and Hattie Kennedy, (MD) Oct. 18, 1895

Page 189
W.S. Grable and Allie Faulkner, Wayne Co., (MD) Dec. 8, 1895
Caloway Leonard and Lucyh Mackey, (MD) Nov. 10, 1895

Page 190
James W. Fowler and Sarah McMillan, (MD) Dec. 8, 1894
John R. McLone, Butler Co., and Allie Shehan, (MD) Dec. 18, 1895

Page 191
John McMillan and Ada Pitman, (MD) Dec. 15, 1895
George W. Smith and Birthia C. Helvey, both from Reynolds Co; (MD) Dec. 22, 1895

Page 192
Overton Smith and Mattie Hearst, both from Reynolds Co.;

(MD) Dec. 22, 1895
Henry Kelley and Alice Morlan, (MD) Dec. 15, 1895
Page 193
Firman Moore and Manerva H. Dawson, (MD) Jan. 2, 1896
John Heifner and Trissie Leach, (MD) Jan. 12, 1896
Page 194
Milton R. Makaffer and Ida Bradford, (MD) Jan. 11, 1896
James D. Hall and Issa Nelson, (MD) Jan. 11, 1896
Page 195
W.J. Stephens and Vina Perkins, (MD) Feb. 1, 1896
Lowery Usery and Sarah A. Kennedy, (MD) Feb. 9, 1896
Page 197
Ed Livingston and Sallie Evans, both from Wayne Co., (MD) Dec. 24, 1896
James Martin and Laura A. Littrell, (MD) Mar. 1, 1896
Page 198
William Price and Mary Tubbs, both from Reynolds Co., (MD) Jan. 19, 1896
James Boyer and Minnie Condray, (MD) Feb. 9, 1896
Page 199
W.T. Leach, Wayne Co. and Ruthey B. Kelley, (MD) Mar. 8, 1896
George B. Arney, Wayne Co. and Ida M. Jones, (MD) Mar. 7, 1896
Page 200
Henry Tucker, Sen. and Mrs. Emily E. Williamson, (MD) Mar. 15, 1896
William E. Darris and Emma Sheets, (MD) Feb. 17, 1896
Page 201
George A. Sheets and Parmelia Crowley, (MD) Mar. 15, 1896
J.E. Threlkel and Lulu M. Creagor, both from Shannon Co., (MD) Apr. 4, 1896
Page 202
William Brown and Leona M. Smith, (MD) Apr. 5, 1896
James D. Smith and Dellie Marbery, (MD) Apr. 9, 1896
Page 203
William C. Martin and Nettie Arnold, (MD) Apr. 13, 1896
William O'Kelley and Onie Dacus, (MD) Apr. 25, 1896
Page 204
J.B. Martin and May Campbell,, Howell Co., MO, (MD) May 10, 1896
W.J. Cornelison and Belle Riden, (MD) May 14, 1896
Page 205
A.P. Holland and Rebecca Green, (MD) May 21, 1896
S.F. Riden and Ellen Neely, (MD) May 28, 1896
Page 206

G.W. Flint, Butler Co., and Lou Bay, Shannon Co., Mo (MD) May 24, 1896
John McDermatt and Mary A. Silger, (MD) May 31, 1896
Page 207
J. F. Vansickle and Bessie G. Lipscombs, (MD) May 28m 1896
Albert Adams, Wayne Co., Mo and Rosey Townsend, (MD) Jun. 6, 1896
Page 208
H. C. Harris and Alice Brame, (MD) Jun. 7, 1896
J. H. Morlan and Lizzie Meyers, (MD) May 31, 1896
Page 209
Lemuel Lewis and Cusie Harmers, both from Ripley Co., MO, (MD) Jun. 22, 1896
D.E. Barrett and Callie Massie, (MD) Jun. 21, 1896
Page 210
John Deering and Ida Cox, (MD) Jun. 24, 1896
Ernie Nitz and Julia Cox, (MD) Jul. 1, 1896
Page 211
Frank Bryan and Lou Cockran, (MD) Jul. 3, 1896
Lee Randall, Shannon Co., Mo and Polly Alley, (MD) Jun. 14, 1896
Page 212
V. Dunnegan and Lula Thompson, (MD) Jul. 8, 1896
William Pogue and Ella Gibbs, both from Shannon Co., (MD) Jun. 21, 1896
Page 213
S.R.P. Kearbey and Sary E. Conner, (MD) Jul. 16, 1896, (CMTS) W.C. Conner, bride's father
William Marlowe and Sibbey J. Taylor, both from Reynolds Co., (MD) Jul. 12, 1896
Page 214
Levi Morlan and Mrs. Susie Sanders, (MD) Jul. 22, 1896
Tobe Fitzgerld and Annie Pogue, both from Reynolds Co., (MD) Jul. 29, 1896
Page 215
Absalom Coleman and Lizette Voyles, (MD) Jul. 30, 1896
George Waller, Oregon Co., and Annie Tackett, (MD) Jul. 17, 1896
Page 216
O.F. Going and Cora Norton, both from Shannon Co., (MD) Jun. 25, 1896
Chas. W. Nitz and Augusta Pinz, (MD) Jul. 20, 1896
Page 217
James R. Moss and Martha J. Raymer, (MD) Jul. 26, 1896
Samuel Sanders and Mellie Chitwood, both from Reynolds Co., (MD) Jul. 27, 1896

Page 218
John H.W. Morrison, Reynolds Co. and Julia A. Harris, (MD)
   Aug. 27, 1896
Samuel Tipton and Adia Roy, (MD) Aug. 23, 1896

Page 219
Samuel Harvey and Lydia D. Hanger, Reynolds Co., (MD)
   Aug. 20, 1896
Chas. W. Fisher, Polk Co. and Lelia M. Newby, (MD) Aug. 27, 1896

Page 220
John Provance and Lucinda Shrum, (MD) Sep. 2, 1896
Emmit Smith and Annie Smith, (MD) Sep. 6, 1896

Page 221
William P. Daniels and Susie J. Beaver, Wayne Co., (MD) Sep. 10, 1896
W.E. Williams and Banie Freeman, (MD) Sep. 12, 1896

Page 222
James Newcomb and Mary Brennen,, Paragould, Arkansas, (MD)
   Sep. 21, 1896
Newton Gregory and Ollie Robinson, (MD) Aug. 23, 1896

Page 223
A.J. Pitman and Sarah Radford, (MD) Sep. 13. 1896
J.E. Lee and Minnie Coleman, (MD) Oct. 8, 1896

Page 224
W.P. Jackson and A.F. Close, (MD) Oct. 13, 1896
Joseph R. Bryan and Mary E. Smith, (MD) Oct. 15, 1896

Page 225
William M. Towner and Elizabeth Holloway both from Ripley Co.,
   (MD) Oct. 24, 1896
J.F. Byard and Emma V. Terry, (MD) Oct. 8, 1896

Page 226
Lincoln Charles Carter and Alzona H. Bowers, both from Reynolds Co.,
   (MD) Nov. 1, 1896
John B. Rongey and Josephine Pullium, (MD) Aug. 30, 1896, (CMTS)
   William H. Rongey, groom's father

Page 227
Levi Clyburn and Laura Nickless,, Wayne Co., (MD) Nov. 1, 1896
William Lambert and Sarah Yates, (MD) Nov. 11, 1896

Page 228
C.F. Leonard and Nealie Justice, (MD) Nov.15, 1896
T.W. Cotton and June Lee, (MD) Oct. 15, 1896

Page 229
Noah Thompson and Ettie Brewer, both from Howell Co., (MD)
   Nov. 16, 1896

Page 230

Abigha P. Stratton, New Madrid Co. and Octiea A. Cummings, (MD) Nov. 22, 1896, (CMTS) Consent groom's guardians, A.H. Stratton and Mattie Stratton.
William C. Despain and Ada Dugdale 28 Nov 1896

Page 231

R.H. Huffman and Minnie Smith, (MD) Nov. 29, 1896
O.M. Headlee and Maggie Huett, both from Reynolds Co., (MD) Dec. 6, 1896

Page 232

C.F. McEntire and Judith P. Crook, (MD) Dec. 15, 1896
B. T. Terry and Myra Fitzwater, (MD) Jul. 25, 1896, (RD) Dec. 16, 1896

Page 233

Alfred Rodgers and Susan Smith, (MD) Oct., 1896
Henry Smith and Julia Wormack, (MD) Dec. 10, 1895

Page 234

William F. Short and Alice Smith, (MD) Dec. 24, 1896
B. F. Massey and Mida Baker, (MD) Dec. 24, 1896

Page 235

John P. Carter and Hattie Robb, both from Wayne Co., (MD) Dec 24, 1896
Samuel Crouch and Cora Johnston, (MD) Dec. 20, 1896

Page 236

W. A. Joiner, Wayne Co., MO and Minnie Caruthers, (MD) Dec. 6, 1896
Luther Baker and Stella Maberrry, (MD) Jan. 12, 1897, (CMTS) Consent of
    groom's father

Page 237

W. P. Black and Elizabeth Christian, both from Reynolds Co., (MD) Jan. 15, 1897, (CMTS)
Zimri Yates and Ida Wallis, (MD) Jan. 18, 1897

Page 238

M.J. Robertson and Nora Hoskins, (MD) Jan. 24, 1897
F.C. Duvall and Ella Sissell, (MD) Jan. 24, 1897

Page 239

Barton Secrease and Nathey A. Brinkley, (MD) Jan. 24, 1897
W.T. Brame and Ola O'Dell, (MD) Jan. 24, 1897

Page 240

H.D. Howard and Florence Collins, (MD) Dec. 25, 1896
W.L. Light and Rosa Brewer, (MD) Feb. 17, 1897

Page 241

Charles Maberry and Tana W. Cotton, (MD) Feb. 16, 1897
M.M. Bramlet and Birdie M. Shomaker, (MD) Dec. 27, 1897

Page 242

JohnL. Windes and Rosa L. Brinkley, (MD) Feb. 28, 1897
William Wadlow and Mary L. Myers, (MD) Mar. 2, 1897

Page 243

Johnie Church and Addie Miller, (MD) Mar. 20, 1897
Thomas Chilton and Pollie Chitwood, Reynolds Co., (MD) Mar. 18, 1897

Page 244

Cyrus H. Helvey and Betty Ann Crosga, both from Reynolds Co., (MD) Mar. 10, 1897
Lewis S. Keaster, Oregon Co. and Delia McSpadden, (MD) Mar. 19, 1897

Page 245

Richmond Moore and Janie Dawson, (MD) Apr 7, 1897
Charles Ellis and Oda Sames, (MD) Apr. 22, 1897

Page 246

W.A. Parkham and Lulie Huckshorn, Wright Co., (MD) Apr. 24, 1897
Sidney Fredrick and Stacey Hooper, (MD) Apr. 25, 1897

Page 247

G.A. Barret, Ripley Co. and Cordelia Condray, (MD) Apr. 15, 1897
Marion Green and Bolza L. Gosnell, (MD) Apr. 14, 1897

Page 248

R.A. Duncan Reynolds Co and Anna O'Dell, (MD) Apr. 7, 1897
John Joplin and Paralee Emmons, (MD) May 14, 1897

Page 249

Clarence Fitzgerald and Mrs. Malinda Pogue, both from Reynolds Co., (MD) Jun. 3, 1897
Charles Tinsley and Lattie Stafford, (MD) Jun. 6, 1897

Page 250

John Sanders and Savanner Smith both from Reynolds Co., (MD) Jan. 22, 1897
Henry Yates, Jr. and Martha Bowen, bride, Shannon Co., (MD) May 16, 1897

Page 251

Silas Shreve and Mary E. Henson, (MD) Jun. 2, 1897
Charles Levingston, Reynolds Co. and Adie Hackworth, Wayne Co., (MD) Apr. 8, 1897

Page 252

J.P. Snider and Nettie I. Jones, Shannon Co., MO, (MD) Jun. 20, 1897, (CMTS) Consent of the bride's mother
Samuel G. Richmond and Mary LaRue, (MD) Jun. 23, 1897

Page 253

George W. Cowen and Malinda Shrum, (MD) Jun. 27, 1897
Max Zeebe and Anna Sass, Howell Co., MO, (MD) Jul. 12, 1897

Page 254

William H. Hart and Milly A. Lambert, (CMS) Bride's parents are deceased amd there are no objections, (MD) Jul. 7, 1897
William E. Larkin and Mary England, (MD) Jul. 10, 1897
Page 255
E.M. Vance and Arena A. Brown, (MD) Jul. 6, 1897
David T. Frazier and Florence Barker, (MD) Jul. 15 1897
Page 256
J.W. Crawley and Sada Baker, Shannon Co, (MD) Jul. 15, 1897
Septimus Brown and Josie Rover, (MD) Jul. 25, 1897
Page 257
William C. Russell and Mary Holland, (MD) Jul. 31, 1897
John Maberry, Shannon Co., MO and Allie Rodebush, (MD) Jul. 4, 1897
Page 258
R.S. Hiltibidol and Cora Chilton, (MD) Jul. 25, 1897
W.A. Sanner, Shannon Co., MO and Emma Brame, (MD) Aug. 1, 1897
Page 259
Charles A. Ward and Lula M. Crouch, (MD) Aug. 2, 1897
William C. Russell and Mary Holland, (MD) Jul. 31, 1897
Page 260
J. E. Voyles, Reynolds Co., MO, and Cora Coleman, (MD) Jul. 18, 1897
Jno. H. Bramball and Jennie Massie, (MD) Aug. 12, 1897
Page 261
William Bybee and Addie Renolds, (MD) Aug. 1, 1897
Uriah Stratton and Harriet A. Williams, (MD) Aug. 15, 1897
Page 262
J. I. Million and Martha F. Gresham, (MD) Aug. 15, 1897
Thomas Marlow and Lizzie Fry, (CMTS) Bride's parents are deceased and there is no objection, (MD) Aug. 22, 1897
Page 263
George M. Clark and Adelia Heath, (CMTS) Consent from bride's Father, (MD) Aug. 31, 1897
A.B. Lowe, Jr. and Mintie Woodward, (MD) Aug. 29, 1897
Page 264
George W. Greene and Fannie M. Barns, Shannon Co., MO, (MD) Aug. 22, 1897
Robert Henson and Malissie Brown, (CMTS) Consent from bride's Father, (MD) Sep. 5, 1897
Page 265
Charlie M. Johnson and M. C. Clayburn, (CMTS) Groom's parents are deceased and there is no objection, (MD) Sep. 3, 1897
J. M. O'Kelley and Haley Sartin, (MD) Sep. 14, 1897
Page 266
John L. Brooks, Ripley Co., MO and Josie Hickerson, (MD) Sep. 21,

1897
Ira F. Kerr and Harriett Wood, (MD) Sep. 16, 1897
Page 267
James W. Henry and Martha D. Grindstaff, (MD) Aug. 15, 1897.
H.C. Jasper, Detroit, Wayne Co., MI, and Susie Bell, Bono, AR, (MD) Sep. 27, 1897
Page 268
Harmaon Gaines and Minnie Silger, (MD) Sep. 28, 1897
R. Stafford and Cora Cockran, (CMTS) bride's parents are deceased. There is no legal guardian, (MD) Sep. 16, 1897
Page 269
J. L. Albright and Lillie Cunningham, (MD) Oct. 4, 1897
Benjamin Bowman and Alice Kirkland, (CMTS) Consent from bride's Father, (MD) Oct. 10, 1897
Page 270
Samuel M. Nanna and Anna M. Wynn, (CMTS) Consent from bride's father, (MD) Oct. 18, 1897
Zimri Headrick and Emeline Lane, (CMTS) Both from Shannon Co., MO, (MD) Oct. 14, 1897
Page 271
Alfred H. Wilson and Paulina B. Windes, (MD) Oct. 17, 1897
David Corey and Mrs. Mary J. Worsons, (MD) Nov. 11, 1897
Page 272
Joseph Farrington and Mrs. Ella Dwyer, (CMTS) both from Shannon Co., MO, (MD) Oct. 13, 1897
S.B. Manes and Nora D. Salsman, (MD) Nov. 13, 1897
Page 273
M.O. O'Dell and Ida Thomas, (MD) Sep. 18, 1897
J. M. Jones and Edith Wood, (MD) Nov. 21, 1897
Page 274
Henry Mosier and Mrs. Josiphene Mabery, (MD) Oct. 17, 1897
William Mosier and Haley Thomas, (MD) Nov. 21, 1897
Page 275
W.G. Hinkle and Sarah Freeland, (MD) Nov. 21, 1897
J. W. Carnahan and Lulu Kirkland, (MD) Nov. 28, 1897
Page 276
Charley Butt and Susie Gosnell, (MD) Nov. 28, 1897
J. H. Taylor and Katie Rutledge, (MD) Dec. 5, 1897
Page 277
John Alcorn and Nora Green, both from Shannon Co., MO. (MD) Dec. 8, 1897
John P. Collins and Christia A. Parham, (MD) Dec. 23, 1897
Page 278

E.G. Graham and Susan M. Clark, (MD) Dec. 16, 1897
John Hooper and Mollie Morris, (MD) Dec. 26, 1897
Page 279
Emery A. Summit and Maude A. Ferguson, (MD) Jan. 12, 1898
Peter Sanders and Clara Kohn, both from Reynolds Co, MO, (MD) Dec. 5, 1897
Page 280
P.W. Stacy and Lucinda A. Stratton, (MD) Jan. 16, 1898
James B. Snider and Rosie Eillis, (MD) Jan. 20, 1898
Page 281
A. H. Radofrod and C. I. Moss, (MD) Jan. 24, 1898
Charles A.Headrick and Sarah E. Carr, (MD) Jan. 25, 1898
Page 282
S. B. Beard, Reynolds Co., MO, and Zoe O'Dell, (MD) Nov. 21, 1897
P. W. Hanks and Bicie White, (MD) Feb. 2, 1898
Page 283
Charles W. Crowley and Anna Crawford, (MD) Feb. 7, 1898
R. E. Conley and M.E. Hinch, (CMTS) both from Reynolds Co., MO (MD) Dec. 23, 1897
Page 284
John M. Sanders and Ethel Price, both from Reynolds Co., MO, (MD) Dec. 23, 1897
Monroe Rodgers and Mrs. Vina L. Swezea, (MD) Jan. 16, 1898
Page 285
Anthony Talbert and Emma Hoy, (MD) Feb. 13, 1898
George W. Stratton and Clementine Norman, (MD) Feb. 20, 1898
Page 286
Willie Voyles and Rosie Chilton, (MD) Oct. 31, 1898
Cyrus Helvey and Lizzie Sanders, (CMTS) both from Reynolds Co., MO, (MD) Mar. 6, 1898
Page 287
W. W. Durbin and Fannie Belle Brame, (MD) Jan. 23, 1898
J. H. Reed and Emily Dennedy, (CMTS) consent groom's father, Taylor Reed, (MD) Dec. 25, 1898
Page 288
Robert Smith and Annie Collins, (MD) Mar. 6, 1898
Edward B. Davis and Jennie Maberry, (MD) Mar. 8, 1898

St. Louis County, Missouri, Members of the Webster Groves' Police Force, 1928.
Eugen Piper, Charles Niel, Fred Smith, Marhsall Strassinger, William Grey, Patrick Wheylan, George Linze, Edward Herron, Frank Lenz, Dad carter, Andrew McDonnell, Clarence Brooks.

Stock Certificates
North Missouri Telephone Co.: Georgia B. Mercer, 3 shares @ $50 each,
Dated November 3, 1925. Signed R. H. Muss and Cross T. Cross
(sic).

Ozark County, Missouri, Welch Cemetery, County Road 910
Adams, Ed: (B) Mar.7, 1896
Adams, Bertha: Jun.1, 1961, (D) May 24, 1944
Adans, Liza J.: (B) Feb.20, 1875, (D) Jun.14, 1956
Adams, John: (B) May 15, 1871, (D) Apr.5, 1947
Adams, Charle: (B) Mar.9, 1904, (D) Nov.30, 1933
Adams, Harvey: (B) Oct.13, 1899, (D) Dec.3, 1899
Adams, Mary E.: (B) Jun.9, 1871, (D) Jul.12, 1920
Adams, Issac: (B) Nov.5, 1855, (D) Apr.14, 1926
Barnett, Dorthy Ellen: (B) Sep.6, 1930, (D) Sep.23, 1930
Brown, Kinley: (B) Mar. 1, 1896, (D), Jan.16, 1898
Copelin, Jane: (B) Apr.2, 1857, (D) Jan.31, 1892
Copelin, Samuel A.:No dates
Graves, Walter: (B) Sep.15, 1907, (D) Jan.26, 1911
Gray, Isaac F.: Co. F, Phelps MO Inf., no dates
Herd, Mahaley: (B) Mar. 20, 1865, (D) Dec. 24, 1887
Humbyrd, Ella Mar: (B) May 3, 1909, (D) Mar. 28, 1933
Ledford, Stella: (D) Apr. 9, 1976, Age 68Y, 10M, 28D
Mahan, King D., Co. A, Ozark County USRC MO HQ, no dates
Maritt, Samuel: (B) Nov. 1, 1842, (D) May 20, 1872
Maritt, S. E.: (B) Dec.17, 1867, (D) Jun. 4, 1894
Maritt, James P.: Co B, 6 Prov. En. MO Mil, no dates
Maritt, Z. T.: (B) Apr. 25, 1847, (D) Dec.15, 1893
Marsh, Marie S: (B) Jan.14, 1919, (D) Mar. 7, 1935
Marsh. Barval E.: (B) Jun. 26, 1925, (D) Jan. 30, 1930
Marsh, Myrtlea: (B) Mar. 4, 1903, (D) Oct.1903
Marsh, Samuel P.: (B) Apr. 2, 1882, (D) Feb.5, 1958
Marsh, Nola A.: (B) Oct.13, 1884, (D) Jul.10, 1925
Marsh, Summers: (B) Apr. 12, 1854, (D) May 5, 1890
Marsh, Cinthy: (B) Nov. 7, 1849, (D) Apr. 26, 1927
Marsh, David C.: Co I, 46th MO Inf, no dates
Marsh, D.E.: (B) Mar. 27, 1845, (D) Apr. 14, 1874
Meln, Bery Oatis: (B) Oct. 29, 1905, (D) Sep. 13, 1906
Merritt, Mary Francis: (B) 1849, (D) 1917
Merritt, Josie: (B) 1863, (D) 1924
Peacock, Sarah L.: (B) Aug. 6, 1856, (D) Mar. 4, 1868
Shocky, Perry M.: (B) 1910, (D) 1917

Meln, Bery Oatis: (B) Oct. 29, 1905, (D) Sep. 13, 1906
Merritt, Mary Francis: (B) 1849, (D) 1917
Merritt, Josie: (B) 1863, (D) 1924
Peacock, Sarah L.: (B) Aug. 6, 1856, (D) Mar. 4, 1868
Shocky, Perry M.: (B) 1910, (D) 1917
Shocky infant: (B) 1911
Shocky, Delsie May: (B) Jan. 18, 1912, (D) 1921
Shocky, John Thomas: (B) Mar. 4, 1909, (D) May 22, 1981
Shocky, Liza Jane: (B) 1886, (D)1951
Shocky, Alva: (B) Jan. 4, 1881, (D) Nov. 7, 1956
Walker, Betsey A., wife of P. Walker: (B) Feb. 28, 1845, (D) Jan. 21, 1892
Welch, Millie, wife of Newton: (B) Feb. 2, 1886, (D) May 17, 1959
Welch, Newton: (B) Dec. 4, 1877, (D) Aug. 31, 1966
Welch, Lowell: (B), Jan.6, 1924, (D) Mar.20, 1924
Welch, Lexie Waldo: (B) Nov. 15, 1913, (D) Jun. 27, 1917
Welch, Sgt. Benjamin F.: Co D, 10 MO Cav, no dates
Welch, Capt. William E.: (B) Jan.11, 1843, (D) Aug.31, 1922
Welch, Rebecca N.: (B) Mar. 25, 1851, (D) May 10, 1926
Welch, C. Clinton: (B) Mar. 14, 1910, (D) 1917
Welch, W. Amos: (B) May 24, 1912, (D) Jul. 11, 1917

Christian County, Missouri, Green Valley Cemetery, Highway 14, 6 miles west of Nixa.
Gerard, Henry S.: (B) Jun. 15, 1858, (D) Dec. 10, 1885
Gerard, N. Annie: (B) Nov. 25, 1882, (D) Oct. 19, 1883

Clinton County, Missouri, Index 1840 Census
Eli Adams, (P) 2; Feathergill Adams, (P) 4; William Adams, (P) 2; Isaac Agee, (P) 2; Jacob Aker, (P) 6; Joel Albright, (P) 11; James Allen, (P) 12; John Allen, (P) 12; John Armstrong, (P) 6; John Asher, (P) 9; John Baker, (P) 4; Abner V. Baldin, (P) 7; Isaac D. Baldin, (P) 7; Levy Baldock, (P) 7; John Basey, (P) 9; Joseph Baxter, (P) 12; William Baze, (P) 2; Strother Bell, (P) 1; William Bentley, (P) 15; William Bentley, (P) 15; John Biggerstaff, (P) 4; Samuel G. Biggerstaff, (P) 3; Walker Bivens, (P) 3; James Blackerby, (P) 1; Martin Board, (P) 12; Martin Bogar, (P) 1; William Bogart, (P) 3; Peter D. Bogges, (P) 11; William Bow, (P) 3; John Bozarth, (P) 7; T. W. N. Brassfield, (P) 13; William Brian, (P) 6; David Brient, (P) 14; Samuel L. Brison, (P) 7; Thomas Brooks, (P) 9; George Brown, (P) 9; Jesse Brown, (P) 11; Josiah Brown, (P) 11; Nelson Brown, (P) 1; Tipton Brown, (P) 10; Stephen Buckhanon, (P) 6; David Buckridge, (P) 7; James Buckridge, Sr., (P) 12; Jos. Buckridge, (P) 12; Joel Burnon, (P) 6; John D. Burton, (P) 9; Shered W. Burton, (P) 13; Catherine Calleway, (P) 6; Elisha Cameron, (P) 9; Geo. W. Campbell, (P) 4; Samuel Carrel, (P) 14; C. H. Carter, (P) 4; Lacy Carter, (P) 14; Thomas W. Carter,

(P) 4; Alex Casteel, (P) 2; David Casteel, (P) 2; Joseph Casteel, (P) 2; James L. Cate, (P) 7; Thos. Caudill, (P) 7; G. C. Clardy, (P) 10; James Clark, (P) 12; Benjamin Clegget, (P) 14; Charles Clegget, (P) 14; William Coalter, (P) 11; Nelly Coffman, (P) 5; William Collet, (P) 1; Addam Cook, (P) 3; Levy Cope, (P) 9; Mayson W. Cope, (P) 10; Thompson B. Corum, (P) 7; Anderson Cox, (P) 9; Abrm. M. Creek, (P) 11; Benjamin Culp, (P) 14; George K. Culp, (P) 14; John Culp, (P) 7; William Daley, (P) 6; John F. Daugherty, (P) 1; Ambrose Davis, (P) 5; Truet Davis, (P) 3; Allen Denny, (P) 12; George Denny, (P) 12; J. L. Derraberry, (P) 13; John L. Derraberry, (P) 13; John Deshazer, (P) 2; Robert Deshazer, (P) 2; Vorhees Ditmar, (P) 11; Hiram Dixon, (P) 14; Edward Dodge, (P) 3; Levi Dodge, (P) 1; Mary Dowell, (P) 14; Victory Doze, (P) 8; Robert H. Dubois, (P) 15; Robert H. Dubois, (P) 15; Jamison Duglas, (P) 12; William M. Duglas, (P) 12; William Dunagan, (P) 13; Nathaniel Duncane, (P) 12; Archibald Elliott, (P) 13; James Elliott, (P) 7; John Elliott, (P) 6; Joseph Elliott, (P) 13; William England, (P) 3; Abram Enyert, (P) 5; Noah F. Essig, (P) 5; Bird Estis, (P) 13; Elijah Evanes, (P) 13; Evan Evans, (P) 2; Elizabeth Evens, (P) 8; Mathew Everett, (P) 1; John Faddis, (P) 4; Theoderick Fitzgeril, (P) 4; James Foster, (P) 6; Milton M. Foster, (P) 10; Henry Fox, (P) 6; John Fox, (P) 6; Josiah Fox, (P) 6; Marget Fraker, (P) 9; William Franklin, (P) 10; Thomas Frost, (P) 12; L. J. Frowman, (P) 4; Benjamin Fry, (P) 13; Elijah Fry, (P) 6; Jefferson Fry, (P) 10; Solloman Fry, (P) 13; And. Fuller, (P) 11; William Fuller, (P) 11; James Fulton, (P) 1; John Galleway, (P) 3; David R. Galloway, (P) 10; Charles Gay, (P) 7; Jesse Gay, (P) 14; Greenberry George, (P) 12; Peter R. Gill, (P) 4; George Gilles, (P) 3; Alexander Gorden, (P) 6; Stephan Gorden, (P) 12; James R. Green, (P) 4; Jesse Green, (P) 9; William Green, (P) 14; Isaac Groom, (P) 4; James Groom, (P) 6; William Groom, (P) 4; Augustice S. Gunter, (P) 5; William Haiter, (P) 15; Anna Hall, (P) 9; James Hall, (P) 3; Martin Hampton, (P) 8; Collet Hanes, (P) 11; Pitman Hanks, (P) 4; Elizabeth Harington, (P) 11; W. P. Harland, (P) 7; William P. Harland, (P) 13; Benj. F. Harris, (P) 6; Cyntha Harris, (P) 1; John Harris, (P) 5; John Harsel, (P) 3; David Henderson, (P) 9; James Henderson, (P) 11; John Henderson, (P) 12; Newman Henderson, (P) 10; Samuel Henderson, (P) 4; Wesley Henderson, (P) 11; Thos. Hickson, (P) 8; William Hiett, (P) 4; Samuel Hill, (P) 5; Jesse Hinde, (P) 2; Benj. R. Hoatt, (P) 7; David Hoblet, (P) 10; John Hodman, (P) 3; Jerry Holt, (P) 11; David Homes, (P) 1; Samuel Homes, (P) 1; Alven Howell, (P) 11; Harrison Howell, (P) 15; James M. Howell, (P) 6; John Howell, (P) 12; Washington Huffaker, (P) 12; Jesse G. Huffman, (P) 10; F. C. Hughes, (P) 12; Peace Hughes, (P) 13; Henry Humphrey, (P) 5; Benjamin Hunter, (P) 5; Joseph Hunter, (P) 11; William Hunter, (P) 5; William Hunter, (P) 9; Jesse Irvine, (P) 14; Abner J. Jackson, (P) 13; Elijah Jackson, (P) 5; William J. Jackson, (P) 3; James James, (P) 2; Joseph

Jinkins, (P) 3; Isreal Johns, (P) 10; John S. Johnson, (P) 3; Abraham. Jones, (P) 12; Asa Jones, (P) 14; Churchill Jones, (P) 15; Isaac Jones, (P) 5; Isaac Jones, (P) 12; Marvel M. Jones, (P) 11; John Jonston, (P) 1; Edward Kelley, (P) 11; William Kendrick, (P) 8; Abram Kernes, (P) 2; S. Kimsey, (P) 4; Austin R. King, (P) 11; Benjamin King, (P) 11; Isaac King, (P) 11; Rebeckah King, (P) 11; Oliver Kingsboro, (P) 14; Nicholas Kingston, (P) 5; John Klinger, (P) 4; Jacob Law, (P) 11; William Ledgwood, (P) 12; Juresy Lile, (P) 5; Selvester Linch, (P) 8; Javis Linsey, (P) 12; John Livingston, (P) 3; Samuel Livingston, (P) 4; William Livingston, (P) 3; J. H. Long, (P) 10; James H. Long, (P) 5; James Loomes, (P) 15; James M. Maris, (P) 14; Wesley Martin, (P) 13; William Martin, (P) 9; James Mayson, (P) 1; A. McClintock, (P) 15; Joseph McClintock, (P) 1; Abijah S. McCord, (P) 8; Benjamin S. McCord, (P) 8; James McCorkel, (P) 2; John McCorkel, (P) 9; Samuel McCorkel, (P) 8; James McCoun, (P) 2; James Sr. McCoun, (P) 2; John McCoun, (P) 4; Lawrence McCoun, (P) 2; James McCoy, (P) 10; William McCully, (P) 13; W. G. McDaniel, (P) 8; D. M. McDonald, (P) 5; Caleb McGill, (P) 5; C. McGines, (P) 13; Marshall McGuire, (P) 1; Silas W. McGuire, (P) 1; John McKensy, (P) 1; Murdock McKinsey, (P) 7; Daniel Mckisick, (P) 5; Moses McMahan, (P) 3; Thomas McMichael, (P) 5; Lawrence Metzger, (P) 1; David F. Millagan, (P) 7; Creed Miller, (P) 6; Isaac Miller, (P) 9; Lemuel G. Miller, (P) 3; William Miller, (P) 12; Lydia Mitchell, (P) 13; Spencer Montgomery, (P) 5; Joseph Morey, (P) 5; Nathaniel Morgan, (P) 5; Charles Morris, (P) 8; Richard Mostinger, (P) 14; Hezekiah Musser, (P) 8; John Musser, (P) 8; John G. Musser, (P) 8; Joseph Musser, (P) 8; Simon Musser, (P) 8; Edward H. Nance, (P) 14; Samuel Nash, (P) 3; Allen P. Nelson, (P) 14; Allen Nevil, (P) 14; H. Newby, (P) 10; James Newby, (P) 10; Jonathan Newby, (P) 13; William Newby, (P) 15; Susan Nichels, (P) 1; John Oldaker, (P) 2; David Oneal, (P) 8; Alford Orten, (P) 14; Miles Orten, (P) 14; Olliver Orten, (P) 14; Iri Orton, (P) 15; Iri Orton, (P) 15; Samuel Osburn, (P) 10; John B. Owins, (P) 6; Isaac Parmer, (P) 5; James Parmer, (P) 11; Thomas Parmer, (P) 5; Arthur Parvin, (P) 4; John Patton, (P) 5; Elijah Pearce, (P) 4; John Pearce, (P) 4; Christopher Perkins, (P) 12; Gilbert Perkins, (P) 12; John P. Perkins, (P) 3; Joseph Perry, (P) 6; Leander Perry, (P) 6; Leander Perry, (P) 7; Thaddeus Perry, (P) 6; James Pickett, (P) 1; Barnet Plymire, (P) 7; And. M. Poge, (P) 6; Greenberry Poge, (P) 3; Robert Poge, (P) 3; William Pointer, (P) 1; James Poteet, (P) 5; Aldredge Potter, (P) 6; John Potter, (P) 7; Joshua Potter, (P) 13; Thomas Potter, (P) 12; Willson Potter, (P) 7; William R. Pow, (P) 6; Nathaniel Powell, (P) 9; Roswell Prindle, (P) 8; Charles Prior, (P) 10; Jerym. Prior, (P) 9; M. Walton Prior, (P) 9; William Prior, (P) 9; Nicholas Proctor, (P) 8; Nelson Pullen, (P) 10; H. D. H. Randolph, (P) 5; Ruben Randolph, (P) 10; Willis Ray, (P) 15; Robert T. Ready, (P) 7; John Reed,

(P) 6; William Reed, (P) 8; Mary T. Renfrow, (P) 2; Harvy Richey, (P) 8; William Richey, (P) 8; Benj. W. Riley, (P) 10; Edmond Roberts, (P) 2; Jacob Roberts, (P) 13; Jesse Roberts, (P) 9; Jonathan Roberts, (P) 1; Littleton S. Roberts, (P) 1; George Rodes, (P) 8; Benjamin Roe, (P) 10; Samuel Rolstov, (P) 10; Ezre Rose, (P) 1; John Ruark, (P) 13; Stephan Runels, (P) 12; Caleb Sampson, (P) 9; Daniel Sanders, (P) 14; Robert H. Sanders, (P) 1; Walter G. Savage, (P) 7; John Scarber, (P) 10; Madding ? Scarlt, (P) 11; Geo. W. Shaw, (P) 9; James Shaw, (P) 8; William Shaw, (P) 8; William C. Shaw, (P) 8; Lewis Sheton, (P) 3; Anderson Smith, (P) 9; Charles Smith, (P) 9; Edward Smith, (P) 8; James Smith, (P) 14; Thompson Smith, (P) 4; William V. Smith, (P) 11; John Snow, (P) 12; Grashim Springer, (P) 7; Harvy Springer, (P) 7; Phillip B. Staggs, (P) 8; Rowland Stark, (P) 2; Hiram Stephenson, (P) 6; Plesant Stephanson, (P) 13; Plesent Stephenson, (P) 7; W. E. Stephenson, (P) 13; Clark Stephenson, (P) 3; Jonathan Stone, (P) 7; Joseph Stone, (P) 13; Samuel Stone, (P) 12; William Stoneum, (P) 13; George Strope, (P) 8; Theoffalis Sutton, (P) 4; J. V. Swiney, (P) 13; Poisin (?) Tage, (P) 14; Benjamin Taylor, (P) 9; C. H. Tharp, (P) 15; C. H. Tharp, (P) 4; Bartholamew Thatcher, (P) 15; John Thatcher, (P) 7; William Thornton, (P) 2; William T. Thornton, (P) 2; William Tinney, (P) 1; Jesse Todd, (P) 2; Joab Todd, (P) 2; Simeon Torrey, (P) 2; James Torry, (P) 2; John Tumblin, (P) 14; Winslow Turner, (P) 5; Joseph Vance, (P) 4; William Vance, (P) 4; Mary Vasser, (P) 2; Samuel Vasser, (P) 9; Samuel J. Vasser, (P) 9; Aaron Vice, (P) 1; James D. Wadkins, (P) 3; Jason Wadkins, (P) 1; Lemuel Wadkins, (P) 4; Jacob Walker, (P) 5; Joshua Walker, (P) 11; Joseph Ward, (P) 10; Rabeckah Ward, (P) 7; Thompson Ward, (P) 10; William Ward, (P) 9; Briscoe Warren, (P) 11; Martin Warrin, (P) 9; George J. Watts, (P) 3; George Weese, (P) 10; George Weese, Sr., (P) 10; Landen Weese, (P) 14; William Weese, (P) 10; William Weese, Sr., (P) 10; John V. Welden, (P) 14; Elias T. Welles, (P) 1; Daniel T. Wells, (P) 10; Harrison Welsher, (P) 11; David Whitaker, (P) 9; James Whitaker, (P) 8; Caswell White, (P) 3; Thomas White, (P) 14; John Whitsett, (P) 11; Sarah Whitson, (P) 3; Harvey Whittington, (P) 5; William Whittock, (P) 3; Samuel Wilhite, (P) 13; William S. Wilkerson, (P) 7; Mayson Williams, (P) 13; Oswell Williamson, (P) 4; W. W. Williamson, (P) 8; James Winn, (P) 13; Lewis Wood, (P) 6; Lenord Woody, (P) 2; Hannah Write, (P) 2; Thos. C. Yallerby, (P) 1; Madison Young, (P) 15; Robert E. Young, (P) 6; Sennet Young, (P) 6;

<u>Missourians in Grant County, Kansas, Draft Regristration, World War I</u>
Arnold, Walter Worth: (B) Apr. 23, 1896, (RACE) White, (BP) Pleasant
    Hill, MO
Gordon, George W.: (B) Apr. 21, 1889, (RACE) White, (BP) Camden,

MO
Jarvis, Loren Emory: (B) 12 Sep 1896, (BP)Lawrence Co, MO
King, Charles Nolan: (B) 19 Sep 1887, (RACE) W, (BP) Browning, MO,
King, Orville Leo: (B) 20 Aug 1896, (BP) Excelsior Springs, MO
King, Roy Ruffus: (B) 2 Aug 1894, (BP) Browning, MO
Oliver, Stonewall Jackson: (B) 10 Jul 1892, (BP) Prosperity, MO
Peterson, Sidney L.: (B) 13 Jan 1896, (BP) Cameron MO
Rowden, Archie Lee: (B) 1 Aug 1890, (BP) Missouri
Sutherland, Loren Burton: (B) 7 Jan 1899, (BP) Mendon MO

Ste. Genevieve County, Missouri, 1890 Special Census

Auderland, Richard R.: (RK) Private; Co.: J or F; (REG) 11; (ED) 1864; (DISD) Not Listed; (LOS) Not Listed. (PO) Coffman, MO.
Bader, Joseph: (RK) Private; Mislayed His Discharge. (PO) Ste. Genevieve, MO.. (CMTS) None.
Bantz, ????: (RK) Corporal; Co.: K; (REG) 47th MO Inf.; (ED) Sept. 24, 1864; (DISD) March 1865; (LOS) 6 M. (O) Ste. Genevieve, MO.. (CMTS) None.
Baumgartner, John: (RK) Private; Co.: A; (REG) 2nd MO Inf.; (ED) Sept. 30, 1865; (PO) Zell. (CMTS) None.
Bayer, Vince: (RK) Private; Co.: Not Listed; (REG) MO Inf.; (ED) June 1, 1864; (DISD) 1864; (LOS) 3M. (PO) Lawrenceton, MO.. (CMTS) Bad Eyes.
Beauchamp, Frank: (RK) Private; Co.: K; (REG) 22nd Ohio Inf.; (ED) Aug. 21, 1861; (DISD) Dec. 1864; (LOS) 3Y 3M. 15D, (PO) Ste. Genevieve, MO.. (CMTS) None.
Beauchamp, Michel: (PO) Ste. Genevieve, MO.. (CMTS) None.
Beauvais, Charles Widow of: (RK) Private; Co.: E; (REG) 9th KS Inf.; (ED) Oct. 1861; (DISD) June 17, 1863; (LOS) 1Y 9 M. (PO) Ste. Genevieve, MO.. (CMTS) Charles Beauvais was killed by Bushwackers on June 17, 1863
Beckerman, George: (RK) Private; Co.: C; (REG) 30th MO Inf.; (ED) Sept. 24, 1862; (DISD) Oct. 30, 1864; (LOS) 2Y (PO) Ste. Genevieve, MO.. (CMTS) Double Inguinal Hernia
Bernays, Dr. J. Francis.: (RK) Surgeon; Co.: Hospital; (ED) August 14, 1862; (DISD) December 1864; (LOS) 4Y. (PO) Ste. Genevieve, MO. (CMTS) None.
Berry, Hiram: (RK) Private; Co.: E; (REG) 21st MO Inf.; (ED) Sept. 18, 1864; (DISD) Sept. 1865; (LOS) 1Y (PO) Ste. Genevieve, MO.. (CMTS) Inlarged Destices
Biehl, Charles: (RK) Private; Co.: K; (REG) Jeff Thomson; (ED) June 1861; (DISD) Dec. 1861; (LOS) 6 M. (PO) Ste. Genevieve Co.
Billey, Joisha: (RK) Private; Co.: A; (REG) 5th NY Inf.; (ED) March

1865; (DISD) Aug. 27, 1865; (LOS) 7m. (PO) Kinsey, MO..
(CMTS) Rhumatism
Blanchart, Joseph: (RK) Private; (REG) 1st MO Art.; (ED) Was not at
Home and wife didn't know (PO) Ste. Genevieve, MO. (CMTS)
None.
Brown, Ruben G.: (RK) Private; Co.: A; (REG) 2nd MO Cav.; (ED)
Aug. 26, 1863; (DISD) July 12, 1865; (LOS) 1Y 11 M. 19 D.
(PO) Ste. Genevieve, MO.. (CMTS) None.
Brumier, Francis J.: (RK) Private; Co.: A; (REG) 2nd MO Art.; (ED)
Oct. 2, 1861; (DISD) Oct. 6, 1863; (LOS) 2Y 11 M. 4D. (PO)
Ste. Genevieve, MO.. (CMTS) None.
Buatte, Antoine: (RK) Private; (PO) Ste. Genevieve, MO.. (CMTS)
None.
Burgert, Joseph: (RK) Private; Co.: G; (REG) 8th MO. Cavalry
(ED) August 1864; (DISD) November 1864; (LOS) 2 M.. (PO)
Ste. Genevieve, MO.. (CMTS) None.
Burle, Alexander: (RK) Private; Co.: F; (REG) 86th MO. Infantry
(ED) September 30, 1865; (DISD) None Given; (LOS) 1M 15D
(PO) Wine Garden (Weingarten). (CMTS) None.
Burle, Louis: (RK) Private; Co.: F; (REG) 41st MO. Infantry, (ED)
Sept. 19, 1864; (DISD) July 12, 1865; (LOS) 9 M.. (PO) Ste.
Genevieve, MO.. (CMTS) None.
Burle, Louis (Second Entry): (RK) Private; Co.: E; (REG) 7th Louisiana
Infantry (ED) 1862; (DISD) Not Given; (LOS) 2Y (PO) Ste.
Genevieve, MO.. (CMTS) Taken Prisoner, Enlisted In MO.
Carsoow, Charles F.: (RK) Surgeon Ass.; Co.: Sanitary Com.. (PO) Ste.
Genevieve, MO.. (CMTS) None.
Curtois, Henry: (RK) Private; Co.: K; (REG) 21st MO Inf.; (ED) Sept.
22, 1864; (DISD) Oct. 3, 1865; (LOS) 1Y 11 D. (PO) Ste.
Genevieve, MO.. (CMTS) None.
Dordge, George W.: (RK) Private; Co.: B; (REG) 31st MO Inf.; (ED)
Aug. 11, 1863; (DISD) May 1865; (LOS) 1Y 9 M. (PO) Ste.
Genevieve, MO.. (CMTS) None.
Duvall, John: (RK) Private; Co.: G; (REG) 50th Missouri Infantry
(ED) Feb. 17, 1865; (DISD) Aug. 5, 1865; (LOS) Not Given.
(PO) St. Mary, MO. (CMTS) None.
Eckert, Anton: (RK) Sergeant; Co.: K; (REG) 78th MO Inf.; (ED) Sept.
24, 1864; (DISD) Dec. 1864; (LOS) 3 M. (PO) Zell. MO..
(CMTS) None.
Ellis, Daniel: (RK) Corporal; Co.: C; (REG) 1st MO Inf.; (ED) Jan. 12,
1864; (DISD) Jan 28, 1865; (LOS) 1 Y 16 D. (PO) Ste.
Genevieve, MO.. (CMTS) None
Falk, Jacob: (RK) Private; Co.: A; (REG) 15th MO; (ED) June 6, 1864;

(DISD) March 25, 1866; (LOS) 1Y 9 M. 19 D. (PO) Ste. Genevieve, MO.. (CMTS) Shot Through Right Hand and Right Shoulder at Franklin, TN

Falleby, George: (RK) Private; Co.: Conf.; (REG) Missouri; (ED) Oct. 1864; (DISD) May 1865; (LOS) Not Given. (PO) St. Mary, MO. (CMTS) None.

Fallert, Joseph: (RK) Captain; Co.: K; (REG) 78th MO Inf.; (ED) Sept. 24, 1864; (DISD) Dec. 1864; (LOS) 2 M. (PO) Zell.

Fanton, Alexander: (RK) Corporal; Co.: A; (REG) 15th Il Cavalry (ED) Aug. 10, 1861; (DISD) March 19, 1862; (LOS) 8 M. 9 D. (PO) Ste. Genevieve, MO.. (CMTS) Discharged Disability

Fieh, Michael: (RK) Private; Co.: G; (REG) 37th MO Inf.; (ED) 1861; (DISD) 1861; (LOS) 3 M. (PO) Ste. Genevieve, MO.

Flice, Joseph: (RK) Soldier, U.S. (PO) Ste. Genevieve, MO.

Gattel, George: (RK) Private; Co.: A; (REG) 3rd MO Inf.; (ED) May 1861; (DISD) Sept [?] 1864. (PO) Ste. Genevieve, MO.

Girard, Louis: (RK) Private; Co.: Confederate Soldier. (PO) Ste. Genevieve, MO.. (CMTS) None.

Geisler, John: (RK) Private; Co.: F; (REG) 1st MO Inf.; (ED) Oct. 1861; (DISD) Oct. 1863; (LOS) 2 Y. (PO) Ste. Genevieve, MO. (CMTS) Discharged i Hospital.

Gisi, Augustus: (RK) Sergeant; (LOS) 2 M. (PO) Ste. Genevieve

Godair, John B.: (RK) Private; Co.: H; (REG) 78th Missouri Cavalry (ED) September 24, 1864; (DISD) Dec. 24, 1864; (LOS) 3M. (PO) Ste.Genevieve, MO. (CMTS) None.

Govro, ???? (PO) Ste. Genevieve, MO.. (CMTS) None.

Govro, Bernard Wdow of: (PO) Ste. Genevieve, MO.

Govro, Felix: (PO) Ste. Genevieve, MO.. (CMTS) None.

Gremminger, Christian: (RK) Private; Co.: K; (REG) 117th MO Inf.; (ED) Sept. 27, 1864; (DISD) March 29, 1865; (LOS) 6M. 2D. (PO) Zell, MO. (CMTS) None.

Grieshaber, Kilian: (RK) Sergeant; Co.: F; (REG) 78th MO Cav.; (ED) Sept. 24, 1864; (DISD) Dec. 1864; (LOS) 3 M. (PO) Ste. Genevieve, MO.. (CMTS) None.

Gueth, Andrew: (RK) Private; Co.: A; (REG) MO Inf.; (ED) 1863; (DISD) 1863; (LOS) 3m. (PO) Bloomsdale, MO.. (CMTS) None.

Haricock, Henry H.: (RK) Sergeant; Co.: E; (REG) Not Given; (ED) June 1862; (DISD) March 1865; (LOS) 2 Yrs., 9 Months. (PO) Cape Girardeau, MO. (CMTS) None.

Hehr, Jacob G.: (RK) Private; Co.: A; (REG) 32nd In Inf.; (ED) Aug. 24, 1861; (DISD) 1864; (LOS) 3 Y. 1 M. (PO) Bloomsdale, MO.. (CMTS) Paralyzed, Right Side Since 1870. Prisoner At Stone River

Heller, Widow Annie: (RK) ???? Soldier, U.S. (PO) Ste. Genevieve, MO..

Henneman, Conrad: (RK) Private; Co.: G; (REG) 8; (ED) August 1863; (DISD) December 1863; (LOS) 4M (PO) River Aux Vases, MO. (CMTS) None.

Herter, Charles J.: (RK) Sergeant; Co.: G; (REG) 8th MO Cav.; (ED) Aug. 1863; (DISD) Nov. 1864; (LOS) 1Y 3 M. (PO) Ste. Genevieve, MO.. (CMTS) None.

Herzog, Leon: (RK) Private; Co.: A; (REG) 2nd MO Inf.; (ED) Aug. 1861; (DISD) Sept. 1864; (LOS) 3Y 1 M. 1 Day. (PO) Ste. Genevieve, MO.. (CMTS) None.

Holliday, Robert U.: (RK) Private; Co.: C; (REG) 21st MO Infantry (ED) Sept. 22, 1864; (DISD) Nov. 11, 1865; (LOS) Not Given. (PO) Coffman, MO. (CMTS) Eye And Lung Disease.

Hoock, Frank S.: (RK) Private; Co.: F; (REG) 78th MO Cav.; (ED) Sept. 4, 1864; (DISD) Dec. 1864; (LOS) 3 M. (PO) Ste. Genevieve, MO.. (CMTS) None.

Huber, Paul: (RK) Private; Co.: C; (REG) 64th MO Inf.; (ED) April 1862; (DISD) August 1863; (LOS) 1 M. (PO) Ste. Genevieve, MO.. (CMTS) Fell With Horse and Crippled; Shot Through Right Foot, Pilot Knob

Hurka, Jacob: (RK) Private; Co.: G; (REG) 15th MO Inf.; Also 4th MO Inf.; (ED) Aug. 1, 1861; (DISD) Sept. 21, 1864; (LOS) 3Y 2 M. (PO) Ste. Genevieve, MO.. (CMTS) Eyes Injured Last Year Of Service. Now Blind

James, Scott: (RK) Private; Co.: K48th MO Inf.; (ED) Aug. 1864; (DISD) Feb. 1865; (LOS) 6 M. (PO) Ste. Genevieve, MO.

Joggerst, Phillip (Widow Caroline): (RK) Private; (LOS) 8M. (PO) Ste. Genevieve, MO. (CMTS) None.

Jokerst, Leo A.: (RK) Private; Co.: A; (REG) 2nd MO, Art.; (ED) March 4, 1862; (DISD) March 17, 1865; (LOS) 3Y 13 D. (PO) Ste. Genevieve, MO.. (CMTS) Injuries on both knees in Battle of Nashville

Karl, David: (RK) Private; Co.: A; (REG) 86th MO Inf.; (ED) Sept. 30, 1865; (DISD) ; (LOS) . (PO) Wine Garden

Karl, Felix: (RK) Private; (REG) 100th IL. (PO) Ste. Genevieve, MO.

Kemph, Nobert: (RK) Private: Mislayed His Discharge. (PO) Ste. Genevieve County. (CMTS) None.

Kenner, Francis: (RK) Not Given; Co.: A; (REG) 8th ; (ED) April 1863; (DISD) Nov. 8, 1863; (LOS) Not Given. (PO) St. Mary's, MO.

Keton, Battice Widow of: (RK) Private; Co.: A; (REG) 68th Colored Vol. (PO) Ste. Genevieve, MO.

Kingleman, Benhegold: (RK) ?; Co.: H; (REG) 27th MO Inf.; (ED) 1861; (DISD) April 1864; (LOS) 3y, 6m . (PO) Bloomsdale, MO.

Kinse, Augustus: (RK) Private; Co.: C; (REG) 29th ; (ED) Aug. 22, 1862; (DISD) March 29, 1865; (LOS) Not Given. (PO) St. Mary, MO. (CMTS) None.

Kirzner, Laurenz: (RK) Private; Co.: K; (REG) 78th MO Inf.; (ED) Sept. 24, 1864; (DISD) Dec. 1864; (LOS) 3 M. (PO) Bloomsdale,

Kist, Richard: (RK) Private; Co.: G; (REG) Not Given; (ED) Oct. 1863; (DISD) Nov. 1863; (LOS) 1 MOnth. (PO) Ste. Genevieve, MO.

Klein, Berhard: (RK) Private; Co.: C; (REG) 2nd MO Heavy Art.; (ED) Nov. 1861; (DISD) Aug. 1863; (LOS) 2Y (PO) Ste. Genevieve

Kohm, Frank: (RK) Private; Co.: A; (REG) 13th MO Inf.; (ED) 1862; (DISD) Aug. 1864; (LOS) 3Y 3 M. And Some D. (PO) Ste. Genevieve, MO.. (CMTS) None.

Kramer, Charles: (RK) Private; Co.: H; (REG) 27th MO Inf.; (ED) 1861; (DISD) Oct. 1864; (LOS) 3Y, 4M . (PO) Bloomsdale, MO.. (CMTS) Rupture.

Krus, Jacob: (RK) Private. Confederate Soldier.

Kunkel, Andrew: (RK) Private; Co.: K; (REG) 53rd Il Inf.; (ED) Aug. 1864; (DISD) March 1865; (LOS) 7 M. (PO) Ste. Genevieve,

Labrier, Leon: (RK) Private; Co.: K; (REG) 47th MO Inf.; (ED) August 1864; (DISD) March 1865; (LOS) 7 M. (PO) Ste. Genevieve,

Lachance, August: (RK) Private; Co.: K; (REG) 47th MO Inf.; (LOS) 6 M. (PO) Ste. Genevieve, MO.. (CMTS) None.

Lafleur, Mikel: (RK) Private; (LOS) 9 M. (PO) Ste. Genevieve, MO.. (CMTS) None.

Lalemendier, Albert: (RK) Private; Co.: B; (REG) 21st MO Inf.; (ED) Sept. 1864; (DISD) July 31, 1865; (LOS) 10 M. (PO) Ste. Genevieve, MO.

Lange, Charles: (RK) Private; Co.: K; (REG) 41st MO Inf.; (ED) Aug. 18, 1864; (DISD) June 15, 1865; (LOS) 10m. (PO) Kinsey, MO.. (CMTS) Neuralgia.

Loida, Daniel: (RK) Private; Co.: K; (REG) MO Inf.; (ED) Oct. 1864; (DISD) Dec. 1864; (LOS) 3m., 3 D. (PO) Lawrenceton, MO.

Luckfield, Christ: (RK) Sergeant; Co.: E; (REG) 12th Missouri Infantry (ED) Aug. 12, 1861; (DISD) Sept. 16, 1864; (LOS) Not Given. (PO) St. Mary, MO. (CMTS) None.

Lux, Louis: (RK) ?, (REG) Missouri State Militia. (LOS) 2 M.. (PO) Ste. Genevieve, MO.. (CMTS) None.

Maurice, Bernard: (RK) Private; Co.: B; (REG) 21st MO Inf.; (ED) Sept. 22, 1864; (DISD) Dec. 5, 1865; (LOS) 1Y 2M. 13D. (PO) Bloomsdale. (CMTS) None.

Meyer, Jacob: (RK) Private; Co.: K; (REG) 21st MO Inf.; (ED) Sept. 22, 1864; (DISD) Dec. 5, 1865; (LOS) 1Y 2 M. 13 D. (PO) Zell, MO.. (CMTS) Rheumatism Since 1865, Now Has Disease 3 Years

Miller, Andrew: (RK) Soldier, U.S. (PO) Ste. Genevieve, MO.
Miller, Frank: (RK) Private; Co.: E; (REG) 2nd Missouri Artillery (ED) Nov. 1, 1861; (DISD) Aug. 25, 1863; (LOS) Not Given. (PO) St. Mary, MO. (CMTS) None.
Moffet, Thomas: (RK) Private; Co.: E; (REG) 1st VT Volunteers ; (ED) May 12, 1863; (DISD) May 26, 1866; (LOS) Not Given. (PO) St. Mary, MO. (CMTS) None.
Moore, William J.: (RK) Private; Co.: K; (REG) 47th Missouri Infantry (ED) Aug. 13, 1864; (DISD) March 29, 1865; (LOS) Not Given. (PO) St. Mary, MO. (CMTS) None.
Moser, John P.: (RK) Private; Co.: K; (REG) 11 MO. (PO) Ste. Genevieve, MO.. (CMTS) None.
Muessig, ????: (RK) Private; Co.: A; (REG) 86th MO Inf.; (ED) Sept. 30, 1865. (PO) Wine Garden [Weingarten]. (CMTS) None.
Nager, Lapeold: (RK) Private; Co.: K; (REG) 112th IL Inf.; (ED) May 4, 1864; (DISD) Oct. 26, 1864; (LOS) 6M, 22 D. (PO) Lawrenceton, MO.. (CMTS) None.
Nicken, Peter: (RK) Private; Co.: A; (REG) 21st MO Inf.; (ED) Sept. 22, 1864; (DISD) Sept. 26; (LOS) 1y, 4 D. (PO) Lawrenceton, MO.
Oberle, Franz: (RK) Private; Co.: C; (REG) 2nd MO Inf.; (ED) Sept. 1861; (DISD) Aug. 1863; (LOS) 1Y 11 M. (PO) Ste. Genevieve, MO.. (CMTS) None.
Otte, Henry: (RK) Private; Co.: K; (REG) 47; (ED) August 6, 1864; (DISD) March 29, 1865; (LOS) Not Listed. (PO) St. Mary, MO.
Reese, Edward: (RK) Soldier, U.S. (PO) Ste. Genevieve, MO.
Rosslet, Anton: (RK) Private; Co.: K; (REG) 44th Missouri Infantry (ED) Aug. 31, 1864; (DISD) March 1865; (LOS) Not Given. (PO) St. Mary, MO.
Rossman, Henry: (RK) ?; Co.: E; (REG) 30th Illinois Volunteers; (ED) 1861; (DISD) 1862; (LOS) . (PO) St. Mary, MO. (CMTS) None.
Roth, Christian J.: (RK) Private; Soldier, U.S. (PO) Ste. Genevieve, MO.
Rottler, Valentine: (RK) 1st Lt.; Co.: F; (REG) 78th MO Mounted Inf.; (ED) Sept. 30. (PO) Ste. Genevieve, MO.. (CMTS) None.
Ruebsam, Adam: (RK) Sergeant; Co.: F; (REG) 47th MO Md. Inf.; (ED) Sept. 30, 1865. (PO) Wine Garden, (CMTS) None.
Russell, Frank H.: (RK) Private; Co.: F; (REG) WI (?) Inf.; (ED) Sept. 19, 1861; (DISD) Feb. 29, 1863; (LOS) 1Y 9 M. 10 D. (PO) Ste. Genevieve, MO.. (CMTS) Discharged On Surgeon's Certificate: (RK) Private; Co.: L; (REG) 2nd Cal. Cav.; (ED) Oct. 5, 1864; (DISD) Aug. 10, 1865; (LOS) 10 M. 5 D. (CMTS) Re-enlisted Veteran

Saint Gem, Gustavus: (RK) Captain; Co.: K; (REG) 47th MO Inf.; (ED) Sept. 8, 1864; (DISD) March 29, 1865; (LOS) 6 M. 21 D. (PO) Ste. Genevieve, MO.. (CMTS) None.

St. James, Widow Susan: (RK) Soldier, U.S. (PO) Ste. Genevieve, MO.. (CMTS) None.

Schaettler, Charles: (PO) Ste. Genevieve, MO.. (CMTS) None.

Schafer, Frederic: (RK) Private; Co.: E; (REG) 2nd MO Inf.; (ED) 1861; (DISD) 1862; (LOS) 1Y 2 M.. (PO) Ste. Genevieve, MO.. (CMTS) Ruptured

Schilly, August: (RK) Lieut.; Co.: K; (REG) MO Inf.; (ED) Oct. 1, 1864; (DISD) Nov. 1, 1864; (LOS) 30 D. (PO) Zell, MO.

Schmith, Joseph: (RK) Private; Co.: K; (REG) 78th MO Cav.; (ED) Sept. 24, 1864; (DISD) Dec. 1864; (LOS) 3 M. (PO) Ste. Genevieve, MO.. (CMTS) None.

Schuler, Charles: (RK) Sergeant; Co.: G; (REG) 8th MO Cavalry (ED) Sept. 1863; (DISD) May 1864; (LOS) 8 M. (PO) Ste. Genevieve, MO. (CMTS) None.

Sewald, Michael: (RK) Private; Co.: C; (REG) 2nd MO Art.; (ED) Sept. 1861; (DISD) 1864; (LOS) 2y, 11m, 7 D. (PO) Kinsey, MO.. (CMTS) Asthma.

Sewald, Valentine: (RK) Private; Co.: C; (REG) 2nd MO Art.; (ED) Feb. 22, 1862; (DISD) March 7, 1865; (LOS) 3y . (PO) French Village, St. Francis County, MO.. (CMTS) Rhematism

Siebert, Augustin: (RK) Private; Co.: A; (REG) 43 Il Inf.; (ED) Aug. 21, 1861; (DISD) Feb. 25, 1864; (LOS) 2 Y. 6 M. 4D (PO) Ste. Genevieve, MO.. (CMTS) None.: (RK) Private; Co.: K; (REG) 43 Il Inf.; (ED) Feb. 26, 1864; (DISD) Nov. 30, 1865; (LOS) 1Y 9M 4D

Siebert, Charles: (RK) Corporal; Co.: A; (REG) 2ne Missouri Light Artillery (ED) Feb. 14, 1862; (DISD) 28 Feb. 1865; (LOS) Not Given. (PO) St. Mary, MO. (CMTS) Eye Disease.

Siebert, Lawrence: (RK) Private; Co.: K; (REG) 47th MO Inf.; (ED) Aug. 1864; (DISD) May 1865; (LOS) 9 M. (PO) Ste. Genevieve, MO.. (CMTS) None.

Siebert, Panrataon: (RK) Private; Co.: K; (REG) 78th MO Inf.; (ED) Sept. 1864; (DISD) Dec. 1864; (LOS) 2 M. (PO) Ste. Genevieve, MO.

Simino, John: (RK) Private; Co.: B; (REG) 36th Inf.; (ED) Oct. 3, 1864; (DISD) May 30, 1865; (LOS) 6 M. 27 D. (PO) Ste. Genevieve, MO. (CMTS) None.

Skewes, William V.: (RK) Private; Co.: K; (REG) 47th MO Inf.; (ED) Aug. 1864; (DISD) March 1865; (LOS) 7M. (PO) Ste. Genevieve County. (CMTS) None.

Small, John W.: (RK) Private; Co.: K; (REG) 47th MO Vol. Inf.; (ED) Aug. 12, 1864; (DISD) March 30, 1865. (PO) Ste. Genevieve, MO. (CMTS) None.

Staekly, Joseph: (RK) Private; Co.: F; (REG) 78th MO Inf.; (ED) Sept. 24, 1864; (DISD) Dec. 1864; (LOS) 3 M. (PO) Bloomsdale, MO.

Stoll, Frank X.: (RK) Private; Co.: Not Listed; (REG) Not Listed; (ED) Oct. 1863; (DISD) Nov. 1863; (LOS) 1 Month. (PO) Ste. Genevieve, MO. (CMTS) None.

Stoll, Mike: (RK) Private; Co.: G; (REG) 8; (ED) August 1863; (DISD) April 1864; (LOS) 8 MOnths. (PO) Ste. Genevieve, MO.

Stolte, Henry: (RK) Seaman; Co.: No. 25; (REG) Gov. Navy Colossus; (ED) Jan. 10, 1865; (DISD) Aug. 18, 1865; (LOS) 1Y 7 M. 8 D. (PO) Ste. Genevieve County. (CMTS) None.

Sweek, Adolphus: (RK) Private; Co.: K; (REG) 47; (ED) Aug. 1864; (DISD) Mar. (Nov.?) 1864; (LOS) Not Given. (PO) St. Mary's, MO. (CMTS) None.

Thaumure, Charles: (RK) Private; Co.: B; (REG) 21st MO Inf. (PO) Ste. Genevieve, MO. (CMTS) None.

Thomure, Joseph: (RK) Private; Co.: G; (REG) 21; (ED) Sept. 22, 1864; (DISD) Aug. 21, 1865; (LOS) Not Listed

Trautman, Constantin: (RK) Private; Co.: G; (REG) 33rd MO Inf.; (ED) Sept. 1863; (DISD) October 1863; (LOS) 1 M. (PO) Bloomsdale, MO. (CMTS) None.

Tucker, William: (RK) Private; Co.: Not Listed; (REG) MO Inf.; (ED) Jan. 21, 1864; (DISD) June 17, 1864; (LOS) 5m, 29 D. (PO) Bloomsdale, MO. (CMTS) None.

Vaeth, Peter: (RK) Private; Co.: A; (REG) 86th MO Inf.; (ED) Sept. 30, 1865. (PO) Wine Garden, (CMTS) None.

Valentine, Widow Mary: (PO) Ste. Genevieve, MO. (CMTS) Widow and Draws Pension, But Does Not Know How Long He Served

Valle, Paul.: (RK) Private; Co.: C; (REG) 56th Missouri Colored Infantry, (ED) 1863; (DISD) 1866; (LOS) 3 Y, (PO) Ste.Genevieve, MO. (CMTS) None.

Voelker, Frank X.: (RK) Private; Co.: E; (REG) 2nd Missouri Infantry (ED) Apr. 1861; (DISD) July 1861; (LOS) Not Given. (PO) St. Mary, MO. (CMTS) None.

Vogt, Roman: (RK) Private; Co.: K; (REG) 21st Missouri Infantry (ED) 1864; (DISD) 1865; (LOS) 1Y (PO) Ste. Genevieve, MO. (CMTS) Ruptured.

Vorst, Joseph: (RK) 1st Lieutenant; Co.: A; (REG) 12th Missouri Infantry (ED) May 30, 1861; (DISD) August 30, 1864; (LOS) 3Y 3 M. (PO) Ste. Genevieve, MO. (CMTS) None.

White, John: (RK) Private; Co. ; (REG) 1st MO Art.. (PO)

Ste. Genevieve, MO.. (CMTS) Colored.
Whitlock, John S.: (RK) 1st Sergeant; Co.: C; (REG) 3rd MO Inf.; (ED) May 1863; (DISD) Nov. 1864; (LOS) 6 M. (PO) Ste. Genevieve, MO.. (CMTS) None.
Wilkinson, Major: (RK) Private; Co.: I; (REG) 9; (ED) Sept. 1863; (DISD) Nov. 1866; (LOS) 3 Y, 2 Months. (PO) Ste. Genevieve, MO. (CMTS) None.
Will, George: (RK) Private; Co.: K; (REG) 21st MO Inf.; (ED) Sept. 22, 1864; (DISD) Oct. 30, 1865; (LOS) 1Y 11 D. (PO) Ste. Genevieve, MO.. (CMTS) None.
Willi, Joseph C.: (RK) Corporal; Co.: A. (PO) Ste. Genevieve, MO.. (CMTS) None.
Wolf, John: (RK) Private; Co.: U; (REG) 27th Missouri Infantry (ED) Aug. 12, 1861; (DISD) Sept. 17, 1864; (LOS) Not Given. (PO) St. Mary, MO. (CMTS) None.
Woods, Richard (Dick): (RK) Private; Co.: H; (REG) 56th Missouri Colored Infantry (ED) August 1863; (DISD) October 1864; (LOS) 1Y 2 M.. (PO) Ste. Genevieve, MO. (CMTS) Wounded In Left Arm, Battle of Little Rock

St. Louis County, Missouri, Order of the Eastern Star, Kirkwood Chapter, October, 1913.
Nettie VanDam, Annie E. Dieter, Jeanette C. Kingsland, Malissa Roloff, Bertha E. Tatman, Elizabeth B. Bowles, Robert C. Huckeby, Lillie M. Crow, Hugo S. Jacobi, Edith Walker Hall, Mary C. Johnson, Bernal Tatman, Annie Laurie Mendham, Jennie M. Huckeby, Eva Lyon, Robert W. Roloff, Josephine R. Mendham, Della Coleman, Annie Rosylyn Hawken, Leo. E. Heinzelmann, Kate L. Hawken, Leo E. Heinzelmann, John H. Diester, Peter VanDam

Adair County, Missouri, Marriage Records, 1841-1880
Jacob C. Marsh and Harriet Kelley, (MD) May 1, 1841
Solsberry Miller and Sarah Fin, (MD) Jun. 1, 1841
John Morgan and Denise West, (MD) Jul. 1, 1841
William Mccrew and Harriet Palmertree, (MD) Apr. 11, 1841
Lewis Carpenter and Juliana Bruce, (MD) Aug. 12, 1841
Benjamin Musgrove and Catharine Humphreys, (MD) Oct. 13, 1841
Erastus Rice and Amanda Mason, (MD) Jul. 15, 1841
J. N. Sallee and Margaret Gilbert, (MD) Jan. 17, 1841
John Vincent and Hannah Corneilson, (MD) Dec. 18, 1841

William Willis and Polly Ricerson, (MD) Mar. 18, 1841
Adam Done and Dosha Sloan, (MD) Jun. 19, 1841
Andrew Miller and Caroline Conklin, (MD) Oct. 2, 1841
John Partin and Rachel Hargrave, (MD) Jun. 20, 1841
Hanford Wilscher and Amanda Jane Sneed, (MD) Dec. 22, 1841
Daniel Corneilson and Rebecca Dean, (MD) Jun. 23, 1841
Nelson Yates and Mandy Laphlain, (MD) Apr. 25, 1841
Zachariah Reed and Mary Ann Dilman, (MD) Mar. 28, 1841
Littleton Conklin and Julia Ely, (MD) Oct. 3, 1841
Andrew Mote and Susanna Crain, (MD) Jul. 3, 1841
Stephen L. Spalding and Susan Wilson, (MD) Sep. 3, 1841
John Stagre and Susan Piles, (MD) Mar. 7, 1841
William M. Sloan and Missouri Shobe, (MD) Sep. 8, 1841
Adam Smith and Elizabeth C????, (MD) Jun. 9, 1841
???? Walker and Elizabeth Charlton, (MD) Dec. 1, 1842
Thomas J. Roberts and Lida Sickliter, (MD) Dec. 10, 1842
Morris Adkins and Elizabeth Truitt, (MD) Dec. 10, 1842
Mays Beach and Elizabeth Roberson, (MD) Dec. 15, 1842
Ezekiel Bragg and Tabitha ????, (MD) Feb. 15, 1842
Jacob Meeks and Mary Cunningham, (MD) Feb. 17, 1842
William Massie and Elizabeth Callison, (MD) Sep. 21, 1842
Thomas Wisdom and Mary Hulet, (MD) Jul. 21, 1842
Samuel ????craft and Mary Ann Bristo, (MD) Sep. 22, 1842
Hiram Perkins and Rebecca Williams, (MD) Dec. 22, 1842
Kemp George and Serena Fletcher, (MD) Dec. 23, 1842
James H. Claybrook and Sarah Elizabeth Allen, (MD) Aug. 23, 1842
John D. Kent and Amanda Rogers, (MD) Apr. 24, 1842
Calvin Saling and S??? Riggs, (MD) Mar. 24, 1842
Thomas S. Wright and Mary Eby, (MD) Sep. 27, 1842
William Roader and Nancy Arnold, (MD) Sep. 28, 1842
Paten R. Cunningham and Sally D. Stockton, (MD) Sep. 29, 1842
John Shoemaker and Nancy Bragg, (MD) Apr. 3, 1842
J. Charlton and Margaret C. Walker, (MD) Nov. 30, 1842
Manuel Gillispy and Margaret Minich, (MD) Apr. 30, 1842
Oliver P. Thomas and Rachel Ann Moffitt, (MD) Jan. 4, 1842
Charles Ashbill and Jane Johnson, (MD) May 5, 1842
Horrace McEntire and Narcisses Mil???, (MD) Jul. 6, 1842
Jesse Canada and Polly Morrow, (MD) May 8, 1842
William Heather and Bemether Partin, (MD) Feb. 8, 1842
??? Sally and Sarah Lane, (MD) Jun. 1, 1843
James Shaw and Rebecca Lemmon, (MD) Dec. 1, 1843
Frederick A. Stephens and ??? Kerley, (MD) Apr. 1, 1843
Caleb Norton and Delilah Floyd, (MD) Aug. 10, 1843

James Williams and Sarah Guffey, (MD) Dec. 10, 1843
Ephraim Knowlton and Lida Ann Tillitson, (MD) May 11, 1843
Joseph French and Nancy E. Stockton, (MD) Feb. 12, 1843
Thomas B. Reed and Hester E. Loftin, (MD) Jul. 13, 1843
Jacob Willis and Ellen C. Hamilton, (MD) Jul. 13, 1843
John Dillion and Mary G. Humphreys, (MD) May 14, 1843
???? Jones and Susan Russel, (MD) Jul. 14, 1843
Hannibal W. Shanks and Elizabeth Renn, (MD) May 14, 1843
J. Holt and Sarah Webster, (MD) Jun. 16, 1843
Thomas Kelley and Fredy Wisdom, (MD) Mar. 16, 1843
James Dickerson, Jr., and Ellen Scovel, (MD) Dec. 17, 1843
Robert King and Sharlotta Tillitson, (MD) May 17, 1843
J. Clifton and Cobb,Elizabeth (MD) Jul. 18, 1843
John Hull and Sophia L. Cocrumb, (MD) Nov. 2, 1843
John S. Mikel and Mary Ann Sco???, (MD) Sep. 2, 1843
Charles Payton and Delia Mildred All, (MD) Jul. 20, 1843
Isham B. Dodson and Nancy Jane Murphy, (MD) Aug. 21, 1843
Thomas Hayden and Mary Ann Hayden, (MD) Dec. 21, 1843
Hezekiah Frazy and Celia Partin, (MD) Feb. 22, 1843
William Brower and Sarah Rhoads, (MD) Aug. 24, 1843
Robert Dingle and Catharine A. McAtee, (MD) Feb. 24, 1843
William C. S. Hamilton and Rachel Summers, (MD) Dec. 24, 1843
E. Fletcher and Mrs. Elizabeth Grigg, (MD) Sep. 25, 1843
Jesse L. Morrow and Elizabeth Booth, (MD) Sep. 26, 1843
John Grogan and Hannah Hull, (MD) Dec. 27, 1843
James M. Partin and Aley Vandike, (MD) Feb. 28, 1843
Gasham F. Drake and Maria Louisa Earhart, (MD) Jun. 3, 1843
James Amett and Mehala Saling, (MD) Jul. 30, 1843
Caleb Barret and Sarah Ellen Shortness, (MD) Mar. 30, 1843
James B. Rodgers and Ruth Burnerd, (MD) Nov. 30, 1843
H. Wilcoxin and Amanda Ford, (MD) Mar. 30, 1843
Francis Freeman and Margaret Clem, (MD) Jun. 4, 1843
William R. Seamon and Drucilla Ann Ross, (MD) Oct. 4, 1843
William B. Smith and Suthial Frakier, (MD) Jun. 5, 1843
Benjamin Collin and Cosann Hathaway, (MD) Apr. 6, 1843
Quin Morton and Manerva Buckaloo, (MD) Jul. 6, 1843
T. Christian and Elizabeth Jones, (MD) Jan. 8, 1843
Franklin Ervin and Mary B????, (MD) Nov. 9, 1843
James Vandike and Martha Jane Humphreys, (MD) Feb. 9, 1843
Zachariah Wright and Martha Ann Rodes, (MD) Jul. 9, 1843
Stephen Adkins and Margaret Duffy, (MD) Feb. 9, 1843
William Buford and Mary Jones, (MD) Aug. 1, 1844
Calvin I???? and Martha Shaw, (MD) Oct. 1, 1844

John H???son and Eliza Jane Sleigham, (MD) May 10, 1844
John W. Johnson and Eliza Jane Sleigham, (MD) May 10, 1844
Edward Butts and Lucy Ann Garrett, (MD) Mar. 13, 1844
James Dodson and Jane Canatsy, (MD) May 16, 1844
James Hoglan and Elizabeth Wilson, (MD) Apr. 16, 1844
Thomas Thrailkild and Jane Fulcher, (MD) Oct. 17, 1844
William M. Bown and Mary Ringo, (MD) Jan. 18, 1844
Albin Partin and Rebecca Vandyke, (MD) Mar. 18, 1844
Cyrus Hindman and Mary Floyd, (MD) Feb. 19, 1844
J. Jones and Matilda Gould, (MD) Apr. 19, 1844
John Marney and Rebecca K. Horn, (MD) Mar. 19, 1844
Christopher ???? and C. Corneilson, (MD) Apr. 2, 1844
Jefferson Latham and Nancy Johnson, (MD) Jun. 23, 1844
Hen??? Shook and Eliza Jane Calison, (MD) Oct. 23, 1844
Frederick Heaneley and Christena Ship, (MD) Nov. 24, 1844
George Minic and Sarah Galaspy, (MD) Oct. 24, 1844
Peter H. Summers and Elizabeth Mullins, (MD) Jan. 25, 1844
Washington Wright and Lucinda Brower, (MD) Aug. 25, 1844
Joseph Ford and Nancy Lay, (MD) Nov. 26, 1844
George W. Hall and Elizabeth Grosseloss, (MD) Aug. 26, 1844
Jefferson Allen and Delilah B????, (MD) Dec. 26, 1844
O. C. Dooley and Mary Russel, (MD) Mar. 28, 1844
Lewis Waters and Elizabeth May, (MD) Mar. 3, 1844
Martin Partin and Nancy Nul???, (MD) Mar. 30, 1844
Davis Mccollum and Margaret Eperson, (MD) Jul. 31, 1844
Ellis Evans and Mary Wells, (MD) Apr. 4, 1844
James H. Callem and E. ????, (MD) Jan. 4, 1844
William Mcfetridge and Manerva Bozarth, (MD) Sep. 7, 1844
Jeremiah Biswell and Nancy Morris, (MD) Feb. 8, 1844
Benjamin Mcatee and Helena Beanford, (MD) Oct. 8, 1844
William Parks and ??? ????, (MD) Jan. 1845
James M. Buckaloo and Rezza Ann Furnish, (MD) Apr. 1, 1845
S. Kent and Elizabeth Rogers, (MD) Nov. 1, 1845
John Murphy and Polly Murphy, (MD) Feb. 1, 1845
Aram Earhart and Jane Earhart, (MD) Sep. 11, 1845
John W. Crawford and Elizabeth F. Hase, (MD) Mar. 11, 1845
William Wilson and Jane Hughland, (MD) Aug. 12, 1845
Benjamin An???? and Elvina Bradley, (MD) Feb. 13, 1845
George Emerson and Elizabeth Lyles, (MD) Apr. 13, 1845
Thomas Morris and Sally Ann ????, (MD) Nov. 13, 1845
Joel C. Wilson and Angemina E. Davidson, (MD) Aug. 14, 1845
John Riddle and Mrs. Elizabeth ????, (MD) Jan. 16, 1845
Andrew M. Smith and Jane Judd, (MD) Mar. 2, 1845

Sa??? Mikel and Tabitha Souther, (MD) Jun. 20, 1845
Hiland Bunch and Polly Stockton, (MD) Dec. 22, 1845
John Len??? and Amanda True, (MD) Jul. 24, 1845
John Fugate and Susanna Hamilton, (MD) Jan. 25, 1845
H. Hedrick and Rachel Burns, (MD) May 25, 1845
John D. Turner and Cintha Ann Bozarth, (MD) Feb. 25, 1845
John Whitley and Nancy Jane Stump, (MD) Sep. 25, 1845
John Serat and Nancy Ann Lane, (MD) Aug. 27, 1845
Michael Gun and Anna Best, (MD) Jun. 3, 1845
John Lay and Katharine Capps, (MD) Aug. 31, 1845
John W. Johnson and Malinda Gilstrap, (MD) Feb. 6, 1845
Richard W??? and Rosetta Bundy, (MD) Aug. 7, 1845
James Percill and Jane Willis, (MD) Feb. 9, 1845
James Presley Saterfield and Easter Manerva Yaden, (MD) Mar. 9, 1845
David Dre??? and ??? Kilgore, (MD) Feb. 1, 1846
William Bozarth and Jane Ringo, (MD) Jan. 1, 1846
Reese Broyles and Jane Jackson, (MD) Aug. 1, 1846
John G. Kirk and Manerva Sloan, (MD) Jan. 11, 1846
M. Barnes and Mary Jane Fraze, (MD) Feb. 15, 1846
E. Gates and Elcana D. Hensley, (MD) Nov. 15, 1846
Elcana D. Hensley and E. Gates, (MD) Nov. 15, 1846
Joseph Sholl and Sarah Floyd, (MD) Mar. 15, 1846
William O. Garrett and Lucinda Smoot, (MD) Jun. 18, 1846
Washington Conn and Martha W. Kimbrough, (MD) Mar. 22, 1846
Adam Grogan and M. Ann Asher, (MD) Apr. 23, 1846
William A. Prather and Sarah Ann Courtney, (MD) May 24, 1846
James Boothe and Susanna ????, (MD) Jul. 25, 1846
Peter Staurley and Peggy Ann Gro???, (MD) Jun. 4, 1846
David Duvall and Priscilla Hofler, (MD) Jan. 6, 1846
John Courtney and Elizabeth Miller, (MD) May 8, 1846
Zacharia Crosen and Sally England, (MD) Nov. 9, 1846
James B. Baker and Mary Stevens, (MD) Nov. 1, 1847
Emanuel Patten and July Capps, (MD) Feb. 1, 1847
John W. Wells and ??? Rose, (MD) Jan. 1, 1847
Ambrose Cole and Nancy Moore, (MD) Apr. 11, 1847
Joseph Nesbit and Mary Ho???, (MD) Nov. 14, 1847
Adam Shoemaker and Louisa Holeman, (MD) Feb. 14, 1847
George A. Kreps and Elizabeth Ann Bean, (MD) Feb. 15, 1847
John S. Crandle and Malinda Range, (MD) Sep. 16, 1847
G. M. Kirk and Ann E. Withrow, (MD) Jul. 18, 1847
??? Titus and Mary Chrystal, (MD) Nov. 18, 1847
Thomas M. Lofton and Elizabeth Jane Moore, (MD) Aug. 22, 1847
Frederick Coghill and Elizabeth Kil???, (MD) Sep. 23, 1847

Willis E. G???? and Frances Kirk, (MD) Jul. 28, 1847
Henry M. Barnes and Nancy Allred, (MD) Aug. 29, 1847
Lewis Lay and Mary Capps, (MD) Nov. 4, 1847
Thomas Dodson and Lucinda1 Grogan, (MD) Aug. 5, 1847
Andrew H. Linder and Nancy Samuels, (MD) Nov. 9, 1847
Henry Adkins and Charity Calison, (MD) Aug. 10, 1848
Edward Adkins and Helen A. Bushnell, (MD) Jan. 13, 1848
James. Cain and Lucinda Rice, (MD) Nov. 16, 1848
Jesse Stclair and Selinda McPherson, (MD) May 16, 1848
Richmond Stice and Martha Jane Barnes, (MD) Jan. 16, 1848
Platt Montgomery and Mary Jane Griffin, (MD) Feb. 17, 1848
George Drewry and Margaret A. Rose, (MD) Nov. 19, 1848
William F. Moffitt and Nancy Jane Stice, (MD) Apr. 2, 1848
J???? Cooley and Permelia Williams, (MD) Apr. 20, 1848
Asberry Frey and Elizabeth Sears, (MD) Jan. 23, 1848
Samuel Persha and Mellicent Brashears, (MD) Apr. 23, 1848
A. C. Stukey and Amanda Cunningham, (MD) Jun. 25, 1848
Nelson Grogan and Patsy Phelps, (MD) Mar. 26, 1848
Isaih Franklin and Matilda C. Allred, (MD) Nov. 26, 1848
Asa K. Collet and Bathsheba Cain, (MD) Feb. 27, 1848
James Williams and Delila Lon, (MD) Jan. 30, 1848
Shelton Biswell and Nancy J. Moffet, (MD) Dec. 5, 1848
M. Bradgan and Sally Nelson, (MD) Jul. 6, 1848
Solomon S. P. Kerbey and Californa C. Barnes, (MD) Apr. 6, 1848
David Rorabaugh and Mary Ann Smallwood, (MD) Apr. 6, 1848
Thomas Knight and Amanda Grogan, (MD) Feb. 9, 1848
John Samuels and Elizabeth Williams, (MD) Jan. 9, 1848
Hiram Smith and Sally Phr???, (MD) Nov. 10, 1849
Edward W. Parcels and Rebecca A. Rowlin, (MD) Feb. 11, 1849
Andrew Burnard and Mary Ann Beeman, (MD) Aug. 16, 1849
John Hence and Phebe Ann Eperly, (MD) Jun. 16, 1849
James Overstreet and Mary Ann Dodson, (MD) Oct. 18, 1849
James Murphey and Basitha D????, (MD) Dec. 2, 1849
Major L. Adk???? and Mary Brassfield, (MD) Oct. 2, 1849
Silas Holloway and Charlotte Allred, (MD) Sep. 20, 1849
Elisha Botts and Sarah Holeman, (MD) Oct. 21, 1849
Isaac ????hens and Nancy Ann Bradshaw, (MD) Dec. 27, 1849
Isom Cox and Elizabeth D. Littlepage, (MD) Dec. 28, 1849
James Ringo and Theresa Ann Bozarth, (MD) Mar. 3, 1849
John R. Adkins and Ellen Eliza Neff, (MD) Feb. 4, 1849
Ephraim C. Kreps and Mary Ann Nelson, (MD) Jul. 5, 1849
Greenup Prather and Elizabeth Murphy, (MD) Sep. 8, 1849
James P. Grogan and Milly T????, (MD) Oct. 9, 1849

J. Lay and Easter Capps, (MD) Nov. 9, 1849
Henry M. Davis and Clemenza Goss, (MD) Apr. 14, 1850
Anderson Ivie and Narcissus Grogan, (MD) Dec. 1, 1850
Rev. Henry M. Turner and Sarah A. Eby, (MD) Oct. 1, 1850
Thomas Hickman and Margaret Allen, (MD) Nov. 12, 1850
George W. Adkins and Margaret C. Hannah, (MD) Nov. 14, 1850
Charles S. Kirk and Caroline Withrow, (MD) Jan. 15, 1850
James Williams and Martha Grogan, (MD) May 16, 1850
Henry W. Cail and A. Sloan, (MD) Aug. 18, 1850
John Hodges and Susanna ?????, (MD) Apr. 18, 1850
James B. Rogers and Eliza Beeman, (MD) Mar. 21, 1850
James M. Stout and Louisa Jane McCormick, (MD) Apr. 21, 1850
Kreps ???? and Julie Ann ????, (MD) Dec. 24, 1850
James L. Morton and Charlotte C. Baker, (MD) Feb. 25, 1850
James C. True and Juli Ann Burns, (MD) May 9, 1850
Bright G. Barrow and M. Ferguson, (MD) May 1, 1851
Woolrey Hoover and Ann Marie Criswell, (MD) Nov. 1, 1851
John Rodes and Johns, (MD) Mar.yAug. 10, 1851
Andrew Capps and Lucretia J. Allen, (MD) Oct. 12, 1851
Jacob Gilstrap and Sarah Jane Wilson, (MD) Oct. 12, 1851
Joseph E. Adkins and Martha J. Smith, (MD) Nov. 13, 1851
??? Ford and Martha Ringo, (MD) Nov. 13, 1851
James B. Jackson and Elizabeth Bozarth, (MD) Jan. 17, 1851
Mathew Oliver and Elizabeth Clifton, (MD) Jun. 21, 1851
George W. Burns and Sarah Ann Shipley, (MD) Feb. 23, 1851
James Broyles and ???? Wortman, (MD) Feb. 24, 1851
James Wilson and Anney Clarissa Morelock, (MD) Sep. 25, 1851
Harvey Phelps and Polly Ann Ivie, (MD) Apr. 26, 1851
John Jones and Winnie Margaret Conn, (MD) May 27, 1851
Colden W. Hardin and Julia Ann Alexander, (MD) Apr. 3, 1851
E. Smith and Adolph Sohlop, (MD) Mar. 31, 1851
Adolph Sohlop and E. Smith, (MD) Mar. 31, 1851
William Hansley and ??? Lay, (MD) Oct. 5, 1851
Stephen Wilson and Sarah M. Baty, (MD) Oct. 8, 1851
Jesse Edwards and Elizabeth M Young, (MD) Jan. 1, 1852
??? Greenstreet and Lavina ????, (MD) Oct. 1, 1852
James Coffee and Sophia Cibanon, (MD) Mar. 11, 1852
William Moore and Sarah Gates, (MD) Aug. 12, 1852
??? Scobie and Emily Sargant, (MD) Dec. 12, 1852
Martin I. Collett and L. Sullivan, (MD) Jul. 15, 1852
Andrew I. Miller and Jane ????, (MD) Jul. 15, 1852
George Dodson and Nancy Russell, (MD) Nov. 16, 1852
George M. Meeks and Cynthia Cunningham, (MD) Oct. 17, 1852

Nathan Jeans and F ???, (MD) Jan. 18, 1852
Daniel G. Clem and Sarah Hankins, (MD) Jan. 18, 1852
Ephraim Patterson and Margaret ????, (MD) Nov. 18, 1852
William I. Cook and Rachel Morris, (MD) Mar. 21, 1852
Robert Choat and Mrs. Virginia Maxey, (MD) Oct. 21, 1852
John W. Galyen and Eliza Jane Linder, (MD) Mar. 23, 1852
Nathan Greenstreet and Lucinda Cain, (MD) Oct. 24, 1852
William Ivie and Harriet Stockton, (MD) Jul. 25, 1852
Richard G. Allen and Nancy C. Ledford, (MD) Mar. 25, 1852
Elijah Mariah and H. ????, (MD) Mar. 25, 1852
John R. Wanger and Elizabeth Huffer, (MD) Sep. 26, 1852
Licugus Bozarth and Permelia Palmatory, (MD) Aug. 5, 1852
William Morton and H. Robinson, (MD) Jul. 6, 1852
Alfred W. Greene and ??? Sloan, (MD) Oct. 7, 1852
Joseph W. Hatfield and Matilda J. Partin, (MD) Feb. 8, 1852
J. W. Coghill and Susan Floyd, (MD) Jul. 8, 1852
Joseph Wilson and Frances Hodges, (MD) Aug. 9, 1852
Simon Rorabaugh and Sarah Katherine Smallwood, (MD) Jun. 1, 1853
J. Ford and Leah Ringo, (MD) Jan. 11, 1853
Joel Botts and Maria Krepps, (MD) Dec. 12, 1853
Aaron Collins and Nancy McDowell, (MD) Dec. 12, 1853
Abraham Stice and Rhoda Stice, (MD) Aug. 13, 1853
William J. Hargis and Mary Turner, (MD) Apr. 15, 1853
James Ivie and Mary Jane Brownell, (MD) May 15, 1853
William Lay and Mary Ann Gilmore, (MD) Oct. 16, 1853
Fustin Cubolin and Elmira Pollard, (MD) Nov. 17, 1853
Hardin Douglas and Sarah Andrews, (MD) Aug. 18, 1853
Joseph Parrish and Katheryn Johnson, (MD) Jul. 18, 1853
Peter Deardorff and Nancy Williams, (MD) Dec. 19, 1853
Jackson Gupton and Eliza Standerford, (MD) Oct. 2, 1853
J. W. Harris and Mary Rose, (MD) Dec. 20, 1853
Cersan F. Drake and Rachel Standerford, (MD) Mar. 20, 1853
John Shivley and Rachel Bradshaw, (MD) Mar. 20, 1853
A. Rownines and Rebecca Williams, (MD) Oct. 20, 1853
William Bozarth and Catherine Snyder, (MD) Nov. 27, 1853
Newton Williams and Nancy Sarah Cross, (MD) Dec. 29, 1853
L. Trewit and Lucinda Cizemore, (MD) Jul. 31, 1853
Jonas Shott and Catherine Shoop, (MD) Sep. 4, 1853
John Young and M. Greenstreet, (MD) Aug. 6, 1853
Thomas Wood and Sarah Jane Prather, (MD) Jan. 6, 1853
Elias Harris and Phebe Ann Hence, (MD) Mar. 6, 1853
Dennis Brassfield and Rachel M. Rorahbaugh, (MD) Apr. 7, 1853
James H. Wilson and Augusta Earhart, (MD) Oct. 1, 1854

Joseph Gill and Pheby Garrett, (MD) Dec. 10, 1854
John Burns and Eliza Cox, (MD) Jul. 13, 1854
William C. Buranard and Matilda Jane Dabney, (MD) Dec. 14, 1854
David Smith Alexander and Mary Elizabeth Swetman, (MD) Apr. 15, 1854
Hezekiah Phelps and July Ann Beard, (MD) Aug. 15, 1854
John Osborn and Elizabeth Bell, (MD) Dec. 15, 1854
Josiah F. Dennend and Mary Satterfield, (MD) Dec. 19, 1854
A. Jurbler and Lida Cox, (MD) Apr. 2, 1854
Danie Simpson and Levicia Capps, (MD) Dec. 21, 1854
???? Snyder and Manerva Shaw, (MD) Jun. 22, 1854
John Floyd and Catherine Branstetter, (MD) Mar. 23, 1854
William Withrow and Mary ????, (MD) Mar. 23, 1854
Thomas Hickman and Elizabeth Scobee, (MD) Nov. 23, 1854
A. Phelps and Mary Elendor Moore, (MD) Nov. 23, 1854
John Loe and Margaret Wood, (MD) Dec. 24, 1854
Payden Callison and Susan Callison, (MD) Dec. 26, 1854
Sarah Moore and Calvin ????, (MD) Dec. 26, 1854
Frais M. Cason and Nancy J. Long, (MD) Apr. 27, 1854
Lewis Watters and Mary Ann Wortman, (MD) Aug. 27, 1854
E. C. Jones and Elizabeth Snyder, (MD) Nov. 28, 1854
James Buckaloo and Mary Jane Stice, (MD) May 29, 1854
Samuel E. Gates and Mary Jane ????, (MD) Mar. 3, 1854
Thomas B. Parcels and Rebecca Hubbard, (MD) Aug. 30, 1854
John Q. Dennon and Elizabeth Hankins, (MD) Jul. 4, 1854
Hiram Atkins and Eliza Logston, (MD) May 4, 1854
Henry Howard and Margaret Schraeler, (MD) Aug. 5, 1854
Arrates Billington and Elizabeth E. Leadford, (MD) Feb. 5, 1854
Andrew Jackson Mathis and Sally Jane Allen, (MD) Jun. 5, 1854
James Powers and Priscilla Barrett, (MD) Oct. 6, 1854
Jesse Borman and Elizabeth Ann Woolfork, (MD) Apr. 8, 1854
Simon Shoop and Elizabeth McPheteridge, (MD) Jun. 8, 1854
William Halloway and Mary Stone, (MD) Feb. 9, 1854
George Jackson and Hannah E. Ready, (MD) Feb. 1, 1855
William D. Baty and Eliza Jane Meeks, (MD) Apr. 1, 1855
Simon Epperly and M. Hamlin, (MD) Feb. 1, 1855
Simon Peter Kreps and Catherine Lee, (MD) Sep. 1, 1855
Thomas B. Nelson and ??? ????, (MD) Dec. 10, 1855
John Broyles and Elizabeth Smallwood, (MD) Jun. 10, 1855
George W. Capps and Cighty Malinda Boryls, (MD) Jun. 10, 1855
Cyrus Novinger and Sarah Knouff, (MD) Dec. 11, 1855
Samuel Scobey and Hannah Yae, (MD) Dec. 13, 1855
Edward B. Ruddy and Martha Ann Turner, (MD) Feb. 15, 1855
Z. B. Greenstreet and Martha Stice, (MD) Jul. 15, 1855

Jonathon Ogdon and Catherine Chambers, (MD) Jan. 17, 1855
Isaac B. Thompkins and Sarah ????, (MD) Dec. 19, 1855
David P. Patterson and Missouri Ann Stuart, (MD) Dec. 2, 1855
Benjamin Jackson and M. Elizabeth White, (MD) Mar. 20, 1855
??? Hilt and Sarah Ann Sloan, (MD) Feb. 21, 1855
Thomas Wilson and Mary Shoemaker, (MD) Jun. 21, 1855
Isaac Still and Mariah Dodson, (MD) Apr. 22, 1855
William Rogers and M. Elizabeth Hibbard, (MD) Oct. 24, 1855
Oliver Bain and Mahala Hamlin, (MD) Nov. 25, 1855
Joseph Christian and Daffuneced Romine, (MD) Oct. 25, 1855
Frances Samuel Griffith and R. A. Wright, (MD) Apr. 26, 1855
R. A. C. Wright and Frances Samuel Griffith, (MD) Apr. 26, 1855
I. Baker and Andrew D. Maden, (MD) Jun. 26, 1855
Andrew D. Maden and I. Baker, (MD) Jun. 26, 1855
Henry C. Mathews and Mary Davidson, (MD) Dec. 27, 1855
William M. Ransom and Mary S. Shantz, (MD) Jul. 3, 1855
Charles Groves and Catherine Deep, (MD) Aug. 30, 1855
Elijah Swinford and Susanna McKinny, (MD) Dec. 30, 1855
T. J. Burns and Lucretia Jane Boyd, (MD) Oct. 4, 1855
Nathaniel Williams and Malinda Holman, (MD) Dec. 6, 1855
John D. Holloway and Charlotte Hansacker, (MD) Mar. 8, 1855
Jonas Shott and Ollie McPhetridge, (MD) Aug. 9, 1855
J. Marsh and Lucretia Winscott, (MD) Apr. 1, 1856
E. Phillips and Leonard Ruderford, (MD) Apr. 1, 1856
Leonard Ruderford and E. Phillips, (MD) Apr. 1, 1856
Eliza Denning and William Martin, (MD) Dec. 1, 1856
William Martin and Eliza Denning, (MD) Dec. 1, 1856
T. Jefferson Barnett and M. Painter, (MD) Feb. 1, 1856
George Henry Eizer and Mary Elizabeth Courtney, (MD) Feb. 1, 1856
??? Phillips and Sophia Anspach, (MD) Nov. 1, 1856
N. M. Tull and Risa Linder, (MD) Sep. 1, 1856
William Thornington and Sarah A. Sellars, (MD) May 12, 1856
James C. Clem and Mary A. Rogers, (MD) May 13, 1856
Richard Oliver and Susan Sampson, (MD) Dec. 14, 1856
???? Courtney and Sarah Smith, (MD) Jun. 16, 1856
John Young and Mary T. Adairs, (MD) Apr. 17, 1856
Green Patterson and Jane Brashears, (MD) Aug. 17, 1856
Josiah M. Rogers and Manerva Moore, (MD) Dec. 17, 1856
Almon M. Shively and Mary Cox, (MD) Feb. 17, 1856
Jarrit Suddith and Polly Ann Winscott, (MD) Apr. 19, 1856
Christian Itell and Catherine Etsel, (MD) Mar. 2, 1856
James Watson and Frances Miller, (MD) Aug. 20, 1856
Elijah C. Arnold and Calimted D. Hargrove, (MD) Jan. 20, 1856

George Clemens and Catherine Young, (MD) Oct. 21, 1856
Henry A. Sinclair and Sarah E. McCarty, (MD) Apr. 22, 1856
Joseph Culop and Rebecca McKinney, (MD) Dec. 22, 1856
Joseph Reddow and Catherine True, (MD) Feb. 22, 1856
Don Benedict and Mary Boon Oliver, (MD) Sep. 22, 1856
John Brook and M. Huddleton, (MD) Mar. 23, 1856
M. Huddleton and John Brook, (MD) Mar. 23, 1856
James Morris and Tall Esley, (MD) Jan. 24, 1856
Henry Shook and Catherine Capps, (MD) May 24, 1856
George W. Nelson and Martha Jane Canaday, (MD) Dec. 25, 1856
??? Anspach and Clarrisa Gorgan, (MD) Sep. 25, 1856
Thomas T. Burrus and Elizabeth Ann Brown, (MD) Jul. 26, 1856
Isham Dodson and Elizabeth Moore, (MD) Jul. 27, 1856
D. B. Stuteville and Mary Dickinson, (MD) Jun. 27, 1856
Jacob H. Baysinger and Amanda Miller, (MD) Jun. 29, 1856
James N. Barton and Rachel Ann Earhart, (MD) Apr. 3, 1856
Perry Phipps and Eliza Hargrave, (MD) Jul. 3, 1856
Josiah Morgan and Susan Emily Cox, (MD) Jul. 30, 1856
Horatio S. Parcels and Sarah E. Thomas, (MD) Dec. 4, 1856
Marion Munden and Elizabeth Miller, (MD) Sep. 4, 1856
Jerome Emmons and Mary Ann Filley, (MD) Aug. 5, 1856
Isaac Evans and ??? Asher, (MD) Mar. 6, 1856
John Grogan and Emerine Phelps, (MD) Sep. 6, 1856
William Smith and Sarah A. Link, (MD) Aug. 7, 1856
Wiley Fortner and Mary Eiffort, (MD) May 8, 1856
Alexander D. Hickman and Cyrena Shipley, (MD) Feb. 1, 1857
Hiram Hall and Mahala E. Dockery, (MD) Jul. 1, 1857
Elijah Osborn and Charlotte Gash, (MD) Oct. 1, 1857
James P. Patten and Juliana ????, (MD) Oct. 1, 1857
Stephen G. Ely and Mary Jane Clem, (MD) Dec. 10, 1857
Peter Wortman and Sarah Ellen Wright, (MD) Feb. 10, 1857
James E. Ruggles and Susan McArty, (MD) Sep. 10, 1857
Solomon Sweet and Elizabeth Kinkade, (MD) Aug. 11, 1857
Galaliah Williams and Mary Morgan, (MD) Oct. 11, 1857
John Sage and Amanda Dodson, (MD) Jul. 12, 1857
Elijah Hargis and ??? Ogdon, (MD) Aug. 15, 1857
Jefferson Campbell and Anna Lowery, (MD) Jan. 15, 1857
William Sterling and Mary Lucinda Yates, (MD) May 17, 1857
Samuel Dye and Nancy Lemaster, (MD) Sep. 17, 1857
Elvan, Allen, Jr., and Elizabeth Mary (MD) Oct. 18, 1857
Edmund H. Knapp and Margaret E. Lorton, (MD) Jul. 19, 1857
George D. Moody and Martha Jane Jones, (MD) Apr. 2, 1857
R. Roberts and Mary Ann Clark, (MD) Jul. 2, 1857

Abraham Beeman and Sophia Kolmier, (MD) May 21, 1857
W. P. Darnell and Mary Ann Burnett, (MD) May 21, 1857
David Wisener and Ann McCarty, (MD) Jan. 22, 1857
Reuben D. Tice and Mary ????, (MD) Apr. 23, 1857
Thomas Clark and Susanna McCoy, (MD) Oct. 23, 1857
Burr Musick and Elgivie Sampson, (MD) May 24, 1857
Samuel C. Farmer and Permelia Ann Tolbert, (MD) Feb. 25, 1857
Maj. P. Roberts and Margaret M. Mullenix, (MD) Oct. 25, 1857
James Hatfield and Eveline Greenwood, (MD) Mar. 26, 1857
John Baker and Mary Maxey, (MD) May 26, 1857
Elisha Botts and Elisa R. Jackson, (MD) Apr. 27, 1857
William Baker and Mary A. Everhart, (MD) Aug. 29, 1857
Louis Allred and Clarinda Lycan, (MD) Jan. 29, 1857
David B. Richardson and Unethie Smith, (MD) Nov. 29, 1857
William Goundry and Catherine Close, (MD) May 3, 1857
Jesse Judd and Sarah Jane Close, (MD) May 3, 1857
Joseph Fletcher and Nancy Jane Lightfoot, (MD) Sep. 3, 1857
Joseph W. Hanks and Caroline Smith, (MD) Apr. 30, 1857
John Munn and Manda Knox, (MD) Aug. 30, 1857
Chiles M. Phipps and Nancy E. Dunham, (MD) Dec. 31, 1857
George Wesley Miller and Grace F. Miller, (MD) Jan. 4, 1857
William Baker and Sarah Steel, (MD) Oct. 8, 1857
Thomas A Blanchard and Sally Allen, (MD) Jul. 9, 1857
James N. Neff and Mildred ????, (MD) Apr. 1, 1858
William T. Bird and Martha C. Hanna, (MD) Aug. 1, 1858
John Daniel and Jane McCiva, (MD) Aug. 1, 1858
Thomas A. Morrow and Lucy Ann ????, (MD) Aug. 1, 1858
John Berry and Catharine Darnall, (MD) Dec. 1, 1858
Joseph Wright and Angeline Gardner, (MD) Dec. 1, 1858
William R. Beshears and Ann E. Boarman, (MD) Feb. 1, 1858
E. W. Morelock and Charity Gates, (MD) Jan. 1, 1858
Cyrus Evans and ??? (MD) Mar. 1, 1858
John D. Garard and Sarah Tinstmen, (MD) Oct. 1, 1858
Worden Koonce and Rose Ann McCarver, (MD) Sep. 1, 1858
George Salada and Christena Wright, (MD) Sep. 1, 1858
John Bryant and Murati ????, (MD) Nov. 10, 1858
Edmund L. Clifton and Martha Ann Kimbell, (MD) Oct. 10, 1858
James Garrett and Elizabeth Hovis, (MD) Oct. 10, 1858
William Jackson Wells and Eliza Jane Wells, (MD) Nov. 13, 1858
Harrison F. Hays and Rachel J. Waddill, (MD) Oct. 14, 1858
Levi Griswold and Ebba Lemaster, (MD) Feb. 15, 1858
Robert Harris and Rebecca A. Porter, (MD) Feb. 15, 1858
Ebba Lemaster and Levi Griswold, (MD) Feb. 15, 1858

Milton Gray and Elizabeth Ringo, (MD) Mar. 15, 1858
William Martin and Mary Pangborn, (MD) Mar. 15, 1858
Phillip Shoop and Frances Shontz, (MD) Sep. 16, 1858
Cornelius Knapp and Amassey Ann Elliott, (MD) Nov. 17, 1858
John W. Greathouse and Rebecca Hill, (MD) Jul. 18, 1858
Lawrence Darnell and Malissa Setters, (MD) Nov. 18, 1858
Francis M. Evans and Rachel Asher, (MD) Apr. 19, 1858
Solomon Otto and Fannie Trustman, (MD) Aug. 19, 1858
Gates Sizemore and Sarah Reed, (MD) Aug. 19, 1858
Benjamin J. Bragg and Laura Brownell, (MD) Dec. 19, 1858
Joseph R. Allred and Catherine M. Livingston, (MD) Dec. 2, 1858
David Conner and ???? ????, (MD) Apr. 20, 1858
John W. Morgan and Martha J. ????, (MD) Feb. 20, 1858
Nicholas W. Smith and Jane Osburn, (MD) Jun. 20, 1858
Henry Nelson and Mary Waddill, (MD) Jan. 21, 1858
John Shaffer and Sarah Tracy, (MD) Jun. 22, 1858
Samuel Baker and Harriet Dilts, (MD) Dec. 23, 1858
R. A. Ray and Frances Ellen Beecher, (MD) Dec. 23, 1858
Andrew H., Jr. Linder and Manerva Samuels, (MD) May 23, 1858
Jonathan W. Waddill and Isabella Darrow, (MD) Oct. 24, 1858
George W. Murphy and Rosa Ellen Ensick, (MD) Feb. 25, 1858
James Moore and Minerva Campbell, (MD) Nov. 25, 1858
Franklin Davis and Drucilla Casteel, (MD) Apr. 27, 1858
William Daniels and Lucinda Beech, (MD) Apr. 28, 1858
William Lightfoot and ??? Adkins, (MD) Jan. 28, 1858
William A Cooper and Mary ????, (MD) Jan. 3, 1858
Francis M. Brashears and Sarah Jane McCoy, (MD) Dec. 30, 1858
Lewis S. Musick and Mary Ann Scobee, (MD) Sep. 30, 1858
Samuel McGrew and Elizabeth Smoot, (MD) Jan. 4, 1858
James Frankfort and Amanda Movinger, (MD) Dec. 5, 1858
Edmund M. Breedlove and Marilla Moody, (MD) Sep. 7, 1858
Marilla Moody and Edmund M. Breedlove, (MD) Sep. 7, 1858
Dillon Cole and Dorothy Kolhlmyer, (MD) Aug. 8, 1858
Jeremiah Johnson and Joheptta ???, (MD) Jul. 8, 1858
George W. Keller and Louisa McDowell, (MD) Mar. 9, 1858
John Barnhart and ???? ????, (MD) Apr. 1, 1859
George Smith and Mary D. Asher, (MD) Dec. 1, 1859
J. R. Good and Hanner ????, (MD) Jun. 1, 1859
James Foster and Ellen Evans, (MD) Aug. 11, 1859
Isaac Cromfield and Malinda Sanders, (MD) Jan. 11, 1859
James Round and Mary Catherine Moore, (MD) Sep. 11, 1859
William Thayer and J. Allen, (MD) Mar. 12, 1859
Solomon Goodson and Fannie Grogan, (MD) Nov. 12, 1859

Silas N. Rose and Elizabeth Hubbard, (MD) Apr. 13, 1859
Andrew Scott and Mary Bailey, (MD) Apr. 14, 1859
Alfred M. Fowler and Martha Ann ????, (MD) Jul. 14, 1859
Andrew M. Gregg and Virginia Workman, (MD) May 15, 1859
John McDonner and Rachel Lambright, (MD) Nov. 15, 1859
William Towles and Catherine Knight, (MD) Sep. 15, 1859
John Fowler and Palmonia Emily Cain, (MD) Jan. 16, 1859
William Standley and Susan T. Sulley, (MD) Jun. 16, 1859
William R. Reynolds and Ruth D. Story, (MD) Jan. 17, 1859
Jacob Ludwig and Elizabeth Smith, (MD) Nov. 17, 1859
Dewett Dover and Mary Ann Flerer, (MD) Apr. 18, 1859
Elevin Powell and Elizabeth S. Gregg, (MD) Sep. 18, 1859
John J. Lent and Eliza Ann Lightfoot, (MD) May 19, 1859
Jacob McCoy and Rebecca Watson, (MD) Jan. 2, 1859
James Newcomb and Elizabeth Jane Horton, (MD) Jan. 20, 1859
Eugene Wooley and Mary Beveradge, (MD) Oct. 20, 1859
Charles H. Manite and Susan Stineman, (MD) Aug. 22, 1859
Thomas Branstetter and Sarah E. Withrow, (MD) Dec. 22, 1859
W. F. Davis and Cordelia Morris, (MD) Dec. 22, 1859
William M. Otto and Martha Swetman, (MD) Sep. 22, 1859
Hiram Johns and Martha Sanders, (MD) Aug. 23, 1859
Charles Farr and Ann Pinkerton, (MD) Nov. 23, 1859
Vi Henning and Jane Greenstreet, (MD) Oct. 23, 1859
??? Dolan and Malinda Wortman, (MD) Dec. 25, 1859
Elisha Sawyer and Julia Wales, (MD) Sep. 25, 1859
Joseph A. Myers and Margaret J. Watson, (MD) Jan. 26, 1859
Sandofal Detebitts and Mary Malissa Savey, (MD) Jun. 26, 1859
Hiziekah Patterson and Hannah Green, (MD) Oct. 27, 1859
Nathaniel Billington and Louisa Oretta Brownell, (MD) Mar. 3, 1859
Alphonso Hickerson and Mandy Robbins, (MD) Mar. 3, 1859
Daniel Harris and Martha Decker, (MD) Mar. 31, 1859
Theophilus Roberson and Philadelphia ????, (MD) Mar. 31, 1859
Phillip Earhart and Elizabeth Peak, (MD) Dec. 4, 1859
Harrison Shull and Lydia Reynolds, (MD) Dec. 4, 1859
Rodalph W. Thomson and Linda J. Lutz, (MD) Dec. 4, 1859
S. Ball and Nancy Ogdon, (MD) Oct. 5, 1859
Enoch Williams and Margaret Marks, (MD) Jan. 6, 1859
Frederick M. Shelton and Elizabeth Spenney, (MD) Aug. 8, 1859
James J. Foster and Sarah E. Good, (MD) Oct. 9, 1859
John Alexander and Sarah Elizabeth Kirby, (MD) Jul. 11, 1860
Finley M. Walker and Mary E. Coghill, (MD) Apr. 1, 1860
Moses Furnish and Laura Case, (MD) Jan. 1, 1860
William P. Linder and Nancy Linder, (MD) Jan. 1, 1860

John Sparks and Barbary ????, (MD) Jul. 1, 1860
J. A. Morris and Lucinda Wright, (MD) Mar. 1, 1860
Andrew Walters and Isadora Gleason, (MD) Mar. 1, 1860
John Ray and Rebecca Sloan, (MD) Nov. 1, 1860
Joseph Morrow and C. ????, (MD) Oct. 1, 1860
James A. Harvey and Serena Bagee, (MD) Sep. 1, 1860
Jacob Saner and Lucinda Stinson, (MD) Jun. 10, 1860
John Thunbach and Catherine ????, (MD) Nov. 11, 1860
George W. Salsberry and Polly Rebecca Hodges, (MD) Jan. 12, 1860
J. Knox and Emily J. Lazier, (MD) Sep. 12, 1860
Almond W. Little and Sarah Ann ????, (MD) Jun. 13, 1860
George W. Cain and Christinia Novinger, (MD) May 13, 1860
Joseph R. Matchett and Sarah Jane Dodson, (MD) Sep. 13, 1860
James R. Gilstrap and Eliza ????, (MD) Jun. 14, 1860
Joseph Morrow and Margaret May, (MD) Jan. 15, 1860
Isaac T. Bell and Catherine Simbler, (MD) Mar. 15, 1860
Thomas Parcells and Sarah C. Ferguson, (MD) Apr. 16, 1860
Joseph T. Hickman and Sintha Ellen Hendricks, (MD) Dec. 16, 1860
Simon Shoop and Wilthy Cook, (MD) Dec. 16, 1860
Vanburen Dodson and Mary Ann Gardner, (MD) Sep. 16, 1860
John Cain and Parthena B. Gallion, (MD) Feb. 17, 1860
John Kissner and Catherine Wineman, (MD) Jun. 17, 1860
Ashum Moody and Alice Sandbone, (MD) Jan. 18, 1860
John Hall and Lydia Osburn, (MD) Oct. 18, 1860
Henry Woolery and Nancy McCoy, (MD) Feb. 19, 1860
Robert Willis and Sarah Floyd, (MD) Jan. 2, 1860
Albert Robinson and Elizabeth Elliott, (MD) Sep. 2, 1860
Silas G. Phipps and ??? ????, (MD) Dec. 20, 1860
Jesse Coghill and Mary E. Horton, (MD) Feb. 22, 1860
Elijah W. Bozarth and Martha E. ????, (MD) Jan. 22, 1860
Otis Butworth and Susan Barkhart, (MD) Mar. 22, 1860
Newton L. Drennen and Phebe Corbin, (MD) Nov. 22, 1860
Breckenridge Campbell and Nancy Cheek, (MD) Oct. 22, 1860
Jacob F. Waddill and M. J. Adkins, (MD) Sep. 23, 1860
Jefferson Salsbury and Amanda Slover, (MD) Oct. 24, 1860
Henry Berry and Susan A. Shoop, (MD) Dec. 25, 1860
James Reed and Nancy Lemasters, (MD) Dec. 25, 1860
Newton A. Powell and Mary Jane Walker, (MD) Oct. 25, 1860
William T. Payne and Sarah E. Paul, (MD) Apr. 26, 1860
Thadious W. Bozarth and Elizabeth S. Spivay, (MD) Feb. 26, 1860
Hiram W. Snyder and Eveline Evans, (MD) Dec. 27, 1860
James M. Stubbs and Elizabeth Jane Fletcher, (MD) Feb. 28, 1860
James Stevens and Catherine Roberts, (MD) Nov. 28, 1860

Milton Hickman and Martha Ann Steines, (MD) Jan. 29, 1860
B. F. Law and Susanna L. Mikeal, (MD) Jul. 29, 1860
David C. Morelock and Ann E. Atkins, (MD) Mar. 29, 1860
Ephraim Osburn and Elizabeth Clark, (MD) Jun. 3, 1860
Clinton Withrow and Catherine A. Johns, (MD) Dec. 30, 1860
John Saunders and Jane Scobee, (MD) Sep. 30, 1860
Benjamin A. Dunham and Barbara E. Dye, (MD) Jan. 4, 1860
???? Martin and Jane Fowler, (MD) Nov. 4, 1860
John Brown and Mary Allensworth, (MD) Dec. 5, 1860
Ira G. Harmon and Nancy Nicholas, (MD) Jun. 5, 1860
Horatio Paul and Sarah A. Cornell, (MD) Mar. 5, 1860
George W Chinn and Ellen E. Mosley, (MD) May 6, 1860
H. H. Swasey and Millie E. Campbell, (MD) May 6, 1860
Joseph Burns and Elizabeth Boyd, (MD) Sep. 6, 1860
H. Bird Foster and Martha J. Ferguson, (MD) Sep. 6, 1860
Ellet Moots and Jane Wilcher, (MD) Sep. 6, 1860
Joseph Ringo and Emily M. Foster, (MD) Feb. 9, 1860
Samuel Grigsby and Julia Greenstreet, (MD) Aug. 1, 1861
William Clifton and Elizabeth ????, (MD) Dec. 1, 1861
James R. Davison and M. Houk, (MD) Feb. 1, 1861
M. Houk and James R. Davison, (MD) Feb. 1, 1861
R. W. Lyon and Hettie L. Henton, (MD) Feb. 1, 1861
George W. Stuckey and Margaret M. Cunningham, (MD) Feb. 10, 1861
Samuel Conkel and Mary Ann Gillham, (MD) Oct. 10, 1861
John L. Porter and Mary E. Ivie, (MD) Oct. 10, 1861
Clark Adkins and Louisa ????, (MD) Jun. 13, 1861
Jesse Griffin and Sarah E. Sweet, (MD) Oct. 13, 1861
John W. Owens and Rebecca Mires, (MD) Sep. 13, 1861
Nicholas Kellon and Nancy Catherine Snow, (MD) Apr. 14, 1861
G. H. Parker and Celesta Jane Austin, (MD) Apr. 14, 1861
Francis O. Willborn and Mary ????, (MD) Feb. 14, 1861
Morgan Franabarger and Sarah Cason, (MD) Jul. 14, 1861
John Moore and Frances Peyton, (MD) Mar. 14, 1861
Samuel Dye and Mary Eubanks, (MD) Dec. 15, 1861
Robert S. Waddill and Margaret J. Dunham, (MD) Dec. 15, 1861
Hugh Abernathy and Jane Lay, (MD) Jun. 16, 1861
William H. Herron and Hannah Ownsby, (MD) Feb. 17, 1861
Morgan Williams and Lucy A. Wood, (MD) Feb. 17, 1861
R. W. Moncrief and M. ????, (MD) Nov. 17, 1861
John Loe and Almanda Palmotory, (MD) Aug. 18, 1861
Michael Howeley and Margaret Hall, (MD) Jan. 18, 1861
Oliver Phelps and Emily Eubanks, (MD) Jul. 18, 1861
Stephen G. Workman and Harriet J. Zimmerman, (MD) Mar. 18, 1861

Jasper N. Moore and Sarah Jane Axton, (MD) Sep. 19, 1861
George H. Ford and Jane Cox, (MD) Sep. 2, 1861
W. H. H. Marine and Margaret H. Dooley, (MD) Oct. 20, 1861
James R. Asher and Zerilda McCarty, (MD) Nov. 21, 1861
William Stewart and Margaret Cullup, (MD) Mar. 21, 1861
Robert Jennings and Mahala ???, (MD) Dec. 22, 1861
Lewis Lay and Rebecca Abermathy, (MD) Jun. 22, 1861
William Tull and Manerva Hopson, (MD) Jun. 23, 1861
John A. Good and Rachel Fortner, (MD) Mar. 24, 1861
Henry Bryan and Frances M. Horton, (MD) Dec. 25, 1861
Willis Chandler and Elizabeth Samuels, (MD) Dec. 25, 1861
James McGown and Priscilla Smith, (MD) Jul. 25, 1861
Irie Thomas and Maggie ????, (MD) Sep. 26, 1861
Lewis Brassfield and Sarah ????, (MD) Jan. 27, 1861
Thomas Vanlandingham and Mrs. Henny Truett, (MD) Jan. 27, 1861
Thomas C. Boyd and Amyrd C. Branaman, (MD) Mar. 28, 1861
Thomas Jordan Overstreet and Clemingred M. Branaman,
    (MD) Mar. 28, 1861
James S. Zigler and Margaret Turner, (MD) Dec. 29, 1861
James Wright and Sarah Elliott, (MD) Feb. 3, 1861
S. A. Aderson and C. S. Ritchee, (MD) Jul. 3, 1861
James Cooley and Sarah Ann Bailey, (MD) Mar. 3, 1861
S. P. Moss and S. W. Williams, (MD) Apr. 4, 1861
S. W. Williams and S. P. Moss, (MD) Apr. 4, 1861
Samuel Withrow and Emily Branstetter, (MD) Aug. 4, 1861
Abraham Johnson and L. Miller, (MD) Dec. 4, 1861
Paten Greenwood and Fannie Foster, (MD) Sep. 5, 1861
Peter H. Moore and Susan C. Smith, (MD) Jan. 6, 1861
Thomas Axton and Nancy Jane Paget, (MD) Oct. 6, 1861
Hiram Cole and Sarah Shoop, (MD) Jan. 7, 1861
Silas Flynn and Sarah Scott, (MD) Mar. 7, 1861
??? Willard and Mary E. Wilson, (MD) Dec. 1, 1862
Enoch Williams and Malissa Mark, (MD) Nov. 1, 1862
Isaac Devan and Welthy ???, (MD) Aug. 10, 1862
Jonathan Sanders and Louisa Sanders, (MD) Aug. 10, 1862
John Bawyer and Sarah Ann Stout, (MD) May 11, 1862
Samuel Bell and Lydia S. Dale, (MD) Nov. 13, 1862
Jacob George Linder and Elizabeth Ransom, (MD) Dec. 14, 1862
G. W. Dunham and Mary J. Chowning, (MD) Aug. 16, 1862
John Waters and Lucinda Gilmore, (MD) Feb. 16, 1862
Henry D. Floyd and Margaret Dean, (MD) Jan. 16, 1862
Alexander Clapper and Catherine Smith, (MD) Mar. 16, 1862
Alexander Covey and Frances V. Markey, (MD) Mar. 19, 1862

Peter Collop and Malissa Sneed, (MD) Mar. 2, 1862
James R. Good and Abbey Willey, (MD) Mar. 2, 1862
Peter J. Beets and Margaret Trowbridge, (MD) Apr. 20, 1862
Samuel Smoyer and Caroline Laisure, (MD) Feb. 20, 1862
John E. Nosworthy and A. Elizabeth (MD) Mar. 20, 1862
Elias Owens and Mrs. Nancy Hays, (MD) Aug. 21, 1862
James E. Palmer and Mary Ann Marsh, (MD) Aug. 22, 1862
Willis B. Harlan and Catherine Rorabaugh, (MD) Jun. 22, 1862
James R. Alexander and Elizabeth J. Dennis, (MD) May 22, 1862
Elizabeth J. Dennis and James R. Alexander, (MD) May 22, 1862
William Ivey and Louisa Greer, (MD) Feb. 23, 1862
George F. Williams and Harriet N. Miles, (MD) Jun. 24, 1862
Joseph H. Workman and Hannah E. Gundy, (MD) Mar. 24, 1862
Andrew Grist and Elizabeth White, (MD) Aug. 26, 1862
J. M. Bozarth and Lucy A. Bozarth, (MD) Dec. 26, 1862
William Nelson and Mary M. Cotton, (MD) Jul. 27, 1862
Joseph Meyers and Sarah Cline, (MD) Dec. 28, 1862
Zephaniah Prather and Charlotte Cline, (MD) Dec. 28, 1862
Charles F. Connelly and Louisa ????, (MD) Feb. 28, 1862
Joseph Jefferies and Dicy Miller, (MD) Feb. 28, 1862
Joseph Rutherford and Mary A. Cunningham, (MD) Dec. 4, 1862
Jacob Lewis and Charlotte Mathena, (MD) Jun. 4, 1862
Charlotte Mathena and Jacob Lewis, (MD) Jun. 4, 1862
Henry Glasgow and Rachel R. Gregg, (MD) Feb. 5, 1862
Thomas J. Phipps and Nancy C. Wilson, (MD) Mar. 5, 1862
J. B. Leighton and Mary J. Wisner, (MD) Jun. 8, 1862
Marcious Samuels and Elizabeth Bell, (MD) Oct. 8, 1862
David Abermathy and L. Kellar, (MD) Feb. 9, 1862
L. Kellar and David Abermathy, (MD) Feb. 9, 1862
Russell Swisher and Harriet Wright, (MD) Dec. 1, 1863
George T. Ridings and M. F. Thrasher, (MD) Oct. 1, 1863
George Wetherford and Sarah J. Jennings, (MD) Dec. 10, 1863
James Abernathy and Elizabeth Walters, (MD) Aug. 12, 1863
Harvey Sloan and Margaret C. Ferguson, (MD) May 12, 1863
Benjamin B. White and Mary Cowell, (MD) Sep. 13, 1863
Milton George Bragg and Ellen Roby, (MD) Mar. 15, 1863
A. W. Cunningham and E. F. Mikels, (MD) Nov. 15, 1863
E. F. Mikels and A. W. Cunningham, (MD) Nov. 15, 1863
John Sherwood Pool and Elizabeth Ann Clem, (MD) Apr. 16, 1863
George Ernest and Joan Wise, (MD) Sep. 16, 1863
O. Patterson and Margaret Jane Peyton, (MD) Feb. 19, 1863
George White and Sarah Ann Scobee, (MD) Jul. 2, 1863
Henry J. Conkle and Eliza J. Patterson, (MD) Aug. 20, 1863

B. G. Barrow and Mary Jane Downing, (MD) Jun. 21, 1863
Marion Dewell and Maria Clarinda Lawrence, (MD) Jan. 22, 1863
John William Brownell and Mary Ellen Tracy, (MD) Mar. 22, 1863
Van P. Clem and Louisa Thompson, (MD) Nov. 26, 1863
Caleb F. Hargis and Cina M. Hall, (MD) Dec. 27, 1863
Edward Braden and Aiznla Shelly, (MD) Oct. 27, 1863
Hubbard M. Dunham and Missouri Ann Peyton, (MD) Jun. 28, 1863
??? Shirer and Ardelia Bardwell, (MD) Oct. 29, 1863
Joseph Mikel and Sarah E. Collop, (MD) Apr. 3, 1863
Richard Chaney and Mrs. Maria Hewitt, (MD) Sep. 30, 1863
Patrick Hanlin and Nancy Byrd, (MD) Mar. 31, 1863
Benjamin P. McGoodwin and Sally A. James, (MD) May 4, 1863
David Bauchman and Cordelia Scobee, (MD) Apr. 5, 1863
George King Beecher and Sarah Elizabeth Low, (MD) Apr. 8, 1863
Hiram T. Hall and Torza L. Hargis, (MD) Oct. 8, 1863
A. Phurius and Virginia Ewing, (MD) Aug. 9, 1863
William C. Stewart and Agnes Gregg, (MD) Feb. 1, 1864
Isaac Braden and Mary E. Tharp, (MD) Mar. 1, 1864
Jackson McGrew and Nelly Walters, (MD) Mar. 1, 1864
Samuel M. McClanahan and Martha Seivirn, (MD) Oct. 1, 1864
Richard Denton and J. A Montcrief, (MD) Mar. 10, 1864
David Samples and Mrs. Amanda Wilson, (MD) Apr. 10, 1864
V. Bernerd and M. J. Mikels, (MD) Jan. 10, 1864
M. J. Mikels and V. Bernerd, (MD) Jan. 10, 1864
Greenfield Houston and Norma A. Hargis, (MD) Jun. 10, 1864
J. A. Montcrief and Richard Denton, (MD) Mar. 10, 1864
F. Blanden and Mary A. ????, (MD) Feb. 11, 1864
Charles S. Moody and Martha B. Wilson, (MD) Feb. 11, 1864
Thomas Phillips and Mary Jane Shoemaker, (MD) Oct. 12, 1864
John Johnson and Mary Amanda Waddill, (MD) Jun. 14, 1864
Leonard Moots and Diana Ritcherson, (MD) Oct. 16, 1864
David Morelock and Sarah F. Bradshaw, (MD) Jan. 17, 1864
Mark Musick and Nancy Jane Bruce, (MD) Mar. 17, 1864
James M. Shores and Elizabeth Little, (MD) Jul. 18, 1864
John B. Ledford and Hannah Bauchman, (MD) Apr. 2, 1864
L. W. Garrison and Emily McIntyre, (MD) Aug. 2, 1864
Noah M. Sloan and Mary M. Simler, (MD) Oct. 2, 1864
Peter Butts and Mary Cook, (MD) Apr. 20, 1864
Noah Read and Catherine Burnett, (MD) May 20, 1864
Jacob Affoltier and Catherine Swagart, (MD) Oct. 20, 1864
Tobias Fellar and Anna ???, (MD) Aug. 24, 1864
Jacob Hartman and Enerie Grogan, (MD) Dec. 25, 1864
George Graham and Ann Patterson, (MD) Dec. 29, 1864

Martin L. Reid and Virginia P. Haynes, (MD) Dec. 29, 1864
William H. Dayton and Frances Ann McGorm, (MD) May 29, 1864
Daniel Sallade and Sarah Jane Good, (MD) Jul. 3, 1864
Peyton F. Greenwood and Julie Ann Bryan, (MD) Mar. 3, 1864
Joseph N. Findley and Louisa Jane Wagner, (MD) Nov. 3, 1864
George W. Coghill and ???? Eifert, (MD) Mar. 31, 1864
William H. Brown and Amanda Kreps, (MD) Aug. 4, 1864
Peter Helwig and Mary Greenstreet, (MD) Dec. 4, 1864
John H. Turner and Angelina M. Sloan, (MD) Mar. 6, 1864
James M. Miller and Sarah M. Webster, (MD) Oct. 6, 1864
John Perrine Deaton and Elizabeth Jane Bragg, (MD) Aug. 7, 1864
A. Lininter and Jane Saladee, (MD) Feb. 7, 1864
Nathan Walters and Mary A. Bish, (MD) Jan. 9, 1864
William A. Ownsby and Sarah F. Dodson, (MD) Jan. 1, 1865
Franklin Wise and Hannah A. Gregg, (MD) Jan. 1, 1865
A. L. Woods and Kate Barnes, (MD) Jan. 1, 1865
Charles W. Simler and Elizabeth Fletcher, (MD) Mar. 1, 1865
D. M. Fiske and J. C. Thatcher, (MD) Nov. 1, 1865
David Johnson and Frances Hays, (MD) Nov. 1, 1865
J. C. Thatcher and D. M. Fiske, (MD) Nov. 1, 1865
William Hall and Dulcina Cane, (MD) Oct. 1, 1865
Charles T. Bryan and Sarah Ellen Towles, (MD) Sep. 1, 1865
Isaac Williams and Catherine Willis, (MD) Apr. 11, 1865
James Collison and Rebecca Salada, (MD) Apr. 12, 1865
James Edward Mountain and Glory Grage, (MD) Dec. 12, 1865
R. C. Warner and Sarah E. Roberts, (MD) Mar. 12, 1865
Henry McBroom and Lydia J. Ferguson, (MD) Nov. 12, 1865
Daniel Hughs and Frances Bragg, (MD) Oct. 12, 1865
William Reason Rupe and Malinda Jane Crow, (MD) Sep. 12, 1865
E. Osborn and Margaret Spears, (MD) Nov. 13, 1865
Elias Pursee and Sarah D. Colving, (MD) Sep. 14, 1865
Benjamin F. Snow and Amanda Wilber, (MD) Sep. 14, 1865
Perlin Snow and George W. Wilber, (MD) Sep. 14, 1865
William H. Steele and Mary E. Spencer, (MD) Sep. 14, 1865
George W. Wilber and Perlin Snow, (MD) Sep. 14, 1865
Robert Lienzy Allen and Catherine Shoemaker, (MD) Mar. 16, 1865
John H. Steele and Hannah Keller, (MD) Nov. 16, 1865
William S. Hutson and Therissa Ann Bozarth, (MD) Sep. 17, 1865
John Rose and Mary Alexander, (MD) Aug. 18, 1865
John Gill and S. M. Samuels, (MD) Nov. 19, 1865
George W. Scoby and Nancy Jane Musick, (MD) Nov. 19, 1865
William Gilman and Mary E. Sebole, (MD) Oct. 19, 1865
Stephen Workman and Landrum F. Wheeler, (MD) Oct. 19, 1865

Alexander Morris and Elizabeth Vanpaypon, (MD) Apr. 2, 1865
Jacob R. Cooke and Catherine Rider, (MD) Jul. 2, 1865
Jacob Haffner and Amanda Piper, (MD) Mar. 2, 1865
Peter Brooks and Nancy Ellen Crawford, (MD) May 2, 1865
William Strunkle and Eliza Ann Smoots, (MD) Jul. 20, 1865
George W. Rutherford and Indiana Hampton, (MD) Sep. 20, 1865
Ira Meads and Malona Wilhite, (MD) Jan. 21, 1865
William Anthony and Sarah Hart, (MD) May 21, 1865
J. W. Ancell and Permelia Ivie, (MD) Sep. 21, 1865
Garlin Moore and Elizabeth A. Clifton, (MD) Jan. 22, 1865
David Brummet and Charlotte Lewis, (MD) Apr. 23, 1865
Jacob Novinger and Susanna Novinger, (MD) Apr. 23, 1865
J. N. Beeman and Armida Powell, (MD) Dec. 23, 1865
Jacob Miles and Margaret Sheltley, (MD) Jul. 23, 1865
B. C. Dodson and Margaret Sinder, (MD) Jun. 23, 1865
Thomas Montgomery and Elizabeth Conkle, (MD) Mar. 23, 1865
Thomas E. Halley and Mary Smith, (MD) Dec. 24, 1865
Egbert A. Polley and Elzora Luider, (MD) Dec. 24, 1865
William Henry Mann and Martha Ann McPheteridge, (MD) Jul. 25, 1865
Marion B. Brown and Mary Ann Utt, (MD) May 25, 1865
William J. Killgore and Rebecca Hinton, (MD) Oct. 25, 1865
John Henry Parrot and Caroline Powers, (MD) Jan. 26, 1865
Joseph D. Holeman and Elizabeth Emely Watson, (MD) Aug. 27, 1865
Joseph Leggett and Sarah Linder, (MD) Dec. 28, 1865
Jupiter Webb and Mrs. Rhoda Webb, (MD) Dec. 28, 1865
Daniel McGimes and Elizabeth Seivets, (MD) Jul. 28, 1865
Daniel McGrimes and Elizabeth Seivets, (MD) Jul. 28, 1865
Nelson Wisner and Mary F. Hirkle, (MD) Jun. 28, 1865
John Schsan and Emma F. McFerron, (MD) Nov. 28, 1865
James Parker Pinkerton and Prissa Ann Watson, (MD) Sep. 28, 1865
Joshua W. Bird and Lydia E. Leech, (MD) Apr. 30, 1865
Eamanuel J. Courtney and Elizabeth H. Wood, (MD) Aug. 30, 1865
Alfred Lowe and Martha McMahan, (MD) Jul. 30, 1865
Parker H. Holmes and Abbie Stout, (MD) Mar. 30, 1865
Joseph Bradshaw and Mary Thornton, (MD) Aug. 31, 1865
Benjamin F. Linder and Sarah E. Thompson, (MD) Aug. 31, 1865
William A. Wilks and Margaret E. Hannah, (MD) Jul. 31, 1865
John Stouts and Katheryn A. Smith, (MD) May 4, 1865
Napoleon Wilson and Lidia Morris, (MD) May 4, 1865
Zacheus M. Stanton and Margaret Pryor, (MD) Oct. 4, 1865
George Boley and Sarah Jane Smith, (MD) Aug. 6, 1865
W. H. Griffin and Marion M. Darrow, (MD) Dec. 6, 1865
John William McIntire and Marain Tider, (MD) Dec. 7, 1865

Samuel P. Barnhart and Sfeander ????, (MD) Feb. 7, 1865
Charles Childress and Margaret A. Huffman, (MD) May 7, 1865
Jonathan A. Hill and Elizabeth Ellen Pitt, (MD) May 7, 1865
C. C. Ott and H. L. Walker, (MD) Nov. 7, 1865
H. L. Walker and C. C. Ott, (MD) Nov. 7, 1865
George Markey and Lydia Ann Brummet, (MD) Oct. 7, 1865
Francis M. Emmons and Ann Grason, (MD) Jan. 8, 1865
Francis Marion Waters and Nancy Eleanor Stuteville, (MD) Jan. 8, 1865
W. J. Burris and Sarah Slover, (MD) Feb. 9, 1865
William M. Hughs and C. Branaman, (MD) Feb. 9, 1865
William Lee and Rachel Louisa Eller, (MD) Mar. 9, 1865
Marcus G. Richland and Sarah E. Tharp, (MD) May 9, 1865
John K. Pickens and Rhody Ann Pickens, (MD) Apr. 1, 1866
John Hayes and Hadassah A. Page, (MD) Jan. 1, 1866
George Baty and Margaret Sanders, (MD) Mar. 1, 1866
Henry Volker and Anna Behrens, (MD) Jun. 10, 1866
John W. Bradley and Mary E. Laughlin, (MD) Apr. 11, 1866
Berry Bates and Mrs. Minerva Bates, (MD) Feb. 11, 1866
Reuben Hughbanks and Mrs. Frances Hughbanks, (MD) Feb. 11, 1866
Andrew J. Elmore and Emma Staniford, (MD) Mar. 11, 1866
George R. Brewington and Lyda Freeman, (MD) Nov. 11, 1866
J. R. Davis and Kitty Parcells, (MD) Sep. 11, 1866
James B. Logston and Julia Ann Snow, (MD) Dec. 12, 1866
William P. Nason and Mrs. Sarah Thompson, (MD) Jun. 12, 1866
James N. Dodson and Mary Barnes, (MD) Dec. 13, 1866
John Courtney and Mrs. Mary Maxey, (MD) May 13, 1866
W. H. Dunham and Letta Marquess, (MD) Jan. 14, 1866
Ody Moore and Jane Clifton, (MD) Jan. 14, 1866
David Coop Powell and Sarah Ellen Ross, (MD) Jan. 14, 1866
Robert N. Taylor and Mary Jane Mikel, (MD) Jan. 14, 1866
Mariban Waterman and Mary E. McCoy, (MD) Mar. 14, 1866
John Calvin Presser and Margaret Ann Collett, (MD) Apr. 15, 1866
Henry Stuky and Mrs. Susan Cunningham, (MD) Feb. 15, 1866
Richard W. Davis and Mrs. Cynthia Martin, (MD) Jul. 15, 1866
William H. Watson and Sarah J. Millay, (MD) Mar. 15, 1866
Reuben Keller and Mary Sal??? Conkle, (MD) Aug. 16, 1866
William H. Shelby and Ester Cook, (MD) Aug. 16, 1866
Perry Scott and Mary Ann Powell, (MD) Feb. 16, 1866
O. C. Snider and Mary Ellen Alexander, (MD) Jan. 16, 1866
William Miller and Mary Kimbel, (MD) Sep. 16, 1866
James Wait and Amanda Lee, (MD) Feb. 17, 1866
John Williams and Debby C. Morrow, (MD) Jan. 17, 1866
William Law and Marigain Furnish, (MD) Jun. 17, 1866

Gilbert Steen and Casandra Collier, (MD) Nov. 17, 1866
Albert Easly and Amanda E. Denton, (MD) Oct. 17, 1866
John Porter and Mary Brown, (MD) Oct. 17, 1866
Samuel Wagner and Elizabeth Cook, (MD) Feb. 18, 1866
Edwin P. Hammermen and Mrs. Maggie Thomas, (MD) Jan. 18, 1866
George Halley and Mary Baker, (MD) Jun. 18, 1866
James R. Smith and Ruth Ann Clifton, (MD) Mar. 18, 1866
John Snyder and Jane Purgett, (MD) Mar. 18, 1866
Frederick Markey and Mary Jane Knapp, (MD) Nov. 18, 1866
Samuel Abercromby and Eleanor Linder, (MD) Apr. 19, 1866
John L. Watson and Mary E. Miller, (MD) Aug. 19, 1866
Thomas S. Hamilton and Laura Ellen Ilgenfritz, (MD) Dec. 19, 1866
John L. A. Armstrong and Ellen Gill, (MD) May 19, 1866
James Monroe Andrews and Elizabeth C. Lemons, (MD) Dec. 2, 1866
Henry Otto and Sarah E. Grim, (MD) Dec. 2, 1866
William A. Robinson and Louisa J. Maddox, (MD) Oct. 2, 1866
W. O. H. P. Ammeriman and F. S. Wright, (MD) Dec. 20, 1866
James E. Gordan and Matilda Suteman, (MD) Feb. 20, 1866
James B. Crawford and Mrs. Elizabeth Scott, (MD) Feb. 21, 1866
James T. True and Mary E. Featherly, (MD) Feb. 21, 1866
James W. Novinger and Elizabeth Shoop, (MD) Jan. 21, 1866
E. T. Huffman and Eleanor A. Clark, (MD) May 21, 1866
Benjamin Franklin and Mary M. Lanker, (MD) Apr. 22, 1866
Phillip Sharr and Emiline Linder, (MD) Apr. 22, 1866
John Lorton and Sarah Carolina Crow, (MD) Feb. 22, 1866
Adam Shoop and Chaney Sibley, (MD) Feb. 22, 1866
J. T. Todd and Maggie L. Alexander, (MD) Feb. 22, 1866
George W. Farr and Ann Farr, (MD) Jan. 22, 1866
Jacob Smith and Hannah J. Hamlin, (MD) Jun. 22, 1866
Henry Drake and Sarah Catherine Webb, (MD) Mar. 22, 1866
James F. Johnson and Mrs. Martha Ellmore, (MD) Mar. 22, 1866
James T. Kent and Mary E. Walker, (MD) Mar. 22, 1866
Thompson Dodge and Sarah Arorabaugh, (MD) Sep. 22, 1866
Henry Applegate and Mrs. Susan Buhl, (MD) Sep. 23, 1866
Peter Quindle and Mrs. Catherine Felker, (MD) Jun. 24, 1866
George W. Dunham and Christina Strunk, (MD) Dec. 25, 1866
Noah Anspach and Rena Loe, (MD) Feb. 25, 1866
Carl Nelson and Mary Young, (MD) Mar. 25, 1866
J. N. Meeks and Mrs. Lizzie Linder, (MD) Oct. 26, 1866
William C. Linder and Sarah Catherine Linder, (MD) Dec. 27, 1866
R. L. Bassett and Mrs. Rebecca Greathouse, (MD) Oct. 27, 1866
William L. Adkins and Ellen Nora Branam, (MD) Jan. 28, 1866
James Jones and Mrs. Susan Jones, (MD) Jan. 28, 1866

George W. Pryor and America J. Speer, (MD) Oct. 28, 1866
John R. Hayden and Mrs. Malinda Hayden, (MD) Jun. 29, 1866
John T. Crane and Amanda Stinson, (MD) Mar. 29, 1866
Moses Banses and Eliza Avers, (MD) Aug. 3, 1866
James Musick and Enis Greensteed, (MD) May 3, 1866
Samuel L. Derold and Mary E. Dye, (MD) Dec. 30, 1866
Peter Reese and Sarah Shoop, (MD) Dec. 30, 1866
David H. Ronsesburg and Mary J. Saffle, (MD) Dec. 30, 1866
Silas C. Greenslate and Sarah A. Crosby, (MD) Sep. 30, 1866
Alexander Mackentire and Mrs. Rebecca Kimbel, (MD) Sep. 30, 1866
Gideon A. Richey and Serina Allison, (MD) Aug. 4, 1866
Charles Stodd and Louisa Hayden, (MD) Jan. 4, 1866
Richard Barnhart and Mrs. Ann Campbell, (MD) Mar. 4, 1866
Salem J. Row and Martha Ann Otto, (MD) Mar. 4, 1866
Justin R. Douglass and Mary E. Middleton, (MD) Nov. 4, 1866
R. L. Powers and Debbie Thatcher, (MD) Aug. 5, 1866
Edman Wallis and Amanda Carpenter, (MD) Feb. 5, 1866
Samuel Beach and Catherine ????, (MD) Mar. 5, 1866
Ezra Wilson and Mary Smith, (MD) Sep. 5, 1866
J. M. Asher and Maggie Howe, (MD) Dec. 6, 1866
William Schrader and Mrs. Martha Murry, (MD) May 6, 1866
William R. Cullison and Mrs. Rebecca Johnston, (MD) Sep. 6, 1866
Adron Floyd and Sarah Willis, (MD) Aug. 7, 1866
James H. Gimings and Sarah F. Voss, (MD) Feb. 7, 1866
Harvey Conley and Elizabeth Loe, (MD) Mar. 7, 1866
John D. Correll and Martha Gates, (MD) Oct. 7, 1866
Henry Helwig and Harriet Greenstreet, (MD) Oct. 7, 1866
Isaac Morgan and Mary S. Canada, (MD) Feb. 8, 1866
M. P. Hannah and Margaretta Alexander, (MD) Jul. 8, 1866
George Shoop and Catherine Novinger, (MD) Jul. 8, 1866
James Thomas Herring and Ann Mercer, (MD) Nov. 8, 1866
John W. Hardin and Lucinda Willis, (MD) Dec. 9, 1866
Thomas Tuder and Hannah M. Waddill, (MD) Jan. 9, 1866
Solomon Bachman and Angeline Capps, (MD) Aug. 1, 1867
Thomas Roseberry and Martha Scobee, (MD) Aug. 1, 1867
T. B. C. Coleman and Margaret Ann Bulkley, (MD) Jan. 1, 1867
S. F. Miller and Maggie A. Kennedy, (MD) Oct. 1, 1867
Elvan Allen and Elizabeth Adkins, (MD) Sep. 1, 1867
Richardson Havens and Nancy Scovil, (MD) Dec. 10, 1867
Wilson Borden and Margaret Dulaney, (MD) Feb. 10, 1867
William Roberson and Ida Rebecca Davis, (MD) Jan. 10, 1867
R. H. Livingston and Mary J. Selby, (MD) Mar. 10, 1867
George W. Dixon and Ellen Newman, (MD) May 10, 1867

Thomas Sims and Sarah S. Wysong, (MD) May 10, 1867
William H. Linsey and Emily Clark, (MD) Nov. 10, 1867
Ludwig Baum and Caroline Sanders, (MD) Sep. 10, 1867
Martin Goolsberry and Mrs. Rebecca Ward, (MD) Sep. 10, 1867
Isaac Anspach and Jane Mahewy, (MD) Apr. 11, 1867
Joshua R. Eller and Ann E. Morgan, (MD) Apr. 11, 1867
J. L. Hainline and Lucinda Martin, (MD) Feb. 11, 1867
G. W. Vanhorn and Martha Jane Still, (MD) Feb. 12, 1867
Ambrose G. Capps and Eliza J. Webster, (MD) May 12, 1867
John Zeigler and Norah Bozarth, (MD) May 12, 1867
David H. Bailey and Mrs. Sarah ????, (MD) Sep. 12, 1867
Emanuel R. Pickens and Hannah E. Scobee, (MD) Jan. 13, 1867
William A. Ewing and Sarah E. Reynolds, (MD) Oct. 13, 1867
George W. Cragen and Hester Hays, (MD) Apr. 14, 1867
James H. Hays and Elizabeth E. Allen, (MD) Apr. 14, 1867
Jonas Shoot and Ann Wallis, (MD) Apr. 14, 1867
James Sibole and Christina Sanders, (MD) Feb. 14, 1867
Samuel Zeigler and ???? Bozarth, (MD) Jul. 14, 1867
John P. Marquess and Mary S. Long, (MD) Mar. 14, 1867
John M. Wright and Eliza J. Johnson, (MD) Mar. 14, 1867
Thomas May and Nancy J. Hickman, (MD) Nov. 14, 1867
E. Eubanks and Flora M. Cochran, (MD) Feb. 15, 1867
Jonah Wallace and Susan M. Sloan, (MD) Jun. 16, 1867
William Willey and Martha Grogan, (MD) Jun. 16, 1867
Charles P. Pool and Eveline Dotson, (MD) Feb. 17, 1867
John R. King and Mrs. Mildred Fletcher, (MD) Jan. 17, 1867
Henry Mulch and Sarah Jane McFarron, (MD) Jan. 17, 1867
Lewis J. Atterberry and Julia A Cem, (MD) Oct. 17, 1867
W. M. Gill and Annie Link, (MD) Oct. 17, 1867
Jesse S. C. Hardin and Columbia Lorton, (MD) Oct. 17, 1867
Columbia Lorton and Jesse S. Hardin, (MD) Oct. 17, 1867
Augustus Bolenger and Louise Scobee, (MD) Aug. 18, 1867
Joseph G. Cline and Mary Lante, (MD) Aug. 18, 1867
Edward M. Steel and Nancy E. Hankins, (MD) May 19, 1867
Robert G. David and Eliza Hartford, (MD) Sep. 19, 1867
John Bishop and Sarah Hamlin, (MD) Mar. 2, 1867
Thomas Sanders and Mrs. Elizabeth Wright, (MD) May 2, 1867
Jonathan Russell and Mrs. Nancy Livingston, (MD) Nov. 2, 1867
Jerome Daniel and Rebecca Beets, (MD) Oct. 2, 1867
Benjamin F. Conner and Charlotte E. Sandford, (MD) Sep. 2, 1867
Provine Jerrard and Sina Hayes, (MD) Dec. 20, 1867
George Macer and Molly Payton, (MD) Jun. 20, 1867
John Lehi and Jane Cortrite, (MD) Feb. 21, 1867

Joseph C. McCoy and Mrs. Rhoda Young, (MD) Sep. 21, 1867
Michel Weaver and Eve Hop, (MD) Dec. 22, 1867
Marshall W. Hahn and Emma D. Hart, (MD) Mar. 22, 1867
Charles Wesley Hankins and Martha Frances Scritchfield, (MD) Dec. 24, 1867
Jasper N. Sibole and Phebe M. Cook, (MD) Dec. 24, 1867
Lewis A. Osborn and Narcissus Jane Vanhorn, (MD) Feb. 24, 1867
David Clark and Cordelia A. Barber, (MD) Jan. 24, 1867
John Miller and Mrs. Elizabeth Watson, (MD) Oct. 24, 1867
Andrew J. McVety and Sarah Conley, (MD) Aug. 25, 1867
Francis Switscher and Amanda Donnelly, (MD) Dec. 25, 1867
Samuel D. Robison and Emila Gerick, (MD) Nov. 25, 1867
Thomas Dockery and Julia E. Luider, (MD) Sep. 26, 1867
Thomas A. Brashers and Laura L. Grason, (MD) Oct. 27, 1867
John Friend and Caroline E. Story, (MD) Oct. 27, 1867
Joseph Hardee and Elizabeth Wagner, (MD) Apr. 28, 1867
James W. Jones and Malissa P. Cain, (MD) Apr. 28, 1867
Charles Anderson and Mrs. Elizabeth Rogers, (MD) Dec. 28, 1867
Isaac Gatten and Matilda Epperly, (MD) Jan. 28, 1867
Benjamin F. Owenby and Mary C. Simpson, (MD) Nov. 28, 1867
R. F. Martin and Mary C. Buoy, (MD) Dec. 29, 1867
Eli Sage and Isabella Sargent, (MD) Dec. 29, 1867
Thomas Donnally and July Ann Punco, (MD) Oct. 29, 1867
Dr. John W. Lee and Mary W. Ross, (MD) Aug. 3, 1867
Reuben W. Miles and Elizabeth Poston, (MD) Jan. 3, 1867
F. M. Floyd and Sarah E. Andrews, (MD) Mar. 3, 1867
Elisha Webb and Clarissa E. Archer, (MD) May 3, 1867
William O. Shannon and Orpha J. Hill, (MD) Nov. 3, 1867
Moses A. Mountain and Anna Elizabeth Brewner, (MD) Dec. 30, 1867
John Deeton and Mary R. Musick, (MD) Jun. 30, 1867
John W. Burns and Mrs. Elizabeth Overstreet, (MD) May 30, 1867
Alfred J. Cowell and Louise E Adkins, (MD) May 30, 1867
William C. Post and Elizabeth C. Hays, (MD) Mar. 31, 1867
John O. Waulker and Ann Mann Ware, (MD) Mar. 31, 1867
David C. Ratliff and Lucy J. Adkins, (MD) Oct. 31, 1867
C. W. Swetman and Sarah M. Christian, (MD) Oct. 31, 1867
Augustus Moore and Olney Rosanna Henderson, (MD) Aug. 5, 1867
James Hall and Cynthia Ann Francis, (MD) Dec. 5, 1867
W. R. Paulding and Sarah Hays, (MD) May 5, 1867
Osamouse Waters and Libbie Kinth, (MD) May 5, 1867
David Bruner and Malinda Dabney, (MD) Feb. 6, 1867
Thomas Bruner and Mary Dabney, (MD) Feb. 6, 1867
William W. Setters and Catherine Byrd, (MD) Jan. 6, 1867

C. J. Pollock and Alice Pierce, (MD) Nov. 6, 1867
Henry M. Prather and Roseane Doomey, (MD) Oct. 6, 1867
James Rager and Sarah Fegly, (MD) Apr. 7, 1867
Barnet W. Crimpsley and Jane Rodgers, (MD) Feb. 7, 1867
Elijah C. Dunham and Mary A. Moore, (MD) Feb. 7, 1867
George W. Dodson and Nellie Graves, (MD) Nov. 7, 1867
Jacob Madden and Ricka Stark, (MD) Nov. 7, 1867
Rick Stark and Jacob Madden, (MD) Nov. 7, 1867
James K. P. Morelock and Harriet E. Gilmore, (MD) Jun. 9, 1867
George W. Novinger and Mary Jane Matter, (MD) Jun. 9, 1867
Andrew J. Ludwig and Mary Wakely, (MD) Oct. 9, 1867
G. B. Cunningham and Ann C. Eitel, (MD) Jan. 1, 1868
Andrew Jackson Farr and Catherine M. Pinkerton, (MD) Jan. 1, 1868
William Redinger and Mary Carnagey, (MD) Jan. 1, 1868
William J. Sandry and Catha. Capps, (MD) Nov. 1, 1868
George Spencer and Sarah Antney, (MD) Nov. 1, 1868
Lowlary Hupper and Polly Ann Courtney, (MD) Apr. 10, 1868
Mary J. Cole and Thomas Harp, (MD) Jun. 10, 1868
Thomas Harp and Mary J. Cole, (MD) Jun. 10, 1868
E. R. Damrell and Mary Bishop, (MD) May 10, 1868
H. F. Armstrong and S. J. Bell, (MD) Sep. 10, 1868
Chauncey J. Jerome and Abbie Parker, (MD) Feb. 11, 1868
John H. Morris and Fannie Tull, (MD) Jun. 11, 1868
James Williams and Rachel Pinkerton, (MD) Mar. 11, 1868
Henry S. Hannah and Nancy Lazure, (MD) Oct. 11, 1868
Joseph D., Sr. Holeman and Mrs. ??? Mark, (MD) Oct. 11, 1868
George M. Waddill and Martha A. Sparks, (MD) Dec. 12, 1868
Jasper Wilson and Mary Pool, (MD) Aug. 13, 1868
James Scrivners and Margaret Linder, (MD) Dec. 13, 1868
Isaac M. Crow and Mary E. Conner, (MD) Feb. 13, 1868
Francis Hairl and Mary Elizabeth Alepanter, (MD) Feb. 13, 1868
George Buckner and Louise Pollard, (MD) May 13, 1868
Louise Pollard and George Buckner, (MD) May 13, 1868
Bartlett Asher and Eliza Pnkston, (MD) Nov. 13, 1868
Samuel Montgomery and Sarah E. Sizemore, (MD) Apr. 14, 1868
Abraham Voorheis and Mariah Lowe, (MD) Apr. 15, 1868
Andrew Cole and Hannah Ricketts, (MD) Nov. 15, 1868
Edmond W. Otto and Sarah Sharr, (MD) Nov. 15, 1868
Samuel Elmer Lindsey and Maranda Jane Roberson, (MD) Oct. 15, 1868
Benjamin F. Sibole and Margaret Elze, (MD) Oct. 15, 1868
David Byers and Maria E. Robb, (MD) Feb. 16, 1868
John Hayse and Nancy P. Voorhies, (MD) Feb. 16, 1868
George H. Rutherford and Susanna Shoemaker, (MD) Mar. 17, 1868

Austin Coffey and Eliza Goldsby, (MD) Sep. 17, 1868
Oliver Ridgeway and Emma Orr, (MD) Nov. 18, 1868
Thomas H. Robertson and Charity Sarah Smith, (MD) Oct. 18, 1868
James P. Adams and Mary E. Good, (MD) Jan. 19, 1868
Euriah P. Smith and Laura P. Pinkston, (MD) Jan. 19, 1868
Thomas C. Parker and Frances A. Smith, (MD) May 19, 1868
Simon D. Elsea and Sarah E. Hughes, (MD) Nov. 19, 1868
Peter Vodker and Catherine Cutter, (MD) Nov. 19, 1868
William H. Grule and Molly A. Shecks, (MD) Jan. 2, 1868
Patrick Moran and Martha J. Wilson, (MD) Jan. 2, 1868
Amos L. Woods and Sally T. Ivie, (MD) Jan. 2, 1868
William B. Keown and Ellen A. Potter, (MD) Jul. 2, 1868
William H. Shadwell and Margaret E. Howerton, (MD) Feb. 20, 1868
William H. Atwell and Catherine ????, (MD) Sep. 20, 1868
Salem Roe and Clara Mountain, (MD) Apr. 21, 1868
Peter McGraw and Alvira Hayes, (MD) Jun. 21, 1868
George Eubanks and Narcis Garrett, (MD) May 21, 1868
John M. Johnson and Maria E. Thorson, (MD) Feb. 22, 1868
Hugh Mikel and Amanda J. Low, (MD) Jan. 22, 1868
???? Rolen and Elizabeth Parsells, (MD) Jan. 22, 1868
George Clemmerson and Sarah Taylor, (MD) Mar. 22, 1868
G. A. Coulter and Sintha A. Andrews, (MD) Mar. 22, 1868
Edward E. Hall and Susanna E. Young, (MD) Mar. 22, 1868
Cornelius Weaver and Susan E. Embree, (MD) Nov. 22, 1868
Samuel Cammel and Ann E. Brummett, (MD) Oct. 22, 1868
??? Hewitt and Ida Cochran, (MD) Dec. 23, 1868
M. A. Epson and W. C. Morrow, (MD) Jan. 23, 1868
W. C. Morrow and M. A. Epson, (MD) Jan. 23, 1868
William T. Crowder and Marinda Mason, (MD) Sep. 23, 1868
Alden Moore and Clara McCune, (MD) Sep. 23, 1868
Jerome B. Greenstate and Isabelle C. Christ, (MD) Dec. 24, 1868
Frederick Metz and Martha Z. Johnson, (MD) Dec. 24, 1868
Nelson Thomas and Mrs. Elizabeth Wolf, (MD) Jan. 24, 1868
John Thrasher and Nancy Conkle, (MD) Mar. 24, 1868
Veni David and Mary A. Hartford, (MD) Dec. 25, 1868
Calvin L. Elsea and Elizabeth Dixon, (MD) Dec. 25, 1868
Henry H. Dodd and Margaret Morrow, (MD) Mar. 25, 1868
John A. Truitt and Sarah Ann Dockery, (MD) Nov. 25, 1868
William Cunningham and Elizabeth Darrel, (MD) Jul. 26, 1868
John Still and Mary Ann Hibbard, (MD) Mar. 26, 1868
George W. Notestine and Della Hildreth, (MD) Dec. 27, 1868
James Courtney and Almira D. Maxey, (MD) Sep. 27, 1868
William Waugh and Louisa Thornton, (MD) Sep. 27, 1868

Thomas E. Halley and Loeta M. Clark, (MD) Jun. 28, 1868
Daniel L. Merrill and Dorcas Smith, (MD) Jun. 28, 1868
Garret Miller and Sarah F. Long, (MD) Mar. 29, 1868
Ludwig Schelly and Argda Matt, (MD) Mar. 29, 1868
Caleb Collins and Sarah E. Doley, (MD) Oct. 29, 1868
George M. Mikel and Susan E. Furnish, (MD) Apr. 3, 1868
R. H. Currier and Catherine McKinney, (MD) Dec. 3, 1868
John A. Richardson and Sally E. Baird, (MD) Dec. 3, 1868
James R. Morgan and Sarah A. Culver, (MD) Jun. 3, 1868
Casper Plumer and Icaphena Owenby, (MD) Jun. 3, 1868
John F. Thorp and Barbara C. Sanders, (MD) Aug. 30, 1868
W. H. Corbin and Ruth Verden, (MD) Dec. 30, 1868
Solomon May and Mrs. Eliza Sanders, (MD) Jan. 30, 1868
J. H. Hollenbeck and Fannie Barnes, (MD) Dec. 31, 1868
Timothy Halstead and Manerva A. Cason, (MD) Jul. 4, 1868
Joshua Hale and Jerusha E. Lay, (MD) Oct. 4, 1868
Andrew J. Grayson and Amanda J. Watson, (MD) Apr. 5, 1868
William Banstetter and Angeline Cunningham, (MD) Aug. 5, 1868
Jahyle Roberson and Sadie Lindsey, (MD) Aug. 5, 1868
James Behymer and Mary E. Axton, (MD) Dec. 6, 1868
James Rudington and Viola Haines, (MD) Jul. 6, 1868
George Jacobs and Mary Belles, (MD) May 8, 1868
Benjamin F. Ivie and Martha J. Moss, (MD) Nov. 8, 1868
John H. McCartney and Marada J. Graham, (MD) Nov. 8, 1868
Henry C. John and Rebecca A. Shelley, (MD) Oct. 8, 1868
Thomas B. Gooce and Sarah A. Hawk, (MD) Aug. 9, 1868
William Waters and Mary Jackson, (MD) Jan. 9, 1868
John Calvin and Lida Woods, (MD) Apr. 1, 1869
Thomas Cole and Elizabeth A. Ricketts, (MD) Aug. 1, 1869
David Bricker and Vashtia Bailey, (MD) Jan. 1, 1869
James L. Hart and Mary J. Jones, (MD) Jan. 1, 1869
Lutron Byrns and Elizabeth Airs, (MD) Jul. 1, 1869
Isum B. Dabney and Manery Jane Bernard, (MD) Nov. 1, 1869
Isaac Bellows and Rebecca Turner, (MD) Jan. 10, 1869
Daniel Dumey and M. A. Prather, (MD) Jan. 10, 1869
Samuel R. Dunham and Laura E. Jennings, (MD) Jun. 10, 1869
Cyrus E. Hamler and Priscilla Shoemaker, (MD) Oct. 10, 1869
Columbus Noble and Susan Hardin, (MD) Sep. 11, 1869
Rev. A. J. Garlock and Jane G. Kelly, (MD) Jul. 11, 1869
Robert Davis and Mary E. White, (MD) Jun. 11, 1869
Michael Collins and Malissa Bell, (MD) Mar. 11, 1869
George Huddleston and Aba J. Farlow, (MD) May 11, 1869
Aaron Burges and Susan Fifer, (MD) Nov. 11, 1869

Jones Williams and Lucy E. Stott, (MD) Oct. 11, 1869
Albert Gibson and Mary E. Stanton, (MD) Sep. 11, 1869
David Stonecipher and Louisa Young, (MD) Oct. 12, 1869
William R. Adams and Eliza Nelson, (MD) Sep. 12, 1869
Joseph Miller and Anna Lantz, (MD) Jul. 13, 1869
Z. W. Walker and Elizabeth Brown, (MD) Jun. 13, 1869
Winfield S. Ledford and Martha ????, (MD) May 13, 1869
James M. Smiley and Sarah M. McMahan, (MD) Feb. 14, 1869
Isaiah W. Snell and Catherine E. Fox, (MD) Feb. 14, 1869
T. J. Campbell and E. S. Horton, (MD) Jan. 14, 1869
E. S. Horton and T. J. Campbell, (MD) Jan. 14, 1869
Hiram Shirkey and Ester Jane Lewis, (MD) Jan. 14, 1869
Rufus J. Richey and Nancy Williams, (MD) Mar. 14, 1869
James D. Waddill and Margaret Tuttle, (MD) Mar. 14, 1869
S. P. Truitt and Mary Dorr, (MD) Nov. 14, 1869
James Bell and Euthay Brough, (MD) Feb. 15, 1869
Martin V. Atterberry and Margaret Cem, (MD) Jan. 16, 1869
E. D. Eversaul and Diana Gunning, (MD) Sep. 16, 1869
A. S. Sanford and M. E. Summers, (MD) Sep. 16, 1869
M. E. Summers and A. S. Sanford, (MD) Sep. 16, 1869
Alonzo D. Smith and Marilla J. Campbell, (MD) Jan. 17, 1869
H. C. Branam and Mrs. Ann Bates, (MD) Jun. 17, 1869
Henry F. Millam and Elizabeth Brewington, (MD) Nov. 17, 1869
George L. Daniels and Nancy Trobridge, (MD) Oct. 17, 1869
Porter R. Smith and Susan C. Kirk, (MD) Sep. 17, 1869
William P. Cason and Frances Die, (MD) Apr. 18, 1869
Valentine Judd and Delila Allen, (MD) Apr. 18, 1869
Lewis Linder and Josenia Foster, (MD) Apr. 18, 1869
Benjamin Roberts and Alice Harris, (MD) Apr. 18, 1869
Irvin M. Stewart and Hannah M. Selvy, (MD) Apr. 18, 1869
Jesse Davis and Tempa Chadwell, (MD) Mar. 18, 1869
David Mountain and Elizabeth M. Darr, (MD) Mar. 18, 1869
R. L. Livingston and Mrs. M. Powers, (MD) Oct. 18, 1869
Russell T. Crow and Sarah E. Stewart, (MD) Aug. 19, 1869
John P. Wells and Ann J. Ely, (MD) Dec. 19, 1869
William Walters and Sarah Ellen Huffman, (MD) Jul. 19, 1869
Hugh M. Anderson and Elizabeth A. Woodworth, (MD) Oct. 19, 1869
James A. Alger and Laura A. Butler, (MD) Dec. 2, 1869
J. Henry C. Nupman and Catherine Propst, (MD) Jan. 2, 1869
David F. Hall and Joanah Jeffers, (MD) Jun. 20, 1869
James R. Houghton and Cerelda Hunsaker, (MD) Nov. 20, 1869
Osker Tiffany and Susan Frances Luder, (MD) Sep. 20, 1869
Alonzo F. C. Hannah and Georgeann Vine, (MD) Dec. 21, 1869

Georgeann Vine and Alonzo F. Hannah, (MD) Dec. 21, 1869
Harrison Watson and Catherine A. Young, (MD) Mar. 21, 1869
Edward Mattix and Harret E. Knox, (MD) Nov. 21, 1869
William McPeteridge and Sarah Elizabeth Bozarth, (MD) Nov. 21, 1869
Gabrel Tuttle and Sarah E. Biliter, (MD) Apr. 22, 1869
John H. Hinton and Mary Dulena Gates, (MD) Dec. 22, 1869
Jacob Schafer and Mary Vesper, (MD) Mar. 22, 1869
Daniel Miner and Martha Logston, (MD) Nov. 22, 1869
Richard M. Ringo and Tennessee Haynes, (MD) Nov. 22, 1869
Scott Walters and Lavina J. Lesher, (MD) Apr. 23, 1869
Emma E. Burk and John Leech, (MD) Jan. 23, 1869
John Leech and Emma E. Burk, (MD) Jan. 23, 1869
William Hendrin and Eliza Dunham, (MD) Jul. 23, 1869
Joseph Byrns and Lyda S. Lord, (MD) Mar. 23, 1869
Daniel W. Rigger and Virginia Stutiville, (MD) May 23, 1869
Elijah Snow and Sarah Jane Vice, (MD) Nov. 23, 1869
Wesley Farr and Louise ?????, (MD) Jan. 24, 1869
Jacob Kolmyer and Amana Hunley, (MD) Jan. 24, 1869
Frederick Nalie and Elizabeth Schrader, (MD) Jan. 24, 1869
Marion Munn and Mary B. Walker, (MD) Oct. 24, 1869
D. C. Scott and Emma ????, (MD) Oct. 24, 1869
John Turk and Nancy Mikels, (MD) Oct. 24, 1869
Zena Keller and Christena McGill, (MD) Aug. 25, 1869
John Meek and Jennie Morgan, (MD) Jan. 25, 1869
Jonathan Shott and Margaret Freal, (MD) Jul. 25, 1869
James Wilber Davidson and Manerva Pittman, (MD) Mar. 25, 1869
Thomas Gates and Martha J. Walters, (MD) Mar. 25, 1869
Martha Jane Miles and Henry Sterling, (MD) Sep. 25, 1869
Henry Sterling and Martha Jane Miles, (MD) Sep. 25, 1869
William J. Farris and Martha A. Smith, (MD) Aug. 26, 1869
Samuel Lutz and Julia Slover, (MD) Dec. 26, 1869
William Wilson and Harriet Tipton, (MD) Jan. 26, 1869
Nelson Grogan and Dicy Miller, (MD) May 27, 1869
Enoch Stiver and Elizabeth J. Murray, (MD) Aug. 28, 1869
Milton Thomas Bragg and Nancy Thrush, (MD) Dec. 28, 1869
James G. Dunham and Edurldia Pugh, (MD) Dec. 28, 1869
Allen Brackney and Loretta Hoover, (MD) Jan. 28, 1869
Evans Miller and Lucretia Bland, (MD) Jan. 28, 1869
Samuel T. Furruah and Nora Eveline Brundhee, (MD) Jul. 28, 1869
Stephen Robbins and Ellen Hamilton, (MD) Jun. 28, 1869
James Post and Sarah Jane Stanley, (MD) Mar. 28, 1869
George W. Pulliam and Sarah E. Stuteville, (MD) Nov. 28, 1869
Robert E. Taylor and Margaret Hill, (MD) Oct. 28, 1869

Harvey Kernodle and Della Collins, (MD) Dec. 29, 1869
William F. Willis and Susan Floyd, (MD) Mar. 29, 1869
Sylester Hill and Jane Keller, (MD) Dec. 3, 1869
Andrew Stuart and Margaret Lasure, (MD) Jan. 3, 1869
D. G. Jacobs and Amanda F. Brown, (MD) Mar. 3, 1869
Robert Smith and Samantha Parks, (MD) Aug. 30, 1869
Carey H. Frankum and Anna B. Smith, (MD) Dec. 30, 1869
John W. Wese and Jennie Grant, (MD) Dec. 30, 1869
John R. Horn and Martha Jane Hicks, (MD) Nov. 30, 1869
John Waldon Zeigler and Cynthia Ann Dockery, (MD) Jan. 31, 1869
Samuel B. Lewis and Eliza Anderson, (MD) Oct. 31, 1869
Kinzey Cline and Sarah E. Gillispie, (MD) Jul. 4, 1869
John Sutton and Martha Stevens, (MD) Jul. 4, 1869
Zachariah T. Mann and Miranda Crowder, (MD) Mar. 4, 1869
Charles H. Knapp and Nancy Combs, (MD) Nov. 4, 1869
Thomas Prentice and Nancy Jane Garrett, (MD) Nov. 4, 1869
John Scobee and Lavina Sibole, (MD) Nov. 4, 1869
Jonathan Courtney and Nancy Smith, (MD) Oct. 4, 1869
Hezekiah W. Lyon and Eliza J. Roberts, (MD) Apr. 5, 1869
Jacob Bachman and Elizabeth Claybrook, (MD) Aug. 5, 1869
George Toland and Sarah E. Briddle, (MD) Jan. 5, 1869
John Caskey and Jennie Link, (MD) Jul. 5, 1869
James M. Foster and Lina M. Foster, (MD) Mar. 5, 1869
Charles H. Lee and Laura M. Hargrove, (MD) Jun. 6, 1869
Charles P. Wright and Marisa A. Needles, (MD) Jun. 6, 1869
Arthur M. Hane and Armida J. Frederick, (MD) Dec. 7, 1869
James T. Williams and Amanda Crane, (MD) Feb. 7, 1869
George W. Lord and Nancy A. Smith, (MD) Jan. 7, 1869
P. T. Penington and Setha A. Jones, (MD) Jan. 7, 1869
Harvey Spangler and Emiline Hill, (MD) Mar. 7, 1869
Jerial Bowman and Sally J. Clark, (MD) Nov. 7, 1869
John Ketchum and Bella Dunnington, (MD) Oct. 7, 1869
Marion Still and Ann Andrews, (MD) Sep. 7, 1869
John T. Gillispie and Josephine Herrin, (MD) Apr. 8, 1869
Jefferson Smith and Maggie Chandler, (MD) Apr. 8, 1869
Robert Wallace and Permelia J. Bowens, (MD) Aug. 8, 1869
James Brooks and Sena Hall, (MD) Jul. 8, 1869
Thomas J. Lomax and Mary M. Smith, (MD) Nov. 8, 1869
Willis Little and Jane Bruner, (MD) Sep. 8, 1869
Jacob A. Linder and Mary E. Moss, (MD) May 9, 1869
John Young and Mahala Shoemaker, (MD) Feb. 1, 1870
John Mitchell and Olive Buckley, (MD) Mar. 1, 1870
H. J. Bailey and Nannie J. Elliott, (MD) Feb. 10, 1870

Charles H. Lee and Laura M. Hargrove, (MD) Jun. 6, 1869
Charles P. Wright and Marisa A. Needles, (MD) Jun. 6, 1869
Arthur M. Hane and Armida J. Frederick, (MD) Dec. 7, 1869
James T. Williams and Amanda Crane, (MD) Feb. 7, 1869
George W. Lord and Nancy A. Smith, (MD) Jan. 7, 1869
P. T. Penington and Setha A. Jones, (MD) Jan. 7, 1869
Harvey Spangler and Emiline Hill, (MD) Mar. 7, 1869
Jerial Bowman and Sally J. Clark, (MD) Nov. 7, 1869
John Ketchum and Bella Dunnington, (MD) Oct. 7, 1869
Marion Still and Ann Andrews, (MD) Sep. 7, 1869
John T. Gillispie and Josephine Herrin, (MD) Apr. 8, 1869
Jefferson Smith and Maggie Chandler, (MD) Apr. 8, 1869
Robert Wallace and Permelia J. Bowens, (MD) Aug. 8, 1869
James Brooks and Sena Hall, (MD) Jul. 8, 1869
Thomas J. Lomax and Mary M. Smith, (MD) Nov. 8, 1869
Willis Little and Jane Bruner, (MD) Sep. 8, 1869
Jacob A. Linder and Mary E. Moss, (MD) May 9, 1869
John Young and Mahala Shoemaker, (MD) Feb. 1, 1870
John Mitchell and Olive Buckley, (MD) Mar. 1, 1870
H. J. Bailey and Nannie J. Elliott, (MD) Feb. 10, 1870
W. H. H. Marine and Mary Ann Crawford, (MD) Feb. 10, 1870
Albert Wortman and Mrs. Mary Sorrel, (MD) Mar. 10, 1870
Sampson N. Warner and ??? ????, (MD) Feb. 11, 1870
Albert Ledford and Martha A. Garlock, (MD) Apr. 12, 1870
Peter F. Barnes and Hattie Grant, (MD) Mar. 13, 1870
George W. Ratliff and Mary S. Adkins, (MD) Dec. 15, 1870
John L. Cavitt and Martha Ann Mason, (MD) Mar. 15, 1870
Hezekiah Bowser and Emaline Green, (MD) Jan. 18, 1870
Absalum Cupp and Mary Winn, (MD) Jan. 18, 1870
Joseph C. Reed and Florence Morris, (MD) Feb. 2, 1870
James H. Woodcock and Mary A. Sevier, (MD) Jan. 2, 1870
John Potts and Louise J. Thompson, (MD) May 2, 1870
George W. Chapman and Elizabeth Russell, (MD) Apr. 20, 1870
Homer P. Hilbrant and Clara Ann Godard, (MD) Feb. 20, 1870
Joshua Owings and Mary Roberts, (MD) Feb. 20, 1870
John W. Salade and Matilda Anderson, (MD) Feb. 20, 1870
Thomas Novinger and Elizabeth Ann Novinger, (MD) Jan. 20, 1870
David R. Wharton and Josephine Uber, (MD) Aug. 22, 1870
James S. Gardner and Frances A. Spencer, (MD) Feb. 23, 1870
Frederick Corbin and Mary E. Hankins, (MD) Jan. 23, 1870
Samuel W. Pinkerton and Emily Slover, (MD) Jan. 23, 1870
Robert Bilbey and Sarah Elizabeth Storey, (MD) Mar. 23, 1870
Colman Martin and Emma Riley, (MD) Mar. 24, 1870

Samuel D. Waddill and Cintha C. Utt, (MD) Nov. 22, 1874
Melville A. Church and Malinda A Watson, (MD) Aug. 27, 1874
William M. Hart, Jr., and Susan M. Edwards, (MD) Dec. 27, 1874
Robert S. Waddle and Elizabeth Marquess, (MD) Oct. 8, 1874
Franklin L. McClay and Margaret A. Mauck, (MD) Sep. 5, 1875
David C. Ratliff and Illinois Waddill, (MD) Dec. 8, 1875
Alexander W. Watson and Eliza L. Bond, (MD) Dec. 12, 1876
Philip Miller and Sarah Spencer, (MD) Nov. 23, 1876
George W. Butler and Fannie K. Waddill, (MD) Aug. 31, 1876
Samuel P. Vaughn and Julia A. Voorhies, (MD) Sep. 13, 1877
Jacob Spangler and Mary S. Voorhies, (MD) Dec. 2, 1877
J. L. Watson and Lucy J. Sheeks, (MD) Jan. 13, 1878
Daniel M. Walker and Sarah Lucinda Voorhies, (MD) Feb. 17, 1880
Benjamin F. Mustoe and Charlotte E. Hart, (MD) Dec. 26, 1880
James E. Moore and Maggie E. Carner, (MD) Jul. 3, 1880

St. Louis County, Missouri, *"Kirkwood Monitor," November 10, 1916, Attendees of the Home Guard Circle Dance.*

Mary Webster, Norman Winter, Edna Alexander, Estelle Berg, Nelda Boehm, Lillian Brooks, King Amber, Elmer Berthold, Nelda Burham, Frank Cochran, Nellie Darley, Roberyt Coleman, Monica Dionysuis, Helen Doerr, Wilbur Dice, Lon Fessler, Irene Fick, Harlan Gould, Ruth Finlay, Julius Gratiot, Esther Gabe, Jack Gunn, Rachel Gardner, Dorthy Garvin, Terry Hageman, Fred Hageman, Jean Hamilton, Norma Hamilton, Lillie Haskill, Carl Heidbrieder, Prentice Henderson, Thelma Heizelman, Julius Hoester, Dorothy Hopkins, Charles Heckins, Eliza Hutchison, Alfred Jekel, Oscar Jekel, Arthur Johnson, Franics Jurden, Ellen Kane, Margaret Kinsella, Frederick Kenyon, Olive Kenyon, Bernice Koenig, Mary Litner, Margaret Lorenz. Charlotte Manning, Warren Manning, Carlisle Martin, William Masten, Joyce McLean, Gordon Meimor, Paula Mincke, Elizabeth Moore, Arthur Newell, Grace Pollard, Evelyn Parker, Mary Perry, Frances Prickel, Mildred Prough, Katharine Ethel Reeve, Mary Ryan, Eloise Sanders, Lucille Schultz, James Sentenne, George Signor, Harriet Tatman, Sarduis VanDam, William VanNice, Vincent Venard, Stuart Vickers, Helen Wallace, Mary Wallace, Helen Watson, Lawrence Webster

Schuyler County, Missouri, Queen City Telephone Directory, March, 1916.

Arthur Applegate, John Applegate, T. R. Ashbym Ben Ayers, Will Archer, George Arkinson, Max Aldridge, J. W. Archer, J.M. Brower, D. S. Brower, Leon Bennettm E. W. Bowen, Thomas Bowen, B. P. Burton, Levi Bowen, J. H. Barclay, J. Barnhart, W. C. Biggs, F. R. Baitty, F. M.

Billings, Robert Biurion, Clarence Boggs, S. H. Boles, A. N. Ballinger, Millard Ballinger, U. G. Bronizer, D. C. Bronizer, August Bergman, J. E. Beihel, G. M. Beck, Lewis Bergman, Jr., Ed Boatman, D. C. Baqrr, Mrs. Nancy Beck, G. A. Bookout, Albert Buner, William Bland, Dan Badger (handwritten in), T. J. Blodgett (handwritten in), A. B. Cockrum, J. O. Coffey, W. B.Cook, W. E. Coffrey, Mrs. Marty Carter, Bab Caswell, E. E. Caldwell, Milo Cole,. J. O. Cowell, Olaf Coons, Ray Cole, Levi Cassady, C. C. Crickette, William Calhoon, Ot Cass, A. T. Collins, Irvin Clevinger, J. T. Casper, William Dunham. Mrs. G. Deierling, William Deierling, Barn (sic) Deierling, Harry Duncan, Jacob Deierling, Victor Deierling, William Davis, Samuel Deierling, Logan Daugherty, Earnest Daugherty, Mrs. William Elms, Mrs. James Elms, James Ewing, John Epperson, Samuel Eason, William Emmert, Clarence Erwin, Robt. Epperson, W. H. Funk, Edward Fugate, John Figger, Howard Fortune, Roy Fugate, Arthur Fugate, David Flick, Lee Foglesong, J. W. Gregory, A. H. Gier, Abner Gardner, J. M. George, Chas. Graumsch, George Gilliland, Williard Gardine, Harry George, J. O. Gosser, Lewis Gosser, Allen Graves, Daniel Gillispie, Tyron Gillispie, Dr. W. B. Hight, J. L. Hart, D. A. Haynes, O. A. Hurd, James Howard, David Hyler, W. H. Hampton, C. E. Holloway, R. G. Hubrey, Albert Huff, James Hurd, Albert Hall, William Houston, Newton Hager, Ellis Hager, Everette Hays, Charles Hays, Herman Herboth, J. T. Jones, Irvin C. Jones, Elias Johnson, Bert Johnson, Elijah Johnson, Jr.., Able Johnson, Eli Johnson, Riley Johnson, Elijah Johnson, Sr., Elias John, Jr., Ceph Johnson, Chas. Jones, John Jones, Samuel Johnson,.William Johnson, A. Kuhn, William Knittle, J. W. Kaster, J. W. Keesecker, N. L. Kaster, Geo. King, Earnest, Jno. Knittell, Samuel Knittell, P. L. Klein, Alva Knittell, Myron Linkey, Robt. Lawson, H. E. Lorton, Press (sic) Lowe, J. D. Logston, Paul Ladwig (sic), R. H. Lawson, P. M. Lind, Ed Myers, W. C. Muff, Joe Myers, H. T. Miller, Bert Mitchell, Clem Miller, N. P. Martin, M. C. Myers, J. D. Martin, Dan Miller, O. C. Mallet, F. R. Miller, A. H. Miller, J. F. Miller, J. J. Miller, William Murtin (sic), A. L. Moore, Ira Myers, Jake Myers, Minatee (sic) Myers, Clarence Moulder, Dave Miller, D. B. Miller, Andrew Miller, eva Miller, Jno. Madders, W. E. Manning, Wesley Myers, Z. A. Macombers, James McNaul, J. W. McNaught, George Mccuskey, Mrs. Benn McElroy, A. W. McNabb, Clyde McElhintey, Lloyd McCormick, William McCuskey, William McDowell, Ora McCuskey, Harry O'Brient, William Pierce, Jno. Perry, I. S. Piper, Jno. Patterson, Jno. Peebles, Chas. Peebles, Abe Peery, Boon Pennington, John Payton, Geo. Parks, Fred Peebles, Stephen Prough, Jeff Prough, Walter Phelps, Clark Patterson, Allen Rolston, A. J. Rolston, E. F. Roberts, William Rinehart, Thomas Rice, Geo. Rolston, Geo. Ruddell, W. T. Ray, Jno. Reindel, Margaret Reindel, J. M. Robbins, Earl Robbins, C. O. Riley, L. Ruth, E. C. Sloop, E. N. Sloop, F. C. Sherton, E. Sweeting, Joe

South, Joe Smith, Mrs. B. S. Shirely, Nick Sloop. William Saxbury, Clyde Sharp. Mrs. O. Slaughter, Mrs. Ira Starbuck, Lewis Starbuck, C. W. Starbuck, Boise Shacklette, H. V. Steffey, P.loop. Victor Sloop, W. B. Sloop, J. W. Sloope. Jno. Smith, Henry Smith, William Smith, Dan Smith, J. B. Shipman, Wesley Spears, Mrs. Steen, Mrs. William Sidwell, J. F. Sidwell, Bart Sidwell, Walton Sanders, R. Schmidt, Vern Sidwell, Geo. Smith, Mat Steen, Ross Shirley, E. Slaughter, Baron Slaughter, S. F. Slaughter, Victor Slaughter, William Sanford (handwritten in), Levi Tarrm Dr. B. A. Taylor, William Thomas, J. W. Thomas, James Tarr, Thomas Turner, David Tipton, Earl Tipton, James Tipton, R. L. Tittsworth, galen Tingley, Ward VanMeter, (handwritten in: "Dad"), William Vittetoe (handwrriten in: "Cousin," Robt. Vandiver, Jno. VanMeter (handwritten in: "Uncle"), Jno. VanMeter (hand- written in: "GranDad,"), Jess VanSickle, Mrs. Thomas Vittetoe (hand- written in: "cousin), Van Vittetoe (handwritten in: "Uncle,"), Elzie Vittetoe (handwritten in: "Cousin), H. G. West, Mrs. I. N. Walker, Eska Wright, Nute Welsh, Eli Watts, Jake Young, Dr. W. H. Zieber.

Special Note: Handwritten at the bottom: Doctor that brought me into the world, 1910, Vacinated (sic) me also Naomi.

State of Missouri, Veterinary Department, 1915-1916.

Name	Residence	County
Dr. D. F. Luckey	Columbia	Boone
L. D. Brown	Hamilton	Caldwell
Arthur W. Ewing	Morrisville	Polk
E. J. Johnston	Excelsior Springs	Clay
H. C. Tuck	Columbia	Boone
C. E. Ackerman	Bolivar	Polk
L. B. Adams	Sikeston	Scott
B. B. Alider	Stockton	Cedar
Geo. E. Bartholomees	Sheldon	Vernon
V. C. Bartlett	Browning	Linn
J. L. Becker	Triplett	Charlton
W. F. Berry	Joplin	Jasper
Samuel Black	Chillicothe	Livingston
Horace Bradley	Windsor	Henry
E. Brainard	Memphis	Scotland
R. L. Buell	Vandalia	Audrain
Francis M. Byrd	Parnell	Nodaway
F. M. Cahill	St. Joseph	Buchanan
H. C. Carver	Higginsville	Lafayette
C. L. Cheatham	Clinton	Henry
F. L. Cissel	Perryville	Perry

L. G. Clark	Nevada	Vernon
Henry C. Conrad	Polo	Caldwell
William J. Cozad	Powersville	Putnam
J. G. Coughlin	Edina	Knox
D. W. Criswell	Savannah	Andrew
E. D. Criswell	King City	Gentry
D. E. Crites	Jackson	Cape Girardeau
James Cullison	Charleston	Mississippi
B. C. Davis	Carrollton	Carroll
A. C. Donohew	Boonville	Cooper
E. L. Dudgeon	Platte City	Platte
W. H. Eberle	Silex	Lincoln
J. M. Eisenhower	Schell City	Vernon
Jos. Emonts	O'Fallon	St. Charles
C. H. Gaines	Chilhowee	Johnson
J. W. George	Harrisonville	Cass
A. D. Glover	Newark	Knox
P. H. Gregory	St. Charles	St. Charles
Paul S. Grigsby	Louisiana	Pike
Willard Hampton	Albany	Gentry
E. M. Hendy	Jefferson City	Cole
J. L. Hickman	Brunot	Wayne
Harry Hinds	Hannibal	Marion
Chas. N. Hook	Braymer	Caldwell
W. J. Houser	Carthage	Jasper
D. Mike Howard	Appleton City	St. Clair
A. W. James	Cameron	Clinton
C. N. James	Belton	Cass
J. N. Jerome	Urich	Henry
Carl H. Johnson	Lamar	Barton
Lee R. Johnston	Sweet Springs	Saline
John L. Jones	Blackburn	Saline
H. H. Jonker	Brookfield	Linn
A. T. Kinsley	Kansas City	Jackson
Ota W. Kirby	Cainesville	Harrison
O. U. Lash	Moberly	Randolph
G. H. Leach	Maryville	Nodaway
G. W. Leber	Pacific	Franklin
W. S. Lester	Bethany	Harrison
R. C. Leininger	Pleasant Hill	Cass
W. J. Lopp	Sedalia	Pettis
R. B. Love	Springfield	Greene

H. M. McConnell	Independence	Jackson
J. H. McElroy	Grant city	Worth
Geo. W. McIntyre	Mexico	Audrain
Barney McManus	Bowling Green	Pike
E. P. Maitland	LaPlata	Macon
T. T. Maize	Lancaster	Schuyler
J. S. martin	Centralia	Boone
W. E. Martin	Perry	Ralls
Ray Matkin	Laredo	Grundy
A. M. Miller	Washington	Franklin
B. M. Miller	California	Moniteau
D. B. Morgan	Neosho	Newton
Sam S. Morgan	Richmond	Ray
A. E. Morrow	Liberty	Clay
Fred B. Muir	Lees Summit	Jackson
A. J. Munn	Fayette	Howard
Olin T. Murphy	Kahoka	Clark
W. E. Neil	Kirksville	Adair
F. N. Niederwimer	Montgomery City	Montgomery
Claude T. old	Malden	Dunklin
W. A. Parker	Eureka	St. Louis
Glee Parmenter	Harris	Sullivan
E. E. Peacock	Fairfax	Atchison
James R. Person	Pierce City	Lawrence
G. R. Pittman	Mount Vernon	Lawrence
R. P. Poage	Shelbina	Shelby
C. A. Ponder	Doniphan	Ripley
L. W. Richardson	Adrian	Bates
J. W. Riley	Wright City	Warren
W. N. Russell	West Plains	Howell
F. W. Rutherford	Maysville	Dekalb
O. N. Scott	Mound City	Holt
H. J. Sebaugh	Princeton	Mercer
J. R. Seipel	Poplar Bluff	Butler
S. Sheldon	Trenton	Grundy
E. A. Shikles	Dearborn	Platte
W. C. Shikles	Plattsburg	Clinton
Fred Sifford	Bloomfield	Stoddard
L. C. Smith	Hamilton	Caldwell
Stanley Smith	Columbia	Boone
W. C. Sorber	St. Louis	St. Louis
Oscar Stuart	Paris	Monroe
Seth E. Sullivan	Gallatin	Daviess

A. A. Taylor	Mendon	Chariton
B. A. Taylor	Queen city	Schuyler
J. E. Thomasson	Morrisville	Polk
C. A. Treadway	Ridgeway	Harrison
Thomas B. Tipton	Hume	Bates
B. M. Troxel	Ridgeway	Harrison
H. C. Ward	Fulton	Callaway
W. D. Warmoth	Macon	Macon
W. B. Welch	Marshall	Saline
John L. Wells	Aurora	Lawrence
T. E. White	Sedalia	Pettis
C. C. Whittaker	Oak Ridge	Cape Girardeau
F. A. Wolfe	Linneus	Linn
J. R. Woods	Warrensburg	Johnson
J. L. Wright	Salisbury	Chariton
Ed L. Young	Grandview	Jackson

Lafayette County, Missouri, September 1, 1854
    Hezekiah Waterhouse of Lafayette County, State of Missouri in consideration of $1,025 dollars paid by David Powell have sold, transfered and delivered, one negro woman and child, woman's name is Ruth age is about 25 years, child's age about 18 months which said negroes, I warrant to be Slaves for Life.

Jasper County, Missouri, Vehicle Registration
Millard Bryan, Carthage, Mo. Owner of 16 HP runabout made by Maxwell brisco Co., No.117, dated Aug. 1, 1911, Signed Cornelius Roach, Sec. Of State

Lafayette County, Missouri, Automobile Registration.
Jan. 28, 1935, Ira A. Banks, Higginsville, No. 275556, 1924 Ford, Coupe. Lisc. No. 9837260

Henry County, Missouri, Hickory Grove Cemetery, White Oak Township.
Alexander, Bessie I.: (B) Jun. 13, 1904 , (D) Jul. 21, 1996
Anderson, Nancy A.: (B) Mar. 14, 1864, (D) Sep. 9, 1876
Armstrong, George W.: (B) Dec. 24, 1842, (D) Jul., 18, 1905
Armstrong, Infant: (B) Feb. 3, 1905, (D) Feb. 13, 1905
Armstrong, Infant: (B) Nov. 23, 1906, (D) Dec.18, 1906
Armstrong, Margaret E.: (B) Oct. 17, 1845, (D) Dec. 15, 1914
Armstrong, Thomas Edward: (B) Aug. 8, 1872, (D) Mar. 21, 1876
Barnhart, Tilden M.: (B) 1910, (D) 1991

Barth, Evilena: (B) Mar. 27, 1884, (D) Nov. 13, 1886
Barth, Josie: (B) Mar. 18, 1884, (D) Feb. 25, 1943
Beach, Ann E. Sims: (B) Jan. 31, 1857, (D) Feb. 17, 1916
Beach, James F.: (B) Feb. 3, 1848, (D) Oct. 29, 1926
Beach, Thomas B.: (B) May 26, 1872, (D) Apr. 23, 1873
Bettes, Lillian: (B) Jan. 5, 1919, (D) Jan. . 18, 1985
Blevins, Charles Preston: (D) Sep. 10, 1868, (A) 1M 25D
Blevins, Emily Hayes: (B) Mar. 22, 1844, (D) Apr. 3, 1903
Blevins, George W.: (D) Nov. 1, 1884,
Blevins, Gothaile: (D) Oct., 19, 1882, (A) 4Y 9M 21D
Blevins, Infant: (D) Nov. 5, 1876
Blevins, Nancy E.: (D) Sep. 28, 1857, (A) 17Y 8M 3D
Blevins, Naomi E.: (B) Sep. 29, 1873, (D) Jul. 18, 1958
Blevins, Stephen E.: (B) Nov. 10, 1869, (D) Jan. 5, 1903
Boudinier, Jessie L.: (D) May 13, 1895, (A) 6Y 2M 16D
Boyd, Holmes T.: (B) Dec. 16, 1853, (D) Nov. 6, 1932
Brannock, Anderson G.: (B) Dec. 9, 1843, (D) Dec. 20, 1923
Brannock, John: (D) Oct. 20, 1873, (A) 66Y 1M, 19D
Briggs, Guy S.: (B) 1899, (D) 1982
Brock, Annie J.: (B) Nov., 18, 1877, (D) Jun. 8, 1878
Brock, Ida May: (B) Mar. 8 ?, (D) Jul. 20, 1879
Burgess, Infant: (D) Feb. 20, 1876,
Burgess, Infant: (B) Mar. 15, 1880, (D) Mar. 28, 1880
Burgess, L. L.: (B) Aug. 20, 1855, (D) Feb. 12, 1918
Burgess, M. M.: (B) (B) May 2, 1853, (D) Mar. 21, 18
Burry, Franklin: (B) Sep. 6, 1844, (D) Jan. 31, 1902
Burry, Harriet: (D) Dec. 25, 1878, (A) 32Y 1M
Burry, Susan A.: (B) Apr. 29, 1842, (D) Feb. 13, 1890
Byrd, John H.: (B) 1869, (D) 1909
Carver, Hettie A.: (D) Oct. 11, 1868, (A) 24Y 9M 2D
Clary, Susannah L.: (B) Aug. 20, 1878, (D) Sep. 20, 1880
Colson, Joseph T.: (B) Nov. 2, 1855, (D) May 1, 188?
Converse, George M.: (B) 1849, (D) 1927
Cook, John W.: (D) Nov. 8, 1893, (A) 50Y 10M 25D
Cook, Musy B.: (D) Feb. 21, 1892, (A) 1Y 6M 9D
Cook, Sarah K.: (B) Dec. 17, 1872, (D) Nov. 17, 1873
Cook, William H.: (D) Jul. 10, 1892, (A) 15Y 25D
Cornett, John L.: (B) May 16, 1846, (D) Oct. 10, 1859
Cox, Dixon L.: (B) Feb. 14, 1876, (D) Aug. 29, 1876
Cox, Jessie A.: (B) Nov. 14, 1877, (D) Sep., 18, 1878
Cox, Noah F.: (B) Nov. 24, 1853, (D) Feb. 27, 1923
Craig, Ruby Ellen: (B) May 15, 1921, (D) Jul. 27, 1921
Cummings, Freda Kedigh: (B) Jun. 13, 1909, (D) Jan. 15, 1982

Dickerson, Gladys May: (B) Jan. 25, 1866, (D) Aug. 20, 1871
Douglas, Calbert Noles: (B) Dec. 3, 1907, (D) Oct. 14, 1975
Douglas, Clyde K.: (B) Aug. 3, 1909, (D) Jan. 7, 1968
Douglas, Thomas A.: (B) 1848, (D) 1926
Duncan, Arthur R.: (B) Nov. 10, 1886, (D) Sep. 7, 1887
Dunn, Daniel L.: (D) Sep. 15, 1856, (A) 14Y 9M 20D
Dunn, Infant: (D) Jun. 17, 1914,
Dunn, Nathaniel: (B) Jul. 1861, (D) Nov. 14, 1861
Dunn, Zulima: (D) Jan. 28, 1874, (A) 56Y 22D
Foster, Albert: (B) 1889, (D) 1954
Fugate, Cathorine: (D) Sep., 18, 1895, (A) 70Y
Garrison, C. W.: (B) Jul. 14, 1883, (D) Feb. 18, 1911
Gilbert, George W.: (B) 1854, (D) 1859
Gillilan, James W.: (D) Jan. 17, 1918,
Goodman, Bertha E.: (B) (B) Jan., 19, 1890, (D) Jan. 21, 19
Goodman, Maggie A.: (B) Jan. 29, 1897, (D) Nov. 23, 1898
Greufe, Evelyn F.: (B) Sep. 24, 1919, (D) Jan., 19, 1985
Griffin, William Riley: (D) Aug. 24, 1877,
Groetzinger, Earl W.: (B) Jan. 6, 1890, (D) Mar. 8, 1892
Hackney, Emmett Z.: (D) Dec. 2, 1883,
Hackney, Geo. H. Judge: (B) Jan. 2, 1842, (D) Jan. 23, 1906
Hackney, Jennie C.: (B) Jan. 21, 1870, (D) Mar. 14, 1873
Hackney, Josie K.: (B) Feb. 4, 1903, (D) Sep. 5, 1904
Hackney, Mary B.: (B) 1873, (D) 1962
Hackney, Nannie C.: (B) Apr. 13, 1872, (D) Apr. 8, 1893
Hackney, T. B.: (B) Jan. 28, 1871, (D) Jul. 24, 1925
Hackney, W. Lock: (B) Oct. 9, 1873, (D) Jun. 13, 1903
Hagan, Perry B.: (B) 1871, (D) 1951
Hargrave, Joseph M.: (B) 1902, (D) 1972
Harris, Jess: (B) Apr. 3, 1856, (D) Jan., 19, 1933
Hays, John: (D) Oct. 24, 1893, (A) 73Y 6M 12D
Hays, Mary A.: (D) Feb. 23, 1859,
Hays, Samuel H.: (B) May 8, 1851, (D) Apr. 7, 1912
Hays, Sophia F.: (B) Sep. 27, 1852, (D) Mar. 26, 1872
Hays, Wesley H.: (D) Apr. 3, 1892,
Hays, William Alexander: (B) Apr. 15, 1853, (D) Feb. 22, 1930
Helm, Annie Elizabeth: (B) Jul. 25, 1858, (D) Jul. 28, 1933
Helm, Arthur: (B) Jul. 16, 1880, (D) Jan. 21, 1931
Helm, Benjamin F.: (B) 1853, (D) 1924
Helm, Bessie: (B) Aug. 26, 1882, (D) Jan. 4, 1885
Helm, Eunice: (B) Nov. 22, 1887, (D) Sep. 3, 1889
Helm, Infant Dau: (D) Aug. 11, 1896,
Helm, Jessie: (B) Feb. 16, 1885, (D) Mar. 21, 1964

Helm, Jonathan: (B) Sep. 25, 1850, (D) Oct. 8, 1935
Helm, Kevin R.: (D) Jul. 22, 1963,
Helm, Millard: (B) May 31, 1899, (D) Feb. 7, 1974
Helm, Wesley: (B) Feb. 18, 1852, (D) Dec. 31, 1897
Henny, Edward: (B) Jan. 4, 1865, (D) Jun. 23, 1926
Hudson, Mary Jane: (D) Jan. 30, 1889
Hudson, Thomas: (D) Feb. 22, 1862
Hudson, William F.: (D) Feb. 22, 1862
Hunt, Andrew D.: (B) Dec. 26, 1842, (D) Nov. 25, 1904
Hunt, Arthur A.: (D) May 29, 1885, (A) 1Y 3M 4D
Jacobs, Sam: (B) 1875, (D) 1946
Johnson, S. A.: (D) Sep. 22, 1873, (A) 18Y 6M 20D
Jones, Infant: (D) May 6, 1875,
Jordan, Francis Gale: (B) Mar. (B) 18, 1929, (D) Mar., 19, 1929
Jordan, James Harold: (B) Feb. 5, 1906, (D) Oct. 4, 1990
Jordan, Jerry Franklin: (B) Mar. 9, 1933, (D) Dec. 20, 1977
Jordan, Mamie: (B) Nov. 26, 1908, (D) Dec. 24, 1990
Kedigh, Ben E.: (B) Nov. 20, 1884, (D) Jun., 19, 1973
Kedigh, Christina M.: (B) Nov. 3, 1869, (D) Oct. 20, 1871
Kedigh, Doris E.: (B) Aug. 27, 1925, (D) Apr. 13, 1997
Kedigh, Edith A.: (B) Dec. 5, 1887, (D) Nov. 21, 1978
Kedigh, Frances Gertrude: (B) Feb. 13, 1922, (D) Jul. 8, 1974
Kedigh, George W.: (B) Dec. 21, 1883, (D) Dec. 16, 1918
Kedigh, Jessie Mildred Patt: (B) May 2, 1915, (D) Nov. 3, 199?
Kedigh, Michael: (B) Dec. 11, 1840, (D) Jul. 13, 1925
Kedigh, Omer F.: (B) 1889, (D) 1970
Kidwiler, Charles L.: (B) 1887, (D) 1965
Kidwiler, Lester E.: (B) Sep. 15, 1925,
Kidwiler, William W.: (B) Aug. 28, 1902,
Lewellen, Thelma R.: (B) Dec. 3, 1914, (D) Oct. 17, 1987
Little, Mary: (B) Jul. 25, 1860, (D) Sep. 21, 1936
Long, Infant: (B) May 21, 1878, (D) Aug. 24, 1878
Martin, John E.: (B), 1906, (D) 1990
Martin, Joseph F.: (B) Feb., 19, 1862, (D) Sep. 23, 1877
Martin, William H.: (B) Feb. 24, 1880, (D) Sep. 2, 1881
Mathews, Eva Jane: (B) Mar. 22, 1882, (D) Jun., 18, 1883
Mayes, Sarah Walsh: (B) 1858, (D) 1877
Mciver, Alexander: (D) Feb. 6, 1873, (A) 10Y 11M 8D
Mendenhall, Florence Dunn: (B) Sep. 25, 1885, (D) Sep. 27, 1971
Mendenhall, Wilbur N.: (B) Jun. 20, 1915, (D) Nov. 12, 1973
Middaugh, E. B.: (B) May 25, 1858, (D) Jan. 27, 19(D) 19
Middaugh, Samuel Everett: (B) Jun. 12, 1890, (D) May 20, 1908
Middaugh, Samuel J.: (B) 1859, (D) 1933

Miller, Charles W.: (B) Mar. 28, 1894, (D) Jan. 17, 1966
Miller, Infant: (B) Oct. 10, 1876, (D) Feb. 7, 1877
Miller, John W.: (B) Mar. 5, 1850, (D) Nov. 2, 1908
Mock, Benjamin P.: (B) Mar. 21, 1886, (D) Feb. 27, 1887
Mock, Carrie E.: (B) Jun. 3, 1882, (D) Apr. 12, 1886
Mock, Charles F.: (B) Sep. 15, 1875, (D) May 24, 1897
Mock, Eliza A.: (D) Jun. 25, 1880,
Mock, Emiline E.: (B) Oct., 1872, (D) Dec. 8, 187?
Mock, Jesse P.: (B) 1886, (D) 1966
Mock, Joseph E.: (B) Mar. 14, 1876, (D) Oct. 17, 1877
Mock, Ulysses S.: (B) Oct. 22, 1883, (D) May 5, 1886
Moore, Mary Belle: (B) Dec. 7, 1858, (D) Sep. 3, 1875
Moreland, Eda Belle: (B) Dec. 6, 1882, (D) Sep. 3, 1883
Moreland, Emily Jane: (B) Jun. 15, 1848, (D) Apr. 16, 1885
Moreland, Ida: (B) Nov. 10, 1883, (D) Dec. 12, 1883
Nelson, Maggie C.: (B) 1882, (D) 1888
Nelson, Mildred C.: (B) 1867, (D) 1915
Owens, Clay R.: (D) Jun. 22, 1877, (A) 2M 1D
Owens, Edward: (B) Mar. 31, 1851, (D) Jul. 2, 1922
Owens, L. E.: (B) Dec. 7, 1843, (D) Mar. 28, 1932
Owens, Rachel: (B) Sep. 13, 18(B) 19, (D) Jan. 1, 1890
Owens, T. P.: (D) Aug. 31, 1869,
Owens, William R.: (B) Jan. 1, 1841, (D) Dec. 23, 1923
Palmer, Donald Clyde: (B) Oct. 21, 1931, (D) Apr. 13, 1932
Patt, Charles R.: (B) 1841, (D) 1862
Patt, Claude Lee: (B) Feb. 2, 1911, (D) Oct. 5, 1913
Patt, Jackson M.: (B) Feb. 8, 1850, (D) May 3, 1934
Patt, James Kermit: (B) Aug. 11, 1914, (D) Jun. 3, 1969
Patt, Lee J.: (B) Mar. 14, 1887, (D) Mar. 26, 1942
Patt, Leota Jean: (B) Oct. 11, 1921, (D) Apr. 17, 1939
Potter, Ella: (B) Jul. 14, 1874, (D) Jan. 20, 1875
Pruett, Mary E.: (B) Feb. 3, 1844, (D) Jan. 16, 1875
Raney, Sam, Mrs.: (B) 1868, (D) Sep. 10
Read, D. J. T.: (B) Oct. 20, 1858, (D) Jan. 2, 1859
Read, Harvey A.: (D) Jan. 17, 1897,
Read, John: (D) Aug. 25, 1857, (A) 66Y 4M 22D
Read, Polly Ann: (B) Oct. 8, 1880, (D) Jan., 18, 1910
Reynolds, Infant: (D) Mar. 6, 1876,
Reynolds, Lydia B.: (B) Jan. 29, 1890, (D) May 1, 1892
Reynolds, Mattie D.: (B) Oct. 29, 1887, (D) Dec. 9, 1892
Ridge, George W.: (B) Jul. 3, 1873, (D) Sep. 1, 1949
Riggins, Grace B.: (B) Apr. 21, 1885, (D) Oct. 30, 1908
Robinson, David J.: (B) Jan. 2, 1873,

Rollins, Margaret Kedigh: (B), 1925, (D) 1964
Seaton, Clarence W.: (B) 1898, (D) 1965
Seaton, George H.: (B) 1859, (D) 1928
Seaton, Jeanievie Amanda: (B), 1923, (D) 1969
Seaton, Leota M.: (B) Sep. 14, 1898, (D) Sep. 13, 1988
Seaton, Mary A.: (D) Dec. 24, 1891, (A) 21Y 6M 4D
Seaton, Maurice E.: (B) Oct. 2, 1889, (D) Jun. 13, 1981
Seaton, Pinkie E.: (B) 1920, (D) 1940
Seaton, Robert: (B) 1864, (D) 1957
Sevier, Anna Marguerite: (B) Jun. 12, 1911
Sevier, Clara Barth: (B) 1882, (D) 1943
Sevier, Edward Franklin: (B) 1872, (D) 1951
Sevier, George A.: (D) Apr. 13, 1874, (A) 28Y 10M 1D
Sevier, Infant: (D) Dec. 5, 1906,
Sevier, James W.: (B) Oct. 21, 1866, (D) Oct. 11, 1921
Sevier, Walter F.: (B) Feb. 26, 1894, (D) Apr. 26, 1894
Sevier, William Harold: (B) Oct. 14, 1908, (D) Sep. 15, 1980
Showman, Anna M.: (B) 1891, (D) 1970
Showman, James R.: (B) Apr. 5, 1832, (D) Dec. 30, 1880
Showman, James W.: (B) 1870, (D) 1940
Shroder, Bryan W.: (B) Sep. 23, 1896, (D) Jan. 11, 1977
Shroder, C. A. : (B) 1885, (D) 1969
Shroder, Charles H.: (B) 1858, (D) 1938
Shroder, Estel L.: (B) Sep. 26, 1916, (D) May 27, 1973
Shroder, Fannie: (B) Dec. 31, 1894, (D) Jan. 4, 1895
Shroder, Icy: (B) Dec. 3, 1901, (D) Nov. 8, 1904
Shroder, Jeanne: (B) May 5, 1924, (D) Oct. 29, 1968
Shroder, John: (B) Aug. 14, 1845, (D) Aug. 22, 1926
Shroder, John S.: (B) Dec. 9, 1880, (D) Jan. 2, 1881
Shroder, Johnnie: (B) 1906, (D) 1908
Shroder, Lizzie: (B) Nov. 7, 1844, (D) Nov. 17, 1875
Shroder, Lonnie: (D) 1906
Shroder, Marguerite F.: (B) May 25, 1920, (D) Dec. 31, 1987
Shroder, Omer R.: (B) 1881, (D) 1961
Shroder, Rheuben: (B) Nov. 29, 1904, (D) Apr. 3, 1908
Shroder, Vernon Burton: (B) Sep. 6, 1918, (D) Oct. 15, 1983
Shroder, Walter Eugene: (B) Aug. 11, 1950, (D) Aug. 22, 1950
Shroder, Walter S.: (B) 1884, (D) 1944
Shroder, Zella: (B) Oct. 12, 1898, (D) Nov. 4, 1898
Sims, A. W.: (B) Nov. 20, 1853, (D) Dec. 28, 1873
Sims, Charlie E.: (B) Mar. 5, 1873, (D) May 13, 1873
Sims, Grover: (B) 1884, (D) 1973
Sims, J. W.: (B) Nov. 20, 1853, (D) Dec. 28, 1880?

Sims, John E.: (B) 1860, (D) 1930
Sims, Ruth E.: (B) Jul. 17, 1869, (D) Dec. 20, 1904
Sims, William A.: (D) Mar. 29, 1887,
Smith, Lola May: (B) May 9, 1910, (D) Jan. 4, 1995
Smith, Teddy D.: (B) Aug. 6, 1930, (D) Jan. 20, 1980
Spry, Corbin: (D) Sep. 29, 1890
Spry, George W.: (B) Sep. 16, 1851, (D) Oct. 7, 1915
Staley, Martin V.: (D) Feb. 21, 1862,
Stearns, John A.: (B) Jul. 29, 1869, (D) Oct. 1, 1869
Stevens, Grant: (B) Dec., 18, 1867, (D) Jun. 20, 1949
Stevens, Lurena: (B) Jun. 25, 1907, (D) Jan. 6, 1908
Stevens, Nora Ellen: (B) Nov. 7, 1877, (D) Jan. 16, 1947
Stevens, Porter L.: (B) Feb., 1900,
Stewart, John Westley: (D) Nov. 30, 1871
Stewart, Robert H.: (B) 1873, (D) 1958
Stewart, William Henry: (D) Jan. 11, 1878
Summers, Lillie D.: (B) Mar. 13, 1875, (D) Jun., 18, 1959
Switser, David N.: (B) 1859, (D) 1935
Switser, Mary M.: (B) 1854, (D) 1929
Toalson, Roger Kahn: (B) Nov. 13, 1942, (D) Nov. 15, 1942
Toalson, Tilford Raymond: (B) Oct. 3, 1901, (D) Oct. 1, 1984
Turner, Minnie: (B) Feb. 23, 1868, (D) Aug. 6, 1931
Vanlandingham, Nancy J.: (D) Dec. 10, 1889
Waddell, Elizabeth: (B) (B) Mar. 2, 1816
Waddell, J. T.: (B) Mar. 22, 1812, (D) Sep. 10, 1872
Walker, Minnie F.: (B) Sep. 9, 1875, (D) Aug. 7, 1876
Walker, W. S.: (B) Apr. 22, 1817, (D) Dec. 17, 1882
Walsh, Anthony: (B) 18(B) 18, (D) 1873
Walsh, Margret A.: (B) 1825, (D) 1908
Walsh, William F.: (B) Feb. 23, 1848, (D) Apr. 8, 1933
Warren, Mary A.: (D) Jan. 1922
Fred Warren: (D) Jan. 13, 1922,
Wheeler, Alva Elton: (B) May 15, 1923, (D) Apr. 8, 1978
Wheeler, Alva: (B) Jan. 31, 1903, (D) Sep. 21, 1980
Wheeler, Jack Duane: (B) Aug. 1, 1948, (D) Aug. 3, 1948
Willcockson, George H.: (B) 1834, (D) 1893
Willcockson, James P.: (B) 1876, (D) 1877
Wilson, Bennie P.: (B) 1881, (D) 1952
Wilson, Elsie Marie: (B) Apr. 23, 1915, (D) May 22, 1920
Wilson, H. G.: (D) Feb. 15, 1887, (A) 42Y 11M 27D
Wilson, James Olen: (B) May 1, 1881, (D) Oct. 7, 1975
Wilson, Lena Leota: (B) Aug. 6, 1882, (D) May 9, 1974
Wilson, Louis Riley: (B) 1859, (D) 1932

Wilson, Marion R.: (D) Oct. 14, 1880,
Wilson, Noah E.: (B) Jun. 2, 1885, (D) Mar. 20, 1982
Wilson, Roy L.: (B) 1889, (D) 1919
Wisdom, Anderson: (B) Oct., 18, 1873, (D) Sep. 28, 1952
Wisdom, Arvill A.: (B) 1902, (D) 1958
Wisdom, Charles Edward: (B) 1934, (D) 1945
Wisdom, Ora William: (B) Nov. 29, 1899, (D) Feb. 27, 1984
Wolfe, Daniel: (B) Feb. 8, 1826, (D) Dec. 28, 1889
Wood, Louisa J.: (B) Feb. 4, 1859, (D) Oct. 11, 1869
Wortman, Edmond: (B) Oct. 4, 1809, (D) Oct. 3, 1875
Wortman, Julia Ann: (B) 1848, (D) 1878

Missouri Civil War Soldier's Letter
Washington, April the 21st,1862.
Dear Mother, I thought I would write you a few lines to let you know that I am well and I wish that you could say the same. I received a letter from Loretta the other day and she (say) that you were sick. I am sorry to hear it I tell you. You ask if I got those letters that you sent by Harly. I did, Mother. We were paid Friday up to the first of March, two month pay.I sent fifteen dollars home by the Adams Express Company. I do not know whether it will come to Seth or Frederburgh. I sent it Friday so it will be there before you get this. When you get it you must write back and let me knowquick as you can. It rained Friday night and all day Saturday and Saturday night. We were ordered to leave. We halted about a half a hour to pack up and get ready to start.We started a little before dark and marched about four miles down through Goergetown and it was dark before we got half way there and as I was saying we got through Georgetown. We was orderd back and had a nice time of it. The mud was about four inches deep. When we got back to camp we was about tired out and it has rained ever since. Christian got a letter today giving him the wonderful news that he had another brother, William. I am getting more nonsense than any need of so I must bid give my love to all and keep a good share for yourself. From your everloving son, Henry Klice. Co A, 7 regiment, Missouri Volunteers,

Shannon County, Missouri, *"Shannon County Democrat,"* September 3, 1938.
    Funeral services for J. A. Tohline, age 77, were held at the M. E. Church on Friday August 28th. Mr. Tohline was along time resident of Winona. He died at his home in Fishertown, Monday evening, August 22nd. Born in Stofsjo, Sweden, he arrived in America in 1880. He married on June 20, 1886 to Emma Johnson who came to this country in 1873 from Norrkoping, Sweden. They had seven sons: Mr. Tohline lived in Dent and Shannon Counties.

SURNAME INDEX

----CRAFT, 153
----HENS, 157
ABBEY, 109
ABBOTT, 76 95 114
ABERCROMBY, 174
ABERMATHY, 168-169
ABERNATHY, 167 169
ACINELLI, 109
ACKERMAN, 187
ADAIR, 90
ADAIRS, 161
ADAM, 114
ADAMS, 77-78 109 124 130 132 139-140
  179 181 187
ADERSON, 168
ADEY, 99
ADIER, 129
ADK----, 157
ADKINS, 1 100 153-154 157-158 164
  166-167 174-175 177 184
AFFOLTIER, 170
AGEE, 1 140
AGNEW, 85 88
AHRING, 114
AIRS, 180
AKEMAN, 90
AKER, 140
AKERS, 1 100
ALBERT, 1
ALBRIGHT, 1 90 109 137 140
ALCORN, 1 137
ALDRICH, 1
ALDRIDGE, 1 185
ALEPANTER, 178
ALEXANDER, 1 100 158 160 165 169
  171 173-175 185 190
ALFORD, 1 114
ALGER, 181
ALIDER, 187
ALL, 154

ALLAN, 114
ALLEN, 1 75 85 92 99 115 129 140 153
  155 158-160 162-164 171 175-176 181
ALLENSWORTH, 1 167
ALLEY, 132
ALLISON, 1 100 117 119 124 128 175
ALLRED, 157 163-164
ALREAD, 1
ALSDORF, 114
ALSUP, 1
ALT, 1
ALVEY, 1
ALWARD, 115
AMBER, 185
AMBROSE, 79
AMETT, 154
AMMERIMAN, 174
AMO, 1
AN----, 155
ANCELL, 172
ANDERSON, 1-2 82 100 109 114 177 181
  183-184 190
ANDREAS, 114
ANDREWS, 2 159 174 177 179 183-184
ANGDON, 2
ANMON, 2
ANSPACH, 161-162 174 176
ANTHONY, 2 83-84 172
ANTNEY, 178
APETTE, 2
APPLEBY, 2
APPLEGATE, 77 174 185
ARCHER, 2 100 177 185
ARGA, 2
ARISMAN, 118 120
ARKINSON, 185
ARLEY, 109
ARMOUR, 2
ARMSTRONG, 2 140 174 178 190
ARNEY, 131

ARNOLD, 2 117 131 143 153 161
ARNOTT, 92
ARORABAUGH, 174
ARTERBERRY, 2
ARTHUR, 100
ASBURY, 90
ASHBILL, 153
ASHBURY, 93
ASHBY, 2 109
ASHCRAFT, 2
ASHCROFT, 2
ASHER, 2 140 156 162 164 168 175 178
ASHWORTH, 2
ASKEW, 109
ATKINS, 2 160 167
ATKINSON, 2
ATTERBERRY, 176 181
ATTERBURY, 84
ATWELL, 179
AUD, 2
AUDERLAND, 144
AUFDERHEIDE, 114
AUSTILL, 2 99
AUSTIN, 115 167
AUTRY, 2
AVANT, 2
AVERS, 175
AVERY, 86 88 109
AXLINE, 114
AXTON, 168 180
AYERS, 2 185
Ashlin, 13
B----, 154-155
BACCUS, 2
BACHMAN, 175 183
BACHS, 3
BACON, 3
BADER, 144
BADGER, 186
BADGETT, 3
BAEGERMAN, 114
BAGBY, 3
BAGEE, 166
BAGGETT, 3
BAGWELL, 3
BAILEY, 3 75 78 88 165 168 176 180 183-184
BAILY, 78
BAIMER, 78
BAIN, 3 161
BAIRD, 114 180
BAITTY, 185
BAJER, 114
BAKER, 3 75 101 114 123 125-126 129 134 136 140 156 158 161 163-164 174
BALDIN, 140
BALDOCK, 140
BALDRIDGE, 3 130
BALDWIN, 94
BALES, 128-130
BALISDELL, 83
BALL, 3 109 115 122 165
BALLAGH, 85
BALLARD, 3 116
BALLEW, 91 93
BALLHEIMER, 3
BALLINGER, 186
BALTHASAR, 114
BAMFORD, 114
BAN, 3
BANE, 124
BANISTER, 123-124
BANKS, 3 114 190
BANSES, 175
BANSTETTER, 180
BANTA, 95
BANTZ, 144
BAQRR, 186
BARBER, 3 177
BARCLAY, 128 185
BARCLIFF, 3
BARDSLEY, 3
BARDWELL, 170
BARGER, 3
BARKER, 3 136
BARKHART, 166
BARKLEY, 114
BARKS, 3 114
BARNARD, 114
BARNES, 4 90 101 156-157 171 173 180 184
BARNETT, 4 90 101 109 139 161
BARNEY, 115
BARNHART, 164 173 175 185
BARNHHART, 190
BARNS, 4 136
BARNUM, 99
BARREE, 122
BARRET, 135 154
BARRETT, 4 89 132 160
BARRICK, 101
BARRINER, 4

BARROW, 4 158 170
BARRY, 78 109
BARTH, 4 191
BARTHELS, 114
BARTHOLOMEES, 187
BARTLETT, 187
BARTLEY, 92
BARTON, 4 162
BASEY, 140
BASINGER, 4
BASKET, 101
BASKETT, 98-99
BASS, 4 94
BASSETT, 95 174
BASTEDO, 81
BATES, 4 125 173 181
BATSON, 4
BATTEN, 4
BATTON, 76
BATY, 158 160 173
BAUCHMAN, 170
BAUGH, 4
BAUGMGARTNER, 114
BAUM, 176
BAUMEISTER, 4
BAUMGARDNER, 4
BAUMGARTNER, 114 144
BAWYER, 168
BAXTER, 4 140
BAY, 132
BAYER, 144
BAYES, 4
BAYS, 129
BAYSINGER, 101 162
BAZE, 140
BEACH, 81 153 175 191
BEACHEM, 4
BEALER, 4
BEALKE, 114
BEAMON, 118
BEAN, 156
BEANFORD, 155
BEAR, 90
BEARD, 138 160
BEASLEY, 101
BEAUCHAMP, 144
BEAURY, 114
BEAUVAIS, 144
BEAVE, 114
BEAVER, 133
BEAZLEY, 93

BECK, 4-5 76 109 114 186
BECKER, 114 187
BECKERMAN, 144
BEDFORD, 79
BEDOLL, 4
BEDSWORTH, 114
BEECH, 164
BEECHER, 4 164 170
BEEMAN, 157-158 163 172
BEENCK, 114
BEENTHALL, 4
BEERS, 4
BEETS, 169 176
BEGEMANN, 114
BEHREND, 114
BEHRENS, 173
BEHYMER, 180
BEIHEL, 186
BEILSTEN, 114
BEISHIR, 109
BELAMY, 5
BELCHER, 5
BELL, 5 109 137 140 160 166 168-169 178 180-181
BELLES, 180
BELLEW, 5
BELLOWS, 180
BELTZ, 114
BELVILLE, 101
BENEDICT, 162
BENHAM, 101
BENNER, 5 115
BENNET, 5 82
BENNETT, 76 101 115 123
BENNING, 120
BENSING, 115
BENSON, 115
BENTHALL, 5
BENTLEY, 140
BENTON, 5
BERDING, 115
BERG, 115 185
BERGER, 5
BERGMAN, 186
BERIENT, 5
BERNAL, 109
BERNARD, 180
BERNAYS, 144
BERNERD, 170
BERNEY, 5
BERRINGER, 5

BERRY, 5 125 144 163 166 187
BERRYMAN, 5
BERTHOLD, 185
BERTUCCI, 5
BESAND, 5
BESHEARS, 98 163
BESS, 5
BEST, 5 156
BESTWICK, 92
BETHEL, 101
BETTES, 191
BETZ, 109
BEUMER, 5-6
BEVERADGE, 165
BEVFODEN, 109
BIBLE, 101
BIEHL, 144
BIGGERSTAFF, 86 140
BIGGS, 6 185
BILBEY, 184
BILITER, 182
BILLEY, 144
BILLINGS, 186
BILLINGSLEY, 6
BILLINGTON, 160 165
BILSKY, 6
BINGAMAN, 109
BIRD, 82 101 163 172
BIRDSONG, 6
BISH, 171
BISHOP, 6 101 176 178
BISSETT, 6
BISWELL, 155 157
BIURION, 186
BIVENS, 140
BLACK, 6 85 88-89 101 109 134 187
BLACKBURN, 6
BLACKERBY, 140
BLACKS, 76
BLACKWELL, 6
BLAGG, 6
BLAKE, 101
BLAKEFIELD, 117
BLAKEMORE, 91
BLALOCK, 127
BLANCHARD, 163
BLANCHART, 145
BLAND, 6 182 186
BLANDEN, 170
BLANFORD, 6
BLANKENSHIP, 6 99

BLEADSOE, 80
BLEDSOE, 6
BLEVINS, 191
BLOCKLEY, 122
BLODGETT, 186
BLOMMENKEMPER, 101
BLOODWORTH, 6
BOARD, 6 101 140
BOARMAN, 163
BOATMAN, 186
BOCEK, 6
BODINE, 6
BOEHM, 185
BOEVING, 6
BOGAR, 140
BOGART, 140
BOGGES, 140
BOGGS, 6 186
BOHANNAN, 80
BOISSEVAIN, 81
BOLENGER, 176
BOLERJACK, 89
BOLES, 186
BOLEY, 172
BOLIN, 6 78
BOLLEN, 101
BOLLING, 101
BOLLINGER, 6
BOLY, 6
BOND, 7 185
BONE, 109
BONNER, 109
BOOK, 7
BOOKOUT, 109 186
BOOR, 7
BOOTEN, 7
BOOTH, 154
BOOTHBY, 101
BOOTHE, 156
BOOZER, 7
BORDEN, 175
BORMAN, 160
BORNTRAGER, 7
BORUM, 109
BORYLS, 160
BOSEK, 7
BOSWORTH, 81
BOTTS, 157 159
BOUDINIER, 191
BOULTON, 90
BOUNDS, 7 76 109

BOURDENEAU, 101
BOURROUGHS, 10
BOW, 140
BOWDEN, 59 123
BOWEN, 81 124 126 135 185
BOWENS, 183-184
BOWERS, 123 133
BOWLES, 101 152
BOWMAN, 83-84 119 137 183-184
BOWN, 155
BOWSER, 184
BOX, 7 82 130
BOXLEY, 101
BOYCE, 109
BOYD, 7 93 98 101 125 161 167-168 191
BOYER, 7 76 116-117 119 123 125 127 130-131
BOZARK, 7
BOZARTH, 140 155-159 166 169 171 176 182
BOZWORTH, 101
BRACKEN, 7
BRACKIN, 7
BRACKNEY, 182
BRADEN, 170
BRADFORD, 7 131
BRADGAN, 157
BRADLEY, 155 173 187
BRADSHAW, 126 157 159 170 172
BRADWAY, 86 88
BRADY, 7
BRAGG, 7 153 164 169 171 182
BRAIDY, 7
BRAINERD, 187
BRAKE, 7
BRALY, 101
BRAMBALL, 136
BRAME, 119 132 134 136 138
BRAMLET, 134
BRANAM, 174 181
BRANAMAN, 168 173
BRANCH, 7
BRANDON, 7
BRANDT, 7
BRANNOCK, 191
BRANNON, 8
BRANNUM, 8
BRANSTETTER, 160 165 168
BRASHEARS, 157 161 164
BRASHERS, 177
BRASSFIELD, 140 157 159 168

BRATCHER, 8
BRAUD, 109
BRAWLEY, 116
BRAZNIK, 8
BREEDLOVE, 164
BRENDEL, 109
BRENDLE, 109
BRENNEN, 133
BRENT, 8
BREWER, 89 101 133-134
BREWINGTON, 173 181
BREWNER, 177
BRIAN, 140
BRIBAR, 59
BRICKELL, 8
BRICKER, 180
BRICKETT, 8
BRICKLE, 8
BRIDDLE, 183
BRIDGMAN, 8
BRIENT, 140
BRIGGS, 8 99 191
BRIGHT, 78 80 101
BRIGHTWELL, 8
BRINGOLF, 101
BRINK, 8
BRINKLEY, 121 123 134-135
BRISON, 140
BRISTO, 153
BRISTOL, 120
BRITT, 8
BRITTON, 101
BROADDUS, 95
BROAM, 101
BROCK, 101 191
BROGG, 8
BROKOETTER, 8
BRONIZER, 186
BRONSON, 86
BROOK, 162
BROOKS, 8 117 120 123-124 136 138 140 172 183-185
BROTHERS, 8
BROUGH, 181
BROWER, 154-155 185
BROWN, 8-9 91 99 101 109 116 122 128 136 139-140 145 162 167 171-172 174 181 183 187
BROWNELL, 159 164-165 170
BROWNING, 9 126
BROYLES, 9 101 156 158 160

BRUCE, 9 130 152 170
BRUMIER, 145
BRUMMET, 172-173
BRUMMETT, 179
BRUMMITT, 9
BRUNDHEE, 182
BRUNER, 177 183-184
BRUNNERT, 109
BRUNO, 109
BRUNSON, 9
BRYAN, 9 95 126 132-133 168 171 190
BRYANT, 9 101 163
BRYANUM, 101
BRYSON, 90
BUATTE, 145
BUCHANAN, 9 118-120
BUCHER, 9
BUCK, 101
BUCKALOO, 154-155 160
BUCKHANON, 140
BUCKLES, 120
BUCKLEY, 183-184
BUCKNER, 178
BUCKRIDGE, 140
BUCU, 9
BUCY, 122
BUELL, 187
BUFFINGTON, 9
BUFORD, 154
BUGIST, 126
BUHL, 174
BUHLER, 9
BULKLEY, 175
BULLIS, 76
BUMGARTNER, 114
BUMPUSS, 9
BUNCH, 156
BUNDY, 156
BUNER, 186
BUOY, 177
BURANARD, 160
BURDEN, 101
BURDETT, 91
BURGARD, 95
BURGERT, 145
BURGES, 180
BURGESS, 191
BURGIN, 115
BURGMAN, 10
BURHAM, 185
BURK, 182

BURKE, 10
BURKEEN, 10
BURKETT, 10 95
BURLE, 145
BURNARD, 157
BURNERD, 154
BURNES, 10
BURNETT, 10 101 109 163 170
BURNHAM, 120
BURNLEY, 125
BURNON, 140
BURNS, 101 109 121-122 156 158 160-161 167 177
BURPO, 10
BURRIS, 10 173
BURRISS, 101
BURRY, 191
BURSON, 10
BURTON, 10 95 140 185
BUSBY, 10
BUSCH, 95
BUSCHMAN, 10
BUSHNELL, 83 157
BUSTER, 10
BUTCHER, 99
BUTLER, 10 77 124 181 185
BUTT, 137
BUTTS, 10 155 170
BUTWORTH, 166
BUZBY, 101
BYARD, 133
BYBEE, 136
BYERS, 178
BYORD, 10
BYRD, 10 170 177 187 191
BYRNS, 180 182
BYWATER, 87
C----, 153
CABANESS, 101
CAGEL, 101
CAGLE, 101
CAHILL, 187
CAIL, 158
CAIN, 157 159 165-166 177
CALDWELL, 10 76 186
CALHOON, 186
CALHOUN, 10 110
CALISON, 155 157
CALL, 10 86
CALLEM, 155
CALLEWAY, 140

CALLISON, 153
CALOWAY, 11
CALTRIN, 101
CALVIN, 11 180
CAMBELL, 121
CAMBRON, 11
CAMDEN, 11
CAMERON, 140
CAMMEL, 179
CAMPBELL, 11 110 126 129 131 140 162 164 166-167 175 181
CANADA, 118 153 175
CANADAY, 162
CANAN, 110
CANATSY, 155
CANDLER, 11
CANE, 171
CANLEY, 11
CANNELL, 11
CANTERBERY, 116
CANTRELL, 11
CAPEHART, 101
CAPPER, 11
CAPPS, 156-158 160 162 175-176 178
CARDER, 11
CARDWELL, 11 110
CARGEL, 129
CARICK, 85
CARLISLE, 99 101
CARMACK, 101
CARMICHAEL, 125
CARMON, 11
CARNAGEY, 178
CARNAHAN, 115 137
CARNER, 185
CARNEY, 126
CAROTHERS, 110
CARPENTER, 11 122 152 175
CARR, 78 138
CARREL, 140
CARRICK, 88
CARRICO, 11
CARRINO, 110
CARROLL, 11-12 101
CARSON, 12 80
CARSOOW, 145
CARTER, 12 76 80 99 101 116 133-134 138 140 186
CARTHER, 124
CARTON, 101
CARUTHERS, 12 134

CARVER, 187 191
CARY, 12
CASE, 98 165
CASEY, 12 115 121
CASH, 12 101
CASKEY, 77 183
CASON, 12 160 167 180-181
CASPER, 12 186
CASS, 186
CASSADY, 186
CASSINGER, 12
CASTEEL, 125-126 141 164
CASTILLO, 12
CASTLEN, 110
CASWELL, 186
CATE, 141
CATES, 128
CATHER, 101
CATO, 12 93
CAUDILL, 141
CAVE, 12
CAVITT, 184
CAVNESS, 99
CEM, 176 181
CHADWELL, 181
CHADWICK, 12
CHAFFMAN, 12
CHAFINN, 12
CHALK, 12
CHALLES, 101
CHAMBERS, 99 161
CHANDLER, 92 168 183-184
CHANEY, 12 170
CHAPIN, 116
CHAPMAN, 12 76 101 184
CHARD, 12
CHARLTON, 153
CHATAM, 12
CHATMAN, 13
CHAVEI, 110
CHEATHAM, 187
CHEDIESTER, 13
CHEEK, 166
CHEEKS, 13
CHENAULT, 13 101
CHENOWETH, 13
CHERRY, 13
CHESTER, 101
CHILCUTT, 13
CHILDERS, 101
CHILDRESS, 13 173

CHILTON, 116 118 120 129-130 135-136 138
CHINN, 167
CHITLER, 13
CHITWOOD, 126 128 132 135
CHOAT, 159
CHOSSIER, 13
CHOWNING, 168
CHRIST, 179
CHRISTIAN, 13 91 93 119 124 134 154 161 177
CHRISTOPHER, 13
CHRISTY, 13
CHRONISTER, 13
CHRYSTAL, 156
CHUPP, 13
CHURCH, 135 185
CIBANON, 158
CISSEL, 187
CIZEMORE, 159
CLANTON, 101
CLAPPER, 168
CLARDY, 141
CLARK, 13 81 101 122 129 136 138 141 162-163 167 174 176-177 180 183-184 188
CLARKSON, 93
CLARY, 191
CLAWSON, 13
CLAY, 119
CLAYBROOK, 153 183
CLAYBURN, 120 136
CLAYPOLE, 92
CLAYTON, 123 129
CLEAVER, 13
CLEGGET, 141
CLEM, 154 159 161-162 169-170
CLEMENS, 162
CLEMENTS, 13
CLEMMERSON, 179
CLEMMONS, 127
CLEMONS, 13 110
CLEVELAND, 95 115
CLEVINGER, 186
CLEVLAN, 14
CLIBOURN, 101
CLICK, 14
CLIFTON, 14 154 158 163 167 172-174
CLINE, 14 169 176 183
CLINTON, 93
CLOIN, 14
CLOSE, 133 163
CLOUD, 77
CLOW, 101
CLUBB, 101
CLUPP, 86
CLYBURN, 121 125 133
CLYMA, 88
COALTER, 141
COAN, 88
COATS, 99 101
COBB, 154
COBBLE, 99
COBBS, 101
COBLE, 14
COCHRAN, 14 81 110 176 179 185
COCKRAN, 101 132 137
COCKROM, 127
COCKRUM, 186
COCRUMB, 154
COFFEE, 158
COFFELT, 101
COFFEY, 179 186
COFFMAN, 141
COFFREY, 186
COGHILL, 156 159 165-166 171
COIN, 77
COLCHER, 14
COLDERON, 101
COLE, 14 102 118 123 126 156 164 168 178 180 186
COLEMAN, 14 91 118 120-121 124 126 132-133 136 152 175 185
COLLARD, 14
COLLET, 141 157
COLLETT, 158 173
COLLIER, 14 174
COLLIN, 154
COLLINS, 14 110 116 118 124 134 137-138 159 180 183 186
COLLISON, 171
COLLOP, 169-170
COLSON, 191
COLTER, 14
COLVIN, 92
COLVING, 171
COLWELL, 14
COMBS, 14 80 102 183
COMER, 102
COMSTOCK, 85
CONDRAY, 123 127 130-131 135
CONEFAX, 102

206

CONGER, 14
CONKEL, 167
CONKLE, 169 172-173 179
CONKLIN, 102 153
CONLEY, 94 138 175 177
CONN, 156 158
CONNELL, 110
CONNELLY, 169
CONNER, 132 164 176
CONNOR, 14 102
CONOVER, 14
CONOWAY, 120 123
CONRAD, 102 188
CONVERSE, 191
CONWAY, 93
COOK, 14-15 76 91 102 110 121 141 159 166 170 173-174 177 186 191
COOKE, 172
COOLEY, 15 102 157 168
COOLIDGE, 15
COONCE, 15
COONER, 178
COONROD, 102
COONS, 186
COOPER, 15 102 164
COOPERS, 15
COPE, 141
COPELAND, 15
COPELIN, 139
CORBIN, 166 180 184
CORBY, 82 102
CORDER, 15
CORDON, 15
COREY, 15 124 137
CORFFORD, 15
CORNEILSON, 152-153 155
CORNELISON, 131
CORNELIUS, 15
CORNELL, 167
CORNER, 76
CORNETT, 191
CORRELL, 175
CORTRITE, 176
CORUM, 141
CORWINE, 102
COSTELLO, 110
COSTIN, 15
COTES, 120 122
COTTON, 102 118 121-122 133-134 169
COUCH, 15
COUGHLIN, 188

COULTER, 179
COURTNEY, 156 161 172-173 178-179 183
COVEY, 168
COWARD, 15
COWDEN, 91
COWELL, 169 177 186
COWEN, 118 127 135
COWN, 15
COWSERT, 15
COX, 15 95 102 121 132 141 157 160-162 168 191
COZAD, 188
COZORT, 15
CRABTREE, 16 87 102
CRADY, 16
CRAFFORD, 16
CRAFT, 16
CRAGEN, 176
CRAGLE, 16
CRAIG, 16 110 191
CRAIGO, 102
CRAIN, 16 153
CRALLAY, 121
CRAMBOW, 102
CRANDELL, 120
CRANDLE, 156
CRANE, 92 175 183-184
CRAVENS, 16 102
CRAWFORD, 102 110 138 155 172 174 184
CRAWLEY, 136
CREAGOR, 131
CREASY, 122
CREEK, 16 141
CRENSHAW, 101
CREWS, 16
CRICKETTE, 186
CRIMPSLEY, 178
CRIPS, 16
CRISLIP, 16
CRISTMAN, 102
CRISWELL, 158 188
CRITES, 188
CRIVITZ, 16
CROCKETT, 16
CROFFORD, 16
CROMFIELD, 164
CROOK, 134
CROSBY, 175
CROSEN, 156

CROSGA, 135
CROSS, 16 76 139 159
CROSSFIELD, 16
CROSSIN, 16
CROUCH, 102 115 134 136
CROW, 16 102 152 171 174 178 181
CROWDER, 16 179 183
CROWEL, 86-87
CROWELL, 102
CROWLEY, 127 131 138
CROWNOVER, 124
CRUMM, 102
CRUMP, 16 91
CRUNK, 16-17
CUBOLIN, 159
CULBERTSON, 17
CULLISON, 175 188
CULLUP, 168
CULOP, 162
CULP, 17 141
CULTON, 102
CULVER, 180
CUMMINGS, 134 191
CUMMINS, 121
CUNNINGHAM, 17 102 137 153 157-158 167 169 173 178-180
CUPP, 184
CURD, 76
CURDT, 17
CURNEL, 17
CURRIER, 180
CURRY, 17
CURTIS, 17
CURTOIS, 145
CUTLERBOTH, 115
CUTTER, 179
D'SPAIN, 119
D----, 157
DABNEY, 160 177 180
DABRICO, 17
DACUS, 131
DAGES, 17
DAHIKE, 95
DAILEY, 89
DAIRDA, 110
DAISEY, 102
DALE, 89 102 168
DALEY, 141
DALTON, 17
DAMERON, 102
DAMERSON, 102

DAMRELL, 178
DANIEL, 98 163 176
DANIELS, 17 110 133 164 181
DARBY, 17
DARDEN, 102
DARE, 17
DARHAM, 17
DARLEY, 185
DARNALL, 163
DARNALLY, 90
DARNELL, 163-164
DARR, 102 117 181
DARREL, 179
DARRIS, 131
DARROW, 102 164 172
DAUGHERTY, 141 186
DAUGHETTE, 17
DAVENPORT, 17
DAVID, 83 85 176 179
DAVIDSON, 17 87-88 155 161 182
DAVIOTER, 110
DAVIS, 17-18 76-77 80 92 99 102 120 122-124 138 141 158 164-165 173 175 180-181 186 188
DAVISM, 84
DAVISON, 167
DAWSON, 102 122 131 135
DAYTON, 171
DEAK, 18
DEAL, 18
DEAN, 153 168
DEARDORFF, 159
DEATON, 18 171
DEBOLT, 102
DECKARD, 19
DECKER, 19 119 165
DEEP, 161
DEERING, 132
DEETON, 177
DEGRAFFENREID, 102
DEGROOT, 19
DEHAVEN, 126
DEIERLING, 186
DEITZ, 19
DEITZER, 19
DEKEN, 19
DELANEY, 19 102 124
DELCORE, 130
DELCOUR, 123
DELLER, 110
DELLINGER, 94

DEMARIS, 19
DEMENT, 19
DENHARDT, 19
DENMAN, 76
DENNEDY, 138
DENNERD, 160
DENNEY, 84
DENNING, 19 161
DENNIS, 19 169
DENNON, 160
DENNY, 19 141
DENTON, 170 174
DEOLD, 102
DEPOYSTER, 19
DEPRIEST, 19 127
DERHAM, 102
DEROLD, 175
DERRABERRY, 141
DERRINGTON, 19
DESHAZER, 141
DESPAIN, 134
DETEBITTS, 165
DEVALL, 19
DEVAN, 168
DEWELL, 170
DEWITT, 80
DEWSENBURY, 102
DIAMOND, 19 119
DICE, 185
DICKENS, 19
DICKENSON, 102
DICKERSON, 102 154 192
DICKEY, 19 102
DICKINSON, 162
DICKSON, 116
DIE, 181
DIESTER, 152
DIETER, 152
DIETZER, 19
DIGRAFFENREID, 102
DILLENDER, 102
DILLION, 154
DILLON, 102
DILMAN, 153
DILTS, 164
DINES, 93
DINGLE, 154
DINNING, 126
DINWIDDIE, 93
DIONYSUIS, 185
DITMAR, 141

DIVINNIE, 19
DIXON, 19 141 175 179
DOBBS, 19
DOCKERY, 162 177 179 183
DOCKINS, 19
DODD, 19 179
DODGE, 141 174
DODSON, 19-20 154-155 157-158 161-162 166 171-173 178
DOERR, 110 185
DOGGETT, 20
DOLAN, 165
DOLE, 123
DOLEY, 180
DOLLINS, 20
DOLLISON, 102
DOLZ, 20
DONE, 153
DONICA, 20
DONNALLY, 177
DONNEGAN, 102
DONNELLY, 177
DONOHEW, 188
DONOVAN, 20
DOOLEY, 92 155 168
DOOLIN, 20 83
DOOLITTLE, 110
DOOMEY, 178
DORDGE, 145
DORR, 181
DORSETT, 20
DOTSON, 176
DOTTS, 20
DOUDY, 20
DOUGHERTY, 20 102
DOUGLAS, 20 159 192
DOUGLASS, 20 175
DOUTHETT, 20
DOUTHITT, 20
DOVER, 20 165
DOW, 81
DOWD, 20
DOWELL, 141
DOWLING, 110
DOWN, 83
DOWNEY, 102
DOWNING, 170
DOWTY, 102
DOYLE, 20 127
DOZE, 141
DRAKE, 20 122 154 159 174

DRE----, 156
DRENNEN, 166
DRENNON, 20
DREUALL, 20
DREW, 20
DREWRY, 157
DRIVER, 102
DRURY, 20 92
DRY, 20
DUBOIS, 141
DUCKETT, 20
DUCKWORTH, 20-21
DUDGEON, 188
DUDLEY, 21 79
DUFF, 102
DUFFY, 21 154
DUGDALE, 134
DUGLAS, 141
DUKE, 21 102 128
DULANEY, 175
DULL, 21
DULY, 21
DUMEY, 180
DUNAGAN, 141
DUNBAR, 91
DUNCAN, 21 102 192
DUNCANE, 141
DUNEHOO, 21
DUNHAM, 163 167-168 170 173-174 178 180 182 186
DUNHAPP, 76
DUNLAP, 21 99
DUNLAPP, 21
DUNLAY, 21
DUNN, 21 102 115 192
DUNNEGAN, 129 132
DUNNING, 21
DUNNINGTON, 183-184
DUNNIVAN, 102
DURBIN, 138
DURHAM, 21
DUVALL, 134 145 156
DWYER, 137
DYE, 162 167 175
DYSON, 91
EADES, 96
EAKER, 21
EARHART, 154-155 159 162 165
EARL, 21
EARLEMAN, 21
EARLS, 76

EARLY, 110
EARP, 21
EASLY, 174
EASON, 186
EAST, 102
EASTIN, 21
EASTON, 21
EASTWOOD, 21
EATON, 21 110 124 127
EAVERSON, 81
EBERLE, 188
EBY, 153 158
ECKERT, 145
EDDINGTON, 120 124
EDELMAN, 22
EDGAR, 94
EDINGTON, 21 122
EDMONDS, 102
EDMONSTON, 22
EDWARDS, 22 76 102 158 185
EGGERS, 115
EHLERS, 22
EHRLICH, 110
EHRSAM, 22
EICHSCHLAG, 110
EICKERMAN, 95
EIFERT, 171
EIFFORT, 162
EILLIS, 138
EISENHOWER, 188
EITEL, 178
EIZER, 161
ELAN, 22
ELDER, 22
ELFERS, 22
ELIZABETH, 169
ELLER, 173 176
ELLERMAN, 22
ELLETT, 96
ELLIOTT, 22 90 102 121 141 164 166 168 183-184
ELLIS, 22 135 145
ELLMORE, 174
ELMORE, 173
ELMS, 186
ELSEA, 179
ELY, 153 162 181
ELZE, 178
EMBREE, 179
EMERSON, 22 155
EMERY, 22

EMINS, 122
EMMERT, 186
EMMONS, 124 135 162 173
EMONTS, 188
ENDICOTT, 102
ENGLAND, 127 136 141 156
ENGLEHART, 102
ENGLES, 22
ENGLISH, 17 22
ENLOW, 22
ENNIS, 22 102-103
ENSICK, 164
ENTENMAN, 117 126
ENYERT, 141
EPERLY, 157
EPERSON, 155
EPPERLY, 160 177
EPPERSON, 103 186
EPPLY, 23
EPPRIGHT, 103
EPPS, 22
EPSON, 179
ERB, 78
ERKE, 95
ERNEST, 169
ERVIN, 23 154
ERWIN, 186
ERZNOKNIK, 23
ESLEY, 162
ESMON, 23
ESSE, 90
ESSIG, 141
ESSMAN, 23
ESTEP, 103
ESTEPT, 126
ESTIS, 141
ETHERIDGE, 23
ETSEL, 161
EUBANKS, 167 176 179
EUDALEY, 23
EVANES, 141
EVANS, 23 84 90 93 131 141 155 162-164
EVANSE, 103
EVENS, 141
EVERETT, 23 118 141
EVERHEART, 163
EVERHHART, 23
EVERSAUL, 181
EVERT, 103
EVERY, 23

EWING, 23 92 170 176 186-187
EYE, 23
EZELL, 23
FADDIS, 141
FAGG, 93
FAIRLESS, 23
FAITH, 23
FALK, 145
FALLEBY, 146
FALLERT, 146
FANN, 23
FANTON, 146
FARABEE, 110
FARLEY, 99
FARLOW, 180
FARMER, 23 115 119 163
FARR, 165 174 178 182
FARRINGTON, 137
FARRIS, 110 115 182
FAST, 115
FAUCETT, 23
FAULKIN, 23
FAULKNER, 130
FEATHERLY, 174
FEGLY, 178
FELKER, 174
FELKINS, 23
FELLAR, 170
FELT, 87
FELTS, 23
FERGUSON, 23 103 138 158 166-167 169 171
FERRILL, 23
FESLER, 23
FESSLER, 185
FETNEY, 103
FICK, 185
FIEH, 146
FIELDER, 23
FIELDS, 23 110
FIFER, 180
FIGGER, 186
FILLEY, 162
FIN, 152
FINDLEY, 171
FINLAY, 185
FINNEGAN, 95
FINNEY, 23 128
FISCHBECK, 95
FISHBURN, 103
FISHER, 23-24 82 103 123 133

FISKE, 171
FITZGERALD, 103 132 135
FITZGERIL, 141
FITZPATRICK, 103
FITZWATER, 134
FLANAKIN, 24
FLANERY, 103
FLEMING, 127
FLERER, 165
FLETCHER, 153-154 163 166 171 176
FLICE, 146
FLICK, 186
FLINT, 132
FLORICK, 87
FLOWERS, 99
FLOYD, 24 153 155-156 159-160 166 168 175 177 183
FLYNN, 168
FOGLESONG, 186
FONDLE, 24
FORD, 99 103 110 154-155 158-159 168
FORGY, 103
FORREST, 24
FORSYTH, 82
FORT, 120-121
FORTNER, 162 168
FORTUNE, 186
FOSTER, 24 103 115 120 141 164-165 167-168 181 183 192
FOUST, 24
FOUTS, 24
FOWLER, 24 81 110 118 123-124 126 130 165 167
FOWLKS, 24
FOX, 141 181
FRAKER, 141
FRAKIER, 154
FRANABARGER, 167
FRANCIS, 24 177
FRANCISCO, 24
FRANEY, 24
FRANKFORT, 164
FRANKLIN, 24 117 141 157 174
FRANKO, 24
FRANKUM, 183
FRASHER, 24
FRASIER, 103
FRAY, 24
FRAZE, 156
FRAZIER, 25 110 123-124 136
FRAZY, 154

FREAL, 182
FREDERICK, 25 99 183-184
FREDRICK, 135
FREELAND, 137
FREEMAN, 25 117 119 133 154 173
FREER, 25
FRENCH, 25 103 154
FREY, 157
FRIDAY, 25
FRIEND, 25 177
FRIZZELL, 25
FROST, 25 88 141
FROWMAN, 141
FRY, 25 99 136 141
FUGATE, 156 186 192
FUGIT, 110
FUKGISSON, 103
FULCHER, 155
FULK, 103
FULLER, 25 103 141
FULLERTON, 103
FULLINGTON, 103
FULTON, 25 141
FUNK, 25 186
FUNKE, 25
FURNISH, 155 165 173 180
FURRUAH, 182
FUSON, 25
G----, 157
GABE, 185
GADEN, 25
GAFFENY, 87
GAGE, 25
GAINES, 25 137 188
GALASPY, 155
GALBRAITH, 25 127
GALLAGHER, 77 97
GALLEWAY, 141
GALLIMORE, 25
GALLION, 166
GALLOWAY, 78 141
GALLUP, 86
GALYEN, 159
GAMBILLS, 126
GAMBLE, 25 82
GANDY, 25
GANN, 25
GANNT, 85
GARARD, 163
GARDINE, 186
GARDNER, 25 163 166 184-186

GARLOCK, 180 184
GARRETT, 25-26 76 155-156 160 163 179 183
GARRISON, 26 77 170 192
GARTH, 92
GARVER, 26 103
GARVIN, 185
GARY, 110
GASH, 162
GASSAWAY, 121
GATES, 115 156 158 160 163 175 182
GATEWOOD, 26
GATLIN, 26
GATTEL, 146
GATTEN, 177
GAULTNEY, 26
GAY, 141
GAYLE, 26
GEAN, 26 76
GEBHART, 103 110
GEISLER, 119 146
GENTRY, 86 121 123
GENTZEN, 26
GEORGE, 26 141 153 186 188
GERARD, 140
GERDIS, 26
GERHART, 26
GERICK, 177
GERSHAM, 103
GERTEN, 26
GEVEAR, 103
GIBBS, 26 117 121 132
GIBONEY, 103
GIBSON, 26 79 91 103 181
GIDDINGS, 81-82
GIDEON, 79
GIER, 186
GIFFORD, 26 87
GILBERT, 76 152 192
GILBREATH, 26
GILDERMAN, 83
GILL, 141 160 171 174 176
GILLES, 141
GILLESPIE, 26
GILLHAM, 167
GILLIAM, 26
GILLIHAN, 26
GILLILAN, 192
GILLILAND, 103 186
GILLIN, 26
GILLION, 26
GILLIS, 27
GILLISPIE, 183-184 186
GILLISPY, 153
GILLSTRAP, 103
GILMAN, 27 171
GILMORE, 103 159 168 178
GILSTRAP, 103 156 158 166
GIMINGS, 175
GING, 116
GINNIS, 27
GIRARD, 103 146
GISI, 146
GIST, 103
GITHENS, 27
GIVENS, 27
GLADDEN, 27
GLADIEUX, 96
GLASEBROOK, 27
GLASGOW, 27 169
GLASS, 27 110
GLASSCOCK, 103
GLAVIN, 88
GLEASON, 166
GLENN, 27
GLENSLOSER, 26
GLICK, 96
GLOVER, 27 85 87 188
GOBLE, 27
GODAIR, 146
GODARD, 184
GODDARD, 27
GODWIN, 27
GOFF, 27
GOING, 132
GOINGS, 27 115
GOINS, 27
GOLD, 91
GOLDEN, 27
GOLDERMAN, 84
GOLDSBY, 179
GOLDSMITH, 27
GOLDSWORTHY, 96
GOMER, 27
GONTERMAN, 27
GOOCE, 180
GOOD, 164-165 168-169 171 179
GOODMAN, 27 192
GOODRICH, 27
GOODSON, 129 164
GOOLSBERRY, 176
GOOLSLEY, 118

GORDAN, 174
GORDEN, 141
GORDINIER, 27
GORDON, 27 92 103 143
GOSNELL, 117 127 135 137
GOSS, 27 115 158
GOSSER, 186
GOSSETT, 27 117 121
GOUGE, 99
GOULD, 81 96 155 185
GOUNDRY, 163
GOURLEY, 27
GOVRO, 146
GOWEN, 27 128
GOWER, 27
GRABLE, 27
GRACE, 103
GRAFUS, 121
GRAGE, 171
GRAHAM, 27 86 103 110 122 138 170 180
GRAINGER, 85
GRANGER, 87
GRANT, 103 183-184
GRASON, 173 177
GRATIOT, 185
GRATZ, 28
GRAUMSCH, 186
GRAVENS, 99
GRAVES, 77 90 130 139 178 186
GRAVIS, 28
GRAY, 28 79 96 103 139 164
GRAYHAM, 78
GRAYSON, 180
GREASON, 28
GREATHOUSE, 28 164 174
GREEN, 28 76 119 121-122 124-125 130-131 135 137 141 165 184
GREENE, 119 130 136 159
GREENOUGH, 83
GREENSLATE, 175
GREENSTATE, 179
GREENSTEED, 175
GREENSTREET, 158-160 165 167 171 175
GREENTREE, 28
GREENWALD, 116
GREENWOOD, 28 163 171
GREER, 28 169
GREGG, 165 169-171
GREGORY, 28 133 186 188

GREMMINGER, 146
GRESHAM, 119 136
GREUFE, 192
GREY, 138
GRIDER, 28
GRIDLEY, 28
GRIESHABER, 146
GRIFFEM, 28
GRIFFIN, 121 123 157 167 172 192
GRIFFITH, 28 103 161
GRIGG, 154
GRIGGS, 88
GRIGSBY, 167 188
GRIM, 174
GRIMES, 28
GRINDSTAFF, 92 137
GRISHAM, 28
GRIST, 125 169
GRISWOLD, 82 163
GRIZZLE, 28
GRO----, 156
GROBE, 28
GROETZINGER, 192
GROGAN, 154 156-158 162 164 170 176 182
GROOM, 126 141
GROSS, 125
GROSSELOSS, 155
GROVE, 28
GROVES, 76 120 161
GRUBB, 103
GRUBBS, 91
GRULE, 179
GRUMMETT, 130
GRUNDMAN, 110
GUARD, 28
GUESS, 28
GUETH, 146
GUFFEY, 154
GUFFY, 28
GUINN, 78-80
GULLEDGE, 28-29 76
GULLY, 29
GUN, 156
GUNDY, 169
GUNN, 124 126-127 130 185
GUNNING, 181
GUNTER, 118 141
GUPTON, 159
GUTHRIE, 29 103
H----SON, 155

HAAG, 29
HACKNEY, 192
HACKWORTH, 128 135
HADEN, 103
HAFER, 103
HAFFNER, 172
HAGAER, 29
HAGAN, 91 192
HAGEMAN, 185
HAGEMIER, 110
HAGER, 29 103 186
HAGERTY, 110
HAHN, 29 177
HAINES, 180
HAINLINE, 176
HAIRER, 29
HAIRL, 178
HAISLIP, 29
HAITER, 141
HAKE, 128
HALBERSLEBEW, 79
HALE, 80 180
HALEY, 29
HALFERTY, 29
HALL, 29 92 103 119 124 128 131 141 152 155 162 166-167 170-171 177 179 181 183-184
HALLEY, 172 174 180
HALLOWAY, 160
HALRATH, 29
HALSTEAD, 180
HALTER, 29
HAM, 29
HAMILTON, 29-30 84 103 111 154 156 174 182 185
HAMLER, 180
HAMLIN, 160-161 174 176
HAMMER, 103
HAMMERMAN, 174
HAMMOCK, 111
HAMMONS, 29
HAMPTON, 30 115 117-118 129 141 172 186 188
HANCOCK, 30 79
HANDING, 111
HANDLEY, 111
HANE, 183-184
HANES, 87 141
HANGER, 115 119 133
HANKINS, 159-160 176-177 184
HANKS, 121 138 141 163

HANLEY, 30
HANLIN, 170
HANNA, 163
HANNAH, 158 172 175 178 181-182
HANNAN, 30
HANNARS, 122
HANNERS, 118
HANNOH, 30
HANNUM, 103
HANSACKER, 161
HANSFORD, 103
HANSLEY, 158
HANSON, 103
HAPPY, 103
HARBER, 111
HARDCASTLE, 111
HARDEE, 177
HARDER, 117
HARDESTY, 30
HARDIN, 30 121 158 175-176 180
HARDING, 87-88
HARDUCEK, 30
HARDY, 122
HARE, 103
HARGIS, 159 162 170
HARGRAVE, 153 162 192
HARGROVE, 30 161 183-184
HARICOCK, 146
HARINGTON, 141
HARLAN, 169
HARLAND, 141
HARLEY, 128
HARMAN, 30
HARMERS, 132
HARMON, 30 127 167
HARNED, 30
HARNEY, 120
HAROLD, 30 111
HARP, 80 178
HARPER, 30 96 103
HARRAWOOD, 30
HARRELL, 30
HARRELSON, 30
HARRIGNTON, 30
HARRIS, 30 80 90-92 103 122 125 132-133 141 159 163 165 181 192
HARSEL, 141
HARSHBERGER, 30
HART, 30 115 136 172 177 180 185-186
HARTFORD, 176 179
HARTMAN, 87 170

HARVEY, 31 94 103 123 133 166
HARWELL, 31
HASE, 155
HASKILL, 185
HASKINS, 31
HASSELL, 125
HAST, 31
HASTINGS, 31
HATFIELD, 159 163
HATHAWAY, 31 154
HAVENS, 175
HAVTER, 85
HAWK, 104 180
HAWKEN, 152
HAWKINS, 31 103
HAWTHORN, 31
HAY, 31
HAYDEN, 154 175
HAYES, 31 79-80 173 176 179
HAYMAN, 31
HAYNES, 31 171 182 186
HAYS, 31-32 103 163 169 176-177 186 192
HAYSE, 178
HAZELWOOD, 103
HEACOX, 32
HEAD, 32
HEADLEE, 134
HEADRICK, 32 137-138
HEADY, 32
HEANELEY, 155
HEARST, 130
HEARTLEY, 32
HEARTLINE, 32
HEASE, 32
HEATH, 32 136
HEATHER, 153
HECKINS, 185
HEDRICK, 115 129 156
HEDSPETH, 32
HEFNER, 32
HEFRAAN, 117
HEFTON, 103
HEHR, 146
HEIDBRIEDER, 185
HEIFNER, 131
HEINZELMANN, 152
HEIZELMAN, 185
HELLEMAN, 32
HELLER, 147
HELLUMS, 32
HELM, 32 192-193
HELTON, 32
HELVEY, 129-130 135 138
HELVY, 32
HELWIG, 171 175
HEMBRY, 32
HEMBY, 32
HEMMICK, 32
HEMPHILL, 78
HENCE, 157 159
HENCIL, 32
HENDERSON, 32 103 111 141 177 185
HENDRICK, 103
HENDRICKS, 166
HENDRICKSON, 32-33
HENDRIN, 182
HENDRIX, 33 85 92
HENDY, 188
HENNEMAN, 147
HENNING, 165
HENNY, 193
HENRY, 33 90 94 103 111 137
HENSEN, 119
HENSLEY, 33 156
HENSON, 33 103 129 135-136
HENTON, 167
HENTZ, 111
HERALD, 103
HERBOTH, 186
HERD, 139
HERDLICK, 111
HERLEY, 103
HERMAN, 111
HERNDON, 103
HERRIGNTON, 33
HERRIN, 183-184
HERRING, 96 175
HERRON, 138 167
HERT, 33
HERTER, 147
HERZOG, 147
HESSELRODE, 33
HESTER, 33
HEWETT, 103
HEWITT, 170 179
HIBBARD, 161 179
HICKAM, 94
HICKERSON, 136 165
HICKEY, 103
HICKMAN, 87 158 160 162 166-167 176 188

HICKS, 33 116 183
HICKSON, 33 141
HIETT, 141
HIGGA, 33
HIGGINS, 111
HIGGS, 111
HIGHLAND, 33
HIGHLY, 78
HIGHT, 186
HIGHTOWER, 33
HILBRANT, 184
HILDRETH, 179
HILDRICH, 33-34
HILES, 76 89
HILGARD, 111
HILL, 34 87 99 111 116 121 125 130 141 164 173 177 182-184
HILLHOUSE, 89
HILLIS, 34
HILT, 161
HILTIBIDOL, 136
HINCH, 138
HINDE, 141
HINDMAN, 87-88 155
HINDS, 103 188
HINES, 34 93
HINKLE, 34 123 137
HINTON, 172 182
HIRBY, 34
HIRKLE, 172
HITCHCOCK, 34
HITE, 111
HIXON, 34
HO----, 156
HOATT, 141
HOBLET, 141
HODAPP, 34
HODGE, 34 88 111
HODGES, 158-159 166
HODLER, 34
HODMAN, 141
HODSON, 34
HOELFELER, 111
HOELSCHER, 34
HOERR, 34
HOESTER, 185
HOFF, 34
HOFFMAN, 34
HOFLER, 156
HOGAN, 34
HOGE, 96
HOGG, 130
HOGLAN, 155
HOGUSE, 34
HOHN, 34
HOLCOMB, 103
HOLDEN, 98
HOLDMAN, 111
HOLEMAN, 156-157 172 178
HOLFORD, 35
HOLLAND, 35 131 136
HOLLENBECK, 180
HOLLIDAY, 35 147
HOLLIS, 35 128
HOLLMAN, 35
HOLLOWAY, 35 104 133 157 161 186
HOLMAN, 35 161
HOLMES, 35 172
HOLSAPPLE, 35
HOLT, 141 154
HOMES, 141
HONEA, 121 124
HOOBERRY, 35
HOOCK, 147
HOOD, 35 94 104
HOOK, 188
HOOPER, 120 135 138
HOOPS, 35
HOOVER, 35 158 182
HOP, 177
HOPKINS, 35 84 104 121 185
HOPPE, 35
HOPSON, 168
HORN, 35 111 128 155 183
HORNBECK, 104
HORNSINGER, 104
HORTON, 35 127 165-166 168 181
HOSFELT, 35
HOSKINS, 125 134
HOUGH, 35
HOUGHLAND, 104
HOUGHTON, 181
HOUK, 167
HOUKS, 35
HOUSE, 35 123 129
HOUSER, 188
HOUSMAN, 35
HOUSTON, 77 170 186
HOUTS, 35
HOVER, 35
HOVIS, 163
HOWARD, 35 83 104 117 128 134 160

HOWARD (cont) 186 188
HOWE, 87 175
HOWELEY, 167
HOWELL, 35 141
HOWER, 35
HOWERTON, 179
HOWLAND, 85 88
HOY, 138
HOYLE, 35
HRIBSHEK, 35
HUBBARD, 104 160 165
HUBBS, 35
HUBECK, 35
HUBER, 147
HUBREY, 186
HUCKEBY, 152
HUCKSHORN, 135
HUDDLESTON, 35 180
HUDDLETON, 162
HUDGINS, 35
HUDSON, 35-36 93 193
HUETT, 119 122 134
HUFF, 36 104 186
HUFFAKER, 141
HUFFER, 159
HUFFMAN, 134 141 173-174 181
HUGAN, 125
HUGHBANKS, 173
HUGHES, 127 141 179
HUGHLAND, 155
HUGHS, 118 171 173
HUGHY, 36
HULEN, 92
HULET, 153
HULL, 130 154
HUMBYRD, 139
HUME, 92
HUMMEL, 111
HUMPHREY, 36 141
HUMPHREYS, 96 152 154
HUNLEY, 36 182
HUNNICUTT, 36
HUNSAKER, 181
HUNT, 36 118 193
HUNTER, 36 92-93 118 141
HUPPER, 178
HURD, 186
HURKA, 147
HURLEY, 89
HURT, 104

HUSHAW, 104
HUSKEY, 36
HUSON, 36
HUTCHERSON, 117
HUTCHINGS, 121
HUTCHINSON, 185
HUTCHISON, 36
HUTSON, 36 171
HUTTON, 111
HYATT, 87
HYDE, 36 77
HYLER, 186
I----, 154
ILGENFRITZ, 174
ING, 87
INMAN, 36 79 124
INMON, 78
IRBY, 36
IRNY, 36
IRON, 81
IRVIN, 93 104
IRVINE, 141
IRWIN, 104
ISELEY, 104
ITELL, 161
IVEY, 169
IVIE, 158-159 167 172 179-180
IVY, 36
JACKETT, 104
JACKSON, 36 81 84 104 119-120 133 141 156 158 160-161 180
JACOBI, 152
JACOBS, 88 180 183 193
JAMERSON, 104
JAMES, 36-37 104 119 141 147 170 188
JAMESON, 104
JAMINIK, 37
JANES, 85
JANSEN, 37
JARRETT, 116 120
JARVIS, 144
JASON, 104
JASPER, 137
JASTRAM, 111
JEANS, 159
JEFFERIES, 169
JEFFERS, 181
JEFFORDS, 37
JEKEL, 185
JENKINS, 37 92 111
JENNINGS, 37 98 111 168-169 180

JEROME, 178 188
JERRARD, 176
JETT, 37
JEWEL, 37 86 88
JILES, 37
JIMES, 111
JINKINS, 128 142
JOGGERST, 147
JOHN, 142 180 186
JOHNS, 37 77 142 165 167
JOHNSON, 37-38 78-79 82 86 99 104 126-127 136 142 152-153 155-156 159 164 168 170 174 176 179 185-186 188 193 197
JOHNSTON, 111 121 123 128 134 175 187-188
JOINER, 38 134
JOINES, 38
JOINS, 38
JOKERST, 147
JOLLY, 38
JONAS, 38
JONES, 38 77 83 86 91 100 104 127 130-131 135 137 142 154-155 158 160 162 174 177 180 183-184 186 188 193
JONKER, 188
JONSTON, 142
JOPLIN, 123 129 135
JORDAN, 38 104 123-124 130 193
JOSEPH, 39
JUDD, 155 181
JUDY, 39
JULIAN, 39 121 126
JURBLER, 160
JURDEN, 185
JUSTICE, 39 130 133
KAHRHOFF, 111
KAICH, 39
KANE, 185
KAPFENSTEINER, 111
KARL, 147
KARSNER, 39
KASSINGER, 39
KASTER, 186
KAY, 111
KEARBEY, 39 132
KEASTER, 135
KEATHLEY, 121
KECK, 39
KEDIGH, 193
KEEL, 39

KEENE, 93
KEENER, 39
KEESECKER, 186
KEEVIL, 125
KEIBARDM, 39
KEITH, 39 99 104
KELLER, 164 171 173 182-183
KELLEY, 131 142 152 154
KELLISON, 111
KELLOGG, 39
KELLON, 167
KELLUMS, 39
KELLY, 39 104 180
KELSAW, 39
KEMP, 39
KEMPH, 147
KENDALL, 104 130
KENDRICK, 142
KENNEDY, 39 131 175
KENNER, 39 147
KENT, 39 118 153 155 174
KENWORTHY, 119
KENYON, 185
KEOWN, 179
KERBEY, 157
KERLEY, 153
KERN, 104
KERNES, 142
KERNODLE, 183
KERR, 39 104 137
KERSTING, 39
KERZEK, 39
KESSINGER, 77
KETCHUM, 39 183-184
KETON, 147
KEY, 104
KIDWILER, 193
KIL----, 156
KILBOURNE, 81
KILGORE, 39 156
KILLGORE, 172
KILLIAN, 40
KILLPATRICK, 104
KIMBEL, 173 175
KIMBELL, 163
KIMBROUGH, 156
KIMREY, 100
KIMSEY, 142
KINDER, 40
KINDLE, 121-122
KINDRICK, 40 129

KINDRICKS, 125
KING, 40 77 83 104 142 144 154 176 186
KINGERY, 40
KINGLEMAN, 147
KINGREE, 40
KINGSBORO, 142
KINGSLAND, 152
KINGSLEY, 40
KINGSTON, 142
KINKADE, 162
KINKEAD, 40
KINNARD, 125
KINNEY, 78
KINNINGHAM, 83
KINSE, 148
KINSELLA, 185
KINSER, 100
KINSEY, 40
KINSLEY, 188
KINTH, 177
KIPPER, 40
KIRBY, 165 188
KIRK, 156-158 181
KIRKLAND, 116 137
KIRKLEY, 40
KIRKMAN, 40
KIRKPATRICK, 40 85 111
KIRTLEY, 94
KIRZNER, 148
KISEER, 40
KISER, 40
KISSNER, 166
KIST, 148
KITTREDGE, 40
KLEES, 111
KLEIN, 111 148 186
KLENN, 117
KLICE, 197
KLINGER, 142
KNAPP, 40 162 164 174 183
KNIER, 40
KNIGHT, 40-41 104 157 165
KNITTELL, 186
KNITTLE, 82 186
KNOUFF, 160
KNOWLES, 41
KNOWLTON, 154
KNOX, 111 163 166 182
KOEHLER, 41
KOEHNEMAN, 95
KOENIG, 111 185

KOHM, 148
KOHN, 138
KOLAR, 111
KOLHLMYER, 164
KOLMIER, 163
KOLMYER, 182
KOLODY, 111
KOONCE, 163
KOVACH, 41
KRAMER, 41 148
KRAUSE, 111
KREPPS, 159
KREPS, 156-157 160 171
KREUNEN, 111
KREVITS, 41
KRIEGBAUM, 41
KRUS, 148
KUHN, 186
KULKBRENNER, 41
KUNCE, 120 125
KUNKEL, 148
KUPFERLE, 111
KURZ, 41
LA, 112
LABRIER, 41 148
LACEWELL, 41
LACEY, 115
LACHANCE, 148
LACY, 86 88
LADD, 41
LADE, 41
LADWIG, 186
LAFFERTY, 41
LAFLEUR, 148
LAFORCE, 104
LAFTEY, 120
LAHM, 112
LAISURE, 169
LALEMENDIER, 148
LAMAR, 104
LAMASTHER, 125
LAMBERT, 41 104 128 133 136
LAMBRIGHT, 165
LAMME, 91
LAMPKIN, 41
LANCASTER, 41 104
LAND, 41
LANDRETH, 41
LANDRUM, 41
LANE, 41 120 137 153 156
LANGDON, 42

LANGE, 112 148
LANGLEY, 41-42 104 116 123
LANHAM, 91
LANKER, 174
LANKFORD, 42
LANTE, 176
LANTFORT, 42
LANTZ, 181
LAPHLAIN, 153
LARKIN, 112 136
LARSON, 104
LARUE, 135
LASH, 95 188
LASHLEY, 123
LASURE, 183
LATHAM, 42 155
LATHIM, 124
LAUER, 82
LAUGHLIN, 42 104 173
LAURENCE, 112
LAW, 142 167 173
LAWRENCE, 42 170
LAWSON, 42 79 186
LAWTHERS, 117
LAXSON, 104
LAXTON, 104 126
LAY, 100 155-159 167-168 180
LAZALIER, 42
LAZIER, 166
LAZURE, 178
LEACH, 42 127 129-131 188
LEADBETTER, 118
LEADER, 42
LEADFORD, 160
LEARY, 112
LEATHERMAN, 42
LEBER, 188
LEDBETTER, 42 104
LEDFORD, 104 139 159 170 181 184
LEDGWOOD, 142
LEE, 42 78 104 112 117 123 133 160 173 177 183-184
LEECH, 172 182
LEER, 42
LEGGETT, 172
LEGRAND, 42
LEHI, 176
LEIGHTON, 169
LEININGER, 188
LEMASTER, 104 162-163
LEMASTERS, 166

LEMBERG, 42
LEMING, 42
LEMMON, 153
LEMMONS, 42 100
LEMONS, 104 174
LEN----, 156
LENARD, 129
LENNIX, 122
LENNON, 86
LENT, 165
LENZ, 138
LEONARD, 42-43 127 130 133
LESHER, 182
LESLIE, 43 116 126
LESTER, 188
LEUTERT, 43
LEVALLY, 104
LEVI, 92
LEVICK, 43
LEVINGSTON, 135
LEWELLEN, 193
LEWIS, 43 104 112 118 129 132 169 172 181 183
LIBBERT, 112
LIDDLE, 43
LIGHT, 134
LIGHTFOOT, 127 163-165
LILE, 142
LILLY, 43
LIMBAUGH, 43
LINCH, 142
LINDER, 43 157 159 161 164-165 168 172 174 178 181 183-184
LINDSAY, 43
LINDSEY, 178 180
LINGER, 43
LINGO, 43
LININTER, 171
LINK, 116 126 162 176 183
LINKEY, 186
LINNDER, 174
LINSENMEYER, 115
LINSEY, 142 176
LINVILLE, 43
LINZE, 138
LIPOSEK, 43
LIPSCOMB, 43
LIPSCOMBS, 132
LISKY, 43
LITNER, 185
LITTLE, 43 112 166 170 183-184 193

LITTLEPAGE, 157
LITTRELL, 131
LIVINGSTON, 43 82 131 142 164 175-176 181
LOCKWOOD, 43
LOE, 167 174-175
LOFLIN, 43
LOFTIN, 154
LOFTON, 104 156
LOFTY, 128
LOGAN, 112
LOGE, 43
LOGON, 104
LOGSTON, 160 173 182 186
LOHMEIER, 43
LOIDA, 148
LOMAX, 183-184
LOMBARDO, 112
LON, 157
LONG, 43 93 112 124 142 160 176 180 193
LONGAN, 104
LONGER, 44
LOOMES, 142
LOONEY, 44
LOOP, 187
LOPP, 188
LORD, 182-184
LORE, 118 120
LORENZ, 185
LORTON, 44 162 174 176 186
LOVE, 44 188
LOVELACE, 44
LOVING, 104
LOW, 170 179
LOWE, 136 172 178 186
LOWERY, 44 162
LOWRY, 104
LOWTHER, 104 126
LOYD, 126
LUCAS, 44 90
LUCKENOTTE, 124
LUCKEY, 187
LUCKFIELD, 148
LUDER, 181
LUDLUM, 128
LUDWIG, 165 178
LUGG, 104
LUIDER, 172 177
LUMPKIN, 44
LUMPKINS, 44

LUNDSFORD, 104
LUNDY, 104
LUSK, 44
LUSTER, 44
LUTES, 44
LUTTRELL, 44
LUTZ, 165 182
LUWELLEN, 104
LUX, 148
LUYENDYK, 112
LYCAN, 163
LYLES, 155
LYNCH, 44 99
LYNN, 44
LYON, 152 167 183
LYONS, 44 91
M'CLUGHEN, 78
MABEARY, 125
MABERRY, 117-118 120 123 126 134 136 138
MABERY, 137
MABES, 104
MABIN, 44
MACER, 176
MACKAY, 130
MACKENTIRE, 175
MACKLEY, 44
MACOM, 44
MACOMBERS, 186
MADDEN, 178
MADDOX, 112 174
MADDUX, 44
MADEN, 161
MAGHER, 89
MAGILL, 44
MAGNESS, 117
MAHAN, 139
MAHEWY, 176
MAIN, 126
MAINE, 122-123
MAINES, 44
MAITLAND, 189
MAIZE, 44 189
MAKAFFER, 131
MALADY, 44
MALLET, 186
MALONE, 104
MANES, 137
MANGOLD, 44
MANGRAM, 44
MANION, 45

MANITE, 165
MANLEY, 45
MANN, 45 96 104 112 118 172 183
MANNER, 104
MANNING, 185
MANNS, 45
MANSBRIDGE, 45
MANSFIELD, 45 91 104
MAPES, 77 79
MAPLE, 45
MARBERY, 131
MARGRAVE, 104
MARIAH, 159
MARINE, 168 184
MARIS, 142
MARITT, 139
MARK, 168 178
MARKEL, 45
MARKEY, 168 173-174
MARKHAM, 104
MARKS, 165
MARLER, 45
MARLEY, 45 78
MARLOW, 136
MARLOWE, 132
MARNEY, 155
MARQUESS, 173 176 185
MARRIS, 45
MARRISON, 104
MARRS, 122
MARSCHAND, 45
MARSH, 139 152 161 169
MARSHALL, 45 121
MARSHBANKS, 124
MARTIN, 45 90 104-105 121 131 142 161 164 167 173 176-177 184-186 189 193
MARY, 45 162
MASIE, 105
MASLEY, 45
MASON, 45 105 126 152 179 184
MASSEY, 134
MASSIE, 116 120-122 132 136 153
MASTEN, 185
MASTERS, 45 129
MATCHETT, 166
MATHENA, 169
MATHEWS, 77 80 105 161 193
MATHIS, 45-46 160
MATKIN, 121 189
MATLOCK, 105
MATT, 180

MATTER, 178
MATTHEWS, 105
MATTICK, 46
MATTINGLY, 46
MATTIX, 182
MAUCK, 185
MAULDING, 89
MAUPIN, 105
MAURICE, 148
MAXEY, 105 159 173 179
MAXWELL, 80
MAY, 155 166 176 180
MAYBERRY, 46 100
MAYES, 46 193
MAYHUGH, 46
MAYO, 46
MAYS, 82
MAYSON, 142
MC, 112
MCAFEE, 86 88 93
MCALLISTER, 46
MCARTHUR, 46
MCARTY, 162
MCATEE, 154-155
MCBAIN, 90
MCBRIDE, 123
MCBROOM, 46 171
MCCABE, 46 105 119
MCCAIN, 46 100
MCCALL, 124
MCCANLEY, 79
MCCARTER, 46
MCCARTNEY, 180
MCCARTY, 162-163 168
MCCARVER, 163
MCCAULEY, 46
MCCAULY, 78
MCCAVE, 46
MCCHRISTIAN, 46
MCCIVA, 163
MCCLAIN, 105
MCCLANAHAN, 46 170
MCCLARY, 122
MCCLAY, 105 185
MCCLINTOCK, 142
MCCOLLUM, 46 105 155
MCCONKEY, 46
MCCONNELL, 105 189
MCCORD, 142
MCCORKEL, 142
MCCORMACK, 46

MCCORMICK, 158
MCCOSKIE, 85
MCCOUN, 142
MCCOY, 88 118 142 163-166 173 177
MCCREA, 105
MCCREW, 152
MCCUEN, 105
MCCULLY, 142
MCCUNE, 179
MCCUSKEY, 186
MCDANIEL, 46 105 142
MCDANIELS, 46-47
MCDERMATT, 132
MCDONALD, 105 125 142
MCDONNELL, 138
MCDONNER, 165
MCDOWELL, 85 105 159 164
MCELHANNON, 47
MCELROY, 47 100 189
MCENTIRE, 118 134 153
MCFAA, 105
MCFADDIN, 117
MCFARLAND, 105
MCFARRON, 176
MCFERRON, 172
MCFETRIDGE, 155
MCGEE, 47
MCGHEE, 120
MCGILL, 142 182
MCGINES, 142
MCGINNES, 105
MCGINNIS, 105
MCGONNIGAL, 117
MCGOODWIN, 170
MCGORM, 171
MCGOWEN, 47 100
MCGOWN, 168
MCGRAW, 179
MCGREW, 164 170
MCGRIMES, 172
MCGUIRE, 105 122 142
MCGUIRES, 76
MCINTIRE, 105 172
MCINTYRE, 47 170 189
MCIVER, 47 193
MCKAY, 47
MCKEE, 47 105
MCKENSY, 142
MCKIDDY, 97
MCKIM, 47
MCKINKEY, 47

MCKINNEY, 47 98 100 105 128 162 180
MCKINNY, 161
MCKINSEY, 142
MCKINZIE, 47
MCKISICK, 142
MCLAUGHLIN, 47 105
MCLEAN, 47 185
MCLELLAN, 83
MCLONE, 130
MCMAHAN, 142 172 181
MCMANNIS, 105
MCMANUS, 47 189
MCMICHAEL, 142
MCMILLAN, 130
MCMULLEN, 47
MCNAUGHT, 186
MCNAUL, 186
MCNECE, 47
MCNEECE, 47
MCNEELEY, 123
MCNICE, 47
MCPHATRIDGE, 105
MCPHEE, 115-116 120
MCPHERSON, 157
MCPHETERIDGE, 160 172
MCPHETRIDGE, 161 182
MCQUITTY, 92
MCREYNOLDS, 47
MCRILL, 47
MCSPADDEN, 126 135
MCSPADEN, 115
MCVETY, 177
MCVEY, 47
MCWILLIAMS, 47
MEAD, 90-91 112
MEADLEY, 78
MEADOR, 105
MEADOWS, 77 105
MEADS, 172
MEANS, 105
MEDCALF, 47
MEDDECK, 47
MEDLIN, 47
MEDLOCK, 47
MEEK, 182
MEEKS, 153 158 160 174
MEIMOR, 185
MELIGIAN, 105
MELLOWAY, 91
MELN, 139-140
MELTON, 47-48

MELUGIAN, 105
MENDENHALL, 193
MENDHAM, 152
MENTZOS, 112
MERCER, 48 139 175
MERRELL, 48
MERRETT, 48
MERRILL, 84 180
MERRIMAN, 48
MERRITT, 48 139-140
METZ, 48 179
METZGER, 142
MEYER, 112 148
MEYERS, 48 125 132 169
MICHAEL, 105
MIDDAUGH, 193
MIDDLETON, 48 175
MIDGETT, 112
MIFLIN, 48
MIHAUPT, 112
MIKEAL, 167
MIKEL, 154 156 179-180
MIKELS, 169 182
MIL----, 153
MILES, 48 79-80 105 169 172 177 182
MILHOLLIN, 91
MILLAGAN, 142
MILLAM, 181
MILLAY, 173
MILLER, 48 87 97 105 112 115 135 142 149 152-153 156 158 161-163 169 171 173-175 177 180-182 185-186 189 194
MILLION, 130 136
MILLS, 105
MILNER, 48
MILSTER, 49
MINCKE, 185
MINER, 105 182
MINIC, 155
MINICH, 153
MINKS, 49
MINTEN, 49
MIRES, 167
MITCHEL, 86 88
MITCHELL, 49 105 112 118 123 129 142 183-184 186
MITCHELLE, 49
MITCHNER, 49
MITTELHAUSER, 49
MOBLEY, 49
MOCK, 194

MOFFAT, 86
MOFFET, 149 157
MOFFITT, 153 157
MOLDIN, 87
MONCRIEF, 167
MONDAY, 49
MONICA, 49
MONROE, 126
MONTAGUE, 49
MONTCRIEF, 170
MONTGOMERY, 49 142 157 172 178
MOOD, 94
MOODY, 100 162 164 166 170
MOOMAW, 49
MOORE, 49-50 99 112 126-127 131 135 149 156 158 160-162 164 167-168 172-173 177-179 185-186 194
MOOTS, 167 170
MORAN, 50 179
MOREHEAD, 105
MORELAN, 127
MORELAND, 100 194
MORELOCK, 158 163 167 170 178
MORETON, 105
MOREY, 50 142
MORGAN, 50 105 142 152 162 164 175-176 180 182 189
MORIS, 116
MORLAN, 123 131-132
MORLEY, 50
MORRIS, 50 84 105 119 124-125 138 142 155 159 162 165-166 172 178 184
MORRISON, 50 133
MORROW, 48 50 153-154 163 166 173 179 189
MORSE, 105
MORTON, 154 158-159
MOSBY, 50
MOSER, 127 149
MOSES, 115 142
MOSIER, 137
MOSLEY, 50 167
MOSS, 51 105 116 130 132 138 168 180 183-184
MOSSENGILL, 122
MOSTINGER, 142
MOTE, 153
MOTLEY, 105
MOTON, 51
MOTT, 51
MOULDER, 85

MOUNTAIN, 171 177 179 181
MOUNTS, 105
MOVINGER, 164
MOWERY, 51
MUESSIG, 149
MUFF, 186
MUIR, 189
MULCH, 176
MULLENIX, 163
MULLIGAN, 122
MULLINS, 155
MUMMERT, 124
MUNDEN, 162
MUNGER, 117 129
MUNN, 163 182 189
MURDOCK, 80
MURPHEY, 157
MURPHY, 51 77 105 112 154-155 157 164 189
MURRAY, 51 182
MURRY, 175
MURTIN, 186
MUSGROVE, 152
MUSICK, 163-164 170-171 175 177
MUSS, 139
MUSSER, 105 142
MUSTOE, 185
MYERS, 51 112 135 165 186
MYRANT, 51
MYRICK, 125
NAGEL, 112
NAGER, 149
NALIE, 182
NANCE, 142
NANNA, 116 124 137
NASH, 51 77-78 142
NASON, 173
NATIONS, 51
NEALE, 105
NEEDLES, 183-184
NEEL, 51
NEELY, 51 131
NEFF, 157 163
NEIL, 189
NEILSON, 51
NEISZ, 112
NELSON, 51 105 131 142 157 160 162 164 169 174 181 194
NENTRUP, 51
NESBIT, 156
NESBY, 52

NEVIL, 142
NEVILL, 52
NEWBY, 133 142
NEWCOMB, 133 165
NEWELL, 185
NEWINGTON, 52
NEWMAN, 175
NEWTON, 77
NEXSEN, 98
NICHELS, 142
NICHOLAS, 105 167
NICHOLS, 52 91 105 129
NICHOLSON, 91
NICKEN, 149
NICKLESS, 125 133
NICKOLSON, 105
NIEDERSTRADT, 52
NIEDERWIMER, 189
NIEL, 138
NISWANGER, 52
NITZ, 124 132
NIX, 80
NIXON, 52
NOAH, 52
NOAKES, 105
NOBLE, 52 180
NOE, 112
NOLAND, 105
NOLLMAN, 52
NOLTE, 52
NOLTY, 52
NOON, 52
NORDEN, 52
NORMAN, 52 100 122 138
NORRIES, 122
NORRIS, 105 116
NORSWORTHY, 84
NORTON, 52 132 153
NOSSE, 52
NOSWORTHY, 169
NOTESTINE, 179
NOVAK, 112
NOVINGER, 160 166 172 174-175 178 184
NUL----, 155
NUNLEY, 52 119
NUNNALLY, 125
NUPMAN, 181
O'BRIENT, 186
O'CONNOR, 52
O'DANIEL, 52

O'DELL, 125 128 134-135 137-138
O'FARRELL, 52
O'KANE, 53
O'KELLEY, 131 136
O'NAL, 53
OAKLEY, 52
OBEMEIER, 52
OBERLE, 149
ODELL, 116
ODOM, 52 120
OGDON, 161-162 165
OGLE, 53
OLCUTT, 81
OLD, 53 189
OLDAKER, 142
OLIVER, 53 91 144 158 161-162
OLLER, 53
OLSON, 129
ONEAL, 142
ONMAN, 115
ONSTOLL, 105
OOKES, 53
ORCHARD, 105
ORDWAY, 53
ORR, 179
ORRICK, 123
ORTEN, 142
ORTIN, 89
ORTON, 142
OSBIRNE, 53
OSBORN, 53 105 160 162 171 177
OSBORNE, 53
OSBOURNE, 53
OSBURN, 142 164 166-167
OSBURNE, 53
OSBURNER, 53
OSTER, 53
OSTRANDER, 97
OTT, 173
OTTE, 149
OTTO, 164-165 174-175 178
OVERFIELD, 53
OVERSTREET, 157 168 177
OVERTON, 53 105
OWEN, 53
OWENBY, 177 180
OWENS, 53 100 112 167 169 194
OWINGS, 184
OWINS, 142
OWNSBY, 167 171
OZMANT, 105

PACE, 53 123 128
PAGE, 53 105 173
PAGET, 168
PAINTER, 112 161
PALM, 93
PALMATORY, 159
PALMER, 53-54 90 169 194
PALMERTREE, 152
PALMOTORY, 167
PANE, 119
PANGBORN, 164
PARCEL, 105
PARCELLS, 166 173
PARCELS, 157 160 162
PARGIN, 54
PARHAM, 137
PARKE, 112
PARKER, 54 81 93 98 122 167 178-179 185 189
PARKHAM, 135
PARKHILL, 128
PARKINS, 54
PARKS, 54 155 183 186
PARMENTER, 189
PARMER, 142
PARRISH, 54 159
PARROT, 172
PARROTT, 105
PARSELLS, 179
PARSLEY, 54
PARSONS, 112 122 126
PARTENBERRY, 54
PARTIN, 153-155 159
PARTNEY, 116
PARTRIDGE, 54
PARVIN, 142
PATRICK, 105-106
PATT, 194
PATTEN, 156 162
PATTERSON, 54 125 159 161 165 169-170 186
PATTON, 92 142
PATTY, 54
PAUL, 106 166-167
PAULDING, 177
PAULY, 112
PAVLETICH, 112
PAYNE, 54 166
PAYTON, 54 154 176 186
PEACOCK, 139-140 189
PEAK, 165

PEARCE, 54 106 142
PEARSON, 54
PEASE, 54
PECK, 82
PEDIGO, 54
PEEBLES, 186
PEERY, 186
PENINGTON, 183-184
PENNE, 54
PENNINGTON, 54 106 186
PENROD, 54-55
PENROSE, 55
PENSON, 126
PEPMILLER, 127
PERC, 55
PERCILL, 156
PERDOSIA, 55
PERDUE, 55 106
PEREZ, 113
PERKINS, 55 131 142 153
PERKINZER, 106
PERRINGTON, 106
PERRY, 106 113 142 185-186
PERSHA, 157
PERSON, 189
PERVIS, 55
PETERS, 55 106
PETERSEN, 113
PETERSON, 55 144
PETRE, 85
PETTY, 55 91 106
PETTYPOOL, 55
PEYTON, 92 167 169-170
PFRIMMER, 55
PHELPS, 55 129 157-158 160 162 167 186
PHILLIPS, 55 90 113 161 170
PHIPPS, 162-163 166 169
PHOEBUS, 106
PHR----, 157
PHURIUS, 170
PICKENS, 173 176
PICKETT, 142
PIERCE, 55 80 106 115 178 186
PIETT, 55
PIGG, 55 90 93
PIKE, 100
PILES, 126 153
PILKINTON, 55
PINKERTON, 165 172 178 184
PINKSTON, 55 179

PINSON, 106
PINWELL, 123
PINYERD, 122
PINZ, 132
PIPER, 138 172 186
PIPKIN, 56 106
PITMAN, 56 130 133
PITT, 173
PITTMAN, 182 189
PLATT, 118
PLUMER, 180
PLUNK, 56
PLYMIRE, 142
PNKSTON, 178
POAGE, 189
POELKER, 113
POERS, 56
POGE, 142
POGJAHIN, 56
POGUE, 116 120 132 135
POINTER, 142
POKE, 56
POLLARD, 56 159 185
POLLEY, 172
POLLOCK, 178
PONDER, 56 189
POOL, 56 106 169 176 178
POORE, 56
POPE, 56
PORCH, 56
PORT, 56
PORTER, 56 113 163 167 174
POST, 177 182
POSTON, 177
POTEET, 142
POTILLO, 56
POTTER, 56 113 121 142 179 194
POTTS, 106 184
POW, 142
POWELL, 56 91 100 142 165-166 172-173 190
POWERS, 56 106 125 160 172 175 181
PRATHER, 156-157 159 169 178 180
PRATT, 56 116
PREE, 113
PRENTICE, 183
PRENZEL, 56
PRESON, 76
PRESSER, 173
PRESSON, 56
PRESTON, 76

PREWETT, 106
PRICE, 127 131 138
PRICHARD, 77-79
PRICKARD, 56
PRICKEL, 185
PRICKETT, 56 88
PRIEST, 56
PRIGMORE, 106
PRINDLE, 142
PRIOR, 106 142
PRITCHETT, 106
PROCTOR, 56 91 142
PROFFIT, 124
PROPSE, 56
PROPST, 181
PROUGH, 185-186
PROVANCE, 133
PRUETT, 56 118 194
PRYOR, 172 175
PUCCI, 113
PUGH, 182
PULLEN, 142
PULLIAM, 120 182
PULLIUM, 133
PUNCO, 177
PURCELL, 100
PURGETT, 174
PURSEE, 171
PURSLEY, 80
PURSSLEY, 79
PYLE, 84
PYLES, 56
QUALLS, 56
QUEEN, 57
QUIFFINNE, 57
QUIGLEY, 57
QUINDLE, 174
RADCLIFF, 57
RADER, 106
RADFORD, 133
RADOFROD, 138
RAGAN, 106
RAGER, 178
RAGSDALE, 57
RAINES, 57
RAINEY, 57
RAINS, 77 80 82 106
RALSTON, 106
RAMBA, 124
RAMSEY, 113
RANDALL, 132

RANDALLS, 57
RANDOLPH, 142
RANEY, 106 194
RANGE, 156
RANKIN, 106
RANSOM, 161 168
RASCHER, 113
RATLIFF, 177 184-185
RAULSTON, 57
RAVELETTE, 57
RAWLWY, 57
RAY, 57 76 123 142 164 166 186
RAYMER, 118 129 132
RAYNN, 80
READ, 57 170 194
READING, 57
READY, 142 160
REAMS, 90
REANDS, 106
RECITER, 57
RECTOR, 128
REDDINS, 57
REDDOW, 162
REDFORD, 57
REDINGER, 178
REDMOND, 79-80
REED, 57 85 88 138 142-143 153-154 164 166 184
REEDER, 57
REESE, 57 149 175
REEVE, 185
REEVES, 58 99-100
REID, 113 171
REINDEL, 186
REITMEYER, 113
RELEFORD, 106
RENFRO, 58
RENFROW, 143
RENN, 154
RENOLDS, 136
REPOTEE, 58
RESNIK, 58
RESTLE, 58
REVELLE, 58
REYNOLDS, 58 106 135 165 176 194
RHOADS, 154
RHODES, 58
RICE, 78 106 152 157 186
RICERSON, 153
RICHARDSON, 91 106 113 120 127 163 180 189

RICHEY, 143 175 181
RICHLAND, 173
RICHMOND, 125 135
RICKETS, 106
RICKETTS, 178 180
RICKNER, 106
RIDDLE, 77 155
RIDEN, 131
RIDENHOUR, 115
RIDER, 172
RIDGE, 194
RIDGEWAY, 179
RIDGWAY, 93
RIDINGS, 169
RIGGER, 182
RIGGINS, 194
RIGGS, 153
RIGHTNOWAR, 118
RILEY, 120 143 184 186 189
RINEHART, 186
RINGO, 155-159 164 167 182
RISINGER, 58
RISLEY, 58
RITCHEE, 168
RITCHERSON, 170
RIVES, 126
ROACH, 58 190
ROADEN, 106
ROADER, 153
ROARK, 58
ROBB, 134 178
ROBBINS, 165 182 186
ROBBS, 58
ROBERSON, 58 153 165 175 178 180
ROBERTS, 58 76 78 88 92 94 106 143 153 162-163 166 171 181 183-184 186
ROBERTSON, 58 76 106 116 119 124 134 179
ROBINAON, 58
ROBINETTE, 90 93
ROBINSON, 58 106 133 159 166 174 194
ROBISON, 58 177
ROBY, 169
RODAWALD, 58
RODEBUSH, 136
RODEN, 58
RODES, 143 154 158
RODGERS, 116 120-121 126 134 138 154 178
ROE, 58 143 179
ROESCH, 113

ROGERS, 58-59 92 106 113 153 155 158 161 177
ROHLFING, 59
ROHLFS, 59
ROKTH, 149
ROLAND, 59 108
ROLEN, 179
ROLLINS, 195
ROLOFF, 152
ROLSTON, 186
ROLSTOV, 143
ROMINE, 161
ROMMELL, 59
RONE, 59
RONGEY, 116 128 133
RONSESBORG, 175
ROONEY, 79
ROPER, 59 116
RORABAUGH, 157 159 169
RORAHBAUGH, 159
ROSE, 59 106 121 126 143 156-157 159 165 171
ROSEBERRY, 175
ROSEMAN, 59
ROSON, 106
ROSS, 59 106 113 116 154 173 177
ROSSLET, 149
ROSSMAN, 149
ROSSON, 106
ROTTLER, 149
ROUND, 164
ROUSE, 59
ROUSSIN, 113
ROVER, 136
ROW, 175
ROWARK, 59
ROWDEN, 144
ROWLIN, 157
ROWNINES, 159
ROY, 106 120-121 133
ROYAL, 59
RPBBINS, 58
RUARK, 143
RUBOTTOM, 59
RUCK, 106
RUCKER, 78 106
RUDDELL, 186
RUDDY, 160
RUDERFORD, 161
RUDINGTON, 180
RUDISIL, 59

RUDOLPH, 59
RUEBSAM, 149
RUGGLES, 162
RUMBERG, 126
RUNELS, 143
RUPE, 171
RUSER, 59
RUSH, 59 106 116
RUSHENBORGER, 106
RUSHIN, 59
RUSHING, 59
RUSK, 106
RUSSAVAGE, 113
RUSSEL, 154-155
RUSSELL, 59 95 113 117 136 149 158 176 184 189
RUST, 59
RUTH, 186
RUTHERFORD, 169 172 178 189
RUTLEDGE, 120 122 137
RYAMER, 57
RYAN, 59 125 185
SADDLER, 59
SAFFLE, 175
SAGE, 162 177
SAINT CLAIR, 157
SAINT GEM, 150
SAINT JAMES, 150
SAINTCIN, 66
SAINTCLAIR, 66
SALADA, 163 171
SALADE, 184
SALADEE, 171
SALING, 153-154
SALLADE, 171
SALLEE, 152
SALLY, 153
SALSBERRY, 166
SALSBURY, 166
SALSMAN, 137
SALTZMAN, 59
SAMES, 135
SAMPLES, 106 170
SAMPSON, 143 161 163
SAMS, 128
SAMUEL, 90
SAMUELS, 157 164 168-169 171
SANDBONE, 166
SANDERS, 59-60 100 106 123 128 132 135 138 143 164-165 168 173 176 180 185 187

SANDERSON, 60
SANDFORD, 176
SANDRY, 178
SANER, 166
SANFORD, 181 187
SANNER, 130 136
SANTACRUZ, 113
SAPP, 91
SAPPINGTON, 60 93-94
SARGENT, 158 177
SARTIN, 117 120 136
SARVER, 60
SASS, 135
SASSE, 60
SATERFIELD, 156
SATTERFIELD, 160
SAUER, 60
SAUNDERS, 125 167
SAVAGE, 60 143
SAVEY, 165
SAWYER, 165
SAXBURY, 187
SAYLORS, 60
SCANTLING, 106
SCARBER, 143
SCARLT, 143
SCATES, 60
SCHACH, 60
SCHAETTLER, 150
SCHAFER, 150 182
SCHALK, 60
SCHARLOTT, 113
SCHELLY, 180
SCHENEWERK, 60
SCHILLY, 150
SCHISLER, 60
SCHLOTERBACK, 60
SCHMERBAUCH, 60
SCHMICK, 121
SCHMIDT, 60 187
SCHMITH, 150
SCHRADER, 60 120 175 182
SCHRAELER, 160
SCHROEDER, 60
SCHSAN, 172
SCHUBER, 60
SCHULER, 150
SCHULL, 60
SCHULTZ, 185
SCHUMAKER, 60
SCHUMER, 60

SCO----, 154
SCOBEE, 160 164 167 169-170 175-176 183
SCOBEY, 160
SCOBIE, 158
SCOBY, 171
SCOFIELD, 60
SCOGGINS, 60
SCOTT, 60-61 80 106-107 113 165 168 173-174 182 189
SCOVEL, 154
SCOVIL, 175
SCRITCHFIELD, 177
SCRIVNERS, 178
SCRUGGS, 106
SEAMON, 154
SEARCY, 94
SEARS, 157
SEATON, 195
SEBAUGH, 189
SEBOLE, 171
SECREASE, 121 134
SECREST, 106
SECRETS, 61
SEELEY, 61
SEGASTIAN, 119
SEGER, 61
SEIBERTS, 61
SEIPEL, 189
SEIVETS, 172
SEIVIRN, 170
SELA, 106
SELBY, 93 175
SELLARS, 161
SELLS, 124
SELVY, 181
SEMAR, 113
SENIOR, 93
SENTENNE, 185
SERAT, 156
SERT, 61
SETTERS, 164 177
SEVIER, 81 184 195
SEWALD, 150
SEYMOUR, 93 113
SEYPOHLTOWSKY, 61
SHACKLEFORD, 61
SHACKLETTE, 187
SHADWELL, 179
SHAFFER, 61 164
SHAFFLEY, 61

SHAIN, 61
SHAMBLIN, 61
SHANKS, 61 106 154
SHANNON, 106 177
SHANTZ, 161
SHARP, 61 118 126 187
SHARR, 174 178
SHAW, 61 106 126 128 130 143 153-154 160
SHECKLER, 61
SHECKS, 179
SHEEHY, 61
SHEEKS, 185
SHEELY, 61
SHEETS, 118 120-121 127 131
SHEFFIELD, 61
SHEHAN, 130
SHEHANE, 61
SHELBY, 173
SHELDON, 189
SHELLEY, 180
SHELLY, 170
SHELTLEY, 172
SHELTON, 61 79 106 113 165
SHEPPARD, 61
SHERELL, 123
SHERIDAN, 61
SHERMAN, 61 97
SHERRER, 127
SHERRY, 61
SHERTON, 186
SHETON, 143
SHIFFLEY, 62
SHIKLES, 189
SHIP, 155
SHIPLEY, 158 162
SHIPMAN, 187
SHIPP, 62
SHIRELY, 187
SHIRER, 170
SHIRKEY, 181
SHIRLEY, 106 187
SHIVELY, 62 161
SHIVLEY, 159
SHOAT, 62
SHOBE, 153
SHOCK, 91 93
SHOCKY, 139-140
SHOEMAKER, 106 153 156 161 170-171 178 180 183-184
SHOLL, 156

SHOMAKER, 134
SHONTZ, 164
SHOOK, 155 162
SHOOP, 159-160 164 166 168 174-175
SHOOT, 176
SHORES, 170
SHORT, 62 115 117 134
SHORTNESS, 154
SHOTT, 159 161 182
SHOULDERS, 117
SHOUP, 62
SHOWMAN, 195
SHREEVES, 118 126
SHREVE, 115 135
SHRODER, 195
SHROUT, 62
SHROYER, 106
SHRUM, 62 133 135
SHULL, 62 165
SHULTS, 113
SHURELL, 62
SIBLEY, 174
SIBOLE, 176-178 183
SICKLES, 62
SICKLITER, 153
SIDWELL, 187
SIEBERT, 150
SIECHMEYER, 116
SIECKMANN, 113
SIFFORD, 189
SIGNOR, 185
SILGER, 132 137
SILKWOOD, 62
SIMBLER, 166
SIMINO, 150
SIMLER, 170-171
SIMMERING, 62
SIMMONS, 62 77 100 113
SIMMS, 62 91-92
SIMON, 113
SIMPSON, 62 160 177
SIMS, 79-80 176 195-196
SINCLAIR, 162
SINDER, 172
SINGLETON, 92 97
SINKS, 62
SISCO, 62
SISNEY, 62
SISSELL, 134
SIZEMORE, 62 164 178
SKAGGS, 62

SKELTON, 62
SKEWES, 150
SKIEP, 115
SKINNER, 82
SKYLES, 118
SLABAUGH, 62
SLADE, 63
SLANCE, 63
SLATE, 92
SLATER, 106
SLAUGHTER, 187
SLAWSON, 106
SLAYTON, 63
SLEIGHMAN, 155
SLIGER, 63
SLINKER, 106-107
SLOAN, 63 153 156 158-159 161 166 169-171 176
SLOOP, 186-187
SLOVER, 166 173 182 184
SLOVINSKY, 63
SLY, 107
SMALL, 151
SMALLWOOD, 107 119 157 159-160
SMART, 63 121-122
SMELSER, 124
SMILEY, 181
SMITH, 63-64 78 91 93-94 97 100 107-108 113 116-119 121 123-126 129-131 133-135 138 143 153-155 157-158 161-165 168 172 174-175 179-184 187 189 196
SMITHERS, 64
SMOCK, 64
SMOODY, 64
SMOOT, 156 164
SMOOTS, 172
SMOTHER, 64
SMOYER, 169
SNEATHERN, 64
SNEED, 64 153 169
SNELL, 181
SNIDER, 64 123 125 128 135 138 173
SNODGRASS, 107
SNOW, 143 167 171 173 182
SNYDER, 64 86 159-160 166 174
SOHLOP, 158
SOLI, 64
SOMERLOTT, 64
SOMMER, 113
SOMMERS, 64

SORBER, 189
SORREL, 184
SOUTH, 107 187
SOUTHARD, 107
SOUTHER, 156
SPALDING, 153
SPANGLER, 64 183-184
SPARKMAN, 64
SPARKS, 97 166 178
SPEARS, 107 171 187
SPEER, 175
SPEILMAN, 92
SPELL, 64
SPELTS, 64
SPENCE, 107
SPENCER, 64-65 107 127 171 178 184-185
SPENNEY, 165
SPILLMAN, 93
SPITZIG, 65
SPIVAY, 166
SPRADLING, 65
SPRINGER, 65 143
SPRY, 196
SPURLOCK, 65
STACY, 138
STAEKLY, 151
STAFFORD, 135 137
STAGE, 65
STAGGS, 143
STAGRE, 153
STALEY, 196
STALLINGS, 65
STAMP, 65
STANDERFER, 89
STANDERFORD, 159
STANDLEY, 165
STANIFORD, 173
STANLEY, 65 77 182
STANLY, 107
STANSBURY, 93
STANTON, 107 172 181
STAPP, 120 127
STARBUCK, 187
STARK, 143 178
STAUISLAUCE, 100
STAURLEY, 156
STEALE, 107
STEARNS, 196
STEED, 65
STEEL, 118 163 176

STEELE, 65 171
STEEN, 174 187
STEENKS, 65
STEFFEY, 187
STEINBERG, 65
STEINES, 167
STEPHENS, 79 90 97 116 121 126-127 129-131 153
STEPHENSON, 107 143
STEPP, 65
STERLING, 162 182
STERRETT, 107
STEVENS, 65 156 166 183 196
STEVENSON, 65 127
STEWARD, 65
STEWART, 118 168 170 181 196
STICE, 157 159-160
STIELS, 107
STIERS, 107
STILES, 107
STILL, 161 176 179 183-184
STILLEY, 65
STILLINGS, 78
STINEMAN, 128 165
STINGER, 65
STINSON, 65 166 175
STITH, 107
STITT, 66
STIVER, 182
STOCKTON, 107 153-154 156 159
STODD, 175
STOGDELL, 115
STOKELY, 126
STOKER, 66
STOLL, 151
STOLTE, 151
STONE, 66 124 143 160
STONECIPHER, 181
STONER, 66
STONEUM, 143
STOREY, 184
STORMS, 107
STORY, 165 177
STOTT, 181
STOUT, 66 107 158 168 172
STOUTS, 172
STRASSINGER, 138
STRATTON, 127 130 134 136 138
STRAWN, 91
STRAYHORN, 66
STREET, 66 92 121-122

STRIBLING, 107
STRINGER, 120
STRINGFEL, 66
STRODE, 93
STROPE, 143
STROTHKAMP, 95
STROUD, 66
STRUBLE, 107
STRUNK, 174
STRUNKLE, 172
STUART, 161 183 189
STUCKER, 66
STUCKEY, 167
STUDLEY, 109
STUKEY, 157
STUKY, 173
STULL, 66 108
STULTS, 66
STUMP, 156
STURGEON, 81
STUTEVILLE, 162 173 182
STUTIVILLE, 182
SUDDITH, 161
SUDER, 66
SUGG, 107
SULLENGER, 107
SULLEY, 165
SULLIVAN, 124 158 189
SUMMERS, 62 91 107 154-155 181 196
SUMMIT, 138
SUTEMAN, 174
SUTHERLAND, 66 97 144
SUTT, 66
SUTTON, 66 120 143 183
SWAFFORD, 66
SWAGART, 170
SWAN, 66
SWANK, 66
SWANSON, 67
SWASEY, 167
SWEAZEA, 122 128
SWEEK, 151
SWEENEY, 119
SWEET, 81 162 167
SWEETING, 186
SWERINGIN, 79
SWETMAN, 160 165 177
SWEZEA, 138
SWINEY, 143
SWINFORD, 161
SWISHER, 169

SWITSCHER, 177
SWITSER, 196
SWITZLER, 90
SWORD, 107
SZWABO, 113
T----, 157
TABER, 122
TACKETT, 107 132
TAGE, 143
TALBERT, 138
TALLEY, 67
TALTON, 67
TANNERS, 125
TANNLUND, 84
TAPSCOTT, 107
TARKOW, 113
TARPLEY, 67
TARR, 187
TARRM, 187
TATE, 67 107
TATMAN, 67 152 185
TAYLOR, 67 86 91 97 100 107 113 123
   125 132 137 143 173 179 182 187 190
TEAL, 107
TEEL, 67
TEMPLE, 119
TEMPLEMEER, 67
TENNIS, 79
TERRELL, 107
TERRY, 67 79-80 120 133-134
TESOWICK, 67
THARP, 107 143 170 173
THATCHER, 143 171 175
THAUMURE, 151
THAYER, 164
THEDFORD, 67
THIES, 67
THOMAS, 67 92 107 113 123 129-130
   137 153 162 168 174 179 187
THOMASON, 67
THOMASSON, 190
THOMEURE, 68
THOMPKINS, 161
THOMPSON, 68 98 107-108 132-133 170
   172-173 184
THOMSON, 165
THOMURE, 151
THORN, 68 99
THORNINGTON, 161
THORNTON, 113 143 172 179
THORP, 180

THORSON, 179
THRAILKILD, 155
THRASHER, 169 179
THRAUM, 114
THRELKEL, 131
THRUSH, 182
THUNBACH, 166
THURMAN, 68 107
TIBBS, 68 121
TICE, 163
TIDER, 172
TIDWELL, 68
TIFFANY, 181
TILLITSON, 154
TILLY, 68
TIMMERMAN, 68
TIMMONS, 68
TINGLEY, 187
TINKER, 68 120 127
TINNEY, 143
TINSLEY, 68 119 122 135
TINSTMEN, 163
TIPTON, 133 182 187 190
TISDIAL, 68
TITTLE, 68
TITTSWORTH, 187
TITUS, 156
TOALSON, 196
TODD, 68 78 93-94 143 174
TOHLINE, 197
TOLAND, 183
TOLBERT, 163
TOLIVER, 68
TOLLUM, 68
TOMERLIN, 68
TOMES, 69
TOMLIN, 69
TOMMERLIN, 69
TOMPKINS, 69
TOMURLIN, 69
TORRENCE, 107
TORREY, 143
TORRY, 143
TOUTANT, 69
TOWLES, 165 171
TOWNER, 133
TOWNS, 69
TOWNSEND, 69 107 132
TRACK, 69
TRACY, 164 170
TRAPP, 95

TREADWAY, 190
TREBBLE, 69
TREMBLE, 69
TRENT, 69 83
TRENTLEMAN, 69
TREWIT, 159
TRIPLETT, 85 90 107
TRIPP, 69
TROBRIDGE, 181
TROSS, 114
TROSTLE, 69
TROTT, 77
TROTTER, 89 107
TROUSDALE, 69
TROUT, 107
TROWBRIDGE, 169
TROXEL, 190
TRUE, 156 158 162 174
TRUETT, 168
TRUITT, 84 153 179 181
TRUSTMAN, 164
TRUSTY, 69
TUBB, 69
TUBBS, 131
TUCK, 187
TUCKER, 69 91 107 115 119 127 130-131 151
TUDER, 175
TUIN, 107
TULL, 161 168 178
TUMBLIN, 143
TUNE, 69
TUNNEL, 107
TURK, 182
TURLEY, 69 122 125 128 130
TURNBOUGH, 121
TURNBOW, 118
TURNER, 69 93 100 143 156 158-160 168 171 180 187 196
TURNIPSEED, 107
TUTTLE, 181-182
TWADDLE, 69
TWEEDY, 100
TWITTY, 107
UBER, 184
UEBELEIN, 70
UHL, 70
ULE, 70
UPTON, 70
URICH, 70
USERY, 131

UTT, 172 185
VACH, 114
VAETH, 151
VALE, 83
VALENTINE, 151
VALLE, 151
VANCE, 70 107 115 136 143
VANDAM, 152 185
VANDIKE, 154
VANDIVER, 93 187
VANDOVER, 70
VANDYKE, 120 155
VANHORN, 93 176-177
VANKIRK, 70
VANLANDINGHAM, 168 196
VANMETER, 187
VANNICE, 185
VANPAYPON, 172
VANSEL, 70
VANSICKLE, 132 187
VASSER, 143
VAUGHN, 70 80 185
VENARD, 185
VERBLE, 70
VERDEN, 180
VERMILLION, 116 127-128
VERNON, 107
VESPER, 182
VESTAL, 107
VESTER, 107
VICE, 143 182
VICKERS, 185
VINCENT, 114 116 152
VINE, 181-182
VINSON, 70
VITTETOE, 187
VIVION, 90 107
VODKER, 179
VOELKER, 151
VOGT, 151
VOLKER, 173
VONDER, 114
VOORHEIS, 178
VOORHIES, 178 185
VOSS, 175
VOYLES, 132 136 138
VROMAN, 70
VULKENBURG, 70
W----, 156
WADDELL, 196
WADDILL, 163-164 166-167 170 175

WADDILL (cont)
  178 181 185
WADDLE, 185
WADE, 70 107 114
WADKINS, 143
WADLINGTON, 70
WADLOW, 135
WAGGONER, 70
WAGNER, 127 171 174 177
WAGSTER, 70
WAIT, 173
WAITS, 121
WAKELY, 178
WALDO, 130
WALDON, 107
WALES, 165
WALKER, 70 77-78 81 107-108 114 116
  118 128 140 143 153 165-166 173-174
  181-182 185 187 196
WALLACE, 124 176 183-185
WALLER, 70 125 132
WALLICE, 130
WALLIN, 117
WALLIS, 119 134 175-176
WALLS, 70
WALSH, 196
WALTER, 70
WALTERS, 70 166 169-171 181-182
WALTON, 71 78-79 108
WANDELL, 81
WANGER, 159
WARBINGTON, 71
WARD, 71 92 100 108 116 136 143 176
  190
WARE, 80 108 177
WARMACK, 71
WARMOTH, 190
WARNER, 171 184
WARREN, 71 108 143 196
WARRIN, 143
WASHINGTON, 71 114
WATERALL, 71
WATERHOUSE, 190
WATERS, 71 92 108 155 168 173 177
  180
WATKINS, 71
WATSON, 71-72 108 128 161 165 172-
  174 177 180 182 185
WATTERS, 160
WATTS, 72 143 187
WAUGH, 179

WAULKER, 177
WEAR, 108
WEAVER, 72 177 179
WEBB, 72 83 108 116 119 129 172 174 177
WEBBER, 72
WEBBN, 72
WEBSTER, 154 171 176 185
WEESE, 143
WEISHROD, 72
WELCH, 140 190
WELDEN, 143
WELDON, 115 121 129
WELLEMEYER, 72
WELLER, 72
WELLES, 143
WELLS, 72 98 114 143 155-156 163 181 190
WELSH, 187
WELSHER, 143
WESE, 183
WEST, 72 152 187
WESTON, 72
WETHERFORD, 169
WETHERMAN, 79
WETHERS, 108
WHALEN, 72
WHALEY, 108
WHARTON, 184
WHEATLEY, 72
WHEELER, 77 108 171 196
WHEELING, 72
WHEELIS, 72
WHETLEY, 72
WHEYLAN, 138
WHIFFEN, 72
WHISTLER, 72
WHITAKER, 119 143
WHITE, 72-73 79 86 88 100 108 114 121 138 143 151 161 169 180 190
WHITED, 114
WHITEHEAD, 73
WHITESIDE, 73
WHITHEAD, 108
WHITLEY, 73 156
WHITLOCK, 77 108 152
WHITLOW, 73
WHITMER, 73
WHITSED, 73
WHITSELL, 128
WHITSETT, 143

WHITSON, 143
WHITTAKER, 190
WHITTEN, 108
WHITTINGTON, 73 143
WHITTOCK, 143
WHITWORTH, 73
WICHMAN, 114
WICKS, 73
WIDGGERS, 120
WIDMER, 73
WIGGINGTON, 91
WIGLEY, 80
WILBER, 171
WILCHER, 167
WILCOX, 86 94
WILCOXIN, 154
WILCUTT, 73
WILDER, 125
WILHITE, 100 143 172
WILKENSON, 108
WILKERSON, 73 143
WILKINS, 73
WILKINSON, 152
WILKS, 73 172
WILL, 152
WILLARD, 168
WILLBORN, 167
WILLCOCKSON, 196
WILLCOX, 87
WILLETT, 126
WILLEY, 169 176
WILLHITE, 128
WILLI, 152
WILLIAM, 114
WILLIAMS, 73 77 85 93 99 108 114 120 125 133 136 143 153-154 157-159 161-162 165 167-169 171 173 178 181 183-184
WILLIAMSON, 73-74 93 108 131 143
WILLIFORD, 74
WILLIS, 74 108 119 153-154 156 166 171 175 183
WILLMANN, 114
WILLOUGHBY, 74
WILLS, 114
WILSCHER, 153
WILSON, 74 108 114 117 129 137 153 155 158-159 161 168-170 172 175 178-179 182 196-197
WINDEL, 74
WINDER, 74

WINDES, 135 137
WINDLE, 74 125
WINDOM, 114
WINEMAN, 166
WINN, 143 184
WINSCOTT, 92 161
WINTER, 185
WINTERS, 108
WISDOM, 74 153-154 197
WISDON, 74
WISE, 169 171
WISECARVER, 74
WISEMAN, 74
WISENER, 163
WISNER, 169 172
WITHERS, 108
WITHROW, 74 156 158 160 165 167-168
WITTE, 74
WOERTHER, 95
WOLF, 108 152 179
WOLFE, 88 108 114 120 124 190 197
WOLSEY, 127
WOMACK, 116
WOOD, 74-75 127 129 137 143 159 167 172 197
WOODALL, 75
WOODCOCK, 108 184
WOODRAM, 108
WOODRUFF, 75
WOODS, 75 84 108 152 171 179-180 190
WOODSON, 98 109
WOODWARD, 117 128 136
WOODWORTH, 181
WOODY, 143
WOOLERY, 166
WOOLEY, 165
WOOLF, 128
WOOLFOLK, 91-92
WOOLFORK, 160
WOOLLEY, 94
WOOLSEY, 75
WOOLSON, 108
WOOLY, 75
WOOTEN, 75
WORKMAN, 165 167 169 171

WORLEY, 75 108
WORMACK, 75 134
WORSONS, 137
WORTHINGTON, 99 108
WORTMAN, 158 160 162 165 184 197
WRIGHT, 75 87 93 108 118 153-155 161-163 166 168-169 174 176 183-184 187 190
WRITE, 143
WULF, 114
WUSSOW, 95
WYLEY, 75
WYNN, 137
WYSONG, 176
YADEN, 156
YAE, 160
YALLERBY, 143
YANCY, 89
YATES, 75 85 98 118 128 133-135 153 162
YEAGER, 92
YELLEN, 114
YORK, 75
YOUNG, 75 86 88 99-100 108 143 158-159 161-162 174 177 179 181-184 187 190
YOUNGBLOOD, 129
ZACHARY, 108
ZADNIZ, 75
ZAMPIER, 114
ZEEBE, 135
ZEIGLER, 75 176 183
ZEISER, 95
ZELLERS, 108
ZEVALLY, 108
ZEVELLY, 108
ZIEBER, 187
ZIGLER, 168
ZILLERS, 108
ZIMMERMAN, 75 167
ZOLL, 75
ZOOK, 130
ZUCK, 75
ZUMALT, 75
ZUPPANN, 95

Other Heritage Books by Sherida K. Eddlemon:

Missouri Genealogical Records and Abstracts:
Volume 1: 1766-1839
Volume 2: 1752-1839
Volume 3: 1787-1839
Volume 4: 1741-1839
Volume 5: 1755-1839
Volume 6: 1621-1839
Volume 7: 1535-1839

Missouri Genealogical Gleanings 1840 and Beyond, Volumes 1-9

1890 Genealogical Census Reconstruction: Mississippi, Volumes 1 and 2

1890 Genealogical Census Reconstruction: Missouri, Volumes 1-3

1890 Genealogical Census Reconstruction: Ohio, Volume 1
(with Patricia P. Nelson)

1890 Genealogical Census Reconstruction: Tennessee, Volume 1

A Genealogical Collection of Kentucky Birth and Death Records

Callaway County, Missouri, Marriage Records: 1821 to 1871

Cumberland Presbyterian Church, Volume One: 1836 and Beyond

Dickson County, Tennessee Marriage Records, 1817-1879

Genealogical Abstracts from Missouri Church Records and Other Religious Sources, Volume 1

Genealogical Abstracts from Tennessee Newspapers, 1791-1808

Genealogical Abstracts from Tennessee Newspapers, 1803-1812

Genealogical Abstracts from Tennessee Newspapers, 1821-1828

Tennessee Genealogical Records and Abstracts, Volume 1: 1787-1839

Genealogical Gleanings from New York Fraternal Organizations Volumes 1 and 2

Index to the Arkansas General Land Office, 1820-1907 Volumes 1-10

Kentucky Genealogical Records and Abstracts, Volume 1: 1781-1839

Kentucky Genealogical Records and Abstracts, Volume 2: 1796-1839

Lewis County, Missouri Index to Circuit Court Records, Volume 1, 1833-1841

Missouri Birth and Death Records, Volumes 1-4

Morgan County, Missouri Marriage Records, 1833-1893

Our Ancestors of Albany County, New York, Volumes 1 and 2

Our Ancestors of Cuyahoga County, Ohio, Volume 1
(with Patricia P. Nelson)

Ralls County, Missouri Settlement Records, 1832-1853

Records of Randolph County, Missouri, 1833-1964

Ten Thousand Missouri Taxpayers

The "Show-Me" Guide to Missouri: Sources for Genealogical and Historical Research

CD: Dickson County, Tennessee Marriage Records, 1817-1879

CD: Index to the Arkansas General Land Office, 1820-1907 Volumes 1-10

CD: Missouri, Volume 3

CD: Tennessee Genealogical Records

CD: Tennessee Genealogical Records, Volumes 1-3

www.ingramcontent.com/pod-product-compliance
Lightning Source LLC
Chambersburg PA
CBHW060117170426
43198CB00010B/920